INSIGHT ⊙ GUIDES

INDONESIA

PLAN & BOOK
YOUR TAILOR-MADE TRIP

BRAZIL

CHILE

ECUADOR

TAILOR-MADE TRIPS & UNIQUE EXPERIENCES CREATED BY LOCAL TRAVEL EXPERTS AT INSIGHTGUIDES.COM/HOLIDAYS

Insight Guides has been inspiring travellers with high-quality travel content for over 45 years. As well as our popular guidebooks, we now offer the opportunity to book tailor-made private trips completely personalised to your needs and interests. By connecting with one of our local experts, you will directly benefit from their expertise and local know-how, helping you create memories that will last a lifetime.

HOW INSIGHTGUIDES.COM/HOLIDAYS WORKS

STEP 1

Pick your dream destination and submit an enquiry, or modify an existing itinerary if you prefer.

STEP 2

Fill in a short form, sharing details of your travel plans and preferences with a local expert.

STEP 3

Your local expert will create your personalised itinerary, which you can amend until you are completely satisfied.

STEP 4

Book securely online. Pack your bags and enjoy your holiday! Your local expert will be available to answer questions during your trip.

BENEFITS OF PLANNING & BOOKING AT INSIGHTGUIDES.COM/HOLIDAYS

PLANNED BY LOCAL EXPERTS

The Insight Guides local experts are hand-picked, based on their experience in the travel industry and their impeccable standards of customer service.

SAVE TIME & MONEY

When a local expert plans your trip, you save time and money when you book, even during high season. You won't be charged for using a credit card either.

TAILOR-MADE TRIPS

Book with Insight Guides, and you will be in complete control of the planning process, from the initial selections to amending your final itinerary.

BOOK & TRAVEL STRESS-FREE

Enjoy stress-free travel when you use the Insight Guides secure online booking platform. All bookings come with a money-back guarantee.

WHAT OTHER TRAVELLERS THINK ABOUT TRIPS BOOKED AT INSIGHTGUIDES.COM/HOLIDAYS

Trip to Portugal

Every step of the planning process and the trip itself was effortless and exceptional. Our special interests, preferences and requests were accommodated resulting in a trip that exceeded our expectations.

Corinne, USA   ★★★★★

Trip to Vietnam

The organization was superb, the drivers professional, and accommodation quite comfortable. I was well taken care of! My thanks to your colleagues who helped make my trip to Vietnam such a great experience. My only regret is that I couldn't spend more time in the country.

Heather   ★★★★★

DON'T MISS OUT
BOOK NOW AT
INSIGHTGUIDES.COM/HOLIDAYS

CONTENTS

Travel tips

TRANSPORT

A – Z

Maps

LEGEND
♀ Insight on
📷 Photo story

THE BEST OF INDONESIA: TOP ATTRACTIONS

△ **Borobudur.** Mesmerising Borobudur is the world's largest Buddhist monument. Dating from the 9th century, this gigantic stupa forms the shape of a mandala – a geometric aid to meditation. See page 166.

△ **Yogyakarta (Jogja).** The Javanese art, dance and music cultivated by 18th-century royalty remain alive in Yogyakarta today, blending seamlessly with the modern-day life of students, farmers and handicraft makers. See page 158.

▽ **Orangutans.** The best places to see these magnificent creatures are the rainforests of Tanjung Puting National Park (Central Kalimantan) and Gunung Leuser National Park (North Sumatra). See pages 198 and 317.

△ **Kuta, Sanur and Seminyak beaches.** Visions of Bali almost always include its southern beaches, with Kuta in the limelight for surfers and young partygoers, followed by the trendier scenes at upmarket Sanur and Seminyak. See pages 229 and 231.

△ **Gunung Bromo.** Arrive before dawn to witness the sunrise illuminate one of the world's most remarkable volcanic landscapes. See page 186.

△ **Tana Toraja.** Tucked away in the green highlands of South Sulawesi, Tana Toraja is a land of breathtaking vistas, ancient funerary rituals and graves guarded by wooden effigies. See page 331.

▽ **Lake Toba.** A water-filled ancient caldera, the largest and deepest in the world, Sumatra's beautiful Lake Toba is believed to have been formed by a series of super-eruptions nearly 900,000 years ago. See page 199.

△ **Ikat-weaving villages.** In remote Nusa Tenggara are many islands where ikat textiles are still woven on back-strap looms. Each village has its own motifs and colours, many of which are collected by aficionados. See page 294.

▽ **Komodo National Park.** In addition to its extraordinary reptiles, this remote corner of Indonesia offers some of the best diving and snorkelling in the Asia-Pacific region. See page 285.

△ **Ubud.** The cultural heartland of Bali, Ubud and its environs attract seekers of spirituality, wellness programmes, health foods and tranquillity. Others are drawn by the wealth and handicrafts and artwork produced here. See page 238.

THE BEST OF INDONESIA: EDITOR'S CHOICE

Balinese landscape.

BEST DIVING SPOTS

Raja Ampat, Western Papua. This remote spot has the world's greatest concentration of marine life for a region of its size, according to the World Wildlife Fund. See page 367.

Pulau Menjangan, West Bali. Bali Barat National Park's crown jewel and the most accessible of Indonesia's many magnificent dive spots. See page 253.

Bunaken Marine National Park, North Sulawesi. Well-established, conservation-oriented dive centres abound in Manado, the gateway to the wonders of this national park. See page 341.

Wakatobi, Southeast Sulawesi. Excellent dive sites plus local cultures and wildlife make Wakatobi Marine National Park ideal for groups that include non-divers. See page 339.

Maluku. Currently centred around Ambon, the fabled Spice Islands' diving opportunities are rapidly extending north to Lembeh Strait. See page 352.

Alor. In Nusa Tenggara, Alor's rich reefs attract sunfish (mola-mola), whales, manta rays, whale sharks and migrating orcas; muck diving is also excellent. See page 295.

BEST SCENERY

Rice fields and volcanoes. The area around Tretes, East Java, offers a symphony of green terraces and towering peaks – without a tour bus in sight. See page 184.

Lakes and forests. From the Bukit Tekenang ranger station in West Kalimantan's Danau Sentarum National Park, an ethereal expanse of jungle and water unfurls. See page 321.

Stormy seas. Watch the Indian Ocean crashing beneath the towering white cliffs of Bali's new travel frontier, Nusa Penida. See page 263.

Above the clouds. The mountain village of Batutumonga offers spectacular views across the heart of Tana Toraja, especially at first light. See page 331.

Crater lake. Ascend through dense jungle to the ridge atop Lombok's Gunung Rinjani for fabulous vistas of the crater lake Segara Anak. One for experienced hikers. See page 276.

Sulawesi scuba diving.

MOST UNIQUE CULTURES

Best variety. The tiny, remote islands of the Solor and Alor archipelagos have Indonesia's highest concentration of unique cultures and handicrafts. See page 295.

Asmat. Once justly feared by outsiders, the Asmat of Papua still maintain strong traditions of ritual and woodcarving. See page 363.

Dayak. The Dayaks of Kalimantan's vast rainforests were once known as fierce head-hunters. See page 320.

Javanese. The Javanese are Indonesia's largest ethnic group, and are known for their court cultures and refined manners. See page 61.

Balinese. Vibrant tradition and global connectivity are artfully intertwined in Bali, an island uniquely at ease with past, present and future. See page 62.

Kecak dance performance on Bali.

BEST FESTIVALS

Pasola. An exciting thanksgiving ritual, Sumba's Pasola is mock war on horseback, held on a date determined by the migration of sea worms. See page 295.

Sanur Village Festival. This four-day festival on Bali promises entertainment for all, with an international kite-flying competition, water sports, dance, music and food. See page 383.

Waisak Day. The Buddhist Day of Enlightenment procession held at Borobudur, Central Java, attracts thousands of devotees from throughout Southeast Asia. See page 382.

Labuhan ritual. Hundreds of Javanese in traditional attire form a procession to Parangkusumo beach, south of Yogyakarta, where sacrifices are made to the South Sea Goddess. See page 382.

Independence Day. Every village and town is decorated two weeks before 17 August, Indonesia's Independence Day, with games, food fairs and family fun punctuating the celebrations. See page 383.

BEST BEACHES

Kuta beach, Bali. This leads the list as Indonesia's most famous hang-out beach and stretches north to Legian and Seminyak beaches and beyond. See page 230.

The Gilis. Three tiny dots of land off Lombok's west coast, each of the Gilis is hemmed with coral sand, with calm, clear waters beyond. See page 275.

Derawan archipelago. A favourite for adventurous divers off the east coast of Kalimantan, this small archipelago includes Derawan, Sangalaki and Nabucco islands, dive resorts and white-sand beaches. See page 307.

Pantai Merah. The fabulous Pantai Merah (Pink Beach) on Komodo island gets its name from the prolific red corals in surrounding crystal-clear waters. See page 286.

Togian Islands. In Sulawesi's azure Tomini Bay, the Togian Islands' scenic limestone cliffs and secluded white-sand beaches are also excellent for snorkelling and diving. See page 338.

Maluku. A premier dive destination, the Maluku Islands' shores are lined with sparkling-white beaches, particularly at Ambon and in the Kai archipelago to the southeast. See page 351.

Bali surf.

Legong dance.

UNIQUE ARCHITECTURE

Traditional houses, Tana Toraja, South Sulawesi. Tongkonan traditional houses in Tana Toraja are decorated with carved wooden panels. The more buffalo horns displayed, the wealthier the owner. See page 331.

Restored Art Deco buildings, Bandung. These Art Deco buildings are a remnant of the Dutch colonial era and are still in use today. See page 154.

Minangkabau architecture, West Sumatra. The Tanah Datar area is the best place to see traditional Minangkabau architecture, their distinctive roofs resembling the horns of a water buffalo. See page 113.

Traditional houses, West Sumba. The dwellings here feature steeply pitched roofs where the family's heirlooms are stored. Their four supporting posts are symbolically placed. See page 295.

Torajan house.

BEST PERFORMING ARTS

Ramayana epic. Performed seasonally on an open-air stage at Prambanan temple near Yogyakarta, the Hindu Ramayana epic epitomises Javanese culture. See page 93.

Hornbill dance. In days of yore, Kalimantan's Dayaks welcomed returning warriors with a traditional hornbill dance, now seen at harvest festivals. See page 87.

Contemporary dance. Students at Indonesian Art Institution universities (ISI) in Bali and Yogyakarta often combine contemporary and traditional dance. Performances are open to the public. See page 92.

Gamelan. Originating in West Bali, where competitions are held, jegog instruments are made of giant bamboo, their quality judged by resonance and tone. See page 252.

Wayang kulit. Fiercely complex, loaded with symbolism and requiring long immersion to fully understand, Indonesia's fabled shadow puppetry offers an atmospheric experience for even the uninitiated. See page 91.

BEST SHOPPING

Weaving villages. Visit the far-flung villages of Nusa Tenggara – notably on Flores, Sumba and Rote – for hand-woven ikat textiles. See page 99.

Pottery villages. Banyumulek, Masbagik and Penujak villages, Lombok, for export-quality hand-thrown pottery. See page 110.

Bali boutiques. Numerous small shops along the main roads of Seminyak, for export-quality fashions and home furnishings. See page 231.

Batik. Yogyakarta is the best place to look for traditional motifs in modern patterns and colours. See page 99.

BEST WILDLIFE AND TREKKING

Ujung Kulon National Park. West Java's major wildlife reserve shelters the endangered Javan rhino and numerous other forest species. See page 151.

Bogani Nani Wartabone National Park. In North Sulawesi, this area is home to rare, endemic Sulawesi animals including babirusas, anoas and Sulawesi warty pigs. See page 343.

Kerinci Seblat National Park. Kerinci Seblat in West Sumatra shelters Sumatran elephants and tigers, clouded leopards, Malayan sun bears and tapirs, and over 375 species of birds. See page 210.

Way Kambas National Park. In South Sumatra, Way Kambas is a sanctuary for Sumatran elephants and rhinos, assuring visitors of the chance to spot them. See page 215.

Tanjung Puting National Park. While orangutans are the flagship species of Tanjung Puting, Central Kalimantan, proboscis monkeys are also abundant and fun-to-watch. See page 317.

Grazing rhinos.

TRAVELLERS' TIPS

Indonesia's sheer size and intricate customs can be overwhelming. Below are a few insider tips to help smooth the way. While Java and Bali have good roads and decent infrastructure, in other regions the going is often slow. When planning a trip to Indonesia 'less is more' is always a good rule – don't try to cram in too many far-flung destinations, and keep a check on distances and journey times. Java or Bali alone could easily take up a month of your time.

Indonesia in general is by no means as socially conservative as the Middle East or the Indian subcontinent, but it still pays to dress respectfully away from the beach – covered shoulders and no above-the-knee shorts for men or women. Remove shoes before entering mosques and homes; don a sarong and sash before entering Balinese temples. Though its use is rapidly spreading, outside of tourist areas and big cities, English is still not widely spoken. Indonesians are generally very patient with foreign travellers, and will make great efforts to understand, but learning a few words of Bahasa Indonesia will make life easier, and will always earn a very warm response.

THE BEST OF INDONESIA: PLAN & BOOK YOUR TAILOR-MADE TRIP

Indonesia is an archipelago nation comprising several thousand islands, so to get the most out of a visit it's best to pick just a few. The islands of Java and Flores make for a delightful combination, offering pristine beaches, dramatic landscapes, exotic cultures and a warm Indonesian welcome. See pages 137 and 289.

△ **Day 5, Prambanan.** Yogyakarta is the perfect jumping off point for Prambanan, a 9th-century Hindu temple compound. The ornately-carved temples have sustained structural damage over the years and restorations are ongoing. So while you can wander around these magnificent ruins, be aware that certain areas may be out of bounds. See page 171.

▽ **Day 6, Borobudur.** Take the scenic route across riverbeds and rice fields to the ancient Buddhist temples of Borobudur, which have a long and colourful history. Built in the 8th- and 9th-centuries, the temples were later abandoned, only to be 'rediscovered' in the jungle in 1814. In the 20th-century Unesco stepped in, overseeing a huge restoration project in the 1970s, which utilised a staggering 10 percent of the population of Central Java. See page 166.

△ **Days 1 & 2, Jakarta.** The megatropolis of Jakarta, on the northwest coast of Java, is a good starting point. Take a taxi to the historical quarter of Kota, which bustles with street artists and food stalls. On the second day head for Medan Merdeka, a huge square where the 137m Monas Tower stands. Take the high-speed elevator to the observation deck for impressive city views. See page 139.

◁ **Days 3 & 4, Yogyakarta.** Head east into Central Java and the cultural hub of Yogyakarta. Explore the enormous Keraton, the Sultan's Palace, revelling in the gamelan music, traditional dancing and shadow puppet shows that take place in the inner pavilion. Afterwards, refuel with the Javanese dish of gudeg, a curry of young jackfruit and coconut. See page 158.

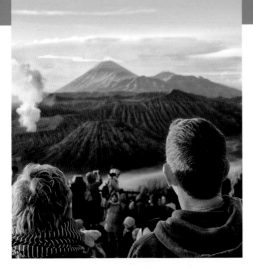

△ **Day 10, Komodo National Park**. The dragons in Komodo National Park, to the west of Flores, are something of an institution. The Park comprises three main islands plus numerous smaller ones, though the best place to see the dragons is the island of Komodo. They shouldn't be hard to spot - the largest living lizards in the world, komodos can weigh up to 70kg and reach three metres in length. See page 287.

△ **Days 7 & 8, Mt Bromo**. Make your way to the east of Java, with its wild, volcanic scenery. Base yourself in the cool highland city of Malang with its colonial Dutch architecture. Rise early on day 8 and head for the Bromo-Tengger-Semeru National Park, where you can begin your ascent of Gunung Bromo, a popular spot to watch the sunrise. See page 185.

▽ ▷ **Day 9, Flores**. The island of Flores is a natural wonderland. Make your way through lush valleys and plantations to Gunung Kelimutu where its three crater lakes constantly change colour. The surrounding coast is great for diving, with manta rays, tuna, octopus, barracuda and colourful reef fish to be spotted. See page 289.

You can plan and book this trip with Insight Guides, or we can help you create your own bespoke trip. Whether you're after adventure or a family-friendly holiday, we have a trip for you, including all the activities you enjoy and the sights you wish to see. All our trips are planned by local experts who help you get the most out of the destination. Visit **www.insightguides.com/holidays** to speak to one of our local travel experts.

Komodo dragons are the largest living lizard.

Mentawai man on Siberut.

Preparing a fishing trap off Alor.

ISLAND NATION

An island nation like no other, Indonesia's diversity is unsurpassed, with modernity and ancient tradition entwined, and historical wonders and cutting-edge metropolises sharing a magnificent tropical backdrop.

At the Banten Mosque in West Java.

Indonesia stretches 5,270km (3,274 miles) from its westernmost point to its easternmost extremity. But while the world's other mega-states are monolithic blocks of territory, this is a galaxy of landfalls, strung across the equator, linking the Indian and Pacific oceans and encompassing all the diversity of an entire continent. Made up of 17,508 islands by the latest official count, none of its attendant superlatives can convey Indonesia's scale or diversity: the world's greatest archipelagic state, largest Muslim-majority nation, third biggest democracy, and most volcanically active country.

Though Indonesia owes its modern borders to the legacy of Dutch rule, it is much more than a colonial construct. In earlier centuries mighty Hindu-Buddhist trading states stitched island to island in a web of commerce and shared cultural references, which reconfigured and continued after the arrival of Islam and Christianity. And the value of its spices tied the archipelago into global networks as long ago as the Roman era. A hardwired multiculturalism is the enduring legacy, with Indian, Chinese, Middle Eastern and European influences all leaving their traces, artfully intertwined with indigenous traditions.

Supremely fertile Java – home to the national capital, Jakarta, as well as more than half of the entire Indonesian population – has always been the lodestar of the archipelago, where the most sophisticated art forms and cultures developed. Since the emergence of international tourism, Java has vied for travellers' attention with its tiny neighbour, Bali, much-mythologised last bastion of Indonesia's ancient Hindu heritage and holidaymakers' paradise isle. But this is just the beginning. Nusa Tenggara and Maluku offer infinite island-hopping opportunities, while Sumatra, Kalimantan, Sulawesi and Papua are each bigger than many European nations, with much surviving wilderness and wildlife – from elusive Sumatran tigers to iconic orangutans.

Indonesia's postcolonial journey has not always been easy, with political turmoil – not to mention frequent natural disasters borne of its unstable geology – very much part of the story. But it has proved remarkably resilient, and is forging ahead in the 21st century as an increasingly self-confident and prosperous democracy. The pace of change is swift here, and old-world images of rice terraces, traditional villages and timeless tradition are counterpointed by Wi-Fi connections in the deepest jungles, and Instagram-obsessed local teens striking poses on remote islands. But certain constants always remain: epic volcanic landscapes, warm humour and a ready welcome, as well as a tantalising taste of spice.

A LAND OF MANY LANDS

The fourth-most populous nation in the world, Indonesia encompasses 6,000 inhabited islands and an extraordinarily diverse mix of cultures and landscapes.

The far-flung islands of Indonesia span an impressively broad spectrum of world history and human civilisation – from ancient Hindu-Buddhist temples to modern luxury resorts, and from remote traditional villages to the immense metropolis of Jakarta. The country's motto, *Bhinneka Tunggal Ika*, usually translated as 'Unity in Diversity', is no mere slogan. The population of around 265 million people is derived from more than 300 ethnic and perhaps several hundred sub-ethnic groups who speak 700 distinct languages and dialects. The common elements are a central government and a national language, Bahasa Indonesia, a derivative of Malay.

The fourth-most populous nation in the world, Indonesia straddles two geographically defined racial groups, the Asians to the west and the Melanesians in the east. The majority are Asians, particularly in the western part of the archipelago. Over the centuries, mostly through commerce and trade, Indians, Arabs and Europeans have mingled with the indigenous people. The largest non-indigenous ethnic group is the Chinese, who control a significant share of the nation's wealth while comprising fewer than five percent of the population. Around 88 percent of Indonesians are Muslim, eight percent are Christian and there are small Hindu, Buddhist and Confucian minorities. In many cases, at least in the rural areas, these beliefs are augmented by centuries-old indigenous traditions.

Indonesia's people are unevenly distributed across the archipelago and more than half inhabit Java and Bali alone, which cover only seven percent of the total land area. With more than 140 million people living in Java – approximately 58 percent of the Indonesian

A grey langur at a Bali temple.

⊘ VOLCANIC FERTILITY

Active volcanoes dominate the landscape of many of the islands, their majestic smoking cones spewing forth millions of tonnes of ash and debris at irregular intervals. Eventually, much of this is washed down to form gently sloping alluvial plains. Where the soil is acidic, the land is infertile and practically useless. But where it is alkaline, as on Java and Bali and a few scattered locations on other islands, it has produced spectacularly fertile land. On both these islands, abundant rainfall fills rivers that originate in the mountains and meander through farmlands. Java and Bali have always been Indonesia's primary rice-growing areas, and thus the centres of population and political power.

population – the demands on its land and resources are considerable.

The archipelago is the world's largest. Its 17,508 islands are strewn across some 5,120km (3,200 miles) of tropical seas, straddling the equator. When superimposed on a map of North America, Indonesia stretches from Seattle to Bermuda. On a map of Europe, it extends east from Ireland to beyond the Caspian Sea.

Four-fifths of this vast area is occupied by ocean, and many of the islands are tiny – no more than rocky outcrops populated, perhaps, by a few seabirds. About 6,000 are large enough to be inhabited, and New Guinea and Borneo (Indonesia claims two-thirds of each) rank as the third- and fourth-largest islands in the world (after Australia and Greenland). Of the other major islands, Sumatra is slightly larger than Sweden, Sulawesi is around half the size of Germany, and Java is a little smaller than England. With a total land area of 1.9 million sq km (733,647 sq miles), Indonesia is the world's 15th-largest nation in terms of size.

VOLCANOES, EARTHQUAKES AND TSUNAMIS

Befitting its reputation as the exotic Spice Islands of the East, Indonesia also constitutes one of the world's most diverse and biologically intriguing areas. Unique geological and climatic conditions have created spectacularly varied tropical habitats – from the exceptionally fertile rice lands of Java and Bali to the luxuriant rainforests of Sumatra, Kalimantan and Sulawesi, and from the savannah grasslands of Nusa Tenggara to the jungle-laced, snowcapped Gunung Puncak Jaya in Papua.

The geological history of the region is complex. The islands are relatively young; the earliest dates from only the end of the Miocene Epoch, 6 million years ago – just yesterday on the geological timescale. Since then, the archipelago has been the scene of violent tectonic activity, as islands were torn from jostling super-continents or pushed up by colliding tectonic plates, and then enlarged in earth-wrenching volcanic explosions. The process continues today – this is part of the Pacific 'ring of fire', with Australia drifting slowly northwards as the immense Pacific plate presses south and west to meet it and the Asian mainland. Indonesia lies

Of Indonesia's major volcanoes, 18 are on Java, 12 dominate Sumatra and two are in eastern Bali. Kalimantan has no volcanoes.

along the lines of impact, a fact reflected in its geography and its seismic instability.

Of the hundreds of volcanoes in Indonesia, over 167 are active, and hardly a year passes without at least one major eruption. On a densely populated island like Java, they inevitably bring

An early-19th-century map of the East Indies.

death and destruction. When Krakatau, off Java's west coast, blew up in 1883 with a force equivalent to that of 10,000 Hiroshima atomic bombs, it created tidal waves that killed more than 36,000 people on Java. The eruption was heard as far away as Sri Lanka and Sydney, and the great quantities of debris hurled into the atmosphere caused vivid sunsets all over the world for three years afterwards. But the Krakatau explosion was less consequential than the truly cataclysmic 1815 eruption of Mount Tambora, on Sumbawa, the largest in recorded history. Around 90,000 people were killed and over 80 cu km (20 cu miles) of ejected material dimmed the sun for many months, producing a disastrous 'year without summer' in distant Europe.

Already in the 21st century several devastating natural disasters have occurred here. The 2004 Indian Ocean tsunami, triggered by a 9.0-magnitude submarine earthquake, originated off the west coast of Sumatra; almost 170,000 people died and 500,000 were displaced in Indonesia alone. Thanks to international aid, early tsunami warning signals are now in place across 28 Indian Ocean countries, drills are regularly held and Indonesia's Disaster Risk Reduction programme has been introduced at international forums.

A tropical forest on the lower slopes of Gunung Rinjani, Lombok.

At a few minutes before 6am one Saturday in May 2006, while many people were sleeping, a 5.9-magnitude earthquake originated deep in the sea along tectonic plate boundaries near Yogyakarta, Central Java. Ninety percent of the homes along the fault line collapsed, killing nearly 6,000 people. Refusing all foreign aid, the Indonesian government provided compensation to those who survived, but it was not enough to rebuild their homes and lives. Years later, even though entire villages have been rebuilt, it is estimated that the survivors owe a debt of US$5.86 million to state-owned banks. In late 2010, Yogyakarta suffered once again, during a sustained eruption of Gunung Merapi, which rained ash on the city and surrounding countryside, and devastated farming communities on the mountain's slopes, killing around 300 people. In 2013, a 6.1-magnitude quake struck the far western part of Sumatra, in Aceh province, killing 29 people and destroying 1,500 buildings. Earthquakes happen on Indonesian islands quite frequently.

The upside to these recent tragedies is that the country has greatly improved its preparedness and response to natural disasters, and is now a consultant to other nations on such matters. In 2011 it sent a relief team to Japan following its 9.0-magnitude earthquake and ensuing tsunami. The Indonesian people were honoured to help, given that Japan had been one of the first to offer consultation and aid in Indonesia's time of need in the past.

Indonesians have also recently become more aware of environmental challenges. Farmers are experimenting with biogas, derived from vegetables, to fuel machinery. Returning to their forefathers' ways, they are using manure instead of chemicals to fertilise crops. Local governments have planted billions of trees. Aid money has been used in some areas to buy solar-powered pumps, providing water to formerly parched areas.

SCATTERED POPULATIONS

As a result of its geographical peculiarities, Indonesia's hundreds of ethnic groups have been isolated from each other right through history, allowing them to evolve independently and resulting in a multitude of languages and traditions. It was not until road systems were put in place that many isolated villages became aware of the existence of other groups relatively close by. Yet while the implementation of a national language in 1945 has been instrumental in uniting millions of dissimilar peoples into one nation, close scrutiny reveals how unique each group is even today.

In addition to their separation through geography, language and cultural traditions, Indonesia's people are divided by more commonplace factors such as wealth, social status, education and health care. Generally speaking, the further away from an urban area a village is, the more likely it is to adhere strictly to ancient traditions and rituals, the closer the family ties, the poorer the health care is, and the lower the education opportunities are likely to be.

At the same time, much of Indonesia has changed enormously in recent years. Modern highway systems connect hamlets to marketplaces and ports more efficiently than ever before. Improved transport includes not only public buses and ferries to help people get

will never be enough of them to go around. The internet has perhaps made the greatest impact of all, connecting citizens of even far-flung areas not only to other Indonesians, but also to the situations and attitudes of the outside world.

All these factors have helped to minimise distinctions between people, for better or worse, but they have also created even larger gaps between those who have access to them and the millions who continue to live in poverty and relative isolation.

Rescue workers search for survivors after Gunung Merapi erupts in 2010.

from one point to another, but there is now increased access to bank loans to finance the millions of motorbikes seen throughout the country. The growing number of budget airlines that reach hitherto inaccessible islands also makes flying more affordable to the growing middle-income group.

Communications, too, have vastly improved over the last decade. Until recently the biggest impact on Indonesians nationwide has been television – nearly every village, no matter how small or remote, has at least one TV and can receive the government-sponsored television channel at the minimum. In the past decade, sales of cellular phones have burgeoned, as the demand for landlines is so great that there

⊘ A DISASTROUS YEAR

Even by Indonesian standards, 2018 was a bad year for natural disasters. On 5 August, Lombok was rocked by a powerful quake. There was severe damage in the north and west of the island, and around 500 people were killed. The following month, a 7.5 undersea quake off Sulawesi prompted a major tsunami – the worst since that in Aceh in 2004 – which devastated the coast around Palu and killed more than 4,000 people. In West Java, meanwhile, which had already experienced a relatively minor quake in January, another tsunami, prompted by a partial collapse of the offshore Anak Krakatau volcano on 22 December, killed more than 400 people.

Prambanan Temple dates from the 9th century, the peak of Sriwijaya power.

DECISIVE DATES

Prambanan Temple.

PREHISTORIC ERA

1.81 million years ago
Solo Man *(Homo erectus soloensis)* inhabits Central Java.

40,000 years ago
Fossil records of modern humans found in Indonesia.

5,000 BC
Austronesian peoples begin moving into Indonesia from the Philippines.

500 BC–AD 500
Dong Son Bronze Age influences Indonesian arts.

INDIANISED KINGDOMS

AD 400
Hindu kingdoms emerge in West Java and East Kalimantan.

850
Sanjaya (early Mataram) seizes control of Central Java; the Sailendras flee to Sriwijaya, southern Sumatra.

860–1000
The golden age of Sriwijaya.

910–1080
Javanese political centre moves to East Java; rise of Hindu kingdoms on Bali.

SINGHASARI AND MAJAPAHIT

1222–75
East Java's Singhasari dynasty founded, gains control of maritime trade.

1294
Singhasari falls to Majapahit kingdom, the most powerful in Indonesian history, which reaches its zenith under Hayam Wuruk in the 14th century.

15th century
Majapahit is conquered by Muslim Demak, ending the Hindu-Buddhist era in Java. Some of the Hindu-Javanese aristocracy moves to Bali.

Mid-16th century
Muslim Banten and Cirebon sultanates established in Java.

Late 16th century
Muslim Mataram kingdom founded in Central Java. The Dutch arrive.

DUTCH COLONIAL YEARS

1602–3
United Dutch East India Company (VOC) establishes trading post in Banten.

1619
Dutch take over Jayakarta (now Jakarta) and rename it Batavia; subsequent sieges by Mataram forces repelled.

1740–55
A major conflict originating in Batavia leads to civil war in Mataram. A new Javanese capital at Surakarta is established.

1755
A Dutch-brokered peace deal sees Mataram divided between two courts, Surakarta and Yogyakarta.

1799–1800
VOC is dissolved; Dutch state assume control.

RESISTANCE AND REPRESSION

1811–16
British interregnum under Thomas Stamford Raffles temporarily replaces Dutch rule in Java.

1812
Raffles engineers an assault on the Yogyakarta Kraton, during which the entire court treasury and archive are looted by the British.

1825–30
Rebel Yogyakarta prince Diponegoro leads the cataclysmic Java War against the Dutch; conflict ends with Diponegoro's capture and exile.

1830–50
Dutch introduce the Cultivation System, a land tax payable by labour or land use. Famine and hardship ensues, but a complex economy develops.

NATIONAL AWAKENING

1908
Dutch-educated Indonesians form regional student organisations; national consciousness takes shape.

1910–30
Turbulent period of strikes, violence and organised rebellions and political awakening.

1927
Sukarno tries to unite nationalists, Muslims and Marxists into a single mass movement. He is imprisoned by the Dutch and later exiled.

WORLD WAR II AND INDEPENDENCE

1942–4
Japanese invade Bali and Java; promise independence.

1945
Japan surrenders. Nationalist leaders Sukarno and Hatta declare Indonesia's independence. Dutch return to resume control; war for independence breaks out.

1949
Dutch acknowledge Indonesia's independence under UN pressure.

Late 1950s
Separatist insurgencies prompt Sukarno to declare martial law and resurrect 1945 'revolutionary' constitution.

SUKARNO AND SUHARTO YEARS

1959
Sukarno dissolves parliament and increases confrontations with foreign powers.

Sukarno and his ministers, 1958.

1965
Nationwide anti-communist pogroms follow a failed military putsch in Jakarta; General Suharto assumes de facto control.

1966
Sukarno persuaded to sign over powers to Suharto, who takes over presidency. Until 1998, Suharto is re-elected six times in rigged elections.

1997
Asian economic crisis begins; rupiah collapses and Indonesia's public and private debts become unmanageable.

1998
Suharto is forced to resign amid mass student uprising as economic chaos continues.

CONTEMPORARY INDONESIA

1998–2001
The reform period gets underway, with three presidents ruling in quick succession.

2002
Terrorist bombs in Bali kill 202 people, devastate the tourism industry and prompt fears of further Islamist violence.

2004
In historic first direct presidential election, Susilo Bambang Yudhoyono (SBY) comes into office. A devastating tsunami sweeps northwest Sumatra; in the aftermath the decades-long Aceh conflict comes to an end.

2008
Suharto dies, ending a major chapter in Indonesian history.

2009
SBY is re-elected by overwhelming majority. Poverty rate drops from 60 percent in 1990 to 14.1 percent.

2010
Amid global economic crisis, Indonesia emerges as the region's third-strongest economy after China and India.

2014
Former Jakarta governor Joko Widodo, popularly known as Jokowi, wins the presidency for PDI-P amid great optimism.

2015
Brazil, the Netherlands and Australia recall their ambassadors from Indonesia after the execution by firing squad of convicted drug traffickers from their countries.

2019
Jokowi wins a second term after a bitter and divisive battle against challenger, Prabowo Subianto. Jokowi announces that the capital of Indonesia will move from Jakarta to the province of East Kalimantan.

BIRTH OF EMPIRES

Indonesians' prehistoric ancestors, Java Man and Solo Man lived in a fertile region that later saw the rise of great maritime empires.

The late 19th-century discovery of hominid remains on Java island took the anthropological world by storm when they were identified as the first scientific evidence on the planet of *Homo erectus*. Early 20th-century findings of more fossils in nearby Sangiran (Sragen) proved to be even older. Indonesia is still throwing up unexpected findings that cast new light on human origins. In 2003 remains were discovered in Flores of a diminutive hominid, Homo floresiensis, quickly nicknamed 'the Flores Hobbit', which may have survived as recently as 12,000 years ago. Scientific debate is ongoing as to whether the Hobbits represent a new species, a late survivor of Homo erectus, or a genetically distinct human population.

When it comes to modern humans, there have been two major migratory waves into Indonesia. One was the Melanesian people who entered, perhaps via land bridges, from the north from mainland Asia. The other was the Austronesians, who were great seafarers and whose populations spread throughout Polynesia and Southeast Asia, extending across the Indian Ocean to Madagascar.

From these beginnings mighty empires arose that stretched as far afield as Cambodia, while the fertile lands of the archipelago would produce spices sought after and fought over, extending Indonesia's influence from Europe to China.

The most striking megaliths in Indonesia are the carved statues of riding men and wrestling animals found on the Pasemah highlands in South Sumatra. No definite date can be given for these.

Homo floresiensis skull.

PREHISTORY

Indonesian archaeological findings have contributed more than their share of controversy in the past. In 1891, a Dutch military physician discovered a fossilised primate jawbone with human characteristics on the banks of the Bengawan Solo River, Central Java. The jawbone was at first discounted by anthropologists who thought it was likely to belong to an extinct species of apes. But in the following year, two more hominid fossils were uncovered. This caused a sensation: together the finds were believed to represent the world's first evidence of Darwin's 'missing link'. Darwin's evolutionary theories were still in dispute at the time and the discovery, dubbed Java Man, was only vindicated with the unearthing of similar fossils outside Beijing in 1921.

It is now thought that the Java Man fossils are about 1.66 million years old. Originally named *Pithecanthropus erectus*, later reclassified *Homo erectus*, it justified migration theories between China and Indonesia. Until later discoveries were made in Kenya, anthropologists theorised that the ancestors of modern humans were Asian in origin.

Then in 1936 German palaeo-anthropologist G.H.R. von Koenigswald discovered a larger collection of fossils in nearby Ngandong village, at

Cave paintings at Maros, Sulawesi.

Sangiran, 18km (11 miles) north of Solo. Dubbed 'Mojokerto Child' (later called Solo Man), the finds were controversial from the outset due to the size of the cranium, debunking previous theories of the intellectual capacity of the now-extinct *Homo erectus*. After exhaustive studies and much debate, most scientists now concede that Solo Man *(Homo erectus soloensis)* was older than Java Man, about 1.81 million years, or about the same age as the Kenya fossils. As a result, it now appears that instead of a single origin of modern man, parallel evolutions occurred in two places at different rates. Interestingly, Solo Man seems to have survived until as recently as 20,000–50,000 years ago, perhaps living alongside early Melanesian settlers, who

began moving into the archipelago from mainland Asia during this period.

Beginning about 20,000 years ago, there is evidence of human burials and partial cremations in Indonesia. Several cave paintings (mainly hand stencils, but also human and animal figures) found in southwestern Sulawesi and New Guinea may be 10,000 or more years old.

The Neolithic centuries – which appear to have begun soon after the end of the last Ice Age, around 10,000 BC – are characterised here, as elsewhere, by the advent of village settlements, domesticated animals, polished stone tools, pottery and food cultivation. In Southwest Sulawesi and the East Timor plain, for instance, pottery vessels and open bowls dating from about 3,000 BC have been found, together with shell bracelets, discs, beads, adzes and the bones of pigs and dogs.

The first agriculturalists in Indonesia probably grew yams before the introduction of rice. In fact, yams are still a staple crop on many eastern islands where the relatively dry climate hampers rice production. Bark clothing was produced with stone-pounding tools, and pottery was shaped with the aid of a wooden paddle and a stone anvil tapper.

Rice production and various other cultural features that survive to the present day arrived in Indonesia with the second wave of migration – Austronesian-speaking peoples who moved southwards from northeast Asia into the region approximately 7,000 years ago. The Austronesians were great maritime travellers, and their expansion eventually went far beyond Indonesia – to the

⊘ THE FLORES HOBBITS

The discovery of *Homo floresiensis*, the so-called 'Hobbit', in the Liang Bua cave in Flores in 2003 was the most significant paleoanthropological discovery so far this century. The date range of the fossils is vast – between 12,000 years and almost 100,000 years. Debate continues as to the exact evolutionary status of the Hobbits, though there appears to be an emerging consensus that they are related to *Homo erectus*. Local people wryly suggest that they were in the know long before the archaeologists – there are old folk tales of a race of tiny people, known as the Ebu Gogo, dwelling in the deepest parts of the Flores forest.

Many Indian traders settled in Indonesia and intermarried with locals. In addition to introducing dance, music, literature, the Sanskrit language and religion, they brought military discipline and the division of labourers into castes.

Pacific islands in one direction, and to Madagascar in the other where the languages spoken today are related to those of western Indonesia.

DONG SON BRONZE CULTURE

It was once thought that Southeast Asia's Bronze Age began with the Chinese-influenced Dong Son bronze culture of northern Vietnam in the 1st millennium BC. However, the discovery of 5,000-year-old copper and bronze tools in northern Thailand raised the possibility of similar developments elsewhere. For now, though, all known early Indonesian bronzes are clearly of the Dong Son type.

The finest Dong Son ceremonial bronze drums and axes are decorated with engraved geometric, animal and human motifs. This decorative style was highly influential in many fields of Indonesian art, and seems to have spread together with the bronze casting technique, as ancient stone moulds have been found as far east as New Guinea.

Who were the Indonesian producers of Dong Son bronzes? It is difficult to say, but it seems small kingdoms based on wet-rice agriculture and foreign trade were flourishing in the archipelago during this period. Articles of Indian manufacture have been found at several prehistoric sites in Indonesia, and a panel from a bronze drum found on Sangeang island, near Sumbawa, depicts figures in ancient Chinese dress. Early Han texts mention the clove-producing islands of eastern Indonesia, and it is certain that by the 2nd century BC, trade was widespread in the archipelago.

INDIANISED KINGDOMS

Beginning in the 2nd century AD, a number of sophisticated civilisations emerged in Southeast Asia – civilisations whose cosmology, literature, architecture and political organisation were patterned on those of India. These kingdoms are known for the wonderful monuments they created:

Borobudur, Prambanan, Angkor, Pagan and others. Yet their creators remain largely an enigma.

The most plausible theory is that Southeast Asian rulers Indianised their own kingdoms – either by employing Indian Brahmans or sending their own people to India to acquire knowledge. Sanskrit writing and texts, along with sophisticated Indian rituals and architectural techniques, afforded a ruler greater organisational control, wealth and social status. They also enabled them to participate in an expanding Indian trading network.

A ceremonial Dong Son bronze drum.

The oldest surviving local references to Indonesian rulers and kingdoms come in the form of inscribed stones. Using the South Indian *Pallava* script, the stone inscriptions were issued by Indonesian rulers in two different areas of the archipelago: Kutai on the eastern coast of Kalimantan, and Tarumanegara on the Citarum River, in West Java near Bogor. Both rulers were Hindus.

There is also the interesting figure Fa Xian, a Chinese Buddhist monk who journeyed to India in the early 5th century to obtain Buddhist scriptures and on his way home was shipwrecked and stranded on Java. Fa Xian noted that what he considered 'heretical' Brahmanist Hinduism, rather than Buddhism, dominated Java at the time.

At the end of the 7th century, a Buddhist king-dom at Palembang took over the vital Melaka and Sunda straits. This was Sriwijaya, which ruled throughout the next 600 years.

SRIWIJAYA'S MARITIME TRADE

The Sriwijaya kingdom relied for existence not on agriculture, but on control of maritime trade. It has been speculated that Sriwijaya rose to prominence as a result of a substitution of Sumatran aromatics – *p'o-ssu* – for expensive Middle Eastern frankincense and myrrh. But

Both Buddhist, Sailendra and Sriwijaya main-tained close relations and controlled Java for about a century. During this time, they con-structed the magnificent Buddhist monuments Borobudur, Mendut, Kalasan and numerous oth-ers in the shadow of Gunung Merapi.

Meanwhile, the Sanjaya line continued to rule over outlying areas as vassals of the Sailendra, building many Hindu temples. Around 850, the Sanjaya prince Rakai Pikatan married a Sailendra princess and seized control of Central Java. The Sailendra fled to Sriwijaya, blocking all Javanese

Borobudur.

Sriwijaya was also located in a strategic position and apparently achieved regular direct sailings to India and China by the late 8th century.

The nearest area suitable for wet-rice agri-culture was in Central Java, where great Indian-ised kingdoms established themselves from the early 8th century onwards. They first supplied Sriwijaya with rice, and then later began to com-pete with that empire for a share of the trade.

SANJAYA AND THE SAILENDRA

The rivalry between Buddhist and Hindu rul-ing families in Central Java bore fruit with the supplanting of the Hindu rulers Sanjaya and his descendants by the Sailendra, a Buddhist line of kings from northern Java.

shipping throughout the South China Sea for more than a century. Rakai Pikatan commemorated his victory by erecting the splendid Prambanan tem-ple, the Hindu equivalent of Buddhist Borobudur.

A succession of Hindu kings followed, but the centre of royal power shifted to East Java around 930. Various factors might account for this. The Sailendra kings, who were installed at Sriwijaya and had shut off the vital overseas trade from Java's north coast, may have threatened to return to Central Java. An eruption of Gunung Merapi may have covered Central Java in volcanic ash. There is also the possibility of an epidemic or of mass migration to the more fertile lands of East Java.

An eastern Javanese empire prospered in the 10th century and attacked and occupied

Sriwijaya for two years. Sriwijaya retaliated later with a huge seaborne force that destroyed the Javanese capital, killed the ruler, King Dharmawangsa, and splintered the realm into petty fiefdoms. It took nearly 20 years for the next great king, Airlangga, to restore the empire.

Airlangga was the dead king's nephew, and he acceded to the throne in 1019 after the Sriwijayan forces departed. He is best known as a patron of the arts and an ascetic. To appease his two ambitious sons, he divided the empire into equal halves, Kediri and Janggala (or Daha and Kahuripan). Kediri became the more powerful and is remembered today as the source of numerous works of old Javanese literature, mainly adaptations of the Indian epics in the poetic *kekawin* form.

Java prospered as never before under the rule of successive East Java empires. At this time, the Javanese were the master shipbuilders and mariners of Southeast Asia. The Singhasari dynasty was founded by Ken Arok in 1222. During his rule of Janggala, Ken Arok revolted against his sovereign, the ruler of Kediri, and set up his new capital at Singhasari. The extraordinary Kertanagara, the last Singhasari king, was a scholar and a statesman of the Tantric Bhairawa sect of Buddhism. In 1275 and 1291, he sent successful naval expeditions against Sriwijaya and wrested control of the maritime trade.

MAJAPAHIT

Kertanagara's son-in-law Raden Wijaya married four of Kertanagara's daughters and established

a new capital in 1294 by the Brantas River (near present-day Trowulan) in an area known for its *pahit* (bitter) *maja* (gourd) fruits. The new kingdom became known as Majapahit. Its extensive system of canals was probably used to transport rice and other goods downriver to the seaports.

Majapahit reached its zenith in the mid-14th century under Wijaya's grandson, Hayam Wuruk, and his able prime minister, Gajah Mada. They controlled the sea lanes throughout the Indonesian archipelago, exerting political and cultural influence, if not outright control, over a vast

The splendour of Prambanan is an indicator of Sriwijaya's wealth.

area. Decline set in almost immediately after Hayam Wuruk's death in 1389. A smouldering struggle for supremacy erupted into civil war between 1403 and 1406, and although the country was reunited in 1429, Majapahit had lost control of the western Java Sea and the straits to a new Muslim power located at Melaka.

Towards the end of the 15th century, Majapahit and Kediri were conquered by the new Muslim state, Demak, on Java's north coast. Although it was many decades before the whole of Java converted to Islam, this marked the end of Hindu-Buddhist dominance in Java. Some of the former Majapahit elite appear to have relocated to Bali.

⊙ KUBLAI KHAN SNUBBED

In the late 13th century, the Hindu-Buddhist king Kertanagara's wealth was so great that Kublai Khan, the Mongol emperor of China, sent ambassadors to demand tribute from Java. Kertanagara not only refused, but disfigured the Mongol envoy, for which gesture the enraged Khan sent a powerful fleet in 1293 to Java.

The fleet landed only to discover that Kertanagara had been murdered by his vassal, Jayakatwang. The Chinese, allied with Kertanagara's son-in-law, Raden Wijaya, stayed in Java for about a year and defeated Jayakatwang. Raden Wijaya then turned on the Mongol generals, drove them off and founded the Majapahit kingdom.

A TRADING POWER

Maritime trade was the conduit that brought foreigners
of many different nationalities, with their ideas,
technology and religions, to Indonesia's shores.

Ancient Chinese chronicles describe the
islands of Indonesia as a wilderness of jungles,
marshes, ferocious wild animals and naked
natives who hunted and fished with poisoned
arrows. Yet a few centuries later, when the Portuguese came to the archipelago, Indonesia's
cities equalled the grandeur of those in Europe.

EARLY TRADE

The Chinese traded in Indonesia from at least
206 BC, and they were later followed by Persians,
Indians, Arabs, Siamese and Burmese. This once-
wild land became a transit point between the
West and the East, where Indonesians exchanged
precious stones, pearls, gold, silk, sandalwood
and spices with foreign merchants. By the 1st
century AD, Indonesian spices were available in
the Roman Empire. No individual traders were
routinely making the journey all the way from
the Spice Islands of Maluku to Europe, however.
Instead Indonesian produce travelled via multiple
way stations across the Indian Ocean, through the
Middle East and into the Mediterranean – a trade
route which endured until the arrival of the Portuguese, hundreds of years later.

Early in the first millennium AD Hinduism
and Buddhism from India began to influence
Indonesia. These religions began as court cultures, gradually extending their influence to
city-dwellers, but largely bypassing the rest of
the population.

> The prices that nutmeg, mace, pepper and cloves
> attracted in Europe were as much as 2,500 percent
> over what traders paid for them in Indonesia.

A wooden dragon carving from a Dayak canoe.

By the 7th century AD, the Buddhist Sriwijaya
dynasty (based in today's Palembang, South
Sumatra) was the greatest maritime empire in
Southeast Asia. It controlled the Melaka Strait
– the narrow channel between Sumatra and the
Malay coast that functioned as a crucial conduit
for all maritime trade between the Middle East,
India and China – as well as the western part of
Indonesia, most of the Malay Peninsula, and even
claimed Sri Lanka. Sriwijaya became the centre
of Buddhist learning for Southeast Asia and had
a university where Chinese pilgrims studied en
route to India. It was heavily involved in trade and
owned ships that sailed to India and China. Sriwijaya's greatest glory occurred in 1200 when,
together with Burma's Bagan kingdom and the

Khmer kingdom in Cambodia, it was one of the three greatest empires in Southeast Asia.

Around the same time, the Javanese kings of the interior had adopted Hinduism from India as their faith. They surrounded themselves with the music, dance, art and language (Sanskrit) associated with that religion, while the ordinary Javanese retained their original beliefs and traditions. In the 9th century, the reigning Hindu Sanjaya dynasty and rival Buddhist Sailendra dynasties merged through marriage, which was when Borobudur and its accompanying Buddhist temples were constructed.

trade routes through South and East Asia. Conversion to Islam ensured that Sumatran rulers could participate in the growing international trade network and receive protection against the encroachments of two aggressive regional powers – the Siamese to the north and the Javanese to the east.

Islam received its greatest boost when, in 1436, a shrewd Melaka king converted to the faith upon returning from an extended stay in China. Until then, Melaka had been a vassal of China ruled by descendants of the Buddhist Sriwijaya dynasty and peninsular kings who had been attacked and

Islam became well established in the 13th century.

TRADE AND ISLAM

Islam arrived in the Indonesian archipelago atop the crest of economic expansion along the trade routes of the East. Although Muslim traders had visited the region for centuries, it was not until Gujarat, an important Indian trading centre, fell into Muslim hands in the 13th century that Indonesian rulers began to convert to the new faith. The trading ports on the northeastern coast of Sumatra immediately saw the advantages of converting and became the first Islamic domains.

Muslim merchants, who controlled the overland Silk Road from China and India to Europe, via Persia and the Levant, had become increasingly powerful. With India's major textile-producing ports in their hands, they began to dominate the maritime

⊘ PROPAGATION BY THEATRE

According to Javanese chronicles, the *Wali Songo*, nine semi-mythical Muslim saints, propagated Islam through the Javanese shadow plays *(wayang kulit)* and gamelan music. They introduced the Islamic confession of faith and the reading of Koranic prayers to performances of the Hindu *Ramayana* and *Mahabharata* epics. There is no historical evidence for this means of conversion, but it serves as an effective symbol of Java's uniquely syncretic culture. Today, Islam is the professed religion of more than 87 percent of all Indonesians and its traditions and rituals affect all aspects of their daily life.

evicted by the Javanese and Siamese during the 14th century. China had proved a valuable patron of Melaka since its founding in 1402, but by 1436, China's influence in the region was on the wane, and the Siamese were again demanding tribute. By 1500, Melaka was to become a major trading port in the region and the greatest emporium in the East.

THE END OF HINDU-BUDDHIST JAVA

During the 15th century, all of the trading ports of the western archipelago were brought within Melaka's orbit, including the important ports

Muslim kingdom of Demak on the north-central coast attacked and conquered the last great Hindu-Buddhist kingdom on Java, Majapahit. They unseated the Majapahit king and annexed the agriculturally rich Javanese hinterlands. Demak then consolidated its control over the entire north coast, emerging as the master of Java by the 16th century.

During the 16th century, Islam continued to spread throughout the Indonesian archipelago, but the whole system of Islamic economic and political alliances was swiftly overturned in the

Java grew wealthy on the proceeds of maritime trade, enabling the construction of major religious buildings, such as the Grand Mosque at Demak.

along the north coast of Java. Traditionally, these ports owed their allegiance to the great inland Hindu-Javanese kingdoms, acting in effect as import-export and shipping agents, exchanging Javanese-grown rice for spices and other luxury items in a complex series of value-added transactions. After about 1400, however, the power of the inland Javanese rulers was rapidly declining, and the coastal rulers were seeking ways to assert their independence and retain the profits of the trade. Gradually, through intermarriage between leading Muslim traders and local aristocrats, relations were cemented with Melaka.

A turning point was reached sometime in the late 15th century when the newly founded

dramatic conquest of Malacca by a small band of Portuguese in 1511.

THE FIRST EUROPEANS ARRIVE

By the time the Portuguese arrived, news of the hitherto closely guarded secret location of the fabled Spice Islands had leaked out, and greed for the riches that possession of nutmeg, mace, cloves, pepper and sandalwood – then as valuable as gold – kicked in. In order to get to the Spice Islands, ships had to pass through the Melaka Strait. Thus, whoever had control over that protected stretch of sea held the keys to those treasures.

The first Portuguese ships were heavily armed men-of-war. Prior to their arrival, the exchange of goods was controlled by a feudal network of nobility and traders, and had been largely peaceful when not affected by piracy and political infighting. However, the Europeans – beginning with the Portuguese – brought a new, aggressive way of doing business backed by firepower, shocking the Indonesians, Arabs, Indians and Chinese who had been working together for centuries.

Portugal's first attack was on Melaka, which fell, but only after a bitter struggle that involved support from as far away as the Ottoman Empire. From Melaka, Portuguese ships proceeded to the rival kingdoms at Ternate and Tidore in Maluku, the world's only source of valuable cloves, and an important base for forays to tiny Banda, the only source of nutmeg. Tidore refused their approaches. About the same time, the Spanish arrived, under the leadership of an exiled Portuguese, Ferdinand Magellan.

The Portuguese were successful at wooing the Ternate king in exchange for their protection against Tidore. Fighting between the Spanish and Portuguese for control of the spice trade continued for 40 years until their governments in Europe agreed on a delineation of spheres of interest. Portugal kept Maluku while the Philippines went to Spain.

By that time there was resistance against the Portuguese. Ternate fort was continually besieged for six more years, while Ambon was eventually deserted. Portuguese Ternate fell in 1574, and Portugal's aura of invincibility was destroyed. Spain had already conquered Brunei and was standing by to take control of Maluku's

spices, and certainly would have except for an astonishing event in Europe: King Philip II of Spain united Portugal to his throne in 1580.

Meanwhile in Java, the mighty Muslim Mataram kingdom was emerging, based close to modern Yogyakarta and set to hold sway over most of the island within a few decades. The major maritime power, meanwhile, was Makassar on the southwest coast of Sulawesi. But while the Portuguese power in Maluku slowly disintegrated, the first English and Dutch ships arrived on the scene.

A statue of the first king of Majapahit (rule 1293–1309) at the Indonesian National Museum, Jakarta.

☉ GREEN CITIES

During the 16th century, Indonesia's cities were physically different from those in Europe, the Middle East, India and China. For the most part built without walls, they were located at river mouths or on wide plains, and relied upon surrounding villages for their defence. An official envoy from the Sultanate of Aceh to the Ottoman Empire explained that Acehnese defences consisted not of walls, but of 'stout hearts in fighting the enemy, and a large number of elephants'.

Indonesian cities tended also to be green. Coconut, banana and other fruit trees grew everywhere, and most of the widely spaced wooden or bamboo houses had vegetable gardens. The royal compound was the

centre for defence and might have walls and a moat. With perhaps no more than 5 million people in the entire archipelago, land had no intrinsic value except what people made of it. In 1613, when the English wanted some land to build a fortress in Makassar, they had to recompense the residents not for the space, but for the coconut palms.

With so few people and so much land, it is not surprising that the urban population of Indonesia in the 16th century at least equalled the agrarian population. Thus, the typical Indonesian of that period was not a peasant, but a town dweller engaged as an artisan, sailor, worker or trader.

Jan Pieterszoon Coen was one of the most influential early Dutch leaders.

THE DUTCH COLONIAL YEARS

The hunt for highly prized spices drew the Western powers to the East, where Indonesia's resource-rich islands were a star attraction.

The saga of the Dutch in Indonesia began in 1596, when four small Dutch vessels, led by the incompetent and arrogant Cornelis de Houtman, dropped anchor in Banten, then the largest pepper port in the archipelago. Repeatedly blown off course and racked by disease and dissension, the de Houtman expedition was a disaster. In Banten, the sea-weary Dutch crew went on a drinking binge and had to be chased back to their ships by order of an angry prince, who then refused to do business. Hopping from port to port along the north coast of Java, de Houtman wisely confined his sailors to the ships and managed to purchase spices. On arrival in Bali, it was decided to abandon the expedition without ever reaching the Spice Islands of Maluku.

Back in Holland two years later, with only three lightly laden ships and a third of the original crew, de Houtman's voyage was nonetheless hailed a success. So costly were spices in Europe that the sale of the meagre cargo sufficed to cover all expenses, even producing a modest profit. This touched off a veritable fever of speculation in Dutch commercial circles, and the following year five consortiums dispatched a total of 22 ships to the Indies.

THE DUTCH EAST INDIA COMPANY

Since the 15th century, ports of the two Dutch coastal provinces in northern Europe, Holland

A Dutch East India Company shipyard.

and Zeeland, had served as entrepôts for goods shipped to Germany and the Baltic states. Many Dutch merchants grew wealthy on this trade and, following the outbreak of war with Spain in 1568, they began to expand their shipping fleets rapidly, so that by the 1590s, they were trading directly with the Levant and Brazil.

Thus, when a Dutchman published his itinerary to the East Indies in 1596, it occasioned the immediate dispatch of de Houtman and later expeditions. Indeed, so keen was the interest in direct trade with the Indies that all Dutch traders soon came to recognise the need for cooperation in order to minimise competition and maximise profits. In 1602, they formed the United Dutch East India Company (known by its

> *As a small country busy fighting its own battles back in Europe, many soldiers who fought in Indonesia on behalf of Holland were not Dutch. Among them were renegades, mercenaries, drunks and thieves; in short, the dregs of society.*

Dutch initials, VOC), one of the world's first joint-stock corporations. It was empowered to negotiate treaties, raise armies, build fortresses and wage war in Asia on behalf of Holland.

In its early years, the VOC met with only limited success. Several trading posts were opened, and Ambon was taken from the Portuguese in 1605. But Spanish and English, not to mention Muslim, competition kept spice prices high in Indonesia and low in Europe. Then in 1614 a young accountant, Jan Pieterszoon Coen, convinced the directors that only a more force-

bombarding and destroying the palace. A siege of the fledgling Dutch fortress began in which the powerful Bantenese and a recently arrived English fleet joined the Jayakartans. Meanwhile, Coen escaped to Ambon, leaving a few men to defend the fort and its valuable contents.

COEN'S CUNNING

Five months later, Coen returned to discover his men still in possession of their post. Although outnumbered 30 to one, they had rather unwittingly played one foe against another by agree-

Dutch warships off the coast of Java in the 18th century.

ful policy would make the company profitable. Coen was given command of VOC operations, and promptly embarked on a series of military adventures that were to set the pattern of Dutch behaviour in the region.

Coen's first step was to establish a permanent headquarters at Jayakarta (now Jakarta), on the northwestern coast of Java, close to the pepper-producing parts of Sumatra and the strategic Sunda Strait.

In 1618, he sought and received permission from Prince Wijayakrama of Jayakarta to expand the existing Dutch post, and proceeded to build a stone barricade mounted with cannons. The prince protested that fortifications were not part of their agreement; Coen responded by

ing to any and all demands, but never actually surrendering their position due to the mutual suspicion and timidity of the three opposing parties. Coen set his adversaries to flight in a series of dramatic attacks, undertaken with a small force of 1,000 men that included several score of Japanese mercenaries. Jayakarta was razed to the ground and construction of a new Dutch town begun, including canals, drawbridges, docks, warehouses, barracks, a central square, a city hall and a church – all protected by a high stone wall and a moat. In short, another Amsterdam.

Coen subsequently learned that during the darkest days of the siege, many of the Dutch defenders had behaved in a most unseemly manner: drinking, singing and fornicating. Worst of all, they had broken open the company storehouse and divided the contents among themselves. Those involved were immediately executed and memories of the infamous siege soon faded – save one. The defenders had dubbed their fortress Batavia (after a semi-mythical European tribe, the *Batavi*); the name stuck.

Coen's next step was to secure control of the five tiny nutmeg-producing Banda islands. He brought an expeditionary force there and rounded up and killed most of the 15,000 inhabitants within weeks. Three of the islands were transformed into spice plantations, managed by Dutch colonists and worked by slaves.

In the years that followed, the Dutch gradually tightened their grip on the spice trade. From Ambon they attempted to negotiate a monopoly on cloves with the rulers of Ternate and Tidore. But the smuggling of cloves and clove trees continued. Traders obtained these and other goods at the new Muslim-ruled port, Makassar, in southern Sulawesi. The Dutch repeatedly blockaded Makassar and imposed treaties barring the Makassarese from trading with other nations, but were unable for many years to enforce them. Finally, in 1669, following three years of bitter fighting, the Makassarese surrendered to the superior Dutch forces.

DUTCH CONTROL

The Dutch achieved effective control of the eastern archipelago and its lucrative spice trade by the end of the 17th century. In the western half of the archipelago, however, they became increasingly embroiled in fruitless intrigues and wars, particularly in Java. This came about largely because the Dutch presence at Batavia disturbed a delicate balance of power in Java.

Batavia came under Javanese attack as early as 1628. Sultan Agung, the third and greatest ruler of the Mataram kingdom, was aggressively expanding his domain and had concluded a successful five-year siege on Surabaya. He now controlled all of Central and East Java, and intended to take West Java by pushing out the Dutch and conquering Banten.

Agung nearly succeeded. A large Javanese expeditionary force momentarily breached Batavia's defences, but was then driven back outside the walls in a last-ditch effort by Coen. The Javanese were not prepared for such resistance

and withdrew for lack of provisions. A year later, Sultan Agung sent an even larger force of 10,000 provided with huge stockpiles of rice for a protracted siege. Coen, however, learned of the stockpiles and destroyed them before the Javanese even arrived. Poorly led, starving and sick, the Javanese troops died by the thousands outside the walls of Batavia. Never again was Mataram a threat to the city.

Relations between the Dutch and the Javanese improved during the reign of Amangkurat I (1646–77). They had common enemies – the

A Javanese painting depicts a battle between Javan and Dutch forces at the Mataram capital, Kartasura (1684).

pasisir trading kingdoms of the northern Java coast. Ironically, the Dutch conquest of Makassar later led to their ally's demise.

The Makassar wars of 1666–9 and their aftermath created a diaspora of Makassarese and Bugis refugees. Many of them fled to East Java, where they united under the leadership of a Madurese prince, Trunajaya. Aided and abetted by the Mataram crown prince, Trunajaya successfully stormed through Central Java and plundered the Mataram capital in 1677. Amangkurat I died while on the retreat, fleeing from the enemy forces.

Once in control of Java, Trunajaya renounced his alliance with the young Mataram prince and declared himself king. The crown prince pleaded for Dutch support, promising to reimburse all military expenses and to award the Dutch valuable trade concessions. The Dutch swallowed the bait and mounted a costly campaign to capture Trunajaya. This ended in 1680 with the crown prince, who styled himself Amangkurat II, being restored to the throne.

But the new king was in no position to fulfil his end of the bargain with the Dutch; his treasury had been looted and his kingdom was in ruins. All he had was territory, and although much of

Thomas Stamford Raffles was lieutenant-governor of Java during the British interregnum (1811–1816).

West Java was ceded to the Dutch, the VOC still suffered a heavy loss.

In 1799, Dutch financiers received stunning news: the VOC was bankrupt. During the 18th century, the spice trade had become less profitable, while the military involvement in Java had grown costly. It was indeed a great war in Java (1740–55) that dealt the death blow to the already delicate Dutch finances. Once again, through a complex chain of events, it was the Dutch themselves who inadvertently precipitated the conflict. The details of the struggle are convoluted, but in a nutshell it began in 1740 with the massacre of the Chinese residents of Batavia, and ended 15 years later, after many bloody

> *Stamford Raffles was a brilliant scholar, naturalist, linguist, diplomat and strategist. He has been credited with rediscovering Borobudur, and he also wrote the monumental History of Java (1817).*

battles, broken alliances and shifts of fortune had exhausted almost everyone on the island.

Indeed, Java was never the same again. Mataram had been cleft in two, with rival rulers occupying neighbouring capitals in Yogyakarta and Surakarta. The VOC never recovered from this drain on its resources.

In the traumatic aftermath of the VOC bankruptcy, there was great indecision in Holland as to the next course. In 1800, the Dutch government assumed control of VOC's former possessions, now renamed Netherlands Indies, but for many years no one could make them profitable. Meanwhile, Napoleon had invaded Holland, meaning that Dutch overseas territory was now fair game for France's enemies.

THE BRITISH INTERREGNUM

In 1811 the British invaded Java, toppled the Dutch, and set up their own administration under the wildly ambitious Thomas Stamford Raffles, who attempted radical expansion of European power and a wholesale overturning of old Dutch economic systems. Bureaucratic anarchy and violent conflict ensued. Raffles wanted to replace the old mercantile system

⊘ EXPLOITATIVE CULTIVATION

The pernicious effects of the Cultivation System introduced by the Dutch in 1830 were apparent from the beginning. While in theory the system called for peasants to surrender only a portion of their land and labour, in practice certain lands were worked exclusively for the Dutch by forced labour. Java, one of the richest pieces of real estate on earth, was transformed into a huge Dutch plantation, imposing unimaginable hardships and injustices upon the Javanese. Private plantations largely replaced government ones after 1870, but some government coffee plantations continued to employ forced labour well into the 20th century.

with its government monopoly on trade, with one in which income was derived from taxes and trade was unrestrained. This enormous task had barely begun when the order came from London, following Napoleon's defeat at Waterloo, to restore the Indies to the Dutch in 1816.

Nevertheless, many of his land-tax ideas were eventually used by the Dutch, and they made possible the later exploitation of Java. The other part of Raffles' project – to achieve European dominance over the Javanese courts – had been more successful, with the bloody sacking and looting of Yogyakarta in 1812. This in turn led to the cataclysmic Java War of 1825–30.

CARNAGE TO CULTIVATION

The causes of the Java War were many and varied, but in later nationalist retellings it was a straightforward struggle against colonialism, and its leader, Pangeran Diponegoro (1785–1855), has been retrospectively proclaimed an Indonesian national hero. He was indeed a charismatic figure: crown prince, Muslim mystic and man of the people.

His guerrilla rebellion against the Dutch and their royal Javanese puppets might have succeeded but for a Dutch trick: luring him out of hiding with the promise of negotiation, Diponegoro was captured and exiled to Sulawesi. The cost of the conflict in human terms was staggering: 200,000 Javanese and 8,000 Europeans lost their lives, many from starvation and cholera rather than from death on the battlefield.

By then, the Dutch were in desperate economic straits, with the government debt reaching devastating amounts. New ideas were sought, and in 1829, Johannes van den Bosch submitted a proposal to the crown for what he called a Cultuurstelsel, or Cultivation System. His notion – partly inspired by Raffles – was to levy a tax of 20 percent (later raised to 33 percent) on all land in Java, and to demand payment not in rice but in labour or use of the land. This would permit the Dutch to grow crops that they could sell in Europe.

Van den Bosch soon assumed control of the East Indies, and from a Dutch perspective his system was an immediate success. In the very first year, 1831, it produced a substantial profit. And within a decade, millions of guilders were flowing annually into Dutch coffers from the sale of coffee, tea, sugar, indigo, quinine, copra, palm oil and rubber. With the windfall profits received from the sale of Indonesian products during the rest of the 19th century, an increasingly sophisticated colonial society developed in Java.

Outside of Java, military campaigns throughout the 1800s extended Dutch control. The bitterest battles were fought against the powerful Muslim kingdom of Aceh in a 30-year war. Both sides sustained horrendous losses. In the earlier Padri War between the Dutch and the Minangkabau of West Sumatra (1821–38), the fighting was almost as bloody. In the east, Flores

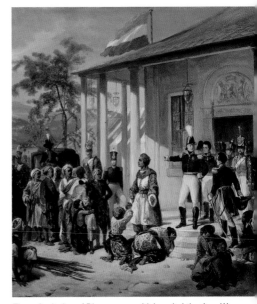

The submission of Diponegoro, which ended the Java War in 1830, as imagined by Dutch artist Nicolaas Pieneman.

and Sulawesi were repeatedly raided and finally occupied by the 1900s.

But the most shocking incidents occurred on Lombok and Bali, where on three occasions (1894, 1906 and 1908) Balinese rulers and their courtiers, armed with only ceremonial weapons, stormed headlong into Dutch gunfire after ritualistically purifying themselves for a puputan ('fight to the finish') rather than acquiesce to Dutch control.

In some ways, the tragic massacres symbolised the abrupt changes wrought by the Dutch: they had achieved the unification of the entire archipelago at the expense of indigenous kingdoms, sultans and tens of thousands of people.

Traffic at dusk, Jalan Medan Merdeka, Jakarta.

MODERN INDONESIA

Indonesia's journey to postcolonial nationhood has been far from straightforward, with much trauma along the way. But in the 21st century its fortunes are decidedly on the up.

At the beginning of the 20th century, signs of change were everywhere in the Indies. Dutch military expeditions and private enterprises were making inroads into the hinterlands of Sumatra and the eastern islands. Steam shipping and the Suez Canal (opened in 1869) had brought Europe closer, and the European presence in Java's cities was growing steadily. New shops, clubs, hotels and homes added an air of cosmopolitan elegance to the towns, while newspapers, factories, gas lighting, trains, buses, electricity and cars imparted a distinct feeling of modernity.

Indeed, thousands of newly arrived Dutch immigrants were moved to remark on the tolerable conditions in the colonies – that is to say, it was just like home, or even better.

But a nascent independence movement was already underway. A small but growing number of Indonesians living in cities were receiving Dutch education. The irony is that Dutch education provided much of the intellectual basis for Indonesian nationalism. As early as 1908, Indonesians attending Dutch schools began to form regional student organisations with political overtones. Small, aristocratic and idealistic, such organisations spawned an elite group of leaders and provided forums for a new national consciousness to take shape.

NATIONAL AWAKENING

In 1928, at the second all-Indies student conference, the concept of a single Indonesian nation (one land, one language, one nation) was proclaimed in the *Sumpah Pemuda* (Youth Pledge). The nationalism and idealism of those students later spread through newspapers and the non-government Dutch- and Malay-language

Early oil exploration in Sumatra.

schools. But while the urban elite grew, the Dutch authorities were preoccupied with the nation's emerging pan-Islamic and communist movements.

The pan-Islamic movement's roots were in the steady and growing stream of pilgrims visiting Mecca and in the religious teachings of the *ulama* (Arabic scholars). What began in Java in 1909 as a small Islamic traders' association (*Sarekat Dagang Islam*) soon became a national confederation of Islamic labour unions (*Sarekat Islam*), with 2 million members in 1919. Mass rallies attracted tens of thousands, and many peasants came to see in the Islamic movement hope of relief from oppressive colonial conditions.

In 1910, the Indonesian communist movement was founded by small groups of Dutch and Indonesian radicals, with support from the working-class people. The movement soon embraced Islam, with many of its leaders gaining control of Islamic workers' unions and speaking at Islamic rallies. Following the Russian Revolution of 1917, they also maintained ties with Comintern (the international communist organisation) and increasingly espoused Marxist-Leninist doctrine.

The period 1910–30 was a turbulent one. Strikes in cities frequently erupted into violence,

imprisoned, he was later released. A general crackdown ensued, and, after 1933, Sukarno and other student leaders were exiled to distant islands, where they remained for 10 years. The prospect of independence seemed elusive.

JAPANESE OCCUPATION

Dutch rule came to a dramatic and abrupt end during World War II, with the Japanese invasion of 1942 – a turn of events that many Indonesians initially saw as a liberation. The Japanese encountered little resistance and, within weeks,

Daily life for Europeans in the colonial period.

and the colonial government arrested many Indonesian leaders. Moderate Muslim leaders soon disassociated themselves from political activities. The rank and file deserted their unions, and while the communists fought on for several years in Java and Sumatra to 1927, they too were crushed.

Leadership of the anti-colonial movement then reverted to the student elite. In 1927, a recently graduated engineer by the name of Sukarno, together with his Bandung Study Club, founded the first major political party with Indonesian independence as its goal. His *Partai Nasional Indonesia* (PNI) grew, and within three years had over 10,000 members. Shortly thereafter, Sukarno was arrested for making 'treasonous statements'. Although publicly tried and

had rounded up all the Europeans and placed them in concentration camps. It quickly became apparent, however, that, like the Dutch, the Japanese had come to exploit the Indies, not to free them. Escalating Japanese rice requisitions created famines and sparked peasant uprisings that were ruthlessly repressed.

However, the Japanese found it necessary to rely on the Indonesians and to promote a sense of nationhood in order to extract their desired war materials. Indonesians were placed in many key positions held previously by Dutch nationals. The Dutch language was banned and replaced by Bahasa Indonesia. Nationalist leaders were freed and encouraged to cooperate with the Japanese. Most of them did.

> *The democratic republic of Indonesia is run by a president and a parliament, the People's Consultative Assembly (MPR). In the past, the president was named by parliament, but since 2004 has been chosen by the people in direct elections.*

When it became clear in late 1944 that Japan was losing the war, the Japanese promised independence to bolster faltering support. Indonesian leaders were brought in for discussions, and close to 200,000 young people were mobilised into paramilitary groups.

INDEPENDENCE DECLARED

The Japanese had promised to facilitate independence, and appointed Sukarno chairman of the preparatory committee with Mohammad Hatta as vice-chairman. But their abrupt surrender following the dropping of atomic bombs on Japan in 1945 came before any concrete moves had been made. Fearing that the momentum would be lost, and under huge pressure from the revolutionary youth, Sukarno and Hatta unilaterally proclaimed *merdeka* (independence) on 17 August.

The following months were a chaotic struggle. News of the Japanese surrender spread like wildfire and millions of Indonesians echoed the call for *merdeka*. The Dutch tried to reclaim the islands (with their British allies initially tasked with accepting Japanese surrender and re-establishing European governance on their behalf). Three Dutch 'police actions' gave the returning colonial forces control of the cities, but each time the ragtag Indonesian army, under the inspired leadership of the youthful commander-in-chief, General Sudirman, valiantly fought back, and global opinion turned against the colonialists.

Finally, in 1949, the United States ceased the transfer of Marshall Plan funds to the Netherlands, and the UN Security Council ordered the Dutch to withdraw from Indonesia and negotiate a settlement. On 17 August 1950 – the fifth anniversary of the *merdeka* proclamation – the new government of the Republic of Indonesia took charge.

Euphoria swept through the cities and towns of Indonesia following the withdrawal of Dutch forces. Mass rallies and processions were held; flag-waving crowds thronged the streets shouting *'Merdeka, Merdeka!'*

The final chapters of early Indonesian nation-building were still to be written, however. The Dutch held on to the western half of New Guinea after granting independence to the rest of Indonesia. Pressure from the United Nations and the threat of all-out war by Sukarno eventually resulted in the transfer of the territory in 1962 and its integration as the country's 26th province, initially renamed Irian Jaya, and later Papua. In 1975,

A pro-independence march in progress.

after Portugal abandoned its colony of East Timor, Indonesia invaded and annexed that territory.

THE SUKARNO YEARS

In Jakarta, the slow and arduous process of constructing a peacetime government began. While the unifying power of the revolution had done much to forge a national identity, the fact of Indonesia's complex ethnic, religious and ideological diversity remained. Moreover, massive economic and social problems faced the new nation – a legacy of colonialism and war. Factories and plantations were shut down, capital and skilled personnel were scarce, rice production was insufficient to meet demand, people were overwhelmingly poor and illiterate, and the population was growing rapidly. A Western-style parliamentary system was adopted to deal with the problems.

From the beginning, however, the existence of more than 30 rival parties paralysed the system. Weak coalition cabinets fell on an almost annual basis, and attempts at cooperation were increasingly stymied by growing ideological polarisation. Sukarno, whose powers as president had been limited by the provisional constitution of 1950, grew frustrated by the deadlock.

A series of separatist uprisings in Sumatra, North Sulawesi and West Java in the late 1950s was followed by military confrontation with newly independent Malaysia in 1963. In 1965, he pulled Indonesia out of the UN, angry that Malaysia was made a member state. Domestically, however, it was Sukarno's nationalistic élan that had helped create a nation out of disparate ethnic groups.

But Sukarno's reliance on charisma alone fostered deep political tensions. While he attempted to offset the growing influence of the military by courting the Partai Komunis Indonesia (PKI, Indonesian Communist Party), the economy crashed. Foreign investors fled, deficits left the

Sukarno reads a statement to the press while his would-be successor Suharto looks on.

gave Sukarno his cue. He declared martial law and gave the army a free hand to crush the rebels. In 1959, with the rebellions under control, Sukarno resurrected the 'revolutionary' constitution of 1945 and declared a period of 'Guided Democracy'.

Under the new political system, power was focused in the hands of the president and the army generals. Militant nationalism became Sukarno's recipe for national integration, and the blame for most of the economic and political problems was placed at the feet of foreign imperialism and colonialism.

In the early 1960s, Sukarno became more militant. The long and successful campaign to wrest control of western New Guinea from the Dutch

government bankrupt, and inflation skyrocketed to 700 percent. Discontent was brewing, and by 1965, Indonesia was a political tinderbox.

THE 1965 POGROMS AND THE RISE OF SUHARTO

In the early hours of 1 October 1965, a group of junior army officers kidnapped and brutally executed six leading generals, in what they claimed was a pre-emptive counter-coup to protect the president from a right-wing plot. However, the rebel officers soon lost the initiative to General Suharto, then commander of the Army Strategic Reserve. In a few hours, Suharto assumed command of the army, crushed the attempted coup and declared the PKI to be the culprit.

A devastating anti-communist purge ensued, facilitated by the military and affected by political and religious groups and citizen mobs. Hundreds of thousands were killed, first in North Sumatra, then later in Java, Bali and Lombok. The blood-letting continued for months. The violence of this period remains a highly sensitive topic in Indonesia, one that has never been properly addressed in public.

Meanwhile in Jakarta, Suharto was slowly pushing Sukarno out of power. On 11 March 1966, Sukarno was persuaded to sign a document bestowing wide powers on General Suharto that charted Indonesia's course for the next 32 years.

Change came quickly. Martial law was declared and order was restored. Marxist-Leninist teachings were outlawed and thousands of alleged communists, including the prominent novelist Pramoedya Ananta Toer, were jailed. Existing political parties were weakened, and in 1967 the new government granted itself the right to appoint one-third of the representatives in the nation's highest legislative assembly. A major realignment in foreign policy restored long-fractured relations with the US and the West, and severed ties with China and the Soviet Union. Building political legitimacy on promises to revive the moribund Indonesian economy, Suharto placed a team of American-trained economists in charge of national finances.

These technocrats guided the rapid reintegration of Indonesia into the world economy, liberalised foreign investment laws and imposed monetary controls. Western aid was sought to replenish the nation's exhausted foreign exchange reserves. By the early 1970s, results began to show. Investors – Americans, Japanese and Indonesian Chinese – moved in to take advantage of Indonesia's vast copper, tin, timber and oil reserves and to set up factories.

Indonesia's mineral wealth made the job easier. Back in 1883, a Dutch planter sheltering from a storm in a northern Sumatran shed noticed a torch burning brightly. On enquiring, he was led to a nearby spring where a viscous black substance lay thick across the water. The

Suharto in the mid-1990s.

Ø DEWI, SUKARNO'S FOIL

As Sukarno's grip on power began to loosen in the early 1960s and Indonesia's economy spun further out of control, his behaviour became ever more erratic and bizarre. He reputedly spent hours talking to spirits and ancestors and consulting seers. His flamboyant political speeches became focused on convoluted neo-colonialist plots. It was at this point that the ageing president found his perfect foil in the stunning young Japanese Naoko Nemoto.

Nemoto was under 20 when she married Sukarno in 1963, becoming Dewi Sukarno, the nation-builder's seventh and best-remembered wife. After his death, she made herself known as an international socialite with a volatile reputation. In the early 1990s, she slashed a Filipino woman with a broken champagne glass at a cocktail party in the USA and served a month in jail. The 50-something Dewi went on to assault a Jakarta gossip columnist and released a book of mid-life nude photographs of herself that both titillated and shocked Indonesia.

She attended lectures by Indonesian politicians abroad and heckled them from the crowd. She also insisted Sukarno's ouster had been the direct result of a CIA plot. Nothing seemed to get her down. Upon emerging from the well-appointed Colorado prison, she said: 'I will treasure [memories of the jail] for the rest of my life.'

discovery led to the formation of Royal Dutch Shell and, eventually, to Indonesia's position as the world's fifth-largest and Asia's sole OPEC producer. Though the dominance of oil fell as the economy matured, it and other natural resources have remained Indonesia's primary source of foreign exchange.

During Suharto's reign, the country also made rapid gains in agricultural production and population control. An intensive family-planning campaign was considered a model for the developing world, and Indonesia managed to reduce the

Jakarta during the attempted coup d'etat in 1965.

birth rate to just over 1 percent annually. Still, Indonesia's main islands of Java and Bali were desperately overcrowded. In response, Suharto revived an old 'transmigration' programme to ship the landless of Java and Bali to Papua, Kalimantan and other sparsely inhabited regions.

THE NEW ORDER

Even as he liberalised the economy, Suharto's so-called 'New Order' regime undermined Indonesia's political institutions and cut off dissenting voices. The new elite exerted total control through the quasi-party Golkar, the political vehicle of the government. Independent newspapers were closed, dissidents were jailed and the military was given a free hand to deal brutally with opponents of the regime. For most of his reign, Suharto delivered on his promise of 'development yes, politics no!' He ensured political survival by stage-managing elections every five years and then ruled by fiat.

But politics had never gone away entirely. By the mid-1990s, gratitude to Suharto for the progress made since 1965 was increasingly being replaced by anger at rampant corruption – particularly the vast business empires carved out by his children and a close circle of cronies. Rioting and religious tension became more intense. In 1996, a ham-fisted effort to discredit Megawati Sukarnoputri, the daughter of Sukarno who had risen to lead the strongest opposition party, backfired and led to rioting in Jakarta that frightened off investors and exposed the strains in Suharto's consensus-based polity. After 32 years of creeping change, Indonesia seemed poised to lurch backwards once more.

The eventual trigger echoed Sukarno's fall 33 years earlier. In July 1997, when Southeast Asia's financial crisis began, conventional wisdom had it that Indonesia, with its tradition of inflation control and restrained spending, would weather the storm better than its neighbours.

But as the rupiah fell alongside other regional currencies, it exposed massive fissures in the economy hidden by the glitter of the boom years. The foundations that the gleaming office towers, five-star hotels and state-of-the-art factories of the New Order rested on were riddled with debt. Corporations alone owed more than US$80 billion to foreign investors.

As banks collapsed and factories closed, prices for food and other basics soared. Millions lost their jobs, and even more saw their economic gains of the previous 30 years evaporate. By the end of October, Suharto was forced into the arms of the International Monetary Fund. The fund arranged a US$40 billion support package, but at a price: the required economic reforms would strike at the monopolies and business groups of his friends and family.

While Suharto dragged his feet over the programme, the rupiah fell to one-seventh of its pre-crisis value, driving inflation and unemployment even higher. Students, the elite and disaffected army officers began to move against him. In March 1998, after Suharto was elected to a new term, opposition groups kicked into gear.

REFORMASI!

Student protests took on a new, more urgent tone with *'Reformasi!'* (Reform) as their rallying cry. On 12 May 1998, six student protestors were shot and killed at Jakarta's Trisakti University, providing the spark for the capital's worst rioting in a generation. Foreigners fled and Jakarta's commercial districts became ghost towns. As flames swept the capital and army troops took charge, Suharto scrambled to hold on. But one by one, his most trusted lieutenants abandoned him. On the morning of 21 May, he resigned. Joyful

over Megawati Sukarnoputri, whose Indonesian Democratic Party-Struggle (PDI-P) had gained the largest vote share.

Partially blind, determinedly informal in style, and avowedly secularist and democratic despite being a hereditary Muslim leader, Gus Dur was famous for his political flip-flopping, intended to confuse his opponents, according to admirers, and also indicative of compromise as a traditionally Indonesian political approach. Despite his personal popularity, his administration was a disaster, and he was impeached by parliament

Student protests in 1998.

students frolicked in the fountain at parliament as Suharto's vice-president and close friend B.J. Habibie was sworn in as his successor.

During Habibie's short rule, he freed the press, allowed an independence referendum in East Timor (now called Timor Leste) and steered Indonesia to a democratic election that ended with his own October 1999 defeat – the first democratic political transition in Indonesian history.

Abdurrahman Wahid, the former head of Nahdlatul Ulama (NU), a 35-million member Muslim social organisation, was Habibie's surprise successor. Though Wahid's National Awakening Party came in fourth in the general election, savvy politicking in the parliamentary assembly that selects the president won him his position

⊘ TRANSITION TO DEMOCRACY

Sri Mulyani Indrawati, Indonesia's former finance minister (2005–10) and former World Bank managing director, played a vital role in the country's evolution in its early years of transition. Her advice to emerging democracies is straightforward: widely publicised new laws must be established quickly, giving citizens freedom of expression and independent elections; corruption must be tackled; and new, independent judges and technical expertise must be found and put into place. Most important, she says, is that Indonesia learned during the process that there are no universal solutions; each country must address its challenges on its own terms.

before the end of his term, to be replaced by Vice-President Megawati.

Despite being the daughter of first president, Sukarno, Megawati's own political credentials were unimpressive, and though she selected a ministerial cabinet of capable advisers, her government did not live up to expectations. She promised to eliminate corruption, rein in the military and reinvigorate the devastated economy. But rather than work on these pressing problems, parliament seemed more concerned with settling old political party rivalries

Susilo Bambang Yudhoyono, Indonesia's first directly elected president.

and differences. Real reform remained stuck in the doldrums. In the meantime, ethnic and religious intolerance flared violently across the archipelago, while separatist movements in both Aceh and Papua were answered with harsh military responses – in spite of promises of greater autonomy. Thousands died in these struggles, but Megawati remained determined to keep Indonesia's immense territories intact as a legacy from her late father.

As a result, not much changed for Indonesia; economic recovery remained stalled, and tourism, the nation's secondary income earner, suffered from the general 'post-9/11' downturn and then from the devastating aftereffects of

terrorist attacks in Bali in 2002. Nonetheless, the outright collapse that many had predicted with the fall of Suharto had not come to pass, and the first subtle signs of recovery were beginning to show.

21ST-CENTURY DEMOCRACY

In 2004 Susilo Bambang Yudhoyono (popularly known as SBY) became Indonesia's first directly elected president. He inherited a government burdened with decades of corrupt practices, enormous human rights violations, insurgencies in outlying provinces and massive foreign debt. But the economy was, at last, beginning to rebound.

SBY's government continued the reform processes that had been underway since 1998. East Timor – by far the most seriously restive province – became independent, and the military was stripped of its police powers and its vast holdings transferred to the state. Indonesia subsequently resigned from OPEC and began diversifying its economy into other areas. Restrictions on the press were now a thing of the past, and a boisterously free media was very much part of the Indonesian scene. SBY's administration has made a dent in the corruption problem, with daily headlines announcing yet another public official's arrest, and new corruption courts being set up across the country to ease the burden on the overwhelmed Jakarta judiciary system. Suharto himself – the ultimate corruptor according to many Indonesians – never stood trial. Whenever the cases against him looked like coming to court, he successfully pled exemption on grounds of ill health. He died in 2008. None of the enormous fortunes his family and cohorts amassed and allegedly stashed in overseas accounts was recovered, much to the chagrin of millions.

AN ECONOMIC POWERHOUSE

By the time of the global economic crisis in 2008, Indonesia's own economy was doing well, and it weathered the storm far better than most western countries, encouraging renewed investment in the aftermath. The spectacular success of China, and to a lesser extent India, are well known, but Indonesia is also a major emerging powerhouse, now firmly established as Asia's third-most successful economy. Reliable markers of prosperity are here in abundance: the mid- to upper-income group is rapidly expand-ing, the banks are stable and the currency is strong. Furthermore, the sizeable population makes an attractive market for manufacturers of practically all products.

SBY further assumed responsibility by tak-ing lead roles in G20 summits with strategies to reduce fuel subsidies, lower greenhouse emissions and protect long-abused forests, while simultaneously directing more cash to poor households and improving education and health care. In 2006, SBY was nominated for the Nobel Peace Prize for his role in the Helsinki Peace Accord, ending nearly three decades of fighting in Aceh. Re-elected by an overwhelm-ing majority in 2009, his effectiveness during his final term of office was hampered by infighting in his coalition government.

As in the US, Indonesian presidents are lim-ited to a maximum of two terms in office. In 2014, Joko Widodo, known as 'Jokowi', from PDI-P replaced SBY as president. A former furniture salesman and self-proclaimed heavy metal fan, as well as a successful former mayor of both Surakarta and Jakarta, his win in the polls was seen to signal a new chapter for Indo-nesia democracy, mainly because he was the first president without links to the Suharto-era political elite or the military. His defeated rival in the presidential race, Prabowo Subianto, was the absolute counterpoint – a former military office who was once married to a daughter of Suharto, and who evoked nostalgia for both Suharto and Sukarno on the campaign trail.

Perhaps inevitably, the euphoria that greeted Jokowi's election, nationally and internationally, was short-lived. He struggled to make good on all his promised reforms, and efforts to cut fuel subsidies for petrol and diesel sparked violent protests and demonstrations in many regions of Indonesia. Jokowi also earned international opprobrium in 2015 following the execution of several foreign citizens who had been convicted of drug trafficking offences.

Elsewhere, the influence of radical politi-cal Islam appears to be on the rise in Indone-sia – with such manifestations as an outbreak of moral panic over LGBTQ activities raising concerns amongst modern secularists, old-fashioned nationalists and minority rights campaigners alike. This has left mainstream

politicians such as Jokowi with the thorny challenge of balancing the appeasement of conservative Muslim demands with the main-tenance of Indonesia's old-established plu-ralist ethos. Addressing this challenge often results in unlikely political alliances, as in the 2019 election when Jokowi chose as his run-ning mate the conservative cleric, Ma'ruf Amin. While critics suggest such approaches are leading to creeping Islamisation and an ero-sion of religious tolerance, others argue that Indonesia's dominant political modus operandi

Acehnese people cheer the signing of a peace pact between the government and Aceh separatists in 2005.

of coalition and compromise successfully reins in more extreme voices.

Other issues aside, the economic situation has remained positive in recent years. Despite renewed uncertainty regionally and internation-ally, infrastructure projects and investments have continued, with Jakarta in particular undergoing a dramatic transformation and see-ing – after decades of broken promises – the establishment of a modern metro system. The 2019 presidential election saw a repeat of the Jokowi-Prabowo contest. It was the most bit-terly fought and divisive election since the fall of Suharto, but Jokowi ultimately triumphed once more with a comfortable majority.

Floating market, Kalimantan.

Hindu blessing ceremony.

Running free at a Balinese wedding ceremony.

THE PEOPLE OF INDONESIA

Anyone travelling through the length of Indonesia will find the complexity and sheer diversity of peoples, languages, cultures and customs astounding.

With over 300 ethnic groups, and numerous sub-groups, it is no easy task to identify all of Indonesia's peoples.

Java houses the largest proportion of Indonesia's total population, with 58 percent, followed by Sumatra with 20 percent and Sulawesi with seven percent. Kalimantan has six percent, as do Bali and Nusa Tenggara combined. Maluku and Papua have a total of three percent – with these figures giving a clear indication of how unevenly population is distributed across the country. Most larger islands are inhabited by numerous different ethnic and linguistic groups. The most heavily populated province is DKI (Special Province) Jakarta with 14,440 people per sq km, and the least crowded is West Papua with eight people per sq km.

Batuan mask makers, Ubud.

ETHNIC GROUPS

The Javanese are by far the largest ethnic group, with 42 percent of Indonesia's total population. Having an ancient court culture based in Central and East Java, with its long history of mighty empires and sheer numbers, it is no wonder that the Javanese tend to dominate the country's bureaucracy, military and politics. The majority of Javanese are Muslims, yet for many their religious and traditional rituals include pre-Islamic and Hindu-Buddhist elements. With a definite segmentation within the culture, every Javanese knows which category he or she falls within – the aristocrats, the merchants and traders, or the peasants – and that is indicated by which level of their hierarchical, three-pronged native language is spoken when addressing others.

West Java has Indonesia's second-largest ethnic group, the Sundanese, who form 15 percent of the population. They too have a long dynastic history, though their cultural traditions are not quite so rarefied as those of the Javanese. Historically, the Sundanese have tended to practice a more orthodox version of Islam than their Javanese neighbours, though such distinctions are less obvious today.

Off the northeastern coast of Java on Madura island, the Madurese also tend to be more orthodox Muslims. They have long had a double-edged reputation, renowned for their bravery and hard-working ethos, but also criticised by other Indonesians for a supposed quick temper and lack of refinement. Overpopulation and poor soils forced many Madurese into the maritime trade during ancient times. Like Javanese, their language is also divided into high, middle and low categories.

Another of Indonesia's major groups is the clan-ruled, monogamous Batak, who inhabit the highlands around Lake Toba in North Sumatra. They are primarily Christians. Outsiders know them for their outspokenness, their former reputation as cannibals, and their passion for singing raucous drinking songs and maudlin, melodic love tunes.

The Bugis and the Banjarese live in the southern part of Sulawesi. They are primarily Muslim seafaring people who are known as good sailors, skilled in shipbuilding, and shrewd businessmen. In the past, they often migrated to earn a living and, at one time, controlled much of the region's maritime trade. They also had a piratical reputation amongst early European seafarers, and one rather unlikely explanation has it that the English term 'Bogeyman' comes from 'Bugis'.

Similar in numbers to the Bugis and the Banjarese are the Minangkabau of the breathtakingly beautiful hills of West Sumatra, whose matrilineal kinship system combined with a staunch belief in Islam and adherence to *adat* (traditional) laws is unique. Their coming-of-age ritual for men, *merantau* (seeking a fortune abroad), has scattered them throughout the archipelago, and they are quickly recognised by their Minang or Padang food restaurants. Known as highly educated, keen entrepreneurs, Minangkabau include well-known writers and political leaders.

On the far northern tip of Sumatra is Aceh, the only province in Indonesia that applies Islamic Sharia law to its Muslim residents (outsiders and non-Muslims are exempt). With its strategic location at the entrance to the Malacca Strait, the gateway to Indonesia's spices and trade with China further east, Aceh was a crucial stopover for merchants from Arabia and India, and was the point of entry for Islam as early as the 13th century, sometimes known as 'Mecca's Veranda'. The Achenese amount to 1.9 percent of the Indonesian population.

Dayak women with extended earlobes.

⊘ AUTONOMY

Under Suharto's New Order regime, 100 percent of revenues earned by the provinces were under the control of the central government. Soon after Suharto fell in 1998, voices were raised, most notably in Aceh (Sumatra), Maluku and Papua, demanding autonomy. In 2000, the Wahid administration granted their wishes, and for the first time taxation, budgeting, infrastructure and trade became locally managed, with the lion's share of revenues remaining in the province. This was good news for some, such as resource-rich East Kalimantan; however, autonomy is not particularly beneficial for poorer areas, which must eke out their existence with loans, grants and other foreign aid.

THE BALINESE

Although the Balinese are arguably the best-known Indonesians, they are a relatively small group in the grand scheme of things, comprising only about 1.5 percent of the total population. They have a unique culture and are the only significant Hindu-majority group in Indonesia (there are also a handful of Javanese Hindus, and some Dayaks in Kalimantan have rebranded their traditional belief systems as Hinduism; Hindu populations elsewhere in Indonesia are generally Balinese migrants). Religion in Bali governs many rituals of life and agricultural cycles.

Balinese society is structured around a hereditary caste system that is far more relaxed

> *Traditional Javanese society requires one to be sopan santun (well mannered). Rukun (harmony) is the primary goal, achieved through knowing one's place in society and acting out one's assigned role.*

than the Indian version. It does, however, carry certain rules of etiquette, as ordained in the Hindu scriptures. At the top is the Brahman caste; only Brahmans are allowed to be high priests. The Satriya form the second strata of society; they are the descendants of warriors and rulers. The merchants and administrative officials, or Wesia, occupy the third rank, and at the bottom are the Sudra, the common people, who account for 93 percent of Bali's population. The Sudras are not deemed inferior or denied access to specific professions; while an upper-caste background does not guarantee a high income or direct access to political power. In Bali, a university professor could be a Sudra and a waiter may turn out to be a Brahman – though the upper two castes are disproportionately represented in local politics and business.

'UNITY IN DIVERSITY'

It was Dutch colonialism that, in its fervour to control the world's spice trade, forced Indonesia's multi-ethnic and multi-religious society into what was to become one nation. Under Dutch rule, selected elites received Western educations, were governed by the same economic and administrative system and experienced similar, if not identical, problems. The Dutch provided a form of social cohesion that enabled the various ethnic groups to come together. The Japanese occupation, although lasting a brief 3½ years, was significant in that it provided Indonesians with military training and further stoked their zeal for independence. To their own ends, the Japanese also actively promoted nationalism, a movement that eventually gained Indonesia its independence and created a nation based on the boundaries of the former Dutch East Indies.

Another factor that helped to unite the ethnic groups was language. Although the language of a minority group, Malay was used widely as a medium of communication between different

ethnic groups in trade relations and in the marketplaces. Campaigners used it to propagate the Indonesian nationalist movement throughout the diverse archipelago. When independence was achieved in 1945, a form of Malay was made into the national language, *Bahasa Indonesia*.

When Suharto ruled Indonesia, a transmigration policy was used not only to redistribute population density, but was also to promote national unity. Java accounts for only seven percent of the Indonesian territory, but 58 percent of the population live on the island. The policy

Becak driver in Togyakarta.

encouraged poor people from Java, Madura and Bali, to migrate to the outer islands, and the resettlement programme created much friction between locals and newcomers. Viewed as largely unsuccessful, the transmigration programme lost its zeal when the central government was regionalised in 2000 and the provinces and regencies were given full autonomy – the resultant Javanese, Balinese and Madurese settler communities endure in far-flung corners of the archipelago.

JAVA AND THE OUTER ISLANDS

Throughout history, ethnic and religious conflicts have occurred between Java/Bali and the Outer Islands, especially after independence.

The people of these inner and outer regions are not only ethnically different, but also dissimilar in their approach to agriculture. The principal farming method in Java and Bali is that of *sawah*, or wet rice-paddy cultivation, while the main method employed in the Outer Islands is *ladang*, or slash-and-burn cultivation.

Until fairly recently, Java and Bali were collectively regarded as agricultural societies, in contrast to the Outer Islands, which were considered maritime. In an agricultural society, the need for close cooperation among villages is paramount, and people tend to be socialistic. In a maritime society, where the livelihood does not depend solely on agricultural products and trade is important for survival, people tend to be more individualistic. This split was emphasised by the aristocratic nature of Javanese society.

DEFINING 'INDONESIANS'

It is difficult to define 'Indonesians' and to generalise about how they think or feel about any given topic. Their particular ethnic upbringing plays its part, but there are vast differences – as there are in every country – between people who are educated and live or work in a metropolis where viewpoints are broader and those who remain isolated in country villages, which may be as much as 50 percent of the population.

Nonetheless, increasing urbanisation, and the rise of digital technology has gone a long way to erode the traditional urban-rural divide. Mobile phone ownership and internet access is widespread, even in remote villages, giving millions of Indonesians direct access to nationwide topics and trends. Families and young people flock to shopping malls and cinemas in their spare time instead of waiting for harvest festivals to create entertainment. Indonesia has the second-largest number of Facebook users in the world and is third among Twitter-ers. These and other social networks not only link people to each other and enable them to voice opinions, they are also an educational link to foreign insights that were once only available to the elite. More Indonesians than ever before are

A portrtait of urban youth, Jakarta.

⊘ CHINESE-INDONESIANS TODAY

There have been Chinese settlers in Indonesia for many centuries, but Chinese migration to the region increased during the colonial period. Many arrived as indentured workers, employed on plantations in Sumatra, but others came seeking to make their fortunes in the towns and cities of the Dutch colony. The Dutch fuelled local hostility by using Chinese entrepreneurs as a buffer between the European elite and the indigenous majority, with Chinese-run revenue collection systems. By the time Indonesia gained independence, an idea of the Chinese minority as disproportionately wealthy and exploitative was deeply ingrained.

After Suharto came to power the association with communist mainland China put more pressure on Chinese Indonesians. The Chinese language was banned, and Chinese people were pressured to adopt 'Indonesian' names and to subscribe to an officially recognised 'Indonesian' religion (with most converting to Christianity). In an ironic twist, some of Suharto's closest associates were supremely wealthy ethnic Chinese tycoons – a fact that only exacerbated popular hostility.

After Suharto's fall, legal discrimination against Chinese Indonesians was rapidly ended, with a resurgence of cultural manifestations. Chinese New Year is now a national holiday, and Confucianism has been added to the list of Indonesia's officially recognised religions.

fluent English-speakers, as well as speaking other non-Asian languages, further widening the gap between those who are educated and those who are not.

University cities, such as Bandung and Yogyakarta, present another aspect of Indonesian identity. With an estimated 50 million university students in the country, when concentrated into smaller towns the ethnicity lines, while never forgotten, become blurred. Bright young students from across the archipelago are thrown together in these environments,

EDUCATION AND HEALTH CARE

Although the number of people living in poverty, according to World Bank parameters, has dropped in the last decade from 60 percent to about 15 percent, many others (perhaps as many as 50 percent, around 120 million people) subsist close to this level.

Providing clean water and sanitation to all, especially those in remote locations, is a substantial challenge and is being addressed largely by international aid organisations. Decentralisation of government from total con-

The school run, Ubud.

many of them away from their villages and families for the first time, and are exposed not only to new ideas through their studies but also to each other's customs and traditions. Nowadays, it is common among more sophisticated families for couples to be of different ethnicities, and even different religions (technically conversion to a single religion is required ahead of marriage, but where family pressure is absent couples can circumvent this). Even among the educated, however, tradition is usually still important, and one wedding ceremony often will be held in the bride's village according to her parents' customs and another in the husband's, followed by a party for the couple's friends in the city where they live.

trol in Jakarta to the regions has helped, and now local administrations are responsible for providing health care to their citizens and for controlling spending.

Foreign funding also assists in training more doctors, nurses and midwives; constructing public clinics that hopefully one day will be accessible to all; and providing nutrition education, maternal and newborn care, as well as immunisations for children.

The Indonesian constitution states that all citizens have a right to free education, but currently the majority of regions only sponsor primary school grades 1–6. Even in the absence of a tuition charge, the cost of books and uniforms is beyond reach for many families.

Nevertheless, primary school enrolment throughout the country is about 96 percent, although it drops to around 50 percent for junior secondary schools. The reasons for this low take-up include lack of access to schools or, particularly in rural areas, the need for boys to work in the fields and girls to look after younger siblings while the parents work.

The good news is that education spending has more than doubled since the fall of Suharto, with more spent on education than any other sector in recent years. But with over 5 million

A Muslim girl on the way to the mosque.

tertiary education students and 53 state and over 400 private universities nationwide, there is still much work to be done. Gaps in access to lower education are filled by private and religious schools – which play a significant role – and in the higher-education realm by vocational secondary schools, colleges and academies. As with health care, foreign funding is significant.

A SHOW OF PATRIOTISM

Regardless of where its citizens live, what their ethnic background is and whether they are wealthy or not, the Indonesian nationalism that was fanned in the run-up to independence is still very much alive today.

When it comes to defending their country's honour in sports arenas, against comments from outsiders that the people perceive to be slanderous or threatening, or when they feel one of their own has been mistreated, Indonesians tend quickly to adopt a patriotic stance. On the downside, many fall short in their ability to examine and analyse opposing points of view and are quick to accept, and repeat, popular opinion. This is the result of a weak education system that is in need of an overhaul. Although some are doing remarkable work, the vast majority of teachers, particularly at lower levels, have come up through the ranks of an archaic system that teaches by rote and punishment rather than encouraging critical thinking. Some progress has been made in training new teachers and reforming their teaching methods, but not nearly enough.

⊘ RADEN AYU KARTINI

Indonesian women have, in part, Raden Ayu Kartini to thank for their equal role in society. She was born into a noble family in 1897. Traditions of the time demanded that Javanese girls of her class be sequestered and protected to prepare them for arranged marriages, often to polygamist husbands who had full authority over them. Not permitted to go to school after the age of 12, Kartini was largely self-educated, learning from Dutch books and magazines through which she developed proto-feminist attitudes. Her letters to Dutch friends railing against Javanese restrictions that robbed women of freedom were published in Holland in 1911, influencing prominent figures. She began

teaching women in 1903, and after her untimely death at the age of 25, other schools for girls were established in her name. Today she is seen as a leader of women's rights, and every year on her birthday, 12 April, her contributions are celebrated.

Women have frequently attained prominence in Indonesian politics. In addition to a former president, high-profile women politicians have included ministers of health, trade, national development planning and women's empowerment. The former managing director of the World Bank, Sri Mulyani Indrawati, is Indonesian, and she has also served twice as the country's finance minister.

Indonesian millennials do not always appreciate the dramatic progress their country has made in the last two decades. Taking for granted the right to speak freely that was denied to their parents, when it is pointed out that Indonesia has the freest press in Asia, they are surprised. Quick to voice dissatisfaction that corruption has not yet been totally eradicated, they fail to note that the judicial system has been overhauled, independent judges have been hired, old judges are being weeded out and transparency is now the key word. They often forget, too, that Indo-

its Olympics-winning badminton teams and female weightlifters. Indonesia's Chris John has won the World Boxing Association's featherweight title 14 times since 2003. Singer-songwriter Anggun Sasmi from Java has had a long and successful career in France, and the US became acquainted with Indonesian pop star Agnez Mo in 2011 when she recorded an album with Michael Bolton, whom she met while co-hosting the 2010 American Music Awards. Indonesian fashion designers are beginning to make a splash overseas, too. An exciting young cou-

Festival preparations, Tabanan, Bali.

nesia has made enormous strides at combating terrorism and that its unexpected success so far with democratisation is being used as a model for other developing countries. Many Indonesians also fail to realise how far human rights – including free elections – have come and that at last the regional and national governments are paying attention to the needs of the poor, education and health care, and how many millions of new jobs have been created.

INDONESIANS ABROAD

An increasing number of Indonesians are attracting attention abroad in a variety of sectors, making them ambassadors for their homeland. Long known internationally are

ture designer, Tex Saverio, created the confection worn by Lady Gaga on the cover of a 2011 US *Harper's Bazaar* magazine, and the novelist Eka Kurniawan has gained a high profile on the international literary circuit since 2015.

Indonesia's journey towards mature and full-functioning democracy is perhaps not entirely complete, and many challenges lie ahead. But in view of their enormous diversity, the hurdles the Indonesian people have overcome are nothing short of amazing. Given that their homeland is the fourth most populous nation on earth, with a burgeoning economy and increasing levels of wealth, it is likely that the rest of the world will be getting to know Indonesians much better in the coming decades.

t Eid al-Fitr festival.

RELIGION

Though the vast majority of Indonesians follow Islam, bare statistics mask a remarkable religious diversity stretching beyond the bounds of the country's six official faiths.

Although Indonesia has the world's largest Muslim population, it is not an Islamic state, with six religions given equal official status. Around 87 percent of its citizens are Muslim. Most of the remainder are Protestant (around seven percent) or Catholic (around three percent). In Indonesia 'Christian' is generally understood to refer to Protestantism; Catholicism is always referred to specifically as Katolik. There are smaller numbers of Hindus, Buddhists and Confucians. Despite the overwhelming numerical dominance of Islam, on the ground Indonesia often seems markedly more diverse. The uneven spread of population density means that more than half of the country's Muslim population is crammed into Java, while large swathes in the east of the country, as well as areas of Sumatra and Kalimantan, have a Christian majority. Even within Muslim-majority areas, towns and cities are generally more mixed, with prominent churches and a handful of colourful Chinese temples.

All Indonesians are expected to record one of the six official religions on their government ID card. Nonetheless, individual degrees of religious devotion vary widely – as in most countries. Also, until very recently, in many rural areas local folk beliefs – often drawing on elements of Hindu-Buddhism or ancestor worship – had more influence than scripture. And even the official 'world religions' tend to take on distinctive 'Indonesian' characteristics: Balinese Hinduism is quite distinct from its Indian counterpart, for example.

INDIGENOUS BELIEFS

Indonesia's indigenous belief systems are many and varied, though certain common themes span the archipelago – with the propitiation of

Balinese temple courtyard.

⊘ ONE GOD

The Indonesian constitution guarantees freedom to worship. Yet, only certain religions have been officially recognised (with Confucianism only added to the list in 2000). Pancasila, the state ideology created by Sukarno in 1945, demanded religions must recognise one god: Balinese, Hinduism and others 'appointed' a supreme being in order to qualify.

It is commonly believed that the one-god proviso was part of Sukarno's efforts to ensure that Indonesian identity was not defined as Islamic. Another theory is that by precluding indigenous belief systems, he could 'civilise' Indonesia's varied peoples, or at least appear to the outside world to have done so.

local place spirits, a concern with male-female symbolic duality, a focus of ritual towards prominent mountains and a devotion to deified ancestors amongst the commonest themes. The influence of these traditions can still be traced in Javanese Islam, with its strong concern for ancestral graves, and Balinese Hinduism with its myriad local deities and spirits. Dramatic funeral ceremonies and lavish burial customs are another manifestation of ancestor-worship. Today very few Indonesians openly declare adherence to an indigenous religion, but it is common

Around 87 percent of Indonesians follow Islam.

to encounter a duality in which an officially recognised world religion is sincerely practiced alongside unique local traditions, ingeniously maintained under the banner of *adat* (custom). In this way ancient belief systems, such as Sumba's *Marapu*, Toraja's *Aluk Todolo*, Kalimantan's *Kaharingan* or Lombok's *Wetu Telu* are able to survive alongside Christianity and Islam.

ISLAM

The most significant of the major religions in Indonesia is Islam, which became the fulcrum for the region's development. By the late 13th century, Islam had gained a foothold in Sumatra and, within a few centuries, had become embedded in Southeast Asia, anchored by a powerful

Islamic commercial and political centre in Melaka during the 15th century.

Although Indonesia has an overwhelming majority of Muslims, religious tolerance and freedom of religion is guaranteed by the constitution. Political parties based on moderate Islamic beliefs have had significant representation in parliament, but they do not dominate, and where they gain power it is typically as junior coalition partners.

The faith is practised in its most orthodox fashion in Aceh, North Sumatra – the only province that applies Sharia law. West Java, Madura, Southeast Kalimantan and western Lombok are also devoutly Muslim regions. Elsewhere, Islam may be the professed religion, but the strict rituals of fasting and prayers may be less rigidly followed than in other Muslim-majority countries – though in recent decades places such as Java, which long eschewed standard Islamic practice, have taken a turn towards to more orthodox observance.

Islam's rituals are intertwined with the basic needs and acts of daily life and define the nature and quality of life itself and of the community. Islamic beliefs and practices are based upon two important touchstones: the *Koran (Qur'an)* and the *Sunnah*. The *Koran* is considered to be the word of God, as spoken to Muhammad (c. AD 570–632) during the last 22 years of his life, through the angel Gabriel. And as it is considered the word of God, the *Koran* in all its 114 chapters is irrefutable and faultless.

The *Sunnah*, less well known to outsiders, reflects the traditional norms regarding assorted concerns and issues, based upon what Muhammad himself did or said regarding those concerns. Although secondary to the *Koran*, it is a fundamental component for most Muslims.

SHARED ABRAHAMIC ORIGINS

Little known among non-Muslims is that Islam accepts most biblical miracles and prophets, in both the Old and New Testaments. Abraham, Moses and Jesus, for example, are important prophets. Adam was the first prophet, later forgiven by God for his sins. According to Islam, Muhammad came later as the last and final prophet, revealing the ultimate, perfected word of God. Islam regards the other Abrahamic religions as essentially representations of the same divine truth, except that Islam is closest to that truth.

For Muslims, Allah (simply the Arabic word for 'God', often used by Indonesian Christians as well as Muslims) is omnipotent and singular, but there are permutations of this fundamental idea throughout Indonesia, where local polytheistic beliefs have been melded with Islam. This modifying of practice and doctrine is not restricted to Islam and is found in all religions.

In common with Christianity, there is a heaven and a hell in Islam. The world's creation was an act of mercy by God, and the purpose of humans is simple: to serve God. But, unlike

Indonesia adapted Indian and all other religions to its needs. For example, the events and people recorded in Hindu epics such as the Ramayana and the Mahabharata have been shifted out of India to Java.

Christian wedding ceremony, Samosir Island, Sumatra.

Christianity, which is more individualistic, Islam has it that humanity's responsibility includes the establishment of social systems that are pure and free from vice and corruption. Allah also judges societies and nations, which are subject to the same transgressions and weaknesses as people.

According to the Koran, people are proud, if not egotistical, and susceptible to selfishness and greed. (Satan is a significant factor in earthly affairs.) Belief in the *Koran* is said to assist people in rising above these inadequacies by establishing an inner ethical bearing called *taqwa*. Through this quality, good and evil, and right and wrong, are recognisable. In the end, a person is judged by *taqwa*, not by earthly deeds or

accomplishments. The role of the Islamic prophets has been to show individuals, as well as whole societies and even nations, the way to *taqwa*.

BALINESE HINDUISM

Most of Indonesia's Hindus live on Bali, where they form more than 90 percent of the Balinese population. Balinese Hinduism has developed local characteristics that distinguish it from Indian Hinduism.

Central to Balinese Hinduism – known as *Agama Hindu Dharma* – is the belief in the balance of two opposite forces, manifested as good and evil; light and dark; male and female; positive and negative; order and chaos, and so on. The two realms coexist and are equally important.

Good, as represented by benevolent gods such as Dewa and Bhatara, is to be emulated, cultivated and esteemed. Worship of these gods is marked by offerings of food, holy water and flowers, dancing and beautiful art pieces. Credit for a bountiful harvest, for example, is given to the popular goddess of rice and fertility, Dewi Sri.

The hierarchy of Balinese gods begins with Sanghyang Widi Wasa, the supreme invisible being who is manifested through the three gods: Brahma, Vishnu (also spelled Wisnu) and Shiva (also called Siva or Siwa). This main god qualifies Agama Hindu Dharma as a monotheistic religion under the terms of Pancasila.

The Balinese live for festive activities, which centre on the village temples, taking place once every 210 days or during a particular full moon in the lunar-solar year, when a communal birthday feast *(odalan)* is held on the anniversary of its consecration. In a typical celebration, delicately carved idols are brought out, wrapped in sacred woven cloths and then infused with the protective spirits of the villages before being borne in a colourful procession to the river or sea to be purified. On return to the temple, mediums tell if the celebrations have been satisfactory to the gods. If so, the villagers pray together and feast throughout the night.

Evil forces, in the form of earth demons, can cause ill fortune such as natural calamity, a breach of human relations or illness, and must be placated with purification offerings and rituals, such as ritual cleansings. Uncleanliness is a state that anyone can stumble into, for example, during menstruation, a long illness, a death in the family or a natural disaster such as a volcanic eruption. Central to the cleansing ritual is the administration of holy water. To the

Villagers celebrating an odalan festival, Bali.

⊘ CHRISTIANITY AND CONFLICT

In most parts of Indonesia a single religion dominates, and while there have been occasional attacks on minorities by radical Islamists (often prompted by unconnected national or international events), the different communities generally coexist peacefully. But in a few places – particularly central Maluku and the Poso area of Sulawesi – Christian and Muslim populations exist in a delicate numerical balance, a situation primed for conflict. In the 1990s and early 2000s both these areas saw intercommunal troubles, typified by tit for tat violence. Peace initiatives have since restored order and helped to diminish old tensions.

Balinese, the mountains are holy because they are believed to be connected to Mount Meru in India and because they are the source of life-sustaining water. Due to this belief, all physical structures – houses, temples and schools – are aligned according to the direction of and proximity to sacred mountains and the sea.

BUDDHISM

Buddhism originated in India, penetrated China, and later entered Java and Sumatra with traders and wandering pilgrims. This contemplative offshoot of Hinduism has cast off the notions of caste differences as well as the myriad array of gods. In its purest form, it offers a practical, moral way of life.

Buddhism's founder was an Indian prince named Siddhartha Gautama, who lived during the 6th century BC. He came to realise that pain and sadness were caused by desire, in itself an illusion. His solution was that by rising above desire and human attachments, human beings can live a life free from suffering. His spiritual recipe, called the Eightfold Path, set out steps to help an individual contain passion and emotion by focusing on wisdom, thought, speech, conduct, livelihood, effort, attentiveness and concentration. For Buddhists, the goal is enlightenment and the bliss that comes with attaining non-attachment. The devotee is then freed from the endless cycles of rebirth and from human suffering.

Today, only small pockets of pure Buddhism remain in Indonesia, such as the monastery across from Mendut temple near Borobudur in Central Java and some tiny communities in Lombok. Most Buddhists in Indonesia are ethnic Chinese who mix Buddhism with ancestor worship, Taoism and Confucianism.

CATHOLICISM AND PROTESTANTISM

Catholicism arrived with the Portuguese in the 16th century, beginning in Maluku, Flores, and Timor. However, once the Dutch VOC came to dominate in the 17th century, Catholic missionary activity was stopped, and many Indonesian Catholics converted to Protestantism. After the VOC collapsed in the early 19th century and Catholicism was legalised in the Netherlands, Catholic priests returned to Indonesia. Flores is the major stronghold of Catholicism today,

> *A Chinese temple in Semarang is dedicated to Sam Po Kong, the deification of 15th-century Admiral Zhengde from China, a Muslim. Both Chinese and Muslims commemorate the temple's founding with a festival each September.*

though there are also small but vibrant Catholic communities in other places such as Java.

Like the British in India, Dutch colonial offi-

Java a significant minority of people who had formerly been nominal Muslims actually converted to Christianity, and even Hinduism, at this point, because they were uncomfortable with the political associations of more orthodox Islam.

CONFUCIANISM

Perhaps one of the earliest religions to arrive in Indonesia, Confucianism was introduced by Chinese merchants and immigrants as early as the 3rd century AD. It is not a religion as such,

Chinese temple at Glodok, Jakarta.

cialdom tended to look askance at missionaries, worrying that their activities would offend local sensibilities, discouraging them in Java and generally tolerating Christianising efforts only amongst 'primitive' peoples – which accounts for the dominance of Christianity in more remote regions even today.

After the 1965 anti-communist coup, all Indonesian citizens were forced to register with the government and carry identification cards naming one of the then five officially recognised religions as their professed faith, and the smaller groups such as Lutherans and Presbyterians listed themselves as Protestant. Likewise, adherents of indigenous faiths were expected to sign up for an 'official' religion. In

but is a philosophy outlining a code of conduct. It is believed that the first Confucian organisation was not formed until the early 20th century in Batavia (now Jakarta). Prior to Suharto's anti-Chinese regime, Confucianism was one of the original six religions which met the government's 'one God' requirement (see page 69), following the declaration of Confucius as a 'god'. It was then banned in 1978 following a decision by the presidential cabinet that it was not, in fact, a religion, and adherents were forced to register as Christians or Buddhists in order to maintain their citizenship. Following the fall of Suharto, fourth president Abdurrahman Wahid declared Confucianism an official religion once more.

CUSTOMS AND RITUALS

The observance of *adat*, or local custom,lies at the heart of Indonesian morality and sense of community, and has been passed down through the generations.

All the religions practised in Indonesia are enmeshed with locally defined customs passed from one generation to another, called *adat*, and the manner in which this intermingling is manifested can be very confusing to outsiders. A classic example is that of a self-declared Javanese Muslim who may also firmly believe in the existence of Hindu-Buddhist deities and in the indigenous folk heroes portrayed in the ever-popular *wayang kulit* shadow play, as well as in a host of ghosts, spirits, demons and genies said to inhabit the worldly environment.

Typically, in addition to fulfilling the requirements of the Islamic faith, traditionalist Javanese hold frequent communal feasts *(selamatan)* to celebrate special occasions and to mitigate the disruptions of unsettling events. They will also seek the advice of a local *dukun*, or mystic, in times of distress, as well as trusting in the magical potency of an inherited *keris* dagger and a variety of other talismans.

An odalan ceremony in Tirta Empul Temple.

FEASTS

Central to the *adat* observances of most Indonesians is the ritual communal feast. In the Javanese *sesaji*, ceremonial foods are offered to the spirits in invitation, but are not eaten, whereas in Bali the food is an offering, publicly consumed to ensure wellbeing and to strengthen solidarity.

The most common example of such a feast is the Javanese *selamatan*, in which special foods are eaten (such as *tumpeng*, an inverted cone of yellow-coloured rice with various dishes), Islamic prayers are intoned, and announcements or requests are made. A *selamatan* may be given at any time and for almost any reason – to celebrate a birth, marriage, circumcision, death or anniversary, to initiate a new project or a new building, or to dispel bad luck or invite good fortune.

In Bali, festive activities centre on the village temple, where a communal birthday feast *(odalan)* is held on the anniversary of its

> Visitors are welcome to attend odalan festivities in Bali, provided they dress and behave respectfully. As each Balinese temple observes this ritual every 210 days, there are plenty to choose from. Most are one-day events.

consecration. Days beforehand, the entire village is engaged in the preparation of elaborate decorations and offerings.

Everyone, from young children to great-grandparents, gets involved with the preparations, for it is a time for socialising as well. Women trim and pin together palm leaves into containers and ritual ornaments, mould coloured rice-dough into symbolic shapes and assemble countless offerings from a dazzling range of materials.

Meanwhile, the men of the village slaughter animals for meat offerings in addition to feeding those helping out in the *odalan*. They also construct temporary platforms and pavilions, repair shrines and climb trees to collect the necessary leaves, flowers and fruits that are used for the offerings.

When the offerings are presented, the deities and spirits consume the invisible essence of the offerings. The physical parts are considered to be 'leftovers' and are eaten by the worshippers at the temple or brought home for a family feast. Clearly, the Balinese have the best of both worlds.

JIWA

These and other types of communal feasts and rituals are frequently intended to enhance the fertility and prosperity of the participants by strengthening, purifying or augmenting something known to many Indonesian peoples as *jiwa* – the spirit or soul thought to inhabit and animate not only humans but plants, animals, sacred objects and also entire villages or nations. These spirits can be malevolent as well as benign, and it is believed that by boosting their own life-giving *jiwa*, people are able to achieve and maintain a fragile balance.

The *jiwa* of human beings is thought by some to be concentrated in the head and hair, and in the past, the Sulawesi Torajans, Kalimantan Dayaks and the Papua Danis sought to promote their own *jiwa* at the expense of an adversary through head-hunting raids. Skull trophies were once regarded as powerful talismans that would enhance the prosperity of a community, and also ward off sickness, war, famine or ill fortune.

A ceremonial first haircut often serves to initiate an infant into human society. The exchange of snippets of hair is an integral part of some Indonesian marriage rites, while human hair curiously features in the costumes of many supernatural characters. Likewise, hair clippings are disposed of carefully (as are nail trimmings), lest they fall into the hands of an enemy sorcerer.

Blood, too, is thought to be infused with *jiwa*, which can be easily transmitted or conferred. On many islands, the pillars of a new house are anointed with the sacrificial blood of animals to render them strong and durable.

Music plays a prominent role in many Indonesian rituals.

⊘ SOCIETY'S GLUE

Adat is often viewed as the glue that binds society and allows it to function with minimal conflict, with all community members having a formally defined perspective on right and wrong. Some *adat* strictures are of a superstitious nature, such as banishing twins of opposite sexes from villages because they are considered to bring bad luck. However, others are practical. In many forest communities, *adat* prohibits cutting certain trees or killing specific animals, thus promoting a balance between human needs and nature. Even in the 21st century, many Indonesians agree that *adat* is of vital importance to their daily lives.

Many Indonesians believe that this soul substance is also found in plants such as banyan trees. An interesting metaphor for human life is the powerful but sensitive *jiwa* associated with the rice plant, which is symbolic of important philosophical values.

When still young, the rice grains are light because they are empty; thus the plant is straight, standing upright as if challenging the sky. This personifies the immature human soul, which is unstable, arrogant and lacking life experience. It also represents the rice plant's

people. Certain rituals are performed before babies are born, for infants and for teenagers to ensure they will be powerful, humble and wise in the future, while remembering their heritage. The ceremonies attempt to imbue these children with good *jiwa*.

All ancient and curious objects, mountains and bodies of water are thought to be imbued with a special *jiwa*. Bezoar stones – mineral deposits found in animals and in the nodes of certain bamboos – are used for magic and healing, while more generally, any object that

A colourful Torajan funeral.

Balinese priestess in a trance.

ingratitude to the life-giving nutrients and water of the earth.

When the plant grows older, the grains become full and heavy and it no longer stands upright but bends to the ground with the weight. This is symbolic of a mature human soul. The more educated one is, the more powerful and wiser. Therefore, like the rice, humans must humble themselves and give thanks to the origins that gave them life. If humans can take on the characteristic of mature rice plants, their *jiwa* will become wiser, calm and humble, capable of accepting inner peace and achieving balance.

This philosophical merit is not reserved for older people, but is also desirable in young

is designated a *pusaka*, or sacred heirloom, is credited with harbouring a vital spiritual essence that requires special veneration and care. Antique *keris* daggers, lances, spearheads, cannons, jewellery, textiles, ceramics, manuscripts, gravestones and masks can all become *pusaka* and may contain a soul of their own or that of a previous owner. Such objects are often in the custody of a king, priest, chief or elder, a link between the living and the powerful ancestral spirits.

A PLACE FOR SOULS

Much of a community's private and public ritual life centres on the management of its human souls, both living and dead. In this, there are generally certain individuals in the communities who possess specialised knowledge or skills in such matters. Special attention is always devoted to funerary rites, in which the dead are ritually venerated and can be transformed into protective clan or village deities.

It is commonly believed that the soul of a person may become detached during life, which can result in illness. Even under normal conditions, it is thought the soul wanders during sleep. Sorcery can entice unwitting souls away.

Cockfights are held at every Balinese temple festival. The blood spilled appeases the hungry forces of evil. Gambling is illegal under Indonesian law, but the police look the other way as cockfighting is considered to be a religious ritual.

Good deaths must also, of course, be attended by a lengthy sequence of elaborate

A cremation ceremony, Bali.

A distinction is made virtually everywhere between good and bad spirits, resulting respectively from good and bad deaths. A bad death, generally premature or violent, releases a vengeful ghost or *hantu* that may bring considerable misfortune on a household or community. The soul of a woman who dies at childbirth is pictured as a bird with long talons that jealously stabs and rents the stomachs of pregnant women. This *kuntilanak* can also assume the shape of a beautiful maiden, who waits at night beneath a banyan tree to seduce and emasculate passing men. Elaborate rituals must then be performed by a shaman to mollify the *hantu* and banish it from the area.

funerary rites. When a person dies, it is universally thought the soul is at first resentful and potentially harmful. Some rites are therefore designed to confuse the soul and dissuade it from returning. It is a widespread custom in Sumatra, Kalimantan, South Sulawesi and Halmahera, for instance, to send the corpse out of the house through a gap in the wall or floor of the house, which is then sealed.

Observers of rituals should respect local customs concerning dress and silence. No one who has witnessed a Balinese funeral procession and cremation, a Torajan funeral sacrifice or a Dayak death ceremony will forget the dignity and colour of the events.

Mie goring is a popular noodle dish.

SPICE ISLANDS CUISINE

Indonesian food is strong in flavours, with a delicious array of fish, unusual vegetables and fruits, and minimal meat. But only the brave should sample the chillies.

Indonesia's cuisine is influenced by the culinary traditions of diverse nations such as China, India, the Middle East and the Netherlands. In fact, Indonesian cuisine is so varied that travellers can be assured of finding at least one dish that becomes a lifelong favourite.

Mealtime for most Indonesians is a quick, private and non-social activity. In most Indonesian homes the food is cooked in the morning to last the whole day. The prepared dishes are placed on the dining table at noon and again at dusk, and family members simply help themselves to a meal whenever they feel hungry. It is only on special occasions, such as on feast days or when having guests over, that the Indonesian family sits and eats together.

The Chinese influence is most evident in the use of stir-fried dishes cooked in a huge steaming wok, while Indonesia's myriad curries show traces of Indian and mainland Southeast Asian influence. Marinated meat on skewers, known locally as *sate*, owes its heritage to the Middle Eastern kebab, while the *rijsttafel* (rice table) traces its roots to Dutch colonial times. In today's Indonesia, each of these various culinary traditions have blended and adapted to form distinctive regional cuisines across the archipelago.

FIVE PILLARS OF THE CUISINE

Rice, coconut, banana, peanut and soya bean are the five pillars of Indonesian cuisine, and it is almost impossible to find a meal that does not include at least one of these items. Rice is the staple food on most of the islands, particularly the more fertile Sumatra, Java and Bali.

There are several kinds of rice in Indonesia: *beras putih* (white rice), *ketan putih* (sticky white rice), *ketan hitam* (sticky black rice) and

Traditional Balinese breakfast in an Ubud market.

beras merah (red rice). Nearly every menu offers dishes prefixed with the word *nasi*, which means they come with rice. Other starches like maize, tapioca, millet and sago are eaten in the drier islands east of Bali and in smaller archipelagos along the coast of Sumatra. On Rote and Sabu islands, the sweet, nutritious juice tapped from the *lontar* palm is a staple.

Coconut and coconut products are central to Indonesian cooking. Almost every meal includes this versatile palm nut in some form. Coconut oil is the common cooking medium while *santan* (coconut milk) is used to thicken and add flavour to soups and curries and as a marinade for meats. Grated coconut is often added to vegetable dishes to provide texture, flavour and an oil base. Fried

Kopi luwak is the world's most expensive coffee. It is made from fermented coffee beans eaten and excreted by luwak (civets). In Lampung and Bali, civets are bred to cash in on the kopi luwak craze.

shredded coconut is served as a condiment. Coconut is also a vital ingredient in Indonesian sweets.

There is an astonishing variety of bananas in Indonesia, ranging from the tiny *pisang mas* to the

Charcoal-broiled sate is known the world over.

larger *pisang lembut* popular in Bali. Bananas can be eaten baked, fried or boiled, and are a popular snack. Even the banana flower is eaten as a vegetable and the leaves are used as wrapping material for steamed meat, fish and vegetables.

Peanuts form an integral part of some meals in the form of a sweet and spicy sauce served with *sate*, *gado-gado* (steamed vegetables) and a host of other dishes. Much of the protein in Indonesian food comes from soya beans. They are eaten boiled or fermented to make *tempe* (soybean cake) and *tahu* (soybean curd). Peanuts are also fried and tossed together with *tempe*, either as a snack or served as a side dish to accompany a main meal.

Fermented soya bean sauces, *kecap asin* (salty) and *kecap manis* (sweet), are important flavouring

agents used with gusto in almost every dish. Most Indonesian restaurants tend to use liberal amounts of MSG (monosodium glutamate) in their cooking, so let the waiter know beforehand if you prefer your food without this flavouring agent.

Indonesians eat a large variety of vegetables. Many greens are picked wild and include tender tapioca, papaya and soya bean leaves, *kangkung* (water spinach) and *bayam* (Asian spinach). Other fruits and vegetables are grown in home gardens, including young jackfruits, papayas and bananas, all varieties of beans, squash and pumpkin, and carrots. Indonesians do not eat much meat for the most part, although it is common to find a few dried fish alongside a mound of white rice. Among other things, the choice of meat is determined by cultural and religious factors.

Main dishes are often accompanied by freshly made *sambal* (a thick chilli concoction), of which there are numerous varieties, ranging from a simple fried diced shallot, garlic and very hot chilli paste to a pungent fried version liberally laced with *terasi* (shrimp paste).

REGIONAL CUISINE

Typically, the food of Java tends to be relatively sweet compared with the spicier flavours of Sumatra and Bali. *Gudeg Jojga*, made with young jackfruit, and *opor ayam*, chicken cooked in coconut milk, represent the sweet foods of Java. The Javanese eat a variety of meats (except pork), and favourite dishes are *soto ayam* (chicken soup), *sop buntut* (oxtail soup) and *ayam goreng* (fried chicken). The Sundanese of West Java prefer fish, grilled, fried or as *pepes* (wrapped in a banana leaf and roasted).

The Balinese favour duck and pork, with dishes including *babi guling* (roast suckling pig) and *bebek tutu* (spiced slow-cooked duck). The Sumatrans eat a lot of beef and buffalo meat. One of the most popular dishes introduced by the West Sumatrans is *rendang* (beef chunks served in a rich and spicy sauce). The traditional Padang restaurant is Sumatra's great contribution to the national cuisine. It offers a bewildering array of tasty local dishes including *ayam* (chicken), *sapi* (beef), *kambing* (mutton), *sayur* (vegetables), *ikan goreng* (fried fish), various curries and maybe an assortment of entrails, plus a substantial serving of steamed rice.

Ayam taliwang, a Lombok dish featuring grilled chicken in hot chilli sauce served with

> *In villages, the centrepiece of the traditional kitchen is a wood-fired stove and rice steamer. Other utensils include a pestle and mortar, wok and banana leaves for wrapping.*

steamed *kangkung*, is familiar throughout Indonesia. South Sulawesi is known for seafood dishes that run the gamut from shrimp, lobster and crab to carp, eel and sea slugs. *Iga sapi bakar* (grilled beef ribs) served with *konro* (rib soup) is on menus throughout the region. The coastal Papuans are said to offer the best *ikan bakar* (grilled fish) in the whole country. However, as in Maluku, their staple food is *pepeda*, sago porridge, eaten with a tuna soup flavoured with lime and turmeric.

EXTREME CUISINE

Some of the Dayaks of Kalimantan consider roast lizard a mouth-watering delicacy, while mice and bats are common fare in Minahasa kitchens in Sulawesi. Dog meat is commonly served during traditional celebrations on Flores, while rabbit and deer *sate* are common in West Java. Cobra meat added to soup and served as *sate* is believed to cure skin diseases and is offered in special restaurants in Java. In Bali, turtle meat is favoured but is now discouraged due to the endangered status of sea turtles. In Central Java, geckos are farmed and processed as crispy snacks, while grasshoppers

are captured to make crackers in Lampung or fried in hot chilli sauce in West Sumatra.

As a general rule, the more rural the area, the higher the chances of having meals prepared with meat and animal parts that may not agree with the palate. Once you go off the beaten track, it is a good idea to check what type of meat has been cooked if you're squeamish. Most Sundanese restaurants feature animal innards on their menus. Fried *ati ampla* (chicken livers and gizzards), *usus* (chicken or cow intestine) and *babat* (tripe) are among the dishes served. The term *jeroan* (meaning 'inside')

Roast suckling pig at Gianyar market, Bali.

⊘ SPICE UP YOUR DAY

It is little wonder that spices are so readily used in the food of the Spice Islands. Spices – known as *bumbu* in Indonesia – can be either wet or dry. The wet type has fresh ingredients like shallots, onions, ginger, garlic and turmeric root ground into a paste, whereas the dry type includes powdered peppercorns, coriander seeds, cinnamon, cumin seeds, candlenut and *terasi* (shrimp paste). *Terasi* is an acquired taste and can be overpowering.

Fresh spices are first ground in a stone mortar and pestle, then fried to release their aroma before being added to meat, poultry or vegetables. Different spices are used with different kinds of meat. Pre-packaged

spices are available in local *warung* and supermarkets. However, in the villages, the woman of the house still prepares spices the old-fashioned way.

No spice mixture is complete without *cabai* (or *lombok*, chillies), as Indonesians love their food *pedas* (hot). The varieties include the long red *tabia lombok* with its sweet flavour, the chunky red and yellow *tabia Bali* and the dynamite bird's-eye chillies. If you are unused to really spicy food, ask that it be prepared without chillies. In addition to being spicy, Indonesian food can be rather aromatic, as fresh bay leaves, lime leaves, basil and lemon grass are common ingredients. The best samplers are found in the Padang restaurants.

is widely understood in Java to mean animal innards. *Gulai otak*, a curry dish made with cow brains, is easily found in Padang restaurants.

VEGETARIAN

Favourite vegetarian dishes include *gado-gado* (vegetable salad with peanut sauce) and *cap cai* (wok-fried vegetables), the latter being ubiquitous in Chinese restaurants. *Lotek* from West Java is similar to *gado-gado* with cooked vegetables, while *karedok* is raw vegetables, and is found on menus in Bogor. Both *lotek*

buy meat. In *arem-arem*, for example, *tempe* is combined with bean sprouts and chunks of compressed, glutinous rice covered with sweet soya sauce mixed with coconut water, and garnished with chopped peanuts and grated coconut.

NATIONWIDE DISHES

One of the best ways to sample a wide variety of Indonesian food is to order *nasi rames* or *nasi campur*. These samplers are platefuls of steamed rice, chicken, fresh and preserved vegetables, fried egg, roasted peanuts, shred-

Unusual meats, such as these bats, are often sold in village markets.

and *karedok* are served with a delicious peanut sauce. *Karedok* is more strongly flavoured than either *gado-gado* or *lotek* thanks to the pungent lesser galangal, a rhizome from the ginger family. *Pecel* from Madiun, East Java, is a popular vegetable salad. Minahasans eat sautéed *bunga papaya* (papaya flowers), while the Sundanese like plain raw vegetables, such as *lalab*, a combination of cabbage, cucumbers, cassava and papaya leaves, basil and aubergine. *Sayur lodeh* (mixed vegetables in coconut milk) originated in Jakarta but is popular throughout Java.

Protein-rich *tahu* and *tempe* are also enjoyed by vegetarians, and both are served in a variety of ways throughout the archipelago, as they are popular with villagers who cannot afford to

ded coconut, fiery *sambal* sauce, and oversized crispy *krupuk* (fried prawn crackers).

The best-known rice dish is *nasi goreng*, fried rice with an assortment of vegetables and chicken, prawns or meat, or a combination of all three. If the word *istimewa* (special) appears, it means the dish comes with a fried egg on top. A cone-shaped mound of *nasi kuning* (yellow rice) cooked with turmeric, coconut milk and spices is served on feast days on a banana leaf-lined platter. *Mi* (noodles) made from rice or wheat flour is another staple. In *mi goreng* (fried noodles), the noodles are fried in coconut oil with meat, vegetables and perhaps egg, with hot chilli shrimp paste and lime on the side. Both *mi goreng* and *nasi goreng* are popular breakfast dishes.

Lontong and ketupat are rice cakes that substitute for steamed rice and are usually eaten with sate and soto (soup). Sate ayam (chicken), sate sapi (beef) and sate kambing (mutton) are common throughout Indonesia, while sate rusa (deer) and sate kelinci (rabbit) are found in West Java. Soto comes in two varieties: one is clear soup flavoured with spices and the other has coconut milk added.

FRUITS AND SWEETS

The array of fresh tropical fruit available in Indonesia often astounds visitors. There are more than

Coconut milk, sticky rice, tapioca, mung beans, palm sugar and bananas are common dessert ingredients. Each island has its version of tiny cakes stuffed with sweetened mung beans, shaved coconut or banana, in a variety of colours made with sticky rice cooked in coconut milk. Indonesians primarily use dark-brown palm sugar as a sweetener for desserts and other dishes.

Look for kue lapis, the Indonesian version of a light layered cake made of rice flour and fragrant coconut palm sugar, and bubur ketan hitam

Red-hot chillies at a market in Samarinda, Kalimantan.

40 varieties of bananas (pisang), pomelos (jeruk Bali), mangoes and pineapples (nanas), plus an array of lesser-known delicacies. Durians might best be described as spiky green bowling balls; decidedly an acquired taste, the pale flesh within is rated a delicacy by those who can overlook the noxious smell. Rambutans are red or yellow, have a hairy exterior and a flavour very similar to lychee. And the skin of the salak (which has a crisp texture and sharp flavour) closely resembles that of a snake. Passion fruit (markisa) is a delicious refreshing fruit full of tiny, edible seeds. Other delicious local fruits include thirst-quenching watermelons (semangka), mangosteens (manggis) and rose apples (jambu air). The local tart green apples are surprisingly juicy and excellent to eat.

⊙ FESTIVAL FOODS

Almost every celebration in Java features nasi tumpeng, a cone of steamed turmeric rice that symbolises a mountain, which is usually served with several side garnishes. Babi guling (suckling pig) is the main dish at ceremonies across Bali, North Sumatra and North Sulawesi. The Chinese minority celebrate Cap Go Meh 15 days after Imlek (Chinese New Year) with favourites including lontong cap go meh (special rice cakes) and opor ayam (chicken stewed in coconut milk). When Muslims celebrate Idul Fitri at the end of the fasting month, their festival foods almost always include ketupat Lebaran (Idul Fitri rice cake) with side dishes such as semur daging (beef stewed in soya bean sauce).

(black rice porridge cooked in coconut milk and sweetened with palm sugar). Delicious pancakes of all sorts, filled with fruit or palm sugar and shredded coconut, are commonly available. *Bubur kacang hijau* (green pea porridge) is also topped with coconut milk and palm sugar, as is *kolak* (steamed bananas, cassava and sweet potato stewed in coconut milk and brown sugar). *Kue pisang*, a coconut milk pudding laced with steamed bananas, is sold wrapped in banana leaves (or nowadays, in plastic) in almost all traditional markets.

pavements of busy streets and in marketplaces with rows of tables and rickety looking benches. Not the most romantic setting, but here most of Indonesia's favourite dishes can be enjoyed at cheap prices. Standards of hygiene are low, however, and refrigeration virtually non-existent, so cast-iron stomachs are a pre-requisite for sampling street fare.

A popular dessert or snack is *es campur*, the Indonesian equivalent of the ice-cream sundae. *Es campur* does not have a nationally accepted set of ingredients, but shaved ice is usually the

Balinese sweets.

Fruit juice vendor, Lombok.

SNACKS

Snacking is a way of life in Indonesia. Children cannot resist *krupuk* or a plate of *rujak* (spicy fruit salad). Fried *(goreng)* or steamed *(rebus)* foods are popular snacks, and can include *pisang* (banana), *tahu* (soy bean curd), *ubi* (sweet potato) and *singkong* (cassava).

Food vendors ply their trade in practically all the streets, attracting customers by twanging a metal chime, beating a low wooden gong or a steam whistle. They serve *bakso* (meatballs), *bakpao* (steamed buns stuffed with meat) or simply a bowl of noodles.

People also get their meals and snacks at traditional Indonesian eating places known as *warung*, makeshift foodstalls set up on the

base. A number of things can be poured over the ice, including syrup and coconut milk, bits of fruits, cubes of brightly coloured gelatine, jackfruit, fermented tapioca and various other sweet titbits.

Es cendol is another great refresher during hot weather, with green-coloured rice-flour jelly served in iced coconut milk and palm sugar. In Central Java it is called *es dawet*. *Es pisang ijo* and *es palu butung* come from Makassar, South Sulawesi, with bananas as the main ingredient, topped with a rice-flour porridge, coconut milk and pandan leaf sauce.

Western food and other speciality cuisines are available at the more popular tourist destinations and in major cities, and Kentucky Fried

Chicken, McDonald's and Pizza Hut are increasingly ubiquitous.

DRINKS

Indonesians often drink sweetened hot black tea with their meals, but iced tea (es teh), local coffee (kopi), fruit juices and bottled sodas are usually also available. Typically, drinks come pre-mixed and tend to be very sweet, so do ask to have the sugar on the side. Sweetened bottled tea, referred to as teh botol regardless of the brand, is widely sold in roadside coolers.

easily found in coastal areas where coconut trees grow. It can be served plain or with added sugar or vanilla syrup with ice.

In the highlands, where temperatures can be quite chilly, hot drinks are favoured by locals. The Sundanese in West Java's highlands drink bajigur, a mixture of palm sugar with coconut milk. Bandrek is another hot drink made with ginger and palm sugar and can be mixed with milk or coffee. In other parts of Java, ginger is also used in hot beverages, such as wedang jahe or ginger tea.

Rijsttafel, a reminder of Dutch rule.

Fruit juices may be ordered fresh or pre-packaged. Among the popular choices of fresh juices are watermelon, papaya, pineapple and avocado. Fresh es buah is a mix of fresh fruits such as watermelon, papaya, pineapple and apple.

Local alcoholic beverages include Bintang beer (whose roots are traceable to the Dutch Heineken), tuak (palm wine), brem (rice wine), badek (rice liquor) and arak, the most potent of rice spirits. Visitors are cautioned against buying locally made spirits, as they can be laced with added ingredients – even gasoline – to give them an extra kick and can cause illness or even death.

Kelapa muda, a drink made from fresh young coconuts, replaces body fluids quickly and is

⊘ RIJSTTAFEL

Much Dutch culinary influence has faded away since independence, but a remnant of it remains in the rijsttafel, a more elaborate form of the Sumatran nasi Padang.

Rijsttafel (literally, rice table) is a series of meat and vegetable courses, served with rice and spicy condiments, presented at the table with much ceremony by a string of sarong-clad waitresses.

Expect about five to six courses in a typical rijsttafel, a far cry from Dutch colonial days when the serving might include as many as 350 separate dishes. Due to the elaborate nature of this meal, it is offered primarily at tourist restaurants and hotels.

DANCE AND THEATRE

The most refined Indonesian performing arts are in Java and Bali, where court theatre has evolved as a highly stylised retelling of the classics. Other islands have their own traditions.

There is such a variety of dance and dramatic tradition throughout Indonesia that it is impossible to speak of a single, unified tradition. Each Indonesian ethnic and linguistic group possesses its own unique performing arts. Nevertheless, there are certain shared features among the groups.

Dance, storytelling and theatre are ubiquitous in Indonesia, elements of a cultural life that is all-encompassing and fulfils a wide variety of sacred and secular needs. Dancers, shamans, actors, puppeteers, storytellers, poets and musicians are members of the community, performing vital roles in informing, entertaining, counselling and instructing their fellows in the well-established ways of tradition.

RITUAL DANCES

Most ethnic groups have ritual dances performed to mark rites of passage – births, funerals, weddings, puberty – and agricultural events, as well as to exorcise sickness or evil spirits, and, in the past, to prepare for battle or celebrate victory. The primary purpose of these dances is to appease the spirits. The Batak *datuk* (magician) of North Sumatra, for example, holds a magic staff as he treads with tiny steps over a design he has drawn on the ground. At the climax of this dance, he hops and skips,

The Barong dance dramatises the struggle between good and evil.

thrusting his staff into an egg on the ground. The **Hornbill dance**, performed by Kalimantan Dayaks for many generations, celebrated warriors returning from battle. Nowadays used as part of harvest festivals, the dancer, adorned with hornbill feathers, makes slow movements as though stalking and attacking the enemy.

More refined ritual dances are performed by a select group, but in village dances, often all the males or females in the community join in. Female movements are generally slow and deliberate, with tiny steps and graceful hand movements; men lift their knees high and use their hands as 'weapons', often in imitation of traditional martial-arts movements *(pencak*

Some dance schools teach boys to perform dance roles usually played by females. In the Javanese town of Wonosobo, the lengger dance features men dressed as women, while the male Buginese bissu of South Sulawesi dances in a trance as a woman.

silat). Accompaniment is provided by chanting, pounding of rice mortars *(lesung)*, and bamboo chimes or flutes.

Group dances often involve the entrancement and possession of participants, best known of which is the Balinese *Barong*. The *Barong-Rangda* dance-drama is a contest between the opposing forces of good and evil in the universe, represented by a good lion-like beast called Barong and the evil witch Rangda. The battle ends in a temporary quelling rather than complete victory.

Barong. The riders begin in an orderly fashion, trotting in circles, until one of them becomes entranced and behaves like a horse, charging back and forth wildly, neighing, and eating grass or straw. The others might follow his lead, and sometimes there is a confrontation between the masked animal and the horsemen. Eventually, the riders are brought out of the trance by their leader, and all ends well.

Another well-known trance dance from East Java is the *reog*, which tells the story of a prince who wants to marry a beautiful princess. He

The kecak dance at Pura Luhur Uluwatu, Bali.

In the Balinese *sanghyang* trance dances, the performers are possessed by gods and animal spirits. In the *sanghyang dedari*, or heavenly maidens dance, two young girls dressed in white enter a circle of 40 to 50 chanting men, the *kecak* chorus. The girls dance in unison with eyes shut, then when they are finally possessed by goddesses they are clothed in glittering costumes and borne aloft on the shoulders of the men, touring the village to drive out evil.

In Central Java, one trance dance is variously known as *kuda kepang*, *kuda lumping* and *jatilan*, and consists of one or more riders on hobby horses made of plaited bamboo, accompanied by musicians, masked clowns and perhaps also a masked lion, tiger or crocodile similar to the

wears an enormous mask weighing 30–40kg (66–88lbs) adorned with a tiger or leopard head and peacock feathers, held in place by the performer's teeth. The dancer – the *singa barong* – goes into trance while demonstrating his strength and prowess in his efforts to impress the lady. On some occasions, children or young ladies ride on top of the mask to impress the audience. In other versions of the *reog*, young boys or girls riding hobbyhorses, similar to the *jatilan* horses used in Central Java, accompany the *singa barong*.

COURT DANCES OF JAVA

Before the turn of the 20th century, all traditional rulers of the coastal and inland kingdoms maintained palace dance and theatrical troupes. But following the Dutch conquests, most court traditions lapsed into obscurity. Only in Central Java are courtly performances and royal patronage of dancers, actors and musicians still found and appreciated.

Java has by far the oldest known dance and theatre traditions in Indonesia, as depicted in stone carvings dating from the 8th and 9th centuries. The walls of Borobudur, Prambanan and others are adorned with numerous reliefs depicting dancers and musical entertainers, from market minstrels and roadside revellers to sensuous court concubines and prancing princesses.

Most of the traditional dances in Central Java are attributed to rulers of one of several Islamic dynasties, particularly those of the 16th to 18th centuries, with rulers having dances choreographed for special occasions. One renowned Javanese court dance is the *bedoyo ketawang*, performed in the Surakarta palace on the anniversary of the Susuhunan's coronation. This is a sacred and private ritual dance said to have been instituted in the early 1600s celebrating a reunion between the descendant of the dynasty's founder and the powerful Goddess of the Southern Ocean, Kanjeng Ratu Kidul.

Nine female palace dancers perform the stately *bedoyo ketawang*, attired in royal wedding dress, and it is so sacred that they may rehearse only once on a given day. Until recently, no outsiders were permitted to witness the performance, as it is believed that Kanjeng Ratu Kidul herself attends and afterwards 'weds' the king.

Another court dance from Solo, *serimpi*, was traditionally performed only by princesses or daughters of the ruling family. It portrays one or two duelling pairs of warriors, reflecting the balance of negative and positive cosmic forces. Following the rise of dance schools in the early 1900s, the *serimpi* became the standard dance taught to all young women.

FOLK DANCES

Outside the courts, there have always been dances performed by the common people.

In the Javanese kuda lumping, dancers often go into a trance.

⊘ BALINESE DANCE

There are clear indications that dance and drama closely tied to religion have played a central role in Indonesian life since time immemorial. Other dances, however, are ceremonial, teach life lessons, or are simply for entertainment.

In Balinese dance, the Indian influence is evident in the facial expressions. Balinese costumes, with their glittering headdresses and elaborate jewellery, are of Hindu-Javanese origin and, as in Java, Balinese dancers adopt the same basic stance. Javanese court dances, however, are performed with slow, controlled, continuous movements, with eyes downcast and limbs close to the body. In contrast, the Balinese dancer is charged with energy, eyes wide and darting, feet lifted high, arms up, moving with quick, cat-like bursts that are startling.

Dances have evolved over long periods of time, and their original uses are now intertwined. In Bali, the *legong keraton* was originally a court dance developed for royal amusement, but it is now seen frequently at temple ceremonies. The *baris* warrior dance, often performed in groups and with weapons, appears to have developed out of a ritual battle dance. A solo *baris* performance is a true test of wits for the dancer and musicians, who must respond to each other's signals to produce the quivering bursts of synchronised energy that are the essence of the dance.

Thought to be too crude to be performed for royalty, these dances are relatively free of restrictions and change with the times.

Some folk dances, for example, are primarily for courtship. They are usually offshoots from fertility rites and women take the initiative, as in *gandrung* from Lombok. A female dancer selects male partners for short dance duets by tapping them on the shoulder with her fan. A similar dance, *joged bumbung*, is performed in West Bali. In Kalimantan, young Dayak women perform graceful dances holding bunches of hornbill

attention of young people who were no longer interested in time-honoured dance.

Very popular, and now a Unesco cultural heritage treasure, is the *saman* dance from the Gayo highlands, near Aceh. Often called the 'thousand hands' dance abroad, between eight and 20 male or female performers kneel on the floor in a line. There is no music; instead, the exuberant cadence is created by clapping hands, pounding the floor and slapping the chest, with one person reading a barely audible narrative in order to maintain the cadence. Energetic and

Young Dayak women performing.

feathers as bachelors watch, hoping the ladies will approach them. Even staunchly Muslim Aceh (North Sumatra) has its dance traditions; the *serampang dua belas* is performed by mixed pairs, telling the 12 steps (*dua belas*) of introducing young people who are about to enter marriage.

From the 1950s, Indonesian performers began studying abroad, each bringing home new elements that they introduced into traditional dances or used to create new ones. The *jaipong* from Bandung, West Java, is considered by some to be vulgar, but its creator, Gugum Gumbira, views it as humorous and spontaneous. Building on the past with *sarong*-clad female performers using some traditional body movements, the dance was intended to attract the

dynamic, the performance requires excellent coordination to keep the rhythm going.

THEATRE

Some theatrical traditions incorporate dance to such an extent that they are typically referred to as 'dance-dramas'. In Java, all theatre seems to have its roots in the *wayang* (puppet) tradition, evident from the fact that all traditional Javanese theatre, whether performed by actors or by puppets, is referred to as *wayang*. Performed by actors on a stage, *wayang topeng* (mask drama) and *wayang orang* (dance drama) are the most traditional, with many of the tales, choreography and characters' movements borrowed from the shadow play.

Wayang topeng may have been inspired by ancient masked dances, but it was not introduced in the courts of Yogyakarta until the early 20th century, by the *pedalangan* (shadow puppetry) community. In Bali, mask plays are still popular, as they are in the courts of Central Java, and in some villages in the east and west of the island. Like puppet plays, masked performances are often used on television and in village performances to convey messages to the public, particularly satirical ones.

The highly stylised Javanese *wayang orang* or *wayang wong* (literally, human *wayang*)

A shadow puppet, Denpasar.

dance-dramas are said to have been created in the 18th century by one or another of Central Java's rulers. *Wayang orang* became a part of the state ritual in these kingdoms, performed in an open pavilion to commemorate the founding of the dynasty and the coronation of the king, as well as at lavish royal weddings. The great age of *wayang orang* was during the 1920s and 1930s, when productions lasted days and would often employ 300 to 400 actors.

To keep up with the times, traditional dance and drama has in some cases blended with modern forms of entertainment to suit contemporary tastes. Javanese *kethoprak* (also spelled *ketoprak*) has connections to *wayang wong* because it uses classical costumes and gamelan music, but the dialogue is spoken rather than sung, the dancing is minimal and risqué humour is used to attract younger audiences. The topics are usually love stories, Javanese heroic romances or tales borrowed from Chinese folklore, and are frequently seen on television as well as at open-air venues. Evolving from this genre in order to relieve stress during times of political and economic change after Suharto's fall, *kethoprak* humour today remains slapstick and full of lowbrow puns and cross-dressing.

MODERN TRENDS

Although traditional dance and drama face competition from modern entertainment, many educated Indonesians are dedicated to keeping these arts alive. There are government and privately sponsored arts high schools

⊘ PUPPET THEATRE

Thought to be derived from ancestral worship, puppet theatre is limited to a few locations in Indonesia.

The remarkable life-sized Batak *sigale-gale* puppet of North Sumatra is manipulated from below with cords and pulleys during funeral ceremonies. It is attributed to a local childless woman who, in somewhat macabre fashion, made an image of her dead husband and animated it to communicate with his soul. Some figures have water-filled sponges at the eyes to make them weep. Traditionally, at the end of the funeral, spears and arrows were shot at the figure to drive away evil spirits.

In Central Java, *wayang kulit* uses flat leather puppets that are perforated and fitted with movable arms for

Ramayana and *Mahabharata* stories. In West Java, *wayang golek* (wooden rod puppets) perform tales from Indian epics and Islamic Amir Hamzah or Menak romances.

Balinese *wayang* refers to many types of shadow-puppet theatre with different repertoires. *Wayang Ramayana* stages stories from the epic of the same name, while *wayang parwa* performs episodes from the *Mahabharata*. An 11th-century Javanese exorcist legend of black magic is the focus for *wayang Calonarang*.

In Lombok, *wayang Sasak* works flat leather puppets to depict Islamic Menak romances, which were introduced from Java during the 17th century to spread the teachings of Islam.

and academies in Java and Bali and two fully accredited universities, one in Jogja and the other in Denpasar. With state-of-the-art visual, performing and recorded media arts, these schools are turning out not only traditional, but also contemporary performers, choreographers, musicologists and ethnomusicologists, as well as photographers, film-makers and interior designers.

While it might seem that the students at these schools would be primarily interested in contemporary arts, many Indonesians – and some

A Snuff Puppets Company production.

foreigners – attend specifically to delve more deeply into traditions. Someone yearning to become a *dalang* (puppeteer), for example, has to study Kawi (Old Javanese) and Sanskrit, and master vocal techniques to give personalities to each puppet character while simultaneously enrapturing the audience, sending the desired messages and ensuring their voices are strong enough to be heard. In addition, they need to learn hundreds of tales from the *Ramayana* and *Mahabharata* epics (see page 93), and many will learn to make their own puppets. Some students will study several genres until they find the right niche to pursue.

In the performing arts realm, tourism helps by providing a commercial demand for the

> *Excellent examples of performances mixing traditional and contemporary dance-drama can be seen on stage at Bali Safari & Marine Park in Gianyar and seasonally at Borobudur. Both use stunning costumes, animals and magnificent lighting effects.*

arts. A new generation of Indonesian choreographers, familiar with Western classical and modern dance, is now producing art-drama-dance (*sendratari*, literally translated as ballet), which is essentially a traditional dance-drama, minus the dialogue, that incorporates some modern movements and costumes. One of the most popular is the *Ramayana* ballet spectacular performed on a large stage in front of the elegant 9th-century Prambanan temple complex near Jogja.

Also emerging from these schools and academies are theatre groups such as Teater Koma (Theatre Comma), which has been active since 1977. Its shows were often banned during the Suharto era for lampooning the government – both the system and leaders – but they persevered and today attract audiences that reach across the population, from university students to professionals to diehard theatre fans. In a lavish Chinese opera production staged in 2011, a series of 7th-century Chinese tales were woven together, incorporating elaborate costumes and make-up, and also brought in Javanese puppets and traditional martial arts. The dialogue in the four-hour-long production included the satirical jabs that Teater Koma is known for.

The new generation of performers is also credited with finding overseas venues for local troupes and for inviting artists from abroad to combine talents with Indonesian actors, actresses and dancers, creating original contemporary work. One such collaboration between the Snuff Puppets Company of Melbourne, Australia, and Jogja artists has been ongoing for several years and has created a new genre using life-sized puppets, theatrical dances, popular music and cross-cultural dialogue about traditions and mythology in changing societies.

INDIAN MORALITY EPICS

Central to Javanese and Balinese drama are the two great Indian epics, the Ramayana and the Mahabharata, stories of love and the triumph of good over evil.

The *Ramayana* and the *Mahabharata* epics are the basis of the most important wayang stories in Java and Bali. These gripping tales, one about an ever-lasting love and the other about a great war, are products of India that entered Java with the propagation of Hinduism.

Filled with high drama, they are morality plays, which over the ages have contributed greatly to the establishment of traditional Indonesian values. Their fascination lies partly in the complex moral themes posed: life is never a case of absolutely black or white. Good heroes may have bad traits, and bad characters may have redeeming qualities. Although the forces of good do triumph over evil in the end, more often than not, the victory is incomplete; both sides suffer losses, and though a king may win a righteous war, he may lose all his sons as well.

THE *RAMAYANA*

The *Ramayana* is filled with examples on how to lead a good life. Written by the poet Valmiki about 2,000 years ago, it tells the story of Prince Rama, who had been predetermined by the gods to be a hero, but would be put to the test many times. Rama is, in fact, an incarnation of the god Vishnu, and it is his destiny to kill the evil ogre king Ravana.

Owing to palace intrigues, Rama, his beautiful wife Sita (also spelled Shinta or Sinta) and his brother Laksamana are exiled to the forest. An ogre named Marica takes the form of a golden deer, luring Rama and Laksamana away. Ravana then carries off Sita to his island kingdom, Lanka. Rama's search for Sita is helped by the monkey god Hanuman and the monkey king Sugriva. Eventually, a full-scale assault is launched on the evil king and Sita is rescued. Sita, in turn, proves her chastity during captivity in a trial by fire before Rama accepts her.

THE *MAHABHARATA*

The *Mahabharata*, which was written after the *Ramayana*, is a collection of stories centring on a long-standing feud between two family clans, the Pandava and the Korava. The feud culminates in an epic battle during which the five Pandava brothers come face-to-face with their 100 cousins from the Korava clan. After 18 days of fighting, the Pandava emerge victorious and the eldest brother becomes king.

The great war portrayed in the *Mahabharata* is believed to have been fought in northern India in the 13th century BC. The war became a focus of legends, songs and poems, and at some point the vast collection accumulated over centuries was gathered

Acting out the Mahabharata.

into a narrative called *The Epic of the Bharata Nation* (India), or *Mahabharata*.

Important events that take place include the appearance of Krishna, an incarnation of Lord Vishnu, who becomes the adviser of the Pandava; the marriage of Prince Arjuna of the Pandava to the Princess Drupadi; the Korava's attempt to kill the Pandava; and the division of the kingdom into two in an attempt to end the rivalry between the groups.

In one scene during the great war, Arjuna becomes despondent at the thought of fighting his own flesh and blood. Krishna, his charioteer and adviser, then explains to him that the soul is indestructible and that whoever dies shall be reborn, so there is no cause to be sad.

GAMELAN MUSIC

The trance-like rhythms of the gamelan have earned its fame as a unique musical form. The contemplative Javanese strains contrast with Bali's sparkling sounds.

Gamelan music is comparable to two things: moonlight and flowing water. It is pure and mysterious like the first and ever-changing like the second. Since 1893, when Claude Debussy first heard a Javanese ensemble perform at the Paris International Exhibition, the haunting and hypnotic tones of the gamelan have fascinated the West. This music has been studied by scholars – the earliest were Jaap Kunst and Colin McPhee – and is now recognised as one of the world's most sophisticated musical arts.

The term gamelan derives from *gamel*, an old Javanese word for handle or hammer, as most of the instruments in the orchestra are percussive. The interlocking rhythmic and melodic patterns found in gamelan music are said to originate in the rhythms of the *lesung* – the wooden mortars used for husking rice. Others ascribe the patterns to the chanting of frogs in the rice fields after dusk.

No one knows exactly when the first gamelan came into being. The manufacture of bronze gongs and drums is associated with the Dong Son bronze culture that is thought to have reached Indonesia from Indochina in the 3rd century BC. Since then, large bronze gongs have formed the heartbeat of this distinctive music, with a deep and penetrating sound that can be heard for miles on a quiet night.

JAVANESE GAMELAN

Gamelan ensembles are most commonly performed to accompany dance and theatre. *Karawitan* is the Indonesian term coined in the 1950s by Ki Sindusawarno, the first director of the music conservatory in Surakarta, for the entire range of Javanese and Balinese performing arts incorporating gamelan music.

Gamelan instruments.

In Java, *karawitan* and related arts reached the height of refinement in the courts of the 18th and 19th centuries resulting in slow, stately and mystical music, designed to be heard in the large audience hall of the aristocratic home and to convey a sense of awesome power and emotional control.

Between five and 40 instruments make up a gamelan ensemble, and most of them are never played alone. Two instruments, the *rebab* (a two-stringed bowed lute, probably of Middle Eastern origin) and the *suling* (bamboo flute), are non-percussive and were probably later additions to the ensemble.

A basic principle underlying all gamelan music is that of stratification, in which the density of notes played on each instrument is determined by its register; higher instruments play more notes than lower ones.

Instruments are grouped according to their function. Gongs, for example, establish the basic foundation of the composition, while mid-register metallophones carry a basic melody and other instruments provide more elaborate versions of that melody. The *kendhang* – wooden drums with skins stretched over both ends – control the tempo of the piece. Some musicians compare the structure of gamelan music to a tree. The roots, deep, sturdy and supportive, are the low registers; the trunk is the melody; and the branches, leaves and blossoms, the delicate complexity of the elaborating melodies.

In Central Java, the main *balungan* (skeletal melody) of a piece is played on the *saron* (small- to medium-size metallophones, with six or seven keys lying over a wooden trough resonator) and on the *slenthem* (metallophones with bamboo resonators). Faster variations on the *balungan* are played

A gamelan performance at Borobudur.

⊙ THE FAHNESTOCK AND SMITHSONIAN RECORDINGS

The Fahnestock brothers, Bruce and Sheridan, sailed for Indonesia on the 42-metre (137ft) schooner *Director II* in 1940 with state-of-the-art recording equipment and 15 scientists. They had 3km (2 miles) of insulated microphone cable to enable them to record on shore while the equipment remained on board. Unbeknown to the public, the Fahnestocks were also spying for President Roosevelt, noting the sea defences of Java under cover of making the recordings.

The boat sank off Australia in 1941, but not before the discs were taken to New York. Bruce was killed in New Guinea during the war; Sheridan became a publisher. The original recordings were donated to the US Library of Congress, which accepted them as part of its Endangered Music Project. A selection of the recordings has been released by Rykodisc as *Music for the Gods – The Fahnestock South Sea Expedition, Indonesia.*

In the 1990s, with funding from the Ford Foundation, a joint team of American and Indonesian ethnomusicologists with the Indonesian Performing Arts Society (MSPI), in cooperation with the Center for Folklife Programs and Cultural Studies of the Smithsonian Institution, made recordings of lesser-known music traditions throughout the archipelago, including Sumatra, Riau, Flores, Papua, Kalimantan, Sulawesi and Maluku. This unprecedented project is available in a series of 20 audio CDs and notes.

The haunting melodies of the Sundanese kacapi suling permeate restaurants and stores across the country. The ensemble comprises two zithers (kacapi) plus a bamboo suling, which play soothing, melancholic melodies.

simultaneously on the elaborating instruments: the *bonang* (a set of small, horizontally suspended gongs), *gender* (similarly built to the *slenthem*, but with two octaves), *gambang* (a wooden xylophone) and *celempung* (a zither with metal strings). Together with the *suling*, the *rebab* and the vocalists, they create the complex, rich sounds unique to gamelan music.

VOCALS

Vocal parts in an ensemble were introduced in Java only in the 19th century and it is now common to have soloists as well as a chorus. Female *(pesinden)* singers are popular, but the sound of their voices is regarded merely as another element in the overall texture of the ensemble.

A common misconception of gamelan compositions is that they are improvised. This impression arises perhaps because written scores are rarely used. Most compositions *(gendhing)* have formal structures, but may be performed differently depending on the particular occasion. There are thousands of pieces, and every region

of Java has its favourites. Each *gendhing* has its own name, often corresponding to the character, dance or ritual for which the *gendhing* is played.

Gamelan musicians were traditionally taught by other musicians in their spare time, without any reference to written scores. In the Central Javanese palaces, a system of notation was developed. Some court musicians began to teach outsiders in the early 20th century. Since independence, government music academies have been founded and students now learn in a more formal setting.

Gamelan instruments at the Keraton, Yogyakarta.

⊙ CONTEMPORARY SOUNDS

Aside from the classical beauty of gamelan music, Indonesia's popular music plays an important part in the social scene: ranging from *keroncong, dangdut, jaipongan, campursari* through pop, jazz, blues, and Javanese-language hip hop. Portuguese-influenced *keroncong*, which combines ukulele, cello (plucked), violin, mandolins, guitars and bamboo *suling*, was originally associated with the lower classes in Jakarta, but later gained respectability when it adopted nationalist themes during the war for independence. The romantic ballads remain popular today. The unmistakable driving beat of the enormously popular *dangdut*, originally influenced by Indian film songs, has swept the country and now gone

international. There is no question that *dangdut* is the choice of the masses. *Jaipongan* combines Sundanese instruments and Western rock music, while *Campursari* mixes Javanese gamelan instruments with keyboard, electric bass and drums for popular sing-along songs performed both in the traditional *wayang kulit* performances as well as at wedding receptions and parties.

With at least 400 Sundanese, Javanese and Balinese gamelan sets scattered throughout the world, gamelan music can now be considered truly international. The annual Yogyakarta Gamelan Festival invites groups from Indonesia, Southeast Asia, Japan, New Zealand, Europe and America to perform their own compositions.

At the village level, it is often difficult to distinguish amateurs from professionals. Many village artists are experts in the music of their region, but no special status is assigned to them, nor are they paid suitable fees for their services.

Some musicians are itinerant, making the rounds of traditional performances, be they theatrical or ceremonial, including the ever-popular *wayang kulit* circuit.

COURT GAMELAN

Although gamelan instruments can be made of iron and brass, the best instruments are hammered out by hand from bronze. The highly decorative wooden frames and stands are made from teakwood, while the best wood for the drums is jackfruit. Good examples of Javanese court gamelan can be seen in the Keraton (Sultan's Palace) and the Museum Sono Budoyo in Yogyakarta (Jogja), and the Puro Mangkunegaran in Solo (Surakarta).

Once a year during the Sekaten festival, celebrating the Prophet Muhammad's birthday, the ancient court *gamelan sekaten* of Jogja and Solo that date to the 14th-century Majapahit kingdom perform in front of the Grand Mosque for one week, in clear defiance of fundamentalist Islamic beliefs regarding music, but in testimony to the enduring eclecticism of the Javanese culture.

BALINESE GAMELAN

In Bali, the gamelan exhibits overwhelming variety. Dozens of completely different types of ensembles exist, some of which are found all over the island, others of which are restricted to isolated areas. Balinese musical performances are noted for their capriciousness, stridency and rhythmic vitality – particularly in contrast to the slow and measured gamelan performances of Java.

One of the most frequently encountered ensembles in Bali is the gamelan *gong kebyar*. *Kebyar* refers to a particularly flashy music style that originated in North Bali in the early 20th century, but the ensembles that play it have since expanded their repertoire to include other styles. In the *gong kebyar*, four different gongs mark the musical phrase. They are, in order of descending size: the gong, *kempur*,

kempli and *kemong*.

The melodic theme is carried by two pairs of large metallophones: the *jegogan* and *calung*. Several *gangsa* (high-pitched metallophones) ornament the theme, and the reyong (Bali's version of the Javanese *bonang*) is played by four musicians producing a rippling stream of visceral, syncopated figurations. A pair of *kendhang* drums leads the group, interlocking with each other to produce spectacular rhythms. The drummer of the lower-pitched *kendhang* is generally the leader, teacher and composer

Legong dance performances are accompanied by gamelan music.

for the ensemble. A set of shimmering cymbals *(cengceng)* and several bamboo flutes *(suling)* complete the ensemble.

Balinese gamelan are normally owned and maintained cooperatively by village music clubs *(sekaha)*. The Balinese religious calendar prescribes a hectic schedule of performances for temple festivals, and the provincial government has taken an active role in preserving lesser-known musical styles that may be in danger of extinction.

Island-wide, inter-village musical competitions have provided an impetus for Balinese composers and performers constantly to expand the expressive essence of the music.

Traditional batik, Brahama Tirta
Sari Studio.

TEXTILES

Indonesia's great variety of peoples has produced an equally wide array of textiles that express cultural identity and powerful symbolism.

Indonesia is one of the world's greatest producers of fine traditional textiles. One of the oldest expressions of traditional art, handmade cloth is a vital component of Indonesian culture. Textiles are not only mere articles of clothing, but are also important to the cultural heritage of the country, as spiritually charged talismans, and symbols of wealth and status.

To understand the true value and meaning of Indonesian textiles, we have to examine their cultural context and the belief systems of the people who produce them. The materials, colours and motifs, along with rituals for their creation and use, all serve as powerful messages that convey wealth, social status, religious belief, the marriage contract and a connection to the spirit world.

Traditional textiles are works of art created by craftspeople who incorporate a medley of technical skills: weaving, dyeing and embroidery using any choice of natural fibres, including bark, cotton and silk. Some are embellished with shells, beads and gold or silver threads, but use methods and techniques that have changed very little over centuries.

Inside Yogyakarta's Batik Museum.

SYMBOLIC SIGNIFICANCE

The process of manufacturing textiles is interwoven with taboos that define gender-role responsibilities to ensure the harmony of the community. Spinning, dyeing and the weaving of yarn are regarded as symbolic of the process of creation, and of human birth in particular. Weaving is generally an exclusively female activity. Men are permitted to participate only in the dyeing of certain colours of the thread, analogous with their role in human conception. The dyeing process is carried out in the utmost privacy, behind partitions set up around the work area. Pregnant, menstruating or sick women are excluded from this work.

A traditional cloth produced with natural dyes once took many years to complete. The main natural dyes used in traditional textiles are indigo (*Indigofera tinctoria*), mengkudu (*Morinda citrifolia*), soga (a brown dye from root and bark) and mud dyes. Today, because of time and economic constraints, many textiles are coloured by chemical dyes.

In some areas, the mounting of threads on the loom is done on an auspicious day, otherwise the threads would break and bring bad luck. In several coastal villages, this means a full moon and a high tide. If a death occurs in the village, weaving stops at once to prevent the spirit of the departed from exacting vengeance by bringing sickness upon the weaver and causing the threads to lose their strength. Finished products are usually sanctified by metaphysical and psychological associations, and therefore regarded as powerful objects that can protect the weaver, cure illness, bring rain and are often necessary for life-cycle rituals.

INFLUENCES AND DEVELOPMENT

Cotton and silk have been used for making cloth for the past 3,000–5,000 years. As the spice trade developed over the last two millennia, Arab, Indian and Chinese traders discovered they could obtain valuable spices in exchange for Indian cotton and silk. Indonesians in turn found they could barter their easily gathered cloves, nutmeg, peppers and aromatic woods for fine textiles from the traders.

Many of the techniques and motifs in Indonesian textiles were adapted from foreign examples. As early as the 14th century, Indian fabrics were imported on a large scale, and the Indian textile revolution extended to fabrics that were considered rare and valuable, or even magical. The single most influential cloth is the Indian *patola*, a double-ikat silk fabric produced in Gujarat. Widely reproduced in Indonesia, it was incorporated into the ceremonial lives of many Indonesians and formed part of the costumes of kings on several islands, including Java. As fewer *patola* were imported after 1800, weavers throughout Indonesia set about producing replicas. Today, the eight-pointed-flower or *chabadi bhatt* design is seen everywhere.

⊘ INDIGO DYE

Indigo dye from Indigofera tinctoria is the most widely used natural blue dye in the world. The recipe for the dye was once a guarded secret, but today it is known across the archipelago. The dye is prepared in a vat and goes through a fermentation and oxidation process. Indigo leaves are first soaked overnight in earthenware jars of water. The leaves are then removed and lime is added, causing chemical reduction. Cotton or silk threads dyed in this vat are then hung up to oxidise. This process is repeated until the desired colour intensity is achieved and the indigo threads deemed ready to be woven.

Indonesian textile decoration methods fall into three major categories: dye-resist, woven and embellished techniques. There are two dye-resist processes: the wax on cloth batik and the tie-and-dye process of warp, weft and double ikat. Warp and weft ikat are produced by the Batak (North Sumatra), in the Nusa Tenggara islands, East Java, Kalimantan and South Sulawesi. Weft ikat is produced in Bali, West Lombok, East Java, Palembang, Sumatra and in South Sulawesi, while double ikat is only produced in Bali. Woven decoration includes supplementary warp and weft, tapestry,

Traditional methods of batik making, Brahama Tirta Sari Studio, Yogyakarta.

tablet-weaving, embroidery, appliqué, beadwork and shellwork. Embellished techniques include supplementary weft such as *songkets*, supplementary warp and warp-wrapping.

BATIK

Batik is Indonesia's renowned textile art, especially Javanese batik, which is regarded as the world's finest. In the technique, dye-resist wax is applied to the cloth to prevent the dye from penetrating certain areas, thus resulting in a pattern in the negative. Finely detailed batik *tulis* ('written' design) is made possible with a tool called a *canting*. The *canting*, a small copper cup with a spout through which melted wax flows, is

Geringsing is said to have protective powers. Kings once presented geringsing garments to warriors prior to battle.

royal family, many locals will choose not to wear batik printed with motifs that were originally regarded as sacred to the royal court.

Batik *cap* is produced with the use of a metal printing block. The *cap* stamps are built out of thin strips of copper and wire soldered to an open frame. The *cap* is dipped into heated wax before it is pressed firmly onto the cloth. The advent of batik *cap* revitalised the industry in the 1890s, making mass-produced cloths that were affordable to all and creating an export trade from Java to the Outer Islands. For more on batik, see page 104.

mounted on a handle and is wielded like a pen, allowing the artist to execute designs.

The first step is to draw a design on a piece of silk or cotton cloth. Areas not to be coloured in the first dyeing are covered with wax. This process

Symbolic hinggi ikat from Sumba are used as dowry gifts and in funeral rituals.

alone can take hundreds of hours. The cloth is then immersed in dye and dried off. With natural dyes, repeated immersions and dryings are necessary, and a single dyeing can take months to complete.

For subsequent dyeings, either more wax is added to seal areas of the first dye before over-dyeing with a second colour, or the cloth has to be de-waxed and waxed again. Wax is removed by boiling in water or by being scraped off. Dyeing and drying follow, and the process is repeated as many times as there are number of colours on the cloth.

In Central Java, certain motifs were once reserved for the royal court, such as the *parang rusak barong*, a broken sword design that consists of diagonal rows of interlocking scrolls. Today, out of respect for the descendants of the

IKAT

Warp ikat is a traditional method of weaving in which the warp threads (on the length) of a cloth are tie-dyed prior to weaving. The process of spinning cotton threads and preparing the dyes, binding the warp threads in a pattern that will resist the dye, and then repeatedly immersing, drying and re-binding them to achieve the desired colour requires tremendous skill and patience. In the hands of a master weaver, the end result is intricate, detailed motifs executed in deep, rich colours. Weaving is done on a backstrap loom, with either discontinuous warp threads affixed to the loom's beams or a continuous warp bent around the beams so as to create a tube of cloth. While one beam is attached to a grounded object (tree or house post), the other is secured to the weaver with the tension maintained by a strap placed around the weaver's back as she sits on the ground. String heddles are employed to create individual sheds, and sometimes a bamboo comb is introduced to maintain the spacing of a discontinuous warp.

The most famous warp ikats are the *hinggi* from East Sumba. These cloths are known for their rich colours, fine details and bold, horizontal fields of stylised human and animal figures.

> *The sacred maa cloths of the South Sulawesi Torajans are kept in special baskets and are essential for major rituals. Some maa are thought to be effective vessels for fertility spirits, and opening a powerful cloth is said to bring immediate rainfall.*

Ikat from South Sulawesi.

Normally produced in pairs, one to wrap around the body and one to drape over the shoulders, they have served as valuable trade goods for centuries and were exported extensively by the Dutch in the 19th century. *Hinggi* textiles are used in Sumba to seal a marriage contract and in funerals; it is not uncommon to wrap the body of a nobleman or woman in as many as 100 textile pieces.

The neighbouring island, Timor, is known for its brilliantly coloured warp ikat embellished by supplementary techniques such as *sotis*, a float weave using contrasting colours and usually woven into small panels. There is also the complex process of *buna*, which resembles heavy embroidery.

Another well-known warp ikat is the red, brown and white *ulos ragidup* (pattern of life) cloth of the Sumatran Bataks. This is presented by the father of the bride to the mother of the groom, who later presents the cloth to her daughter-in-law when she is seven months pregnant with her first child, as an *ulos ni tondi* or 'soul cloth'.

Weft ikat (resist-patterning of the crosswise threads) occurs primarily in Bali and the coastal trading areas of Gresik in East Java, Palembang and elsewhere in South Sumatra. Weft ikat is usually woven on a 'fly shuttle' handloom.

The Palembang and Bangka weft ikat are extremely sophisticated, done on silk in rich tones of red, blue and yellow, often with supplementary gold threads in the weft. Indian, Javanese and Chinese motifs are all employed, sometimes simultaneously.

Today, weft ikat is a thriving cottage industry, with great amounts of cloth woven in bright colours and floral or geometric designs. A special weft ikat textile, *kain limar*, woven with gold threads, is worn by boys on the day of circumcision, a special rite among Muslim Palembang and Sumatran families.

GERINGSING

The rare double ikat, known as *geringsing*, is made in Tenganan, a small village in East Bali, one of only three places in the world to produce this labour-intensive textile. The other two places are India and Japan. It can take several years just to complete a single *geringsing* piece. Both warp and weft threads are tied and dyed, then woven to produce an integrated motif on the finished fabric. Red being the predominant colour in most *geringsing*, the background is indigo overdyed with red to produce a midnight black.

Considered by the Balinese to be sacred, *geringsing* is used in many important ceremonies throughout the island, including tooth filings. In Tenganan, wearers of the cloth are thought to be protected from evil and illness, as *geringsing* means 'without sickness'.

SONGKET

Songket – cloth of gold or silver – is an ornately brocaded textile that has gold or silver threads worked into it. On a silk or cotton base, 'floating' metallic weft threads are woven in to create a raised pattern that almost resembles embroidery. Areas with the best *songket* are Bali and Palembang, and those produced by the Minangkabau are sought after as well.

Palembang songket features gold threads woven onto bright red silk to form a fine geometrical pattern that often covers the entire cloth, while the Minangkabau's silver-threaded *songket* has a background of wine-red or black silk. Wearing *songket* became a sign of physical and spiritual blessings.

Once a cloth favoured by the royal class, *songket* (also known as *tanuk*), is worn today in a formal headdress by the Minangkabau women of West Sumatra. It serves as a display of wealth and the way it is folded also indicates which village the wearer is from.

BARK CLOTH

Bark cloths found among upland tribes in Kalimantan, Sulawesi and Papua display a high degree of artistry and techniques that date to the prehistoric era.

The Torajans boil and ferment the inner bark of *Pandanus*, mulberry or other trees before beating – with special wooden and stone mallets – the resultant pulp into extremely soft and pliable sheets. This cloth (*fuya*) is then dyed, painted or stamped using natural pigments.

Certain groups in Kalimantan, Flores, Sulawesi and Timor produce warrior tunics from fibres by twining them, a simple process in which two weft fibres are alternately wrapped above and below a passive warp.

Songket weaving at Sukarara weaving village, Lombok.

⌀ LURIK

References in old Javanese Hindu inscriptions (AD 851–82) mention striped and checked textiles that are today known as *lurik*. In Java, what remains of the *lurik* weaving culture is centred in Jogja, Solo and Tuban, with the most obvious examples of *lurik* being the traditional coats worn by the palace guards at the Yogyakarta Keraton. However, the isolated Badui of West Java still weave *lurik* for their daily attire, and there are a handful of weavers in Banyumas, who call their cloth *kluwung*. Sadly, in Kudus in the northeastern part of Java, which once had a fairly wide range of motifs, only a few remain today. On Bali, these textiles are called *keling* and *saudan*, and remain ritually important.

Each motif on *lurik* cloths is defined by a specific palette and organisation of stripes and each has a symbolic meaning, is considered sacred, or thought to possess magical powers. Ancient rice paste-resist patterns on *lurik* textiles were probably the first Javanese batiks. *Lurik* is thought to pre-date tie-and-dye ikat textiles, though the origin of the latter is unclear.

Hand-woven *lurik* disappeared from favour with the advent of mechanised fabric factories producing a wider range of designs and colours at cheaper prices, but today it is experiencing a comeback thanks to a new generation of Indonesians who have great respect for old traditions.

📷 BATIK: ART ON FABRIC

Batik is the great leveller in Indonesian society. It is the formal attire of Jakarta urbanites, as well as for rustic villagers working the fields.

Batik is one of the most prominent expressions of cultural identity in Indonesia. Nowhere in the world has the art of batik evolved into such high standards, fine-tuned over the centuries under the patronage of the Javanese royal courts. Today, the making and wearing of batik remains a source of national pride, a vital and unifying medium found in every conceivable form: sarong, dress, shirt, scarf, table-cover, wall hangings and more.

The Indonesian word batik (from tik, meaning dot) was originally a term used to describe the dye-resist technique; today, the term is used for both the process and the decorated fabric. The value of each piece is determined by the method of creation; the most highly prized and expensive is the labour-intensive batik *tulis* (literally 'to write') using a canting tool. The best pieces are created by small cottage-industry workshops in Java. A cheaper alternative is the block-printed batik, produced using a metal printing stamp called *cap*. Batik *cetak* (printed batik) is mass-produced screen-printed fabric imitating traditional designs.

Each area of Java has its own unique style of batik, which communicates ethnic identity and social status, while the folds of the *kain panjang* (waistcloth) convey one's gender. Special motifs with symbolic meanings, once reserved for the royal courts of Java, are today worn by all for ceremonies such as weddings, circumcisions, childbirth and burials.

The motifs created on the north coast of Java and Madur are known as pesisir batik. As exemplified by the Cirebo batik, pictured, foreign influence through maritime trade brought changes to the traditional Javanese motifs, resulting in brighter colours and new designs.

A wooden or copper block called a cap is dipped into hot wax and meticulously applied to the cloth, ensuring that a residual wax left on the cloth will not damage the motif.

While Javanese batiks are exported across the world, they are also found in every marketplace in Indonesia. A Torajan boy in Sulawesi shields himself from the weather with a batik kain panjang (sarong) from Java.

Traditional methods of batik making (canting) at the Brahama Tirta Sari Studio, Jogja.

Cultural treasures

The strong designs in dark colours of Central Java are distinguished by the white background on Jogja batiks versus the pale-yellow backdrop of Solo pieces. The batiks of Southwest Java differ, with red, greenish-blue and black in Tasikmalaya and russet and golden brown against dark indigo in Banyumas.

In Pekalongan, on Java's north coast, batik is characterised by flora and fauna motifs in pastel colours, while further west in Cirebon a multicultural mix of designs – Chinese, Indian, Arab and Central Java – is used. In Madura, East Java, designs are stylised to comply with Islamic restrictions on representation.

Contemporary batiks range from classic designs in modern colours to the colourful beach sarongs found in Bali.

reet stalls selling batik, Jogja. Mass-produced, printed brics called batik cetak, are made into clothing, cessories and souvenirs.

A traditional Javanese court motif is used on batik sarongs of wayang golek puppets from West Java.

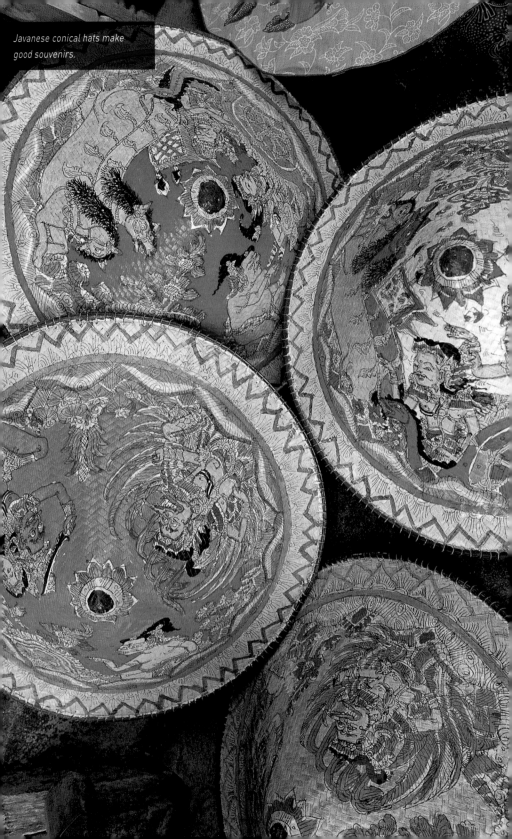

Javanese conical hats make good souvenirs.

INDONESIA'S HANDICRAFTS AND ART

Many handicrafts produced by Indonesian artisans are exported worldwide, and art collectors flock to Jakarta auction houses to buy paintings produced by the new generation of Indonesian artists.

As a crossroads for maritime trade, the Indonesian archipelago has for centuries been subject to foreign cultural influences, most notably Indian, Arab, Chinese and Dutch, as is evident in the art and culture of the coastal areas, the royal courts and in the architecture of ancient Hindu and Buddhist temples. In the remote interior and outer islands, many tribes lived in relative isolation until as recently as the 20th century, producing 'primitive' art that was a medium of expression of their indigenous beliefs.

Indonesian creative arts are primarily seen as a manifestation of the peoples' spiritual beliefs. As a result, traditional Indonesian art is suffused with spiritually charged talismans. Creative arts serve to establish social and cultural identity, and fulfil social rites of passage such as birth, puberty, marriage and death.

In Central Java, the *loro blonyo*, painted wood statues that represent Dewi Sri, the goddess of fertility, and her consort Sedono, are placed in the home of newly married couples. Many objects of art are produced as the bride's dowry, such as the *mamuli* of Sumba, a decorative metal object given by the groom's family to the bride's family in exchange for textiles and other goods. A *mamuli* will also be placed in a grave for wealth in the afterlife.

Indonesia is a treasure-trove of handcrafted items. Many artisans carry on the timeless tradition of fine craftsmanship, using traditional iconography passed on from one generation to the next. In many villages and tourist destinations, the main streets and local *pasar* (markets) are full of artisans working at their trades in the open. Few other countries offer the opportunity of direct encounters with so many craftsmen practising skills that are centuries old.

Hand-crafted shadow puppets.

The production process is usually divided between what is considered male and female. Male energy items use substances that are hard and strong or created with fire, as in the crafts of ironsmiths and woodcarvers. Female energy is expressed through what is soft and flexible, as in the weaving of textiles, basketwork and beadwork. There is no power struggle or competition between the sexes, but rather a desire to maintain the balance between the two in a unified symbol of an ordered universe.

PUPPETS AND MASKS

Indonesia is well known for its shadow puppets, or *wayang kulit*, flat puppets made of buffalo hide with finely chiselled, painted details, and rod puppets, or *wayang golek*, with carved and painted wooden faces. Puppets are typically used for performances of the *Ramayana* and *Mahabharata* Hindu epics, which impart complex yet subtle lessons in social behaviour. The oldest and best-known puppet makers are found in the environs of Yogyakarta (Jogja) and Surakarta (Solo), Central Java.

Ceremonial masks are found on many of the islands and are believed to access the spiritual essence of the wearer's soul. Bali is famed for

Wood carving in Krebet.

elaborately decorated and highly expressive *topeng*, carved softwood masks used in sacred temple ceremonial dramas. Cirebon masks from Java are used in theatrical pageants. Central and East Javanese masks celebrate the lives of past Javanese royalty. The Dayaks of Kalimantan make oversized wooden masks, *hudog*, with bulging eyes and large beaked noses, that are used in a ceremonial dance to keep maleficent spirits from taking over the 'soul' of the rice. The Bataks of Lake Toba make carved masks and wooden hands that are symbols of their ethnic identity, copied from the *si gale-gale*, a life-sized puppet used in pre-Christian funeral ceremonies as artificial mourners for those who died childless.

WOODCARVINGS

Prized by museums and collectors throughout the world, many of Indonesia's woodcarvings are masterpieces of primitive art. Every island maintains a unique tradition, and today most produce countless 'copies' of traditional sculptures, usually out of tropical hardwood. The woodcarvings of the Asmats of Papua are some of the most impressive of Indonesian 'primitive' art. Decorative carved shields serve as vessels for ancestral spirits, and large spirit poles are the homes of the spirits of departed ancestors. In Sumatra, Batak ancestor statues called *si baso nabolon* are placed in the loft of a traditional house and serve as protectors against evil spirits. Kalimantan's Dayaks produce large carved wooden guardian poles, *hampatong*, with a stylised crouching ancestor figure, usually with an outstretched tongue; they are placed at the front of Dayak longhouses for protection against evil spirits.

The Javanese are known for their refined furniture-making skills, while the Balinese are known for their highly ornamental motifs found on doors, windows and posts.

From the 1600s, European and Chinese influences appeared in the form of enormous frame beds used for wedding ceremonies, embellished with carved panels of flowers and birds and painted in the style of Chinese wedding beds. Today, furniture shops are filled with cabinets, beds, tables, chairs, chests and wall panels made of tropical woods.

⊙ DAYAK BABY CARRIER

Several ethnic groups, known collectively as Dayak, inhabit the Kalimantan interior and produce powerful and expressive art that maintains balance and harmony with the spirits of the supernatural world. Many Kenyah and Kayan Dayak baby-carriers are highly decorative works of traditional art. Carved out of wood with spiritually protective designs or made from rattan and embellished with ancient sacred beads and coins, they bear the claws and teeth of wild jungle animals and serve to protect the young child carried within. The amount of detail in the motif also indicates social stature.

STONE AND METAL

Religious stone statues of Hindu gods and Buddha have been carved for centuries in Java and Sumatra (excellent examples are found in Jakarta's National Museum). Newly made copies of these masterpieces are still produced in Central and East Java, as well as Bali. Batubulan village on Bali is dedicated to the creation of stone statues. Fashioned in *paras*, a soft ashy stone, Hindu gods are produced alongside fanciful garden statues. On other islands such as Nias, stone statues of ancestors are found.

In 1975 in a painting entitled Ken Dedes, named after a Majapahit Empire queen, Indonesian artist Jim Supangkat shocked Jakarta by depicting the revered lady bare-breasted and curvaceous, wearing unzipped jeans and high heels.

Dutch coins, rattan trim and the teeth of wild boar. At one time, *parang ilang* or *mandau* were used for head-hunting by Dayaks. Today, the fin-

Stone-carving at Batubalan, Bali.

Metalwork was introduced to Indonesia during the Dong Son Bronze Age around the 3rd century BC. To this day, metal items are produced either by forging or by wax-casting. One of the most revered examples of metal art is the ornamental dagger, *keris*, decorated with silver, gold or precious stones and thought to possess magical powers. Unfortunately, there are few *empu* or master-smiths left today, and this dying art form is the preserve of a few ironsmiths in Central and West Java as well as in Kusamba, Bali, where a new *keris* can be commissioned.

Kalimantan and the Nusa Tenggara islands produce a functional cutlass, or *parang*, which usually has an ornate hilt of carved wood. The scabbard is sometimes decorated with old

est *parang* are used ceremonially. Swordsmiths forge *parang* from scrap metal and employ bellows; the blade is repeatedly beaten, folded and hardened in cold river water.

Gold- and silversmithery have a long history in Indonesia. Early travellers were impressed by the riches and quality workmanship of the royal courts: parasol fittings, the bejewelled golden *keris* and exquisite ornate boxes fashioned of gold. Traditional jewellery is an important part of the bride price and each island produces its own distinctive style, ranging from the delicate filigree work of Bali and Java to the bold and expressive beaten gold of the Outer Islands. Indonesian gold- and silversmiths are masters of several decorative and labour-intensive techniques such as *repoussé* or embossing. For centuries, Balinese royal courts have expressed sacred and temporal power through art.

Kamasan village is still a centre for Balinese court arts, producing objects of silver and gold for ceremonial use. Statues of Hindu deities, offering bowls and containers for holy water, are embellished with intricate designs and mythological figures. A thriving business is modern silverwork for the tourist market. Celuk village in Bali is lined with rows of homes and shops producing silver jewellery and objects, while in Java, the silver centre is Kota Gede near Jogja. Most pieces are made with 90–95 percent pure silver, some set with semi-precious stones imported from Kalimantan.

BASKETRY AND POTTERY

Indonesia has an inexhaustible supply of useful plant products derived from bamboo, coconut palms, rattan, *pandan* (screw pine), breadfruit trees, reeds and grasses. Basketry serves as a functional craft; fishing traps, baskets, backpacks, hats and all manner of useful containers are made. Men help to gather the materials, but it is traditionally the women who work the weaving or plaiting, usually with great speed and aesthetic and technical refinement.

In Lombok, bark and rattan boxes are used to transport wedding clothes, while large rectangular or round boxes made of palm leaf are decorated with split seashells and used for storing rice. The baskets of Sumatra are embellished with fine gold leaf and lacquer, while those made in Kalimantan display superb rattan palm-weaving skills.

Pottery has been made since Neolithic times. Earthenware vessels such as bowls and *kendi* (water pitchers), decorative roof gables, animals and figures of Hindu deities serve both a functional and a decorative purpose. Terracotta pottery is usually only produced in villages that specialise in the craft and only by women who make the clay vessels. Lombok pottery, with entire villages now producing the high-quality earthenware, is exported worldwide.

Pottery is a popular craft in Indonesia.

⊘ LOMBOK POTTERY

Lombok is well known for many of its traditional handicrafts, in particular earthenware pottery. With the assistance of the Indonesian and New Zealand governments, the Lombok Crafts Project was established two decades ago. Three villages initially received funds to build workplaces, warehouses and showrooms, and were supplied with technical and design advice as well as marketing and business ideas. The result was a thriving cottage industry producing high-quality decorative and functional pottery that continues today, with many women in Banyumulek and Masbagik villages (see page 278) owning lucrative businesses.

The grey-brown clay used for the pots is obtained by women from local riverbeds. They work it by hand, using a round stone and wooden paddle instead of a potter's wheel, a method that has changed little over the centuries. Geometric patterns are incised with a sharp bamboo stick.

The pots are left in the sun to set before being fired. Placed in a pit in the ground, they are covered with rice straw and husks that burn out quickly and leave a thick ash coating that retains the heat for the final stages of firing. A second firing using coconut husks, dung and wood turns the pottery jet black. After it cools, the finished product turns a rich red-brown.

Comic strips drawn by Indonesian artists appear in newspapers in Jakarta and Malaysia. Today's comic artists are adept at social commentary, particularly regarding the foibles of the government, which was forbidden until 1998.

TEXTILES

The making of high-quality handloom textiles (see page 99), such as ikats, is the work of women and a skilled art, as is batik *tulis*. Today, mass-produced 'copies' of traditional work are made for the tourist market using quick chemical dyes, and are found in most hotel shops and markets.

Beadwork is associated with agricultural fertility and femininity, and except for Sulawesi's Torajans, all beadwork is done by women. The Dayak regard beads as having magical power and use them in the necklaces worn by shamans and to embellish ritual objects such as baby-carriers. Antique beads came from as far away as Venice, introduced by the Portuguese and Dutch, while today most of the beads are from Japan.

INDONESIAN ART

In Java, one of the first modern painters of note was Raden Saleh (1816–80), who spent 20 years in European courts and later painted some memorable portraits of the royal families of Central Java.

In Bali, paintings were of religious objects commissioned as decorations for palaces and temples until the early 20th century. When European artists Walter Spies and Rudolph Bonnet promoted painting as an art form in Ubud, the Balinese began to depict naturalistic scenes of everyday life for the first time. Various local artist associations developed thereafter, including the Pita Maha Artists of Ubud (1936–42) and in the 1960s, the Young Artists group, which is known for its portrayal of Balinese life in vivid oils, inspired by Dutch artist Arie Smit.

Simultaneously, Yogyakarta and Bandung became the two crucibles of modern Indonesian art, and many accomplished artists appeared on the scene. Soedjojono (1913–86), Hendra Gunawan (1918–83) and Affandi (1907–88), for example, were strongly united in expressing

their desire for independence from colonial rule and in propagating a strong national awareness. After the Dutch left, Suharto's regime quashed all freedom of expression, and underground art colonies flourished. When his iron-fisted rule ended in 1998, artists were at last at liberty to express themselves openly, which they have taken great pleasure in doing ever since.

Today, there are two government-owned fully accredited art universities – one in Jogja (Yogyakarta) and the other in Denpasar, Bali – as well as an arts high school in Solo. Together with the Fine

Two women in a garden at the Neka Art Museum, Ubud.

Arts department of the Bandung Institute of Technology, they are producing performing and visual artists who are creating cutting-edge themes with a freshness not often seen in the West.

In these cities, public spaces and galleries brim with expressions of unfettered enthusiasm on every possible topic. Jogja, in particular, gives artists – who see themselves as autonomous, removed from government or museum support – plenty of elbow room in which to discourse, debate, work and display. At the same time, a burgeoning art-auction market has evolved, with wealthy Indonesians joining foreigners as collectors. Agus Suwage and Entang Wiharso are both currently collectibles of international acclaim.

Tongkonan dwelling, Tana Toraja, Sulawesi.

ARCHITECTURE

Architectural designs tracing Indonesia's evolution from the 9th century until the present day reflect its rich cultural heritage.

Indonesian architecture is a reflection of its various cultures, the influence of foreign arrivals and regional adaptions of universal styles. Its history can be traced through the remains of the ancient temples and bathing places of Hindu-Buddhist rulers, the mosques introduced by Muslim traders, the European influence brought by colonialists, and the palaces of the last sultans. It is remarkable, however, that in many regions traditional houses *(rumah adat)* are still being constructed today in styles similar to those used centuries ago.

TRADITIONAL HOUSES

Although all of Indonesia's varied ethnic groups have their own versions of *rumah adat*, many share similarities that are believed to have originated in east Asia 6,000 years ago among the Austronesian group of related-language speakers that spread throughout Southeast Asia, the Pacific and Madagascar.

Built without nails from organic materials that grew nearby, the houses had four main hardwood posts, each with a symbolic meaning, and steep, thatched roofs suitable for shading residents from the tropical sun in the dry season and from torrential downpours when it rained. Most were also raised on stilts for ventilation and as protection from rival clans and marauding beasts in the thickly forested surrounds. *Rumah adat* had a separate cooking area, usually at the back of the house, which consisted of a stone base where meals were cooked in earthenware pottery over a wood fire. Strangers would never have been invited into the family quarters of the house, but would be greeted on a verandah, or if there was none, a small front room at the entrance, until sufficient meetings confirmed whether the visitor was friend or foe.

Batak architecture on Samosir Island, Sumatra.

Because natural materials suitable for building were abundant in the forests, houses were more or less disposable. When the bamboo, thatching or timber began to rot, a new house was built and the old one left to disintegrate, or by that time perhaps area game had played out and hunter-gatherers simply moved on. The entire community played a role in building a new house, with each member having a particular speciality.

Another recurring feature in *rumah adat* was communal living, with the house being the primary focus for extended families and communities for social contact as well as for protection from tangible and intangible forces, such as spirits. Examples of community houses can still be seen among the Dayaks in Kalimantan, the North Sumatran Bataks, the Torajans in Sulawesi, and in the Mentawai islands off the west coast of Sumatra.

There are other distinctive features among Indonesia's ethnic houses. The Minangkabaus and Torajans favour enormous roofs shaped like boats or saddles, and their buildings are also recognisable for their intricate exterior carvings. The elaborate, stilted *lumbung* (rice barns) of the Sasak on Lombok are known for their bonnet-shaped roofs. The *rumah adat* of

Sasak rice barn, Lombok.

Java and Bali are not built on stilts, however the pyramid-shaped roofs of Java's *joglo* and *limasan* houses contain the same four, symbolic hardwood piles used in other traditional houses, while Balinese homes are a collection of buildings within a high-walled compound. Many of these traditions continue today.

HINDU-BUDDHIST ARCHITECTURE

The examples of Hindu-Buddhist architecture (9th–15th century) that remain are temples – primarily in Central and East Java – and royal bathing pools in Bali. Many others had wooden frameworks that have long since collapsed. As the great empires of that era lapsed and structures were abandoned, many fell

victim to looting, either by the local people for construction materials or by treasure hunters. A number of them were also lost to volcanic eruptions. In Java, it is still a common occurrence for a farmer ploughing his field to unearth a statue or part of a wall that belonged to one of these buildings.

Although this form of architecture was inspired by India, local influences created a uniquely Indonesian style. The *candi* (temple, shrine or mausoleum), for example, was usually a towering stone structure built on a base. At the top was a stepped-pyramid roof (*meru*), as seen in Bali. These structures were representations of Gunung Meru, which in Hindu-Buddhist mythology is the abode of the gods. And each of them – as exemplified in Dieng plateau and at Prambanan – had niches containing statues of the deities to whom the shrine was dedicated, representative of the caves where the gods were believed to reside on holy Gunung Meru.

It is interesting in Central and East Java, where the greatest number of temples remain, to be able to see how the architecture evolved. Java's oldest temples, dating from the early 8th century, are found on the cool heights of the Dieng plateau. It is believed that there were once as many as 400 *candi* here, but only eight are left standing. Dieng's temples are small and rather plain, and the *kala* heads – the toothy mythical demon seen over Balinese doors today – are not particularly ornate. Yet a century later, the magnificent Hindu Roro Jonggrang rose out of the Prambanan plains around AD 856. At about the same time, Buddhist Borobudur was constructed (AD 750–850), and instead of being set on a stone base, a natural plateau was selected, the purpose of both types of base being to elevate the structures, making them appear even more magnificent than they already were.

Shortly after Borobudur was completed, temple architecture disappears in Central Java, shifts to Sumatra, and reappears in East Java in 1250. The structures almost continually being uncovered at Trowulan, even in the 21st century, are believed to be the 14th-century Majapahit Empire capital, a large city with public bathing places and water systems. For the first time, structures that appear to have been dwellings are made of brick rather than organic materials and are very similar

Borobudur's reliefs feature depictions of daily life, including dwellings, which provide a valuable record of Java's 9th-century architecture. This would otherwise have been lost, due to the perishable construction materials used.

to the houses seen throughout Bali today. By 1450, the Hindu-Buddhist kingdoms had been replaced by Muslim sultanates.

as it had always been. Early mosques had four central posts like *rumah adat*, supporting a pyramidal roof, similar to the Javanese *joglo* and *limasan* houses, and the roofs were multi-tiered, as are contemporary Balinese temples. Domes did not appear atop mosques until the 19th century. The Grand Mosques at Aceh (1881) and Medan (1906) appear to be the beginning of the Moorish-style domed architecture, and since then Indonesian mosques have followed global Islamic design.

Cemeteries were placed behind mosques

Taman Tirtagangga water park, East Bali.

ISLAMIC INFLUENCE

Beginning in the 12th century, Islam entered the archipelago with traders in coastal areas of Sumatra and Java. As with Hindu-Buddhist places of worship, the concept of mosques may have come from afar, but the architecture was strictly Indonesian, as existing architectural styles were modified to meet Muslim requirements. New structures also had to be added, such as cemeteries, because cremation – the preferred method of disposing of the dead until that time – was forbidden by Islam.

By the 17th century the 'new' religion had penetrated most of the archipelago, with trading ports and palaces the main architectural focus, leaving rural housing much the same

or on top of a hill, which can be traced to an ancient Austronesian tradition of reverence to ancestors. Surrounding mosques with walls provided a link to Java's Hindu-Buddhist past, with the walls being similar to those that surround modern Balinese temple complexes. The Grand Mosques in Demak (1474) and Kudus (1549) are two of Indonesia's oldest, and it is thought that the minaret at Kudus may replicate the tower of an earlier Hindu temple. Kudus's minaret is not used for the vocal calls to prayer usually associated with mosques, but houses the large drum traditionally used in Indonesia to summon the faithful. Similarly, drum towers exist throughout Bali, though not in mosques; the one at

Pura Penataran Sasih at Pejeng contains a 2,000-year-old bronze drum from the Dong Son era.

Since royal palaces (*keraton* in Javanese, or *istana* in Indonesian) were at the centre of religions, they also adopted some Islamic features. The only *keratons* that remain are less than 200 years old, so it is not known how Islam affected early royal architecture. However, judging from existing examples in Java and Bali, it appears that Islam did little to influence them. None of the palaces were grand affairs, rather their power was expressed by symbolic alignment with water sources and mountains and with symmetry. The most imposing structure in the Yogyakarta *keraton* is the *pendopo*, a pavilion restricted to honoured guests where the ruler sat during ceremonial occasions, which has a traditional Javanese tiered roof supported by four posts, as in *joglo* houses. The residences surrounding the *keraton* within the inner walls of the city were occupied by the sultan's immediate family members and aristocracy. Beyond the walls were those who had regular dealings with the court, and outside that was the rural population, placing the sultan in the centre of the 'universe'.

While the *keratons* at Yogyakarta, Surakarta and Cirebon are generally Javanese, they have also borrowed elements of other styles. A gateway at the Cirebon *keraton* is repeated in both Yogyakarta and Surakarta, with arched entries from the Hindu-Buddhist era, a 'cloud and rain' motif adopted from the Chinese, heavy emphasis on Javanese symbolism and European gazebos. Balinese palaces resemble Javanese *keratons* somewhat, with a central pavilion (*bale*, in Balinese) placing the king at the centre and symbolic symmetry to emphasise power and sovereignty. At the Ubud palace, the central pavilion was replaced with a courtyard and a building where the king resided. At Karangasem, the pavilion 'floated' (*bale kambang*) in a pond.

COLONIAL ARCHITECTURE

In the 16th century, new architectural features began to appear in Indonesian ports, introduced by European merchants and adventurers. In some cases, new elements were integrated with local traditions; in others, they remained purely European. The best examples of Portuguese architecture are scattered throughout Timor. The Protestant church in Semarang (built 1778–1814) is mixed, with a Byzantine cupola and Baroque bell towers.

At the onset, the Dutch emulated cities from their homeland without taking into consideration the tropical climate. At Batavia (now the Kota area of Jakarta), canals were constructed and city townhouses with few windows were

Medan's Masjid Raya.

built in rows, and all were enclosed in solid walls as protection from local revolts and attacks from other Europeans. The fortress housed the governor, officers, barracks, offices, a church and European merchants. Towns grew up beyond the fortress walls.

In 1870 the Dutch opened private enterprise, resulting in a building boom. Many examples of Dutch architecture remain, particularly in Java: railway stations in neo-Gothic style still stand in Semarang and Jakarta, along with bank buildings, warehouses and trading centres in Jakarta, Semarang, Surabaya and a few in Medan, Makassar and Singaraja. Dutch tree-lined avenues are clearly visible in Bandung. As the cities grew, wealthy merchants began building country estates to escape the congestion. Better adapted to the climate, a new type of colonial architecture was born called the Indies Style. The four posts and the pyramid roof with overhanging eaves of the *joglo* were incorporated, and verandahs and porticoes appeared. European elements, such as neoclassical columns around the verandahs, were added, along with typical 18th-century Dutch-style windows for ventilation.

MODERN ARCHITECTURE

By the 20th century, the Dutch had introduced many other architectural styles, such as Art Deco, best seen in Bandung. Modernist buildings, popular in Europe at the time, were the trend. Contemporary Indonesian architects were of two types: those who had been trained overseas and apprentices who had learned at home under the tutorship of foreigners. Thus, after Indonesia's independence architecture remained Modernist for several decades, with then-president Sukarno determined to erect modern cities equal to those in Europe and America. Factories, airports, office buildings and housing were constructed in rapid succession to keep up with the demands of a growing economy. The trend continued under Suharto's rule, and by the 1970s downtown Jakarta resembled every other major city in the world.

By the 1980s, following a boom in world oil prices which were directed towards

development, a new generation of Indonesian architects was encouraged to create a national identity. There was a return to incorporating traditional styles, but it was limited to adding one or two local features to Modernist buildings, such as the multi-tiered roofs on the University of Indonesia and the *joglo* structures at Yogyakarta's Gadjah Mada University. Taman Mini Indonesia Indah (Beautiful Indonesia in Miniature) theme park in Jakarta was constructed during this era, housing examples of indigenous architecture from

The Keraton at Jogja features a range of architectural styles.

☉ CHINESE ARCHITECTURE

A few of the Chinese shophouses, of the type still seen in Singapore, survive in parts of Jakarta. They are well adapted for the tropics, with high ceilings, ventilation grilles, airwells and extended eaves. Various old *klenteng* (Chinese temples) remain as places of worship in Jakarta, Yogyakarta, Semarang and Banten, as well as some outside Java, such as in Singaraja (Bali). Their symmetrically aligned courtyards and walled compounds follow *feng shui* principles that align buildings with natural landscape features. Roofs are swept up at the ends and are typically decorated with dragons. Their red colour – identified with fire and blood – symbolises prosperity, good fortune and virtue.

each of its provinces to promote the country's rich cultural diversity. While this has at least preserved local designs, it did little to influence a new national identity, apart from resorts frequented by tourists with expectations of local environments.

As Indonesia continues to urbanise in the 21st century, its architects have kept up with global trends, and commercial skylines are filled with postmodern glass buildings, innovative designs and atrocities, as in all major cities. Today's innovative Indonesian architects are taking environmentally friendly designs to new levels, a trend that is hoped to continue.

Sumatran orangutan in Gunung Leuser National Park.

AMAZING BIODIVERSITY

Indonesia's volcanoes and forests, unique flora and fauna, and plethora of marine life make it an ideal destination for outdoor activities and adventures.

The great tropical rainforests of Indonesia comprise some of the world's oldest and richest natural habitats, home to a fabulous variety of flora and fauna, including many species found nowhere else on earth. Indicative of this wealth of biodiversity is the fact that new species are still being discovered in the jungles of Papua, Sumatra and Sulawesi. There are also large areas of pristine mangrove forest and swamp, montane forests and savannahs, and thousands of miles of coastline harbouring colourful coral reefs.

The deep oceanic trench between Bali and Lombok that extends northwards to the east of Borneo marks a separation in the types of mammals and birds found in Indonesia. Named the Wallace Line in honour of the great 19th-century naturalist Sir Alfred Russel Wallace, to the west of the line the bulk of the fauna is of Asian origin; that in Papua and parts of Maluku is mainly Australian. The intervening transition zone known as Wallacea (Sulawesi, Nusa Tenggara and parts of Maluku) features a fabulous mishmash of species (see page 334).

Gunung Bromo, with Gunung Semeru in the background.

WEST OF THE WALLACE LINE

Kalimantan and Sumatra contain Indonesia's greatest expanses of jungle. Together with the forests of Sulawesi, Maluku and Papua, they are second in size only to the Amazon and house an astonishing variety of animals and birds. The Asian fauna west of the Wallace Line includes large mammals such as elephants in Sumatra and rhinos in both Sumatra and Java, the Javan rhino being one of the world's rarest creatures. Big cats include leopards and small populations of tigers in Sumatra. Orangutans are found in Sumatra and Kalimantan, along with gibbons, slow lorises and tarsiers in the mid-storey. Along the riverbanks

in Kalimantan there are proboscis monkeys that chatter noisily and belly-flop from tree to tree.

Leopards also inhabit the Javan forests, and several smaller cats can be found in Sumatra. Kalimantan's jungles still shelter a few clouded leopards and reclusive sun bears, and Sumatra has Malayan tapirs, though they are rarely seen.

On Java and Bali endemic birds include the Javan hawk eagle, Javan scops owl, Javan kingfisher and Javan barbet, but the rarest of all the avifauna is the Bali starling, currently making a successful comeback after years at the brink of extinction. Sumatra and Kalimantan host spectacular hornbills; the red jungle fowl lives in the forests of Sumatra, Java and Sulawesi; ornate Argus pheasants perform elaborate mating dances in Kalimantan; and the strutting green peacock is found only on Java.

These and other species can be seen in western Indonesia's national parks: 12 in Java and eight in Kalimantan. There is one national park on Bali and 11 in Sumatra.

THE TRANSITION ZONE

Moving east from Lombok into Nusa Tenggara, the climate becomes drier and lowland jungles are replaced by deciduous monsoon forests and open savannah. This transition zone between Asia and Australia, formed by explosive volcanic eruptions and with deep channels between the islands, has few large mammals, but birds of both origins are abundant. Lesser sulphur-crested cockatoos, sunbirds, drongos and bee-eaters are representative, with the most unusual species being a mound-building megapode. The coral reefs in this region are rich, with at least 1,000 fish species and 250 hard corals found in Komodo National Park alone.

The most remarkable creature in Nusa Tenggara is the world's largest monitor lizard, *Varanus komodoesnsis*, reaching up to three metres (10ft)

The forests of Kalimantan provide a habitat for sun bears.

◎ MOST VISITED NATIONAL PARKS

A Forestry Department *surat jalan* (travel permit) is required before entering a national park. Most will have an on-site Forestry Department office, where permits can be issued on the spot. Popular parks include:

Ujung Kulon, West Java. Best accessed by chartered boat from Carita beach, a Unesco World Heritage Site and habitat of the Javan rhino. The park includes Anak Krakatau.

Bromo-Tengger-Semeru, East Java. Reached from the north by road from Pasuruan, home to active volcanoes Bromo and Semeru. Spectacular scenery.

Bali Barat, West Bali. Arrive via northern or southern trans-Bali highway. First-rate diving and snorkelling at Menjangan island, birdwatching and trekking.

Komodo, Nusa Tenggara. Take a chartered boat from Labuanbajo, Flores or Sape, Sumbawa. A World Heritage and a World Network of Biosphere Reserves Site, it protects the Komodo dragon.

Gunung Leuser, North Sumatra. Transit through Medan. A World Heritage and World Network of Biosphere Reserves Site with Sumatran orangutans, tapirs and other forest wildlife.

Tanjung Puting, Central Kalimantan. Fly to Pangkalanbun, drive to Kumai and go upriver by chartered boat. A World Network of Biosphere Reserves Site with good populations of orangutans and proboscis monkeys.

in length and weighing up to 150kg (331lbs). The number of Komodo dragons has dwindled to fewer than 3,000 confined to a few islands in the park.

In addition to Komodo, there are five other national parks in Nusa Tenggara. Three of them surround volcanoes: the active Gunung Rinjani on Lombok, the dormant Kelimutu on Flores, and the vast Tambora on Sumbawa, responsible for one of the most destructive eruptions of all time in 1815. There are more than a dozen other active volcanoes in the region.

ENDEMIC ODDITIES

The greatest concentration of biological oddities in the Wallacea transition zone is to be found in Sulawesi, created as an island when plate tectonics flung together diverse fragments of the northern and southern landmasses. Most of the island's mammals, including deer, monkeys, some civets and some tarsiers, are of obvious Asian origin; however, the two types of cuscus found here – the lesser and the bear cuscus – are marsupials and typically Australian. Additionally, some of Sulawesi's species are endemic and occur nowhere else in the world (see page 334).

In Lore Lindu National Park are the world's smallest buffalo, anoa, and the curved-tusked babirusa – literally 'pig-deer'. Thought to be extinct until the late 1970s, the Sulawesi palm civet still exists, and there are at least five endemic species of macaques. Sulawesi's endemic avifauna includes two species of hornbills – the spectacular Sulawesi hornbill has a brilliantly colourful beak and casque. Among the 70 or so species originating from both the Asian and the Australian regions are kingfishers, drongos, babblers, cockatoos and sunbirds.

The wide variety of marine life at Bunaken National Marine Park (see page 341) ranges from bannerfish, orbicular batfish and bumphead parrotfish to massive Napoleon wrasse, dogtooth tuna, pilot whales and giant green sea turtles. Seahorses, ghost pipefish, mimic octopus and many varieties of nudibranch dot the shallows.

Sulawesi's mountainous interior is dotted with enormous lakes and forests. Situated on the island's extreme north arm are eight major volcanoes. Eight national parks protect Sulawesi's treasures: Bunaken and Wakatobi are marine preserves attracting serious divers, and Lore Lindu is a World Network of Biosphere Reserves site.

East of Sulawesi is Maluku, the fabled Spice Islands that first drew Europeans to Indonesia. These days the area is best known for its incredible snorkelling and diving, with giant sea turtles and dugongs sharing the sea with colourful reef fish. Crocodiles, pythons and monitor lizards lurk topside, along with the endangered blue-tongued Ambon lizard related to the Australian sailfin variety.

A green turtle.

☉ RAINFOREST PRODUCTS

Products from Indonesian forests have been exported for centuries. Rattan was sold to China, where it was made into cordage. 'Dragon's blood', a red resin from rattan, was used for medicine and to stain Dayak basketry. Other resins included camphor, highly prized for incense and medicine; damar, for varnish and sealing wax; and benzoin, a resin used in perfume and medicines. Birds contributed plumage, which appeared on the hats of European elite, and hornbill 'ivory' is still carved into ornaments or ground up by the Chinese as an aphrodisiac. Rainforests also yield beeswax and honey, as well as *lac*, insect secretions used in making shellac.

Managed tourism can help conservation. Human presence deters illegal poachers and loggers, and tourist revenues can be used to maintain park security.

Many of the islands are richly forested and house a plethora of birds: the salmon-crested cockatoo, red-breasted pygmy parrot, red-flanked lorikeet, red lory and a rare bird of

The crimson sunbird, an eastern Indonesian species.

paradise, to name a few. Near the Banda Sea seabirds include masked, red-footed and brown boobies, frigate birds and red-tailed tropicbirds.

There are several volcanoes and two national parks in Maluku, Aketajawe-Lolobata and Manusela, both established to protect marine life.

EASTERN INDONESIA'S AUSTRALASIAN SPECIES

Remote Papua, the western half of New Guinea island, together with some of the eastern Maluku islands, have a floral and faunal diversity equal to that of Kalimantan, with at least half of the known species endemic.

In the interior, Papua's terrain comprises thickly forested hills and montane jungles, with

magnificent valleys stretching in between. Indonesia's highest mountain, Puncak Jaya (formerly called Carstenz Pyramid), is in the Lorentz National Park, towering 4,884 metres (16,024ft) and capped with permanent ice fields. In the south, in Wasur National Park, expansive savannahs, lowland forests and extensive swamplands dominate the landscape. All coastal areas are fringed by virtually untouched mangroves.

So large and dense is the Papuan forest that new species are still being discovered. In the Foja Mountains west of Jayapura, 8 million hectares (nearly 20 million acres) of undeveloped rainforest make it an Eden for species generation and as a carbon storehouse.

Also in Papuan forests are monotremes – egg-laying mammals such as echidnas – as well as marsupials: terrestrial and tree varieties of kangaroos, and wallabies, possums, large-eyed cuscus, and bandicoots, with many of the marsupials occupying the role monkeys hold in western Indonesia forests.

'Magnificent' barely begins to describe the avifauna, with lowland forests dominated by noisy cockatoos and hornbills. At slightly higher altitudes are flocks of 40 species of parrots and the large black palm cockatoo. Waterbirds such as spoonbills, magpie geese, black-necked storks and cranes wade in the swamplands of Wasur National Park. Most spectacular of all are Papua's 42 species of birds of paradise, 36 of which are native to the island of New Guinea. The largest bird is the flightless cassowary, which frequents forests where ample fruit can be found.

⊘ INDONESIA'S RAINFORESTS

Two thousand years ago, tropical rainforests are thought to have covered as much as 12 percent of the Earth's land surface, but today the figure is below five percent, and falling. The largest unbroken stretch of rainforest is found in the Amazon basin of South America, with Brazil containing about one-third of the world's remaining tropical rainforests. The only other large tracts are found in central Africa and Indonesia, and the still-extensive jungles of Sumatra, Kalimantan and Papua are the last refuge for many endangered species. Elsewhere in South East Asia, forest cover has been reduced into a patchwork of smaller forests, where species diversity is reduced.

⚲ CONSERVATION IN ACTION

Indonesians have enthusiastically embraced the need to protect their country's environmental riches, and the results are finally beginning to show.

From the time the phrase 'climate change' was coined, Indonesia, due to its enormous expanse of forests and its long history of rampant illegal logging, has been top of the hit list for activists, and their efforts are beginning to pay off. In recent years the government has implemented legislation and law enforcement and has improved forest management to ensure that all timber and its various products intended for export are produced from legal and sustainably harvested sources.

In addition, recent studies have shown that only 20 percent of deforestation is the result of the conversion of forest land to large-scale commercial agriculture – for example palm oil plantations. Their findings have tended, instead, to attribute environmental degradation to the millions of poor people who use the forests for food, fuel and shelter. The many NGOs working in Indonesia are now focusing on training villagers to do other jobs, thereby improving livelihoods and reducing greenhouse emissions caused by forest destruction and degradation.

Marine conservation also includes protecting shorelines from erosion by planting extensive mangrove forests to reduce shoreline abrasion and seawater intrusion, which are exacerbated by climate change and can help lessen the effects of tsunamis.

Natural disasters greatly impact on Indonesia, which has more than its share of earthquakes, volcanic eruptions, landslides and tsunamis. Hardest hit are the poor – the vast majority of the population – who live in vulnerable areas on the coast, on mountain slopes prone to mudslides and on low-lying flood plains.

Growing awareness of environmental issues, particularly among young Indonesians, is beginning to make a difference. Green groups, bike-to-work programmes, school nature clubs and Scouts groups are gaining popularity. There is an increasing number of backpacker organisations comprising young professionals, and

Reduce, Reuse, Recycle campaigns instigated by corporate responsibility initiatives are influencing neighbourhoods to pitch in.

There remains a great deal of work to be done, but Indonesians have proven themselves to be fast learners. More focus on reducing poverty and increasing education will impact on many problematic areas of this rapidly developing country, and protecting the environment is certainly one of these. Elsewhere, grassroots protest movements have emerged, utilising social media and bringing together committed activists, academics and local communities to challenge environmentally unsound developments. A recent plan – currently stalled – to

Logging in Kalimantan.

reclaim land for resort development in southern Bali's natural Benoa Harbour, destroying some of this heavily urbanised region's last surviving mangroves, was met by sustained protests.

With some 55,000km (34,000 miles) of coastline and sharing maritime borders with 10 countries, Indonesia has also taken a lead in setting up the Coral Triangle Initiative, establishing a protected area of 3.5 million hectares (8.6 million acres) in the Savu Sea – a migration route for half the world's whale species and home to vast expanses of rare corals.

Huge challenges remain, with corruption, powerful business lobbies, and the ceaseless rise of the palm oil industry among the issues. But there is certainly an improved commitment to environmentalism.

WORLD HERITAGE SITES

Indonesia is unique in that it is the only country in Southeast Asia that has eight of its landmarks declared as Unesco World Heritage Sites.

The United Nations has listed eight of Indonesia's natural and cultural wonders as Unesco World Heritage sites, one of which, in Sumatra, is earmarked as a Natural Heritage in Danger.

The Buddhist **Borobudur** monument (see page 166) in Central Java, built from around AD 788, fell into disrepair after the centre of royal power shifted from the region. Its restoration was completed by Unesco and Indonesia between 1973 and 1983.

Prambanan (see page 171), also in Central Java, is the largest Hindu temple complex in Indonesia. Completed in AD 856, some 244 temple remains are still found in the outer compound.

Ujung Kulon National Park (see page 151), West Java, has around 50 endangered Javan (Lesser) one-horned rhinoceros and Java's largest lowland rainforests. The offshore Krakatau island is part of the park.

Komodo National Park (see page 285) in Nusa Tenggara is primarily the home of the protected 2,740 carnivorous monitor lizards known as the Komodo dragons.

Lorentz National Park, Papua (see page 365), the largest protected area in Southeast Asia, is one of the few areas in the world to have snow-capped mountains in a tropical environment.

In 2011, three of Sumatra's national parks were named **Tropical Rainforest Heritage of Sumatra** for their great potential for long-term conservation of the distinctive and diverse biota. Sadly, it also bears the label 'World Heritage in Danger'.

In 2012, Unesco enlisted **'the Cultural Landscape of Bali'** as a World Heritage Site. The Subak – the unique Balinese rice farming culture – is a manifestation of the *Tri Hita Karana* cosmological doctrine. All the sites of the cultural landscape demonstrate the capability of the Balinese to make these doctrines a reality, practiced in their daily life.

Lorentz National Park is home to numerous isolated tribes, including the Amungme, Western Dani, Nduga, Ngalik, Asmat (Sempan, Komoro), Mimika and Somohai. is one of the most ecologically diverse national parks in the world.

The six lower terraces at Borobudur are carved with Buddhist bas relief scenes. Three upper tiers with 72 lattice-work miniature stupas each contain Buddha images that are unique in Buddhist art.

The Sangiran Homo erectus site, Central Java.

Sangiran Early Man Site

In 1891, on the banks of the Bengawan Solo River near Surakarta (Solo), Central Java, Dutchman Eugene Dubois unearthed the site of Sangiran Early Man – one of the world's first known specimens of *Homo erectus* (upright man), the 'missing link' that proved Darwin's evolution theory. The more complete remains (sometimes called Solo Man) found by G.H.R. von Koenigswald in 1936 are now thought to be as many as a million years older than Dubois's find, as old as those discovered in Kenya.

Many other fossils have been unearthed in the area, ranging from 1.2 million to 500,000 years old. Unesco proclaimed Sangiran a World Heritage Site in 1996, declaring this one of the most important places in the world for understanding human evolution.

883, Krakatau exploded and sunk, re-emerging in '7 as Anak Krakatau, 'Child or Krakatau'. It remains ve with frequent eruptions, and is part of Ujung Kulon ional Park.

The skull of 'Java Man' is displayed at Jakarta's National Museum.

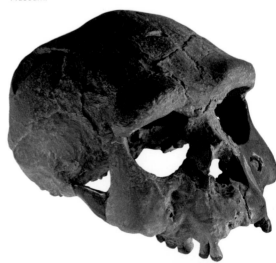

Ora Beach Eco Resort, Seram Island.

The colourful black-capped Lory.

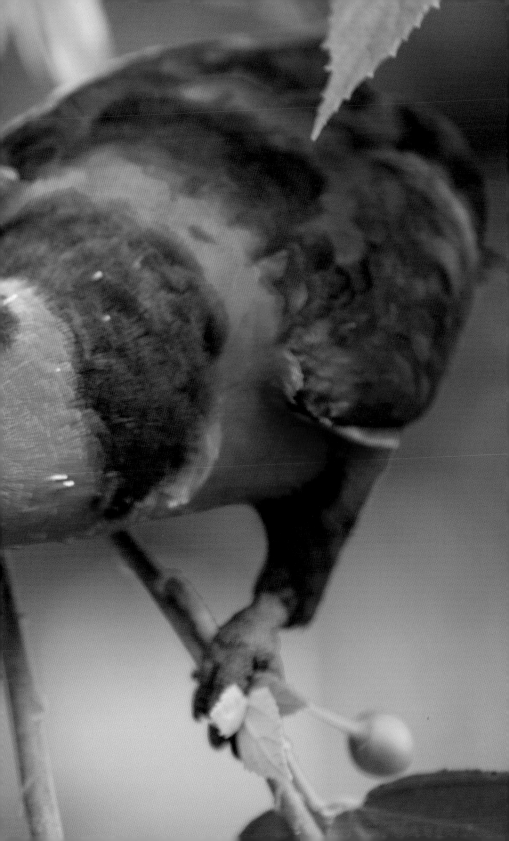

Kawah Ijen crater lake.

INTRODUCTION

A detailed guide to the entire country, with principal sights cross-referenced by number to the maps.

A sasak rice barn, Lombok.

Indonesia's choice of attractions and terrains is so vast that it has to be experienced to be believed. It is a country of over 17,000 islands – large and small – which wraps itself around one-eighth of the world's circumference.

Java is home to over half of the nation's population, no mystery considering the land's fertile volcanic landscape. Some of the country's most elegant aesthetic endeavours are here: music, dance and drama, textiles and antiquities. The capital city, Jakarta, a traffic-clogged metropolis, is not especially beautiful by day, but at night its electrified skyline can be elegant. To many Indonesians, it is the city of hope, the one place that best exemplifies a prosperous, forward-looking nation.

To the west, the large island of Sumatra is where spice traders first anchored after passage from India and China. The terrain is not especially good for farming, but there are verdant jungles, still-plentiful wildlife, and a colourful mix of the country's most independent ethnic groups.

East of Java lies Bali, for many travellers the epitome of an exotic tropical paradise. Beyond is Lombok, and then Nusa Tenggara, or what the Dutch called the Lesser Sundas, a chain of volcanic islands with some tremendous scenery, both terrestrial and marine.

Due north of Java is Kalimantan, Indonesia's portion of mystical Borneo. Bisected by the equator, Kalimantan was once synonymous with remoteness, inaccessibility and head-hunters; today it suggests timber wealth and oil frontiers, although vast tracts of forest remain, home to orang-utans and numerous other species.

Further east are a series of increasingly remote outposts. Sulawesi is home to the remarkable Toraja people (who bury their dead in the limestone cliffs), exceptional wildlife, fabulous scenery and amazing coral reefs. Scattered across the tropical seas beyond are Maluku, formerly The Moluccas, the original Spice Islands. Their lucrative crop of nutmeg, cloves and mace was the subject of battles between European powers. Finally, the final frontier of this island nation is New Guinea, the western half of which belongs to Indonesia. Called Papua, it was a land of unknown peoples and mountain valleys until early in the 20th century. Even today it remains remote and distinct from the rest of Indonesia.

Things in Indonesia don't always work on schedule. As you travel through this vast and beautiful country, large doses of patience and a good sense of humour will stand you in good stead.

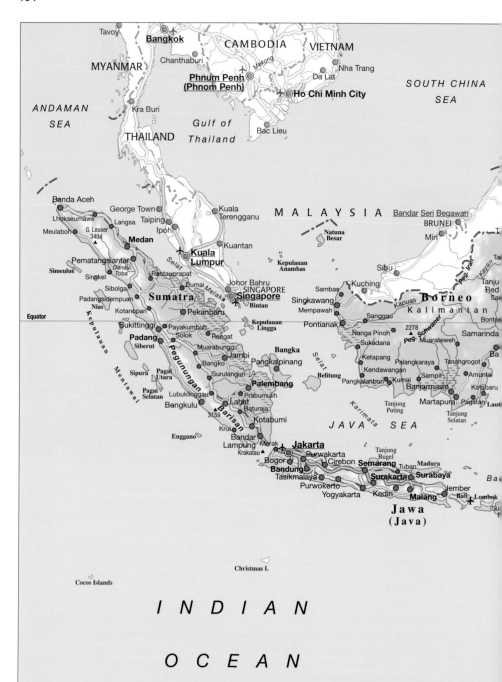

Tavoy

Bangkok

CAMBODIA

VIETNAM

MYANMAR

Chanthaburi

Nha Trang

**Phnum Penh
(Phnom Penh)**

Da Lat

Ho Chi Minh City

SOUTH CHINA
SEA

*ANDAMAN
SEA*

Kra Buri

Gulf of

Bac Lieu

THAILAND

Thailand

Banda Aceh

George Town

Kuala
Terengganu

M A L A Y S I A

Bandar Seri Begawan

Lhokseumawe

Langsa

Taiping

BRUNEI

Meulaboh

G. Leuser
3404

Ipoh

Medan

Kuantan

Natuna
Besar

Miri

Pematangsiantar

*Danau
Toba*

**Kuala
Lumpur**

Kepulauan
Anambas

Sibu

Simeulue

Singkel

Rantauprapat

Tanju
Red

Sibolga

Dumai

Johor Bahru

SINGAPORE

Sambas

Kuching

Borneo

Padangsidempuan

Nias

Kotanopan

Sumatra

Singapore

Bintan

Singkawang

K a l i m a n t a n

Sa

Equator

Pekanbaru

Mempawah

Sanggau

Bonta

Bukittinggi

Payakumbuh
Solok

Kepulauan
Lingga

Pontianak

Nanga Pinoh

2278
Peg.

Samarinda

Padang

Rengat

Sukadana

Muarateweh

Siberut

Muarabungo

Ketapang

Palangkaraya

Tanahgrogot

Ba

Sipura

Pagai
Utara

Jambi

Bangko

Surulangun

Bangka

Pangkalpinang

Kendawangan

Pangkalanbun

Kumai

Sampit

Amuntai

Pagai
Selatan

Lubuklinggau

Palembang

Belitung

Banjarmasin

Kotabaru

Bengkulu

Prabumulih

Lahat

Baturaja

Martapura

Pagatan

Laut

3159

Tanjung
Puting

Tanjung
Selatan

Enggano

Kotabumi

Krui

J A V A   S E A

Bandar
Lampung

Merak

Jakarta

Krakatau

Bandung

Bogor

Purwakarta

Cirebon

Semarang

Tanjung
Bugel

Tuban

Madura

Tasikmalaya

Surakarta

Surabaya

Ba

Purwokerto

Yogyakarta

Kediri

Malang

Jember

Bali

Lombok

Jawa
(Java)

Christmas I.

Cocos Islands

I N D I A N

O C E A N

Barrow I.

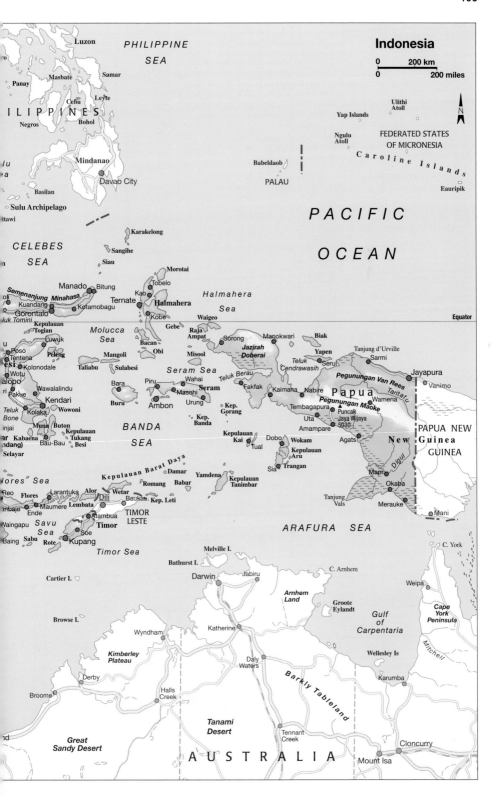

Luzon

PHILIPPINE
SEA

Indonesia

0 _____ 200 km
0 _____ 200 miles

Masbate   Samar

Panay

Cebu   Leyte

ILIPPINES   Bohol

Negros

Mindanao

Ulithi
Atoll

Yap Islands

Ngulu
Atoll

FEDERATED STATES
OF MICRONESIA

N

Davao City

Babeldaob

PALAU

Caroline Islands

Eauripik

Basilan

Sulu Archipelago

itawi

PACIFIC

OCEAN

CELEBES
SEA

Karakelong

Sangihe

Siau

Manado   Bitung

Morotai

Tobelo

Kao

Semenanjung Minahasa

Kuandang

Gorontalo

luk Tomini

Ternate

Kotamobagu

Kobe

Halmahera

Halmahera
Sea

Waigeo

Equator

Kepulauan
Togian

Luwuk

Molucca
Sea

Gebe

Raja
Ampat

Sorong

Manokwari

Biak

Poso

Tentena   Peleng

Bacan

Obi

Misool

Jazirah
Doberai

Yapen

Tanjung d'Urville

Sarmi

esi Kolonodale

Mangoli

Teluk
Cendrawasih

Serui

Wotu

Taliabu   Sulabesi

Seram Sea

Fakfak

Teluk Berau

Jayapura

alopo

Bara

Piru

Wahai

Kaimana   Nabire

Pegunungan Van Rees

Vanimo

Pakue

Wawalalindu

Buru

Masohi

Seram

Papua

Tarutu

Kendari   Wowoni

Ambon

Urung

Kep.
Gorang

Tembagapura

Pegunungan Maoke

Wamena

Kolaka

Muna Buton

Kep.
Banda

Puncak
Jaya Wijaya
5030

Teluk
Bone

injai   Kepulauan
Tukang
ar Kabaena Besi

BANDA

Kepulauan
Kai

Uta

Amampare

PAPUA NEW

ndang)

Bau-Bau

SEA

Tual

Dobo Wokam

Agats

New Guinea

GUINEA

Selayar

Kepulauan
Aru

lores Sea

Kepulauan Barat Daya

Damar

Yamdena

Sia Trangan

Reo Flores

Larantuka Alor Wetar

Romang

Babar

Kepulauan
Tanimbar

Mapi

Digul

Okaba

Ende Maumere Lembata

Dili

Baukau Kep. Leti

Tanjung
Vals

Merauke

Mani

anbajo

Atambura

TIMOR

Waingapu

Savu
Sea

Soe

Timor

LESTE

ARAFURA SEA

Baing Sabu

Rote Kupang

Timor Sea

Melville I.

C. York

Bathurst I.

Cartier I.

Darwin

Jabiru

C. Arnhem

Weipa

Arnhem
Land

Groote
Eylandt

Cape
York
Peninsula

Browse I.

Katherine

Gulf
of
Carpentaria

Mitchell

Kimberley
Plateau

Wyndham

Daly
Waters

Wellesley Is

Derby

Barkly Tableland

Karumba

Broome

Halls
Creek

Tanami
Desert

Great
Sandy Desert

AUSTRALIA

Tennant
Creek

Cloncurry

Mount Isa

Java has a long seafaring
tradition.

JAVA

Although it covers only 6 percent of the total area, Java is Indonesia's heartland, and its political and economic centre.

Traditional batik, Yogyakarta.

For 1,000 years, from the time of the great Hindu-Buddhist empires up to the early 1800s, Java's population of 3.5 million remained relatively stable. Wet-rice cultivation was the basis of civilisation, and as long as the population was small, farmers produced vast surpluses. Then in the 19th century a forced-labour cultivation system instigated by the Dutch to increase food supplies resulted in a spiralling birth rate. By 1900, the population had soared to 28 million and today stands at around 140 million.

This is an island unlike any other in the archipelago. Its interior remains farmland, the soil made fertile by nutrient-rich ash deposits from 30 active volcanoes that rise magnificently amid the rice fields. Java is Indonesia's most densely populated island. Around half of its inhabitants still live in rural areas, with many still making a living as farmers or fishermen. At the other end of the spectrum are its major cities: Jakarta, the nation's capital and the nucleus of Indonesian business, finance and politics, is here. A bustling metropolis, its people live among glittering skyscrapers, pricey shopping malls and bumper-to-bumper traffic. Surabaya, Indonesia's second-largest city, is a sprawling commercial centre and the primary trading port for the islands to the east. On the north coast is Semarang with its intriguing mix of descendants of traders from afar.

Gunung Bromo and Gunung Semeru at dawn.

In the interior, the island's remaining forests are now limited to its 12 national parks protecting some of the Earth's rarest creatures. Trekking, climbing, birdwatching and wildlife-spotting at Gunung Bromo, Ujung Kulon and Gunung Merapi attract adventurers and naturalists. Two parks – Kepulauan Seribu and Karimunjawa – are marine preserves, luring water-lovers to their shores; Alas Purwo has some of the best surfing this side of Hawaii.

At the heart of Java is Yogyakarta, where painters, gamelan musicians, batik artists and dancers study and perform. Its rich courtly culture, refined manners, elevated language and proud traditions make it the traditional wellspring of Javanese culture. Outside its realm are Borobudur and Prambanan and countless smaller temples, remnants of glorious past kingdoms.

Gridlocked traffic along Jalan Sudirman.

JAKARTA

The charms of this huge sprawling metropolis are well hidden, but Jakarta dwellers are proud of the cultural and intellectual life in their ever-changing, chaotic capital city.

The gargantuan capital of a huge nation, for many Indonesians Jakarta ❶ is a city of promise. The lure of jobs and a better life has caused the city's population to escalate at an alarming rate to over 10 million. Chronic traffic congestion, haphazard planning and sheer scale lend the place an often chaotic feel. But central Jakarta has been considerably cleaned up in recent years, with proper pavements and pedestrian crossings making for easier navigation on foot, and attractive flowerbeds lining the main streets. Real progress is also being made with the public transport network, with upgraded suburban trains, a proper modern bus network and a new MRT system. The staggering size of the high-rise business buildings and shopping malls, meanwhile, is a powerful indicator of contemporary Indonesia's economic importance. Though individual tourist attractions are scattered thinly, the city has a rich cultural life, with an abundance of performing and visual arts. And its greatest saving grace remains the easy-going, welcoming atmosphere and ready humour that endures at street level, despite the surrounding mayhem.

Jakarta sprawls across a vast area. Just south of the harbour on Jakarta Bay and Ancol recreation park is Kota,

the old Batavia area, where remnants of Dutch colonial rule reside. Heading south are *Pecinan* (Chinatown) and busy Glodok, the electronic, gadget and computer centre of the city. A major north–south artery, Jalan Hayam Wuruk, merges into Jalan Gajah Mada, lined with shops, restaurants, hotels and nightlife, ending at the huge expanse of Lapangan Merdeka (Freedom Square), the heart of Central Jakarta.

The busy Jalan Thamrin-Sudirman corridor, south of Lapangan Merdeka,

◉ Main attractions

Taman Fatahillah
(Fatahillah Square)
Monas
National Museum
Taman Ismail Marzuk
Masjid Istiqlal (Istiqlal Mosque)
Taman Mini Indonesia Indah
(Beautiful Indonesia in Miniature Park)
Kepulauan Seribu
(Thousand Islands)

⊙ Maps on pages 140, 146, 150

Lighting incense in a Chinese temple, Glodok.

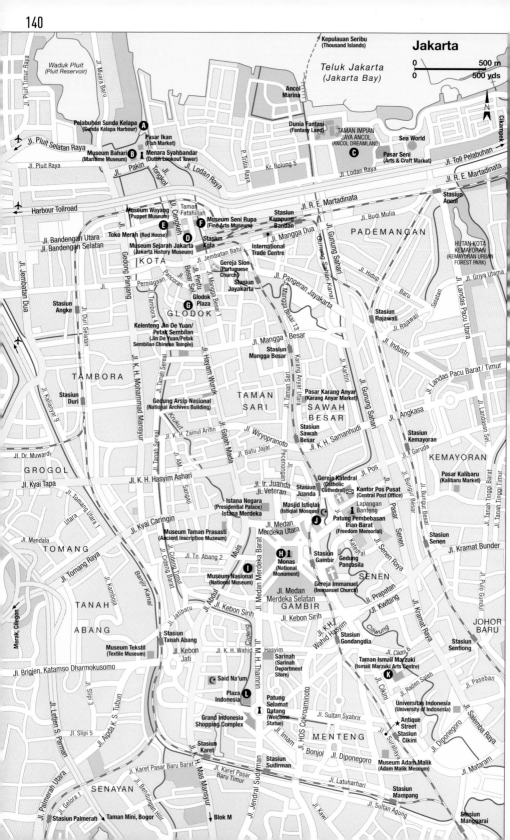

is one of two major Central Business Districts (CBDs), a wall of glimmering glass and steel with some of the most interesting high-rise architecture in Southeast Asia. This traffic-clogged thoroughfare in turn connects with Jalan Rasuna Said and Gatot Subroto, the second CBD and a golden triangle for national and international companies, banks, hotels, shopping malls and embassies.

Surrounding the city mayhem on all sides are residential areas, ranging from upper- and middle-class streets to the most basic shanties. Scattered throughout are pockets that seem frozen in time, including diminutive residential districts with market gardens and makeshift *kampung* (village) dwellings that impart something of a village atmosphere to many back alleys.

JAKARTA'S HISTORY

Starting out as a simple harbour town called Sunda Kelapa in the 14th century under the Hindu Pajajaran kingdom, the settlement now known as Jakarta grew into a major seaport as the lucrative maritime trade expanded with Indian, Chinese and Arab traders. In 1522, the Portuguese arrived in search of the legendary Spice Islands, followed later by the English and Dutch. The seaport was conquered in 1527 by the combined forces of the neighbouring Banten and Demak kingdoms, renaming the area Jayakarta or 'City of Victory'.

But it was the Dutch who had bigger designs, taking Jayakarta by force in 1619, and claiming the land in the name of the VOC (East India Company). The Dutch governor-general, Jan Pieterszoon Coen, moved his headquarters here from Ambon and ordered construction of a new town named Batavia. It was to be the seat of the Dutch empire in Asia for the next 350 years.

Under the VOC, Batavia's fortunes rose and fell. It grew rich during the 17th century on an entrepôt trade in sugar, spice, tea, textiles, porcelain, hardwoods and rice, then declined in the 18th century as the VOC itself edged towards bankruptcy. At the beginning of the 19th century most of Old Batavia was demolished to provide building materials for a new city to the south called Weltevreeden, around what is now Lapangan Merdeka. The fashionable architectural styles of the period blended with newly laid out tree-lined boulevards and extensive gardens to produce an elegant colonial cityscape, traces of which endure today.

During the Japanese occupation of World War II, Batavia was renamed Jakarta. Following the nation's postwar independence struggle, hundreds of thousands of Indonesians flooded in from the countryside and outer islands. Jakarta quickly outstripped all other Indonesian cities in size and importance, becoming the unrivalled political, cultural and economic centre of the new nation.

The 19th-century Dutch Lookout Tower.

A drawbridge over a Kota canal.

Sunda Kelapa's graceful schooners are being fast supplanted by modern freighters.

AROUND THE WATERFRONT

Hail a taxi and start your tour where the city's history began, the old spice trading seaport **Sunda Kelapa Harbour** . Early morning is the best time to walk along the 2km (1.25-mile) wharf. Though the ships that moor here are now all motorised, they are still built to the traditional wooden model of the pinisi schooners of the Bugis, fabled seafarers from Sulawesi, and they still handle much of Indonesia's interisland trade. Local boatmen offer tours of the harbour, though it is necessary to bargain to ensure a fair price.

The area around Sunda Kelapa is rich in history, and the best way to survey the area is on foot. Near the river stands a 19th-century **Dutch lookout tower** (Uitkik), constructed on the site of the original customs house of Jayakarta. Behind the lookout stands a long two-storey structure dating from VOC times, now the **Museum Bahari** (Maritime Museum; Jalan Pasar Ikan No. 1; tel: 021-669 3406; Tue–Fri 9am–3pm,

Sunda Kelapa Harbour.

Sat–Sun 9am–2pm). This warehouse, now a maritime museum, was built by the Dutch in 1646 and was used to store coffee, tea and Indian cloth. Inside are displays of traditional sailing craft from all corners of the Indonesian archipelago, as well as some old maps of Batavia. Down a narrow lane and around a corner behind the museum lies the **Pasar Ikan** (fish market), beyond which are numerous stalls selling nautical gear.

Further east along the waterfront is a giant seaside recreation area, **Taman Impian Jaya Ancol** (Ancol Dreamland), featuring beachfront hotels, restaurants, a golf course, bowling alley and an arts and crafts market. There are also several theme parks, including **Sea World** (tel: 021-645 2976; daily 9am–6pm), which has a tropical oceanarium, and **Dunia Fantasi** (tel: 021-645 3456; daily 10am–6pm) featuring rollercoasters and other rides. The whole complex gets very crowded at weekends. Close by is **Ancol Marina**, from where ferries depart to various islands (see page 147).

THE OLD CITY

South of the port districts is the area known as **Kota**, heart of the old 17th-century Dutch settlement at Batavia, originally a walled town modelled on Amsterdam. Most of Old Batavia was demolished at the beginning of the 19th century, but the town square area survived and has been restored and renamed **Taman Fatahillah** (Fatahillah Square). Adjacent colonial buildings have been converted into museums, and the whole neighbourhood has been considerably gentrified in recent years. There are several fashionable cafes on the surrounding streets, and the main square bustles at weekends with street entertainers, old-fashioned bicycle rentals, artists and food vendors.

Start at the **Museum Sejarah Jakarta** D (Jakarta History Museum; tel: 021-692 9101; Tue–Sun 8am–3pm). This was formerly Batavia's city hall (*Stadhuis*), completed in 1710 and used by successive governments until the 1960s. It now houses memorabilia from the colonial period, notably 18th-century furnishings and portraits of VOC governors, along with many prehistoric, classical and Portuguese-period artefacts. Dungeons visible from the back of the building were used as holding cells where prisoners were made to stand waist-deep in sewage for weeks awaiting their trials. Executions and torture were once commonplace in the main square as judges watched from the balcony above the main entrance.

The **Museum Wayang** E (Puppet Museum; tel: 021-692 9560; Tue–Sun 8am–3pm) is on the western side of the square. It has many puppets and masks, some of them rare buffalo-hide shadow puppets (*wayang kulit*), along with a collection of *topeng* masks, and tombstones of several early Dutch governors.

The **Museum Seni Rupa** F (Fine Arts Museum; tel: 021-690 7062; Tue–Sun 8am–2.30pm) occupies the former Court of Justice building, completed in 1879. Its collections include paintings and sculptures by modern Indonesian artists, and an important exhibition of rare porcelain, featuring many Sung

The Museum Wayang on Fatahillah Square.

Kampung Tugu.

⊘ FORGOTTEN PORTUGUESE

Nestled between busy Tanjung Priok harbour and the Cilincing warehouse district is one of Jakarta's oldest neighbourhoods. Kampung Tugu's residents are descendants of Southeast Asia's long-established Portuguese community. Enslaved by the Dutch after they conquered Melaka (in modern Malaysia) in 1641, they were later freed on condition of taking Dutch names and converting to Protestantism. They became known as *Mardijkers*, 'liberated people', a term which eventually gave rise to the Indonesian word for freedom, *merdeka*. The village's 17th-century church, featuring a distinctive bell tower, is still in operation.

The community embraces its four-centuries-old Portuguese heritage, with ancient rituals such as the *Rabo-Rabo* ceremony on New Year's Day. Another celebration, *Mandi-Mandi*, takes place on the first Sunday in January, with communal prayers, followed by the application of powder to one another's faces as a sign of mutual forgiveness. The ritual ends with beer and performances of *keroncong* music. The band is comprised of ukuleles, guitars, violins, flutes and cellos. It is thought that the sound that the ukulele makes (*crong... crong*) was the origin of the name *keroncong*.

'Tugu' may refer to a stone inscription dating back to King Purnawarman of the Tarumanegara kingdom which was found in a nearby canal. Another explanation is that it comes from the middle syllable of *Por-tugu-ese*.

Jakarta History Museum.

A famous former resident.

celadon pieces from the Adam Malik collection, ancient Javanese water jugs *(kendhi)*, and terracotta pieces dating from the 14th century.

Before leaving the area, walk over to the 16th-century Portuguese cannon mounted on the north side of Taman Fatahillah. Si Jagur, 'The Robust One', as it is called, is regarded by many as a fertility symbol, perhaps because of the fist that is cast into the butt end of the cannon, with a thumb protruding between its index and middle fingers (an obscene gesture in Indonesia). Nearby is Café Batavia, once a warehouse, now with eclectic furnishings and window tables that offer excellent views of the square.

Next, walk behind the Museum Wayang to view two Dutch houses dating from the 18th century. Across the canal and to the left stands a solid red-brick townhouse (Jl. Kali Besar Barat No. 11) that was built around 1730 by the then soon-to-be governor-general. The design and particularly the fine Chinese-style woodwork are typical of old Batavian residences. Three doors

to the left is another house from the same period. Nearby is a historical drawbridge on the Kali Besar River called Jembatan Pasar Ayam (Chicken Market Bridge), as the area was once a market for poultry and vegetables.

Jakarta's **Chinatown** is immediately adjacent to the former European centre just to the south of the Old City in an area now known as **Glodok** , and is the centre for electronics, household goods and herbal medicines. The main streets are unremarkable, but the convoluted back alleys are thoroughly atmospheric, with a number of colourful Chinese temples, and some lively market areas.

FREEDOM SQUARE

A circumnavigation of Central Jakarta begins at the top of the **Monas** (National Monument; Tue–Sun 9am–5pm). A 137-metre (450ft) tall marble obelisk is set in the centre of **Lapangan Merdeka** (Freedom Square). There is an observation deck at the top surmounted by a 14-metre (45ft) bronze flame sheathed in 33kg (73lbs) of gold symbolising the spirit of freedom. It was commissioned by Sukarno and completed in 1961 – a combination Olympic Flame-Washington Monument with the phallic overtones of an ancient Hindu-Javanese *lingga*. The museum in the basement contains 12 dioramas depicting historical scenes from a nationalistic viewpoint. A high-speed elevator rises to the observation deck, where on a clear day there is a fabulous 360-degree view of Jakarta.

Double back north to pass behind the Presidential Palace, situated between Jalan Medan Merdeka Utara and Jalan Veteran. The palace building consists of two 19th-century neoclassical villas situated back to back. The older of the two, the Istana Negara, faces north and was built by a wealthy Dutch merchant around 1800. It was taken over some years later to serve as the town residence of the Dutch governor (whose official residence was then located in Bogor). The south-facing Istana Merdeka was added in 1879 as a reception area. President Sukarno resided in the palace and frequently gave lavish banquets in the central courtyard.

On the west side of Medan Merdeka lies one of Indonesia's great cultural treasures, the **National Museum ❶**, on Jalan Medan Merdeka Barat (tel: 021-386 8172; Tue–Fri 8.30am–4pm, Sat–Sun 8.30am–5pm). Founded in 1868 by the Batavian Society for Arts and Sciences, the museum now holds a huge array of antiquities and ethnographic artefacts. The courtyard of the original building is crammed with an impressive mass of Hindu-Buddhist statuary, while the new wing houses well-displayed collections spread over several floors. Highlights include the ceramics section, and the glittering golden regalia of various Indonesian royal houses. Be sure not to miss the excellent, though poorly signposted, fourth floor, accessible by elevator. There is a small café on the ground floor.

CENTRAL JAKARTA SIGHTS

Head eastwards about 1,000 metres (3,280ft) to the imposing white-marble **Masjid Istiqlal ❷** (Istiqlal Mosque) on Jalan Veteran. Opened in 1978 and designed by a Catholic architect from Sumatra, it is the largest mosque in Southeast Asia, standing at the former site of the Dutch Benteng (Fort) Noordwijk. The mosque is open to appropriately dressed non-Muslims for tours outside of prayer times.

Lapangan Banteng (Wild Ox Field) lies just to the east, bounded on the north by the neo-Gothic **Catholic Cathedral** on Jalan Katedral, completed in 1901; note the rather interesting buildings on the east near the Supreme Court (1848) and the Department of Finance (1982), and on the south by the Borobudur Hotel with its lush gardens.

Returning to the eastern side of Lapangan Merdeka, are two more colonial structures: the 1830 Gedung Pancasila on Jalan Taman Pejambon, where Sukarno unveiled the five principles of the Indonesian state (*Pancasila*),

⊘ Tip

Members of the Indonesian Heritage Society conduct free guided tours of the National Museum in English, French and Japanese. Call ahead (tel: 021-572 5870) or check the website (www.heritagejkt.org) for the latest schedule. Tours in English are Tue–Thu and Sat at 10am, with an extra Thursday tour at 1.30pm.

The National Museum.

⊘ BARACK OBAMA

Former US President Barack Obama lived in Menteng, Jakarta between the ages of six and ten. Going by his Indonesian stepfather's name, he was registered in St Francis of Assisi and Besuki Menteng primary schools as Barry Soetoro. As a child he spoke fluent Indonesian, and during his first presidential visit in 2010 he delighted the Indonesian public with a few remembered phrases in the language. Ahead of the visit, a group of expats raised funds and erected a statue of Obama as a child in Taman Menteng (Menteng Park). Although most Indonesians have a deep affection for Obama because of his local connection, there was controversy around the appropriateness of a monument to a foreign politician in a public place. The statue was eventually moved to Besuki Menteng School.

> **Tip**

The best stop for souvenir shopping is Pasaraya department store, packed with items from every corner of Indonesia, from Javanese batik to Dayak woodcarvings and Balinese art.

and the small Immanuel Church on Jalan Medan Merdeka Timur, built in 1835 and resembling a Greek temple.

Southeast of the square, a short ride down Jalan Cikini, are two other noteworthy attractions. **Taman Ismail Marzuki** (tel: 021- 2305 146; daily 7.30am–4pm) is a very impressive cultural centre that presents a programme of drama, dance and music from around Indonesia and the rest of the world. It also has a planetarium. Nearby, **Jalan Surabaya** is the city's so-called 'antique street', with dozens of shops selling everything from *wayang* (puppets) to ship fittings – little of it authentic.

SHOPPING AND DINING

There is no shortage of places in Jakarta to shop in air-conditioned comfort and find something good to eat. Hail a taxi and cruise west across the upper-class residential area, **Menteng**, to the **Welcome Statue**, a busy roundabout with a statue of two waving youths and a fountain. Jalan Thamrin runs north and south here,

turning into Jalan Sudirman a few more blocks south. The roundabout fountain is an urban anchor of Jakarta, built by Sukarno in the early 1960s and a favourite spot for generally peaceful political protests.

Surrounding the roundabout are the **Grand Indonesia Shopping Complex** and **Plaza Indonesia**, two of the best shopping malls in Jakarta, offering designer and local-label goods and a huge array of eateries. Next door to Plaza Indonesia is EX Plaza entertainment centre, attracting a younger crowd. The Grand Hyatt is perched above Plaza Indonesia and is a wonderful place for afternoon tea – a ceiling-to-floor bay window allows you to look out on the heart of the city.

Further north from the Welcome Statue, Sarinah is historic as the first department store in Indonesia, built in 1962. Recently renovated, this five-storey building has fashion and jewellery, art and handicrafts. There are some excellent upscale and midrange restaurants along Jalan K.H. Wahid

Turtles at Kepulauan Seribu.

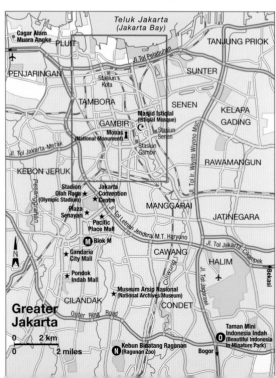

Haysim, running east from Sarinah, and a plethora of cheap street-side food stalls after dark on nearby Jalan Haji Agus Salim.

Further south on Jalan Sudirman, behind the Senayan sports field, home to national football games, is **Plaza Senayan**, another of the city's trendy shopping malls. **Senayan** City opposite Plaza Senayan is yet another shopping haven for branded goods and many food outlets.

The final stop for downtown shopping is **Pacific Place Mall** in the Sudirman Central Business District: branded shops, local and international restaurants, fitness centres, cinemas and megastores in one location.

Away from the city's heart is the middle-class **Blok M** ⓜ, bustling with street stalls and at least seven shopping malls, including Blok M Plaza and Blok M Mall, home of Pasaraya department store, which has a whole floor dedicated to Indonesian handicrafts and batik. In a wealthy southern suburb is **Pondak Indah Mall**. Two kilometres (1.25 miles) north is yet another upscale mall, **Gandaria City**.

SOUTH JAKARTA ATTRACTIONS

Still heading south, about 15km (9 miles) from the centre of the city, is **Ragunan Zoo** ⓝ (tel: 021-7884 7114; Tue–Sun 9am–4pm). Conditions are reasonable by general Indonesian standards; the grounds are pleasant, and the collection includes such iconic species as Komodo dragons, orangutans and Sumatran tigers.

Taman Mini Indonesia Indah ⓞ (Beautiful Indonesia in Miniature Park; tel: 021-8779 2078; Tue–Sun 8am–6pm) covers nearly 100 hectares (250 acres) of land near Kampung Rambutan. While not entirely successful in compressing the entire archipelago into a single attraction, the park none-theless permits you a glimpse of the many thousands of Indonesian islands

you will probably not visit. The various pavilions are each constructed in the traditional architectural style of a different Indonesian province. Housed inside each pavilion are interesting displays of handicrafts, traditional costumes, musical instruments and other artefacts for which each region is known.

In addition, there are at least 30 other attractions here, including a tropical bird park, orchid garden, IMAX cinema, cable car ride, transport museum, swimming pool, and the splendid **Museum Indonesia** (Tue–Sun 8am–6pm) – a three-storey Balinese palace filled with traditional textiles, houses, boats, puppets, jewellery and wedding costumes.

Also inside the park is **Museum Purna Bhakti Pertiwi** (Presidential Palace Museum; Tue–Sun 8am–6pm), established by the late First Lady Ibu Tien Suharto as a showcase for the family's private collection of antiques and art, along with the many diplomatic gifts Indonesia received while her husband was president.

Pasar Ikan's fish market.

ⓞ ISLAND GETAWAYS

One of the best ways to unwind and recapture a taste of the tropics after the bustle of Jakarta is to escape to clear blue waters and white-sand beaches at any one of the 600 small islands off the north coast of Jakarta, known as **Kepulauan Seribu** (Thousand Islands), one of Java's national parks.

Day trips can be taken to Bidadari, Kelor and Kahyangan islands near the coast. On Onrust island, explore the ruins of an old Dutch fort, which has remains of an 18th-century shipyard. Bokor and Rambut islands are home to bird sanctuaries; you need a permit from the national park office, PHKA, in Jakarta. Ferries depart every day from Ancol Marina (see page 142) to various islands between 8am–9am and return between 1.30pm–2pm. They can be contacted via mobile: 085 6163 6724 or on tel: 021-640 1140.

About 100km (60 miles) further out to sea lies a group of islands that have been developed into resorts: Pelangi, Putri, Matahari, Kotok, Ayer and Pantara. Each has fully equipped hotels with beachfront bungalows and restaurants. All bookings to island resorts have to be made in Jakarta through a travel agent. Activities include scuba diving, snorkelling, swimming and fishing. Diving gear can be rented on most of the islands, but check with your travel agent to confirm.

WESTERN JAVA

Homeland of the earthy Sundanese, western Java offers majestic volcanoes, several national parks, a wild and rugged coast and refreshingly cool highlands.

Western Java can be divided into two distinct regions: the volcanic highlands from Bogor east to Tasikmalaya; and the surrounding southern coastal plains. The highlands are dotted with volcanoes, rainforests and national parks, attracting trekkers and those wishing to escape from the lowland heat. There are a scattering of resorts along the scenic southern coast, while the lowland Ujung Kulon National Park on Java's southwestern tip harbours the country's last population of Javan rhinos.

This western region is culturally and linguistically distinct from the rest of Java. Indeed, for locals it is not part of Java at all; it is *Tanah Sunda* (Sunda Land), home of the Sundanese people, Indonesia's second largest ethnic group after the Javanese themselves. Local stereotypes see the Sundanese as less staid and refined than their Javanese neighbours, with an earthier sense of humour. Although also Sundanese, the people west of Bogor prefer to call themselves *Urang* Banten, or Bantenese. Historically, the Sundanese often strained against the dominance of the major Javanese empires, while the region later became a crucible of the colonial agricultural economy. Today traditional *angklung* music, *jaipongan* dances and lively *wayang*

golek performances endure, while Bandung has a well-earned reputation as a hub of modern Indonesia's pop music and entertainment industries.

BANTEN LAMA

Heading west from Jakarta on the Jakarta–Merak toll road for about 1.5 hours is historical **Banten Lama** (Old Banten) ❷, the gateway to the once-grand Banten sultanate. During the 16th and 17th centuries, this was one of Asia's largest and most cosmopolitan trading emporiums. Once a grand

Main attractions
Anyer and Carita beach resorts
Anak Krakatau volcano
Ujung Kulon National Park
Bogor Botanical Gardens
Puncak Pass
Cibodas Botanical Gardens
Gunung Gede-Pangrango National Park
Pangandaran and surrounds
Bandung

Map on page 150

Pilgrims visiting the 16th-century Masjid Agung mosque at Banten.

A fishing village at Banten Girang.

walled city, it went into decline after the emergence of Jayakarta (Jakarta) and the rise of the Dutch.

Today, it is a small town with several interesting historical sites, such as the ruins of a large palace (Surosowan), which has been partially excavated. Looming over the town is the 16th-century Masjid Agung (Grand Mosque) with a five-tiered roof typical of early Javanese Hindu-Islamic style. Climb the staircase to the top for a view. A small museum offers a glimpse into the seaport's great past. The Dutch fortress, Speelwijk, stands at the former river mouth. Between April and August, migratory birds flock by the thousands to the nearby islands of Pulau Dua and Pamojan Besar in Banten Bay.

Across the bridge is the Chinese Klenteng temple, one of the oldest in Java. The ruins of Banten Lama are 10km (6 miles) from Serang, also called Banten Girang (Upper Banten). It is best to go by hired car from Jakarta, or take a Jakarta–Serang bus, alight in Serang and then switch to a public minivan to the site.

WEST COAST BEACHES

From Banten Lama, head south to Java's sandy and secluded west coast beaches (2.5 hours, or 110km/70 miles west of Jakarta). At Cilegon, the road branches off to the right and continues 13km (8 miles) to **Merak**, where ferries depart for Bakauheni on Sumatra.

Branching south towards the beaches, there are numerous pretty bays and low-key developments mainly aimed at weekend trippers from nearby cities. At **Anyer** ❸, several large resorts grace the coastline surrounding Dutch-built Anyer Lighthouse. Continuing 6km (3.5 miles) south is Karang Bolong, a huge rock forming a natural archway to the sea. Its pleasant beach is a popular weekend swimming spot for Jakartans.

Another 10km (6 miles) south is **Carita**, with sandy beaches situated in a lovely cove. Here there is beachside accommodation, a marina and sailing, jet-skiing, diving and snorkelling. In addition to sun, sea, sand and solitude, this palm-fringed coast has stunning sunset views of **Anak Krakatau** (Child of

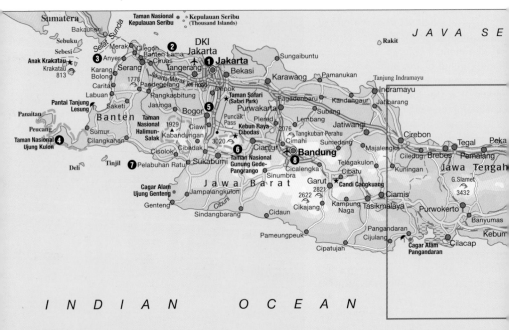

Krakatau). The original Krakatau volcano achieved lasting infamy in 1883, when it erupted with cataclysmic force, ripping out a huge chunk of the earth's crust to form a monstrous 40-sq km (16-sq mile) submarine caldera. The sea rushed in, and tidal waves up to 30 metres (100ft) high swept the coast, claiming more than 35,000 lives. Today, all that remains of the mighty volcano are Sertung, Panjang and Rakata at its crater rim.

In the decades that followed, undersea eruptions continued and a new peak emerged from the sea in 1927: Anak Krakatau. This is itself a highly active volcano, and a particularly violent eruption in 2018 led to a partial collapse of its caldera, triggering a tsunami which killed several hundred people and caused considerable damage in Carita and other coastal communities.

Boats can be chartered from Carita for day trips out to the volcano – best arranged through established travel agents and hotels. The journey takes four hours each way aboard a fishing boat (though some travel agencies have speedboats which make the crossing in under two hours). When volcanic conditions allow, it may still be possible to land on Anak Krakatau, but since the 2018 eruption most tours stick to nearby Rakata Island, a surviving fragment of the original, much larger Krakatau caldera. Rakata offers excellent views of the younger, active peak. Despite damage caused by the 2018 tsunami, there is still good snorkelling off Rakata, and camping is possible on the beaches on the east coast. It is also possible to land and to camp on the smaller Sertung Island, closer to Anak Krakatau itself. Krakatau is regularly monitored by volcanologists. Warnings will be posted if it is unsafe.

UJUNG KULON NATIONAL PARK

A Unesco Natural Heritage Site, **Ujung Kulon National Park ❹** is located south of Carita on the southwest tip of Java. A 420-sq km (260-sq mile) reserve, it is the last refuge for the highly endangered and seldom sighted Javan rhino. The park also has other interesting animals, including leopards, macaques, leaf monkeys, mousedeer, crocodiles

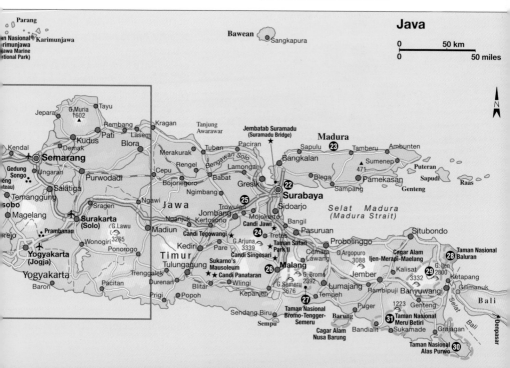

and *banteng* (wild oxen). Much of the area is dense lowland rainforest, open woodlands, and wetlands – excellent for birdwatching – with beaches in the north and south.

Peucang island, north of the mainland portion of the park, has basic bungalows and a restaurant, where deer, monkeys and monitor lizards are a common sight. About 10 minutes by boat from Peucang is Cidaon, the grazing ground for *banteng* and Javan peacocks. The highlight of the park experience is a canoe ride starting from **Handeuleum** island up the Cigenter River, where scientists monitor the Javan rhino activity. **Panaitan**, the largest of the offshore islands, is a good spot for diving and fishing. It's covered by hilly rainforest; there are several prehistoric Hindu statues at Gunung Raksa.

The best time of year to visit is during the dry season, from April to September. A permit is required from the PHKA (national park) office in Labuan (15 minutes south of Carita), where accommodation, guide and transport can also be arranged. It is usually a

5-hour boat ride each way between Labuan and Peucang. Note that this can be a rough crossing in bad weather.

BOGOR

The most scenic of West Java's major routes extends to the south of Jakarta, with the ascent to the dramatic Priangan highlands. First stop is **Bogor ⑤** – only an hour's drive or a short train ride from central Jakarta. Situated about 500 metres (1,640ft) above sea level, the city is appreciably cooler (and wetter) than the coast. The main attraction here is the glorious **Kebun Raya** (Botanical Gardens; tel: 0251-831 1362; daily 8am–4pm). Established by the Dutch in 1817, it became worldrenowned during the 19th century for its wide range of tropical botanical specimens and research into cash crops such as tea, cassava, tobacco and cinchona. The vast park with its rolling lawns, lily ponds and forest groves contains 15,000 species of trees and plants (including 400 types of palms) and orchid nurseries.

The elegant white **Istana Bogor** (Presidential Palace) stands at the northern end of the gardens. Constructed by the Dutch in 1856 as the official residence for the governors-general of the Dutch East Indies, it was a favourite hideaway of President Sukarno and contains paintings and sculpture from his vast collection. Sukarno lived here while he was under 'house arrest' from 1967 until his death three years later. A permit is required to visit the palace, obtainable from the State Secretariat (ask your hotel to arrange).

Bogor is home to a number of traditional craft workshops. Across the road from the Istana and down an alley is Pak Dase's **Sundanese *wayang golek*** (wooden puppet) **workshop** (Lebak Kantin RT 02/VI; tel: 0251-838 3758). Visitors can watch the puppets being made and see performances. Elsewhere, at the family-run **gong and gamelan 'factory'** (Jl. Pancasan 17,

The Istana Bogor within Bogor's magnificent Botanical Gardens.

Bogor; tel: 0251-832 4132), visitors can see how traditional instruments are forged from copper in tin by barefooted men over an open-pit fire.

COOL MOUNTAIN AIR

East of Bogor is a favourite getaway for Jakartans, **Puncak Pass** (puncak means 'summit'). Its cool, clean mountain air offers welcome relief from the oppressive lowland heat, but it can become very crowded over weekends and holidays because of its accessibility to the capital. The main road is lined with small hotels and restaurants, while further on are manicured landscapes of tea plantations. The 168-hectare (400-acre) **Taman Safari** (Safari Park; tel: 0251-825 0000; daily 8am–5pm) is ideal for families. An open-air recreational park where lions, tigers, bears and giraffes forage in the open occupies one section; in the other there are rides for kids, educational animal shows and eateries.

Beyond Puncak Pass, a turn-off to the right leads to **Cibodas Botanical Gardens**, an extension of Bogor's Kebun Raya, and outstanding for its collection of montane and temperate flora from around the world. Next to the gardens' main gate is the entrance to **Gunung Gede-Pangrango National Park** ❻ (closed to trekkers and climbers Jan–Mar and Aug). The oldest national park in Indonesia (founded in 1889) and a Unesco World Network of Biospheres Reserve, it is spread across the upper incline of two volcanoes. Its 15,000 hectares (37,000 acres) are home to rare Javan gibbons and leaf monkeys – both of which are often spotted – as well as a few leopards and a variety of bird species.

Cibeureum waterfall is a 90-minute walk from the park information centre at the main gate. Serious climbers can ascend Gunung Gede (2,958 metres/9,705ft) or Gunung Pangrango (3,020 metres/9,905ft), both requiring overnight stays and appropriate

clothing for cold nights. Technically, hiking permits should be obtained at least two days in advance from the PHKA (national park, tel: 0263-512 776) office in Cibodas, though foreigners are generally able to pay and obtain a permit on the spot.

Good accommodation and food are available in the nearby **Cipanas** mountain resort, a base for hiking through highland forests and tea estates, and other activities.

HALIMUN-SALAK NATIONAL PARK

West of Gede-Pangrango National Park is another range of mountains. **Halimun-Salak National Park** (halimun means 'misty mountain'), established in 1992, covers 113 hectares (280 acres) and is home to endemic Javan eagles, leopards and gibbons, as well as a multitude of insects and reptiles. The easiest access is from Kabandungan, about one hour south of Ciawi, where the head office and visitor information centre is located. Report for a permit, then continue another two hours west

> **⊙ Tip**
>
> In Puncak, stop by the historic Puncak Pass resort, built in 1928, where there are spectacular views of the valley below. Specialities at the restaurant include delicious pancakes and a refreshing drink, *wedang jahe* (hot ginger tea).

Tea-picking near Puncak Pass.

⊘ Tip

For detailed and up-to-date information on trekking routes on the volcanoes of West Java – and hundreds of other peaks around Indonesia, check the brilliant Gunung Bagging website (www.gunungbagging.com). It hosts the first concerted effort to categorise the countries *gunung* (mountains) for trekkers, coining the designation *Ribu* ('thousand') for summits with an all-round prominence of at least 1,000 metres.

A Hindu ritual sacrifice off the coast at Pelabuhan Ratu.

on an unpaved bumpy road to Cikaniki research station for lodging. A guided canopy trail walk and rainforest trek to Citalahab tea plantation are offered.

SOUTH COAST BEACHES

From Ciawi, the road continues south over the pass between Gunung Pangrango and Gunung Salak to the village of **Pelabuhan Ratu** ❼, where the ragged, wind-lashed Indian Ocean foams and crashes onto smooth black-sand beaches. When the boats moor in the morning, the fish market does a roaring trade in freshly caught tuna, prawns, whitebait, sharks, stingrays and other delicacies. A number of good swimming beaches and hotels line the coast for several kilometres past the town, but be warned that the surf and undertow can be treacherous. Pelabuhan Ratu is part of the southern coastline that many locals believe is guarded by the legendary Kanjeng Ratu Kidul, the Queen of the Southern Ocean. Room 308 at the Samudra Beach Hotel remains empty and is reserved for the queen. There is a bat

cave about 1km (.6 mile) out of town; at sunset thousands take to the sky.

BANDUNG, CITY OF FLOWERS

East of Ciawi, the road leads to **Bandung** ❽, another cool escape from Jakarta's oppressive heat. Located in a huge basin 700 metres (2,300ft) above sea level and surrounded by lofty volcanic peaks, it is a prosperous city with over 2.3 million inhabitants. Before World War II, it was a quaint Dutch administrative and university town of about 150,000 and was known as the Paris of Java for its shady boulevards and expensive shops. Although it is now a rapidly growing industrial city, Bandung still has a pleasant climate and fine surrounds. It is often called Kota Kembang (City of Flowers).

Bandung's foremost industry is education, with more than 27 colleges and universities and thousands of students. But there is plenty for travellers, with an abundance of Dutch colonial **Art Deco architecture**, including the magnificent Gedung Sate, built in 1920 and home to the provincial government.

Browsing in factory outlet shops along Jalan Cihampelas, a feast for the eye as well as the pocket, is a popular pastime. Many of the shops have quirky facades fashioned from papier mâché, chrome or plywood. One even has King Kong peering down; another, a dinosaur crashing through a roof.

The **Museum Geologi** (Geological Museum, Jalan Diponegoro No. 57; tel: 022-721 3822; Sat–Thu 9am–3.30pm) is worth a visit for its extraordinary array of rocks, maps and fossils, including replicas of the famous Java Man or *Homo erectus* skulls found in Central Java. The campus of Bandung's Institute of Technology (ITB), Indonesia's oldest and finest university established by the Dutch, is also worth a visit. It has an interesting library built in the 1920s.

Spend some time, too, wandering around Jalan Braga, the old Dutch shopping district, and take a look into the remodelled Art Deco Savoy Homann Bidakara Hotel on Jalan Asia-Afrika. The town's large flower market is also nearby on Jalan Wastukencana. In the evenings, many theatres and clubs present Sundanese dance performances; check with your hotel or tour office for details.

AN ACCESSIBLE VOLCANO

Surrounding Bandung are the Priangan highlands (roughly, 'Abode of the Gods') with vistas of manicured tea plantations, hot springs, waterfalls and the easiest-to-visit volcano in Java, **Gunung Tangkuban Perahu** (Overturned Boat Mountain), 30km (20 miles) north of the city. From Lembang, an old Dutch resort town surrounded by fruit, vegetable and flower farms, head east 9km (5.5 miles) to the park entrance and another 4km (2.5 miles) to the crater's rim. Morning clouds mix with sulphurous fumes rising from a perfect bowl-shaped centre to create a spectacular scene, surrounded by souvenir shops and restaurants. There are also several other smaller craters to hike around; exploration is best carried out during the dry season from April to September. Some 7km (4 miles) beyond Tangkuban Perahu is **Ciater**, where hot springs offer a soothing soak amid tea and clove estates.

Mist-shrouded Gunung Tangkuban Perahu, Java's most accessible volcano.

Krakatau erupting.

⦿ FROM BANDUNG TO PANGANDARAN

The 210km (130-mile) route southeast from Bandung to Pangandaran beach on the southern coast is both scenic and historic. A two-hour drive from Bandung brings you to the mountainous Garut regency. Here, the only Hindu temple in West Java, Candi Cangkuang, is found in Leles village. Guesthouses at the village of **Cipanas** feature naturally heated water flowing from subterranean springs beneath Gunung Guntur. Hikes to another local volcano, Gunung Papandayan, take in steam geysers, bubbling mud pools and fumaroles. The nearby town of **Garut** is known for its distinctive batik.

On the way from Garut to Tasikmalaya is **Kampung Naga**, where villagers still hold to their ancestors' rules and traditional way of life focused on simplicity in living and respect for the environment. **Tasikmalaya** is well known for its cottage industries: colourful paper umbrellas, batik, embroidery and *kelom geulis* (wooden clogs).

A further four-hour drive southeast via Ciamis leads to **Pangandaran**, a low-key beach resort on a narrow isthmus leading to a small nature reserve, home to *banteng*, deer, hornbills and grey langurs. Sunrises and sunsets are particularly spectacular here; local boat owners take visitors for a closer look at the marine park. Thirty kilometres (18 miles) west is **Green Canyon**, where caves and karst landscapes dominate, and the charmingly sleepy village of **Batu Karas**, which has excellent surfing conditions.

Making traditional batik,
Yogyakarta.

CENTRAL JAVA

The glorious past of this volcano-studded region lives on today in the cultural capital of Yogyakarta and the spectacular World Heritage Sites of Borobudur and Prambanan.

Lapped by the Java Sea to the north and the Indian Ocean to the south, the landscape of Central Java is one of fertile agricultural fields dotted with forested volcanoes. The region's highlands, including mighty Gunung Merapi and less volatile Gunung Merbabu, give climbers, trekkers and birdwatchers ample reasons to come often and stay longer. Off the north coast, the Karimunjawa islands attract divers. To the south, the tempestuous Indian Ocean is flanked by beaches – some of black volcanic sand, some white-sand. Part of the south coast is marked by a limestone karst mountain range riddled with caves, very few of which have been explored.

Central Java's 35 million inhabitants live primarily in rural areas, where population densities are high. In the hinterland they are farmers and on the coasts they are fishermen, with a large number of handicraft-makers scattered throughout. North coast Semarang is the only major industrial city.

This region was the heartland of major historical empires – the Hindu-Buddhist Mataram and its later Muslim namesake – and it is still the bastion of refined Javanese culture where the status of storied royal courts endures in the 21st century. Often it is the cultural attractions that draw visitors here: the sombre stillness of ancient Hindu and Buddhist temples, the sequestered courtyards of its 18th-century Islamic palaces and the traditional arts.

Much of interest is concentrated in and around the twin court cities, Yogyakarta (pronounced 'Jogjakarta' and often abbreviated to Yogya or Jogja) and Surakarta (also known as Solo). But Central Java is also home to spectacular rural landscapes, and memorable sights set deep amongst the volcanic uplands: Dieng, the Gedung Songo and the mountains temples of Gunung Lawu.

Main attractions
Yogyakarta
Borobudur
Dieng Plateau
Prambanan
Surakarta (Solo)
Gunung Lawu temples

**Maps on pages
158, 166**

A tobacco crop on the fertile soil of Central Java.

Bedoyo dancers at the Sultan's Palace in Yogyakarta, c.1860.

YOGYAKARTA AND ITS REGION

Sprawling **Yogyakarta** (Yogya or Jogja) is situated at the very core of an ancient region known as Mataram, site of the first great Central Javanese kingdoms. From the 8th to the early 10th century, this fertile plain was ruled by a succession of Indianised kings – the builders of Borobudur, Prambanan and dozens of other elaborate stone monuments. Around AD 900, these rulers suddenly and inexplicably shifted their capital to East Java, and Central Java became a sleepy backwater.

At the end of the 16th century, the area was revived by a new Islamic power based at Kota Gede, east of present-day Jogja. This second Mataram dynasty was founded around 1575 by King Panembahan Senopati.

The Yogyakarta and Surakarta (Solo) sultanates came into being in 1755 after a lengthy civil war. A Dutch-brokered peace treaty saw Mataram partitioned and two separate royal capitals established. These were later partitioned in turn, in part as a European tactic to further diminish their potential power. Surakarta is home to a secondary royal household, the Mangkunegaran, while Yogyakarta's secondary court is the Pakualaman.

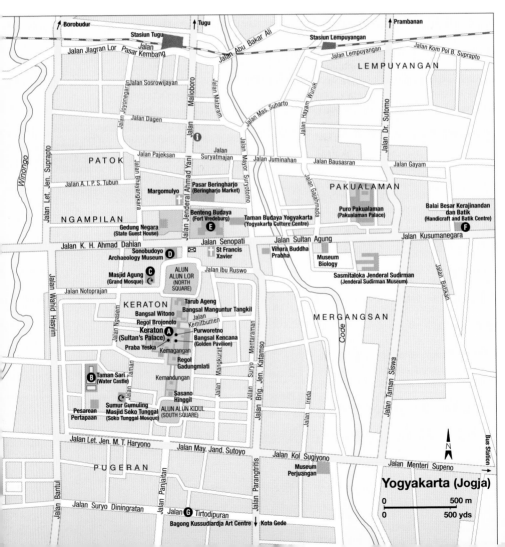

Yogyakarta (Jogja)

0   500 m
0   500 yds

Relations between the royal courts and the European colonialists were often strained. In 1812 the British launched a devastating assault on Yogyakarta which saw the entire palace archive and treasury looted by British forces. Following the return of the Dutch the region was ravaged by the Java War (1825–30), led by the charismatic Yogyakarta prince, Pangeran Diponegoro, for whom streets in towns all over modern Indonesia are named.

In more recent times, Jogja served as the capital of the troubled Indonesian republic for four years during the fight against the Dutch, from 1945 until 1949. The then sultan (Hamengkubuwono IX) was an enthusiastic supporter of the revolutionary movement, and as a reward his kingdom was maintained after independence. Uniquely in republican Indonesia, the Yogyakarta court still has official status, and the reigning sultan is the appointed governor of the surrounding Special Administrative Region. Further east in Surakarta, the court had kept aloof from the republicans, and was later stripped of its legal standing as a consequence.

THE SULTAN'S PALACE

Today, it is Jogja's cultural attractions that travellers come to see – ancient temples, palaces, batik, gamelan, dances and *wayang* puppet performances. Growing in popularity are nature-related activities. The city is a mere hour by plane from Jakarta or nine hours by express train; from Bali, it is 1.5 hours by air or 12 hours by bus. Jogja is easy to get around: there are plenty of taxis, public buses and man-powered *becak* (pedicab).

The first stop is the **Keraton Ⓐ** (Sultan's Palace; Sat–Thu 8am–1.30pm, Fri 8am–noon), a two-centuries-old palace complex that stands at the heart of the city. According to Javanese cosmological beliefs, the ruler is literally the 'navel' or central 'spike' of the universe, anchoring the temporal world and communicating with the mystical realm. In this scheme of things, the Keraton is both the capital of the kingdom and the hub of the cosmos.

A coat of arms at Surakarta's Keraton Kasunanan.

A keris dagger.

A pavilion in the Keraton grounds.

The palace houses not only the sultan and his family, but also the dynastic regalia *(pusaka)*, private meditation and ceremonial chambers, a magnificent throne hall, several audience and performance pavilions, a mosque, an immense royal garden, stables, barracks, an armaments foundry and two expansive parade grounds planted with sacred banyan trees – all laid out in a carefully conceived complex of walled compounds, narrow lanes and massive gateways, and bounded by a fortified outer wall measuring 2km (1.5 miles) on every side.

Construction of the Keraton began in 1755 and continued for almost 40 years, throughout the long reign of Hamengkubuwono I. Today, only the innermost compound is considered the Keraton proper, while the maze of lanes and lesser compounds, the mosque and the two vast squares, have been integrated into the working city. Long sections of the outermost wall remain, and many of the residences inside are still owned and occupied by members of the royal family.

To step within the massive inner walls is to enter a patrician world of grace. In the first half of the 20th century, the interior was remodelled along European lines, incorporating Italian marble, cast-iron columns, crystal chandeliers and rococo furnishings into a classical Javanese setting. The 'Golden Pavilion' or **Bangsal Kencana** (central throne hall) is its most striking feature – a *pendopo* or open pavilion consisting of an ornate sloping roof supported at the centre by four massive wooden columns.

There is much more to see within the Keraton, including the Keraton and Royal Carriage Museums, ancient gamelan sets, and two great *kala*-head gateways.

PURO PAKUALAM

About 2km (1.2 miles) east of the Keraton is Jogja's second palace, **Puro Pakualam**. Following the 1812 British attack on Yogyakarta, in an effort to further undermine the power of the court the then lieutenant-governor, Thomas Stamford Raffles, created a separate

principality within the sultanate. A junior prince and British ally, Notokusumo, was handed this second throne, under the hereditary title Pakualam. The Pakualaman palace remains the official residence of the current prince (Pakualam X) as well as a museum (Tue, Thu and Sun 9.30am–2.30pm); performances are held here too.

TAMAN SARI

Behind the Keraton stand the ruins of the royal pleasure garden, **Taman Sari ❸** (daily 8am–3.30pm). It was constructed over many years by Hamengkubuwono I, beginning in 1758 and then abruptly abandoned after his death. Dutch representatives to the sultan's court marvelled at its large artificial lake, the 'Water Castle' mansion, underground passageways, meditation retreats and series of sunken bathing pools.

The ruins of the mansion occupy high ground at the northern end of the huge Taman Sari complex, overlooking a batik makers' colony. The crumbling walls and a massive gate are all

that remain of the building. A tunnel behind the castle leads to a complex of three restored bathing pools, **Umbul Bindangun**. The large central pool was designed for the use of queens, concubines and princesses, while the small southernmost pool was reserved for the sultan.

Further south, tucked amid a crowded *kampung* (village), lies **Pesarean Pertapaan**, an interesting royal retreat reached by passing through an ornate archway west of the bathing area, then following a winding path to the left. The main structure, a small Chinese-style temple with a forecourt and galleries, is said to be where the sultan and his sons meditated for seven days and nights at a time.

The most remarkable structure at Taman Sari is the **Sumur Gumuling** (circular well), a *masjid* (mosque) with a well as its centrepiece. Folklore says the secret tunnels found there (now collapsed) led to the sea where the sultan could commune with Kanjeng Ratu Kidul, the powerful Goddess of the Southern Ocean, to whom all

The Taman Sari water palace.

Wayang kulit shadow-puppet play at Sonobudoyo Archaeological Museum.

☉ Tip

A good way to explore Jogja is by *becak*, a three-wheeled man-powered pedicab, or *andong* (horse cart). Confirm the fare upfront, then enjoy the ride through scenic backstreets.

Mataram rulers had been promised in marriage by the dynasty's founder and from whom they are said to derive their mystical powers. Access is by an underground passageway, whose entrance lies to the west of the Water Castle. The 'well' is in fact a sunken atrium, with circular galleries facing onto a small, round pool.

Southeast of the Taman Sari lies the smaller of the two grass-covered royal squares (*alun-alun*), rather more peaceful and attractive than its larger northern counterpart. At night food and drink stalls pop up along its edges. It is possible to get up onto the well-preserved ramparts nearby.

JALAN MALIOBORO

Jogja's main thoroughfare, **Jalan Malioboro**, begins in front of the royal audience pavilion, at the front of the palace, and ends at a *tugu* (monument) dedicated to the guardian serpent spirit Kyai Jaga some 2km (1.25 miles) to the north. Jalan Malioboro derives its name from the Sanskrit words *malya bhara*, meaning 'garland bearing', as the royal processional route was always adorned with bouquets during ceremonial occasions.

Today, Jalan Malioboro is primarily a shopping district, though it is also an area of historical and cultural interest. Begin at the northern town square (*alun-alun*) and stroll up the street, stopping first at the **Masjid Agung** ☉ (Grand Mosque), built in 1773, and notice the two fenced-off banyan trees standing in the centre of the square. They symbolise the balance of opposing forces within the Javanese kingdom.

Nearby, on the northwestern side of the square, is **Sonobudoyo Archaeology Museum** ☉ (Tue–Thu 8am–1.30pm, Fri 8–11am, Sat–Sun 8am–noon). Opened in 1935 by the Java Institute, a cultural foundation of wealthy Javanese and Dutch art patrons, today the museum houses important collections of prehistoric artefacts, Hindu-Buddhist bronzes, *wayang* puppets, dance costumes and traditional Javanese weapons.

Proceed northwards from the square through the gates and out across Jogja's main intersection. Immediately ahead on the right stands the old Dutch garrison, **Benteng Budaya** ☉ (Fort Vredeburg; tel: 0274-586 934; Tue–Thu 8.30am–2pm, Fri 8.30–11am, Sat 8.30am–noon), a museum and cultural centre complete with exhibition and performance halls. Opposite, on the left, stands the State Guest House. It was first the Dutch resident's mansion and, during the revolution, was also used as the presidential palace. Further along on the right, past the fort, is the huge central market, **Pasar Beringharjo** (9am–4pm), a rabbit warren of small stalls selling everything from fresh fruits and vegetables to batik, 'antiques' and hardware. Bargain hard here.

Back out on Malioboro, both sides of the street are lined with handicraft shops selling a great range of batik, leather goods and endless knick-knacks. At dusk (4–10pm) the

Getting around by becak (pedicab).

sidewalks explode into an incredible street market of handicraft stalls and food and drink stands. Taste-test some of the traditional snacks such as *onde-onde* (rice flour balls filled with sweet mung bean paste), *lumpia* (spring rolls), *klepon* (green-coloured balls filled with palm sugar) or steamed coconut-coated *putu*.

PERFORMING ARTS

Of the many art forms, *wayang kulit* or shadow-puppet play lies closest to the heart of the Central Javanese. All-night performances for *selamatan* ritual feasts, weddings or ceremonies occur regularly, often in village compounds. In addition to weekly *wayang kulit* plays at the Keraton, there is an eight-hour presentation on the second Saturday of every month at the **Sasano Hinggil** (daily 9am–5pm), near the Keraton. **Sonobudoyo Archaeological Museum** (Jalan Trikora No. 6; tel: 0274-376 775) holds *wayang kulit* shows daily except Sunday (8–10pm, closed the night before public holidays; camera fee). Dance and music performances, both traditional and contemporary, as well as changing visual art exhibitions, are held at **Taman Budaya Yogyakarta** (Jalan Sriwedari No.1; tel: 0274-523 512). Check the programme on arrival to see what is currently on offer.

Court dances are also taught outside the Keraton at a number of private schools and government art academies in the city. The performances within the Keraton itself should not be missed, but also check out **Bagong Kussudiardja Art Centre** (Kembaran Rt. 04 Rw. 21 No. 148 Tamantirto, Kasihan, Bantul, in southern Jogja; tel: 0274-41 4404), a large performing arts complex dedicated to creating new works within the framework of classical music, dance and theatre. Free monthly performances are open to the public.

Perhaps the ultimate Javanese dance spectacular is the Ramayana Ballet, a modernised version of the story of Rama and Sita performed with the floodlit Prambanan temples as a backdrop (see page 171). Tickets can be arranged through most hotels and travel agents in Jogja.

BATIK TOWN

Jogja's most famous handicraft is still batik, now a Unesco Cultural Heritage icon. Visit the **Balai Besar Kerajinan-dan dan Batik ❻** (Handicraft and Batik Centre) on Jalan Kusumanegara. An individually guided tour costs nothing, and is an excellent introduction to the craft's painstaking manufacturing process, as well as to the staggering variety of patterns and colours to be found throughout Java. Batik courses are taught here and at other centres.

Batik cloth is produced and sold all over Jogja, but especially in the south of the city on **Jalan Tirtod-ipuran ❼**, a street with more than 25 batik workshops and showrooms, most of which are happy to let visitors observe production. Many of the city's better-known artists, and a number

Reprising the roles of Rama and Sita in a classical dance-drama.

The extraordinary Sumur Gumuling mosque.

of aspiring ones, also produce batik paintings made with the same resist-dye method, but specifically designed for framing and hanging. For lower-quality souvenir batik cloths and clothing go to Pasar Beringharjo or Mirota Batik, both on Jalan Malioboro.

KOTA GEDE

Long before Yogyakarta was established, **Kota Gede** ⑩, 4km (2.5 miles) southeast of Jogja, was founded in 1575 by Sultan Panembahan Senopati as the first capital of the Mataram Empire, where it remained until his successor moved it to Kerta. During its golden years, Kota Gede attracted a myriad of wealthy traders, including Arab and Dutch, who built mansions in exceptional architectural styles.

A pleasant way to arrive is by *andong* (horse-drawn carriage), about a 20-minute ride from Jalan Malioboro. Now known for its silversmiths, it is an interesting place to stroll around. Accommodation is available in some of the historic buildings, and there is also a restaurant.

Parangtritis beach.

About 500 metres (yards) behind the *pasar* (traditional market) is the **Kota Gede Royal Cemetery** (Mon 10am–noon, Fri 1.30pm–4pm) dating back to Mataram times. Javanese attire, which can be rented from the cemetery attendants, is required to enter to see the graves of Senopati and other important figures. While in the area, you may like to visit **Monggo Chocolate Factory** (Jalan Dalem KG III; tel: 0274-373 192; daily 8am–6pm) to see 'Belgian' chocolate being made, using Indonesia cacao of course.

BEACHES, CAVING AND CLIMBING

The Indian Ocean is less than an hour's drive south of central Yogyakarta. **Parangtritis** ⑪, a wonderful stretch of black sand backed by towering bluffs, is both a popular recreation spot and a place of worship, where the legendary Kanjeng Ratu Kidul, Queen of the Southern Ocean, is said to live. The rip tides are dangerous here, so swimming is forbidden. Nearby is the sacred **Parangkusumo beach**. Every year on 30 Rajab of the Javanese calendar (ask a local to check for you), a ceremony called Labuhan Alit is held to commemorate the coronation of the Yogyakarta Sultan and offerings are given to Ratu Kidul. The beaches can be done in a day trip from Jogja, but basic lodgings are available if you prefer to stay the night. There are great sunsets on Parangtritis hill, east of the beach.

Twenty kilometres (12 miles) southwest of Jogja via Bantul city are **Samas** and **Pandansimo beaches**. Both with the same stormy shores as Parangtritis, Samas is home to a village-run sea turtle conservation project, and Pandansimo is a Javanese pilgrimage site. For swimming beaches, some with white sand, head 60km (40 miles) southeast of Jogja to Baron, Krakal, Kukup, Sepanjang, Drini, Sundak, Ngandong, Siung, Wedi Ombo, Sandang or Ngrenehan. While all are excellent choices for a day of relaxation away from the city's traffic, **Ngrenehan** is the best place to have a swim and enjoy some freshly caught fish cooked to order at a local restaurant. At Ngobaran beach, 5 minutes from Ngrenehan by car, is Kejawen Hindu temple, built in 2005.

North of the beaches rises the **Gunung Sewu mountain range**, a length of karst limestone hills perforated by caves. Only a few have been explored, but with the cooperation of villagers who have developed homestays as part of a community project, two have been sufficiently explored by a local caving group to allow novices to participate in the adrenalin rush. The first, Jomblang, requires a vertical rappel down an inclined wall where there is a surprising subterranean forest, fed by the sun and rainfall entering through an enormous, gaping hole at the entrance. Connected to Jomblang by a horizontal corridor is Grubug, a much riskier descent. A river flowing into Grubug is raftable in the rainy season. Nearby, on Siung beach, enormous limestone walls prove popular with cliff climbers. A paragliding jamboree is held in this area when the winds are favourable, March–April.

North of Jogja is volatile **Gunung Merapi**, popular with climbers. There is also excellent trekking and birdwatching further north on **Gunung Merbabu**. From Kopeng on its southern flank to Kenteng Songo, one of its two peaks, takes between 8 and 10 hours. The drive there via the Selo Pass affords fabulous volcano views.

HANDICRAFTS AROUND JOGJA

The villages around Jogja specialise in handmade crafts. Shopping in the villages where the items are made means the craftsmen – not a middleman – reap the benefits with profits going back into the local area. It's also a good way to get a look at real life in the countryside. South of Jogja are Kasongan and Panjangrejo, which make earthenware pottery; Kota Gede is known for its delicate filigree silverwork; Manding produces leather bags, belts, shoes and jackets; wooden masks and other woodcarvings are

Kota Gede gateway.

found in Sendangsari-Krebet and Patuk; and *wayang* puppets and hand-forged ceremonial *keris* blades are specialities of Imogiri.

For authentic *keris* (ceremonial daggers; see page 175) – not the tourist variety sold at souvenir shops – Empu Sungkowo *(keris* maker) Harum Brodjo (Gatak, Sumberagung, Moyudan, Sleman; tel: 81-2273 1372) is a master craftsman. It takes two months to finish one dagger. You must make an appointment to visit him.

BOROBUDUR AND THE DIENG PLATEAU

The approach to the Unesco World Heritage Site at **Borobudur ⑫** (daily 6am–5pm; licensed guides available) passes through busy roadside communities and rich agricultural countryside. Allow yourself a minimum of two hours to tour the candi (temple), though you could easily spend half a day here. This huge mandala, the world's largest Buddhist monument, was built sometime during the relatively short Sailendra dynasty between AD 778 and AD 856

– 300 years before Angkor Wat and 200 years before Notre-Dame. Yet, within little more than a century of its completion, Borobudur and the other structures in Central Java were mysteriously abandoned as the focus of Javanese royal power shifted to the east.

BOROBUDUR'S RESTORATION

In 1900, the Dutch government established a committee for the organised restoration of Borobudur. The initial task was accomplished between 1907 and 1911 by a Dutch military engineer with a keen interest in Javanese antiquities.

At this time, Borobudur was discovered to be a fragile mantle of stone blocks that had been built upon a natural mound of earth. Rainwater was seeping through the stone and eroding the soft foundation from within, while mineral salts were collecting on the monument's surface, where they acted in conjunction with sun, wind, rain and fungus to destroy it. Grandiose plans for a permanent restoration were never realised, due to the intervention of two world wars and an economic depression.

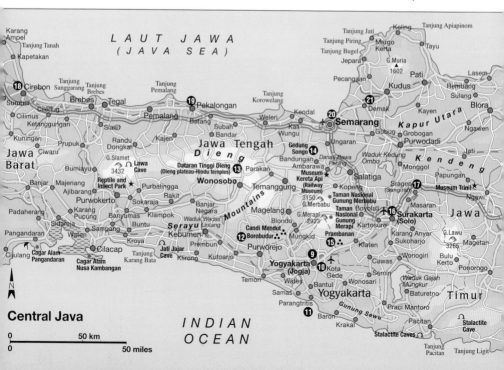

Central Java

During the 1950s and 1960s, it became increasingly evident that Borobudur was structurally endangered. Unesco was called to direct a rescue operation. Technical assistance and financing became available, and the project officially got under way in 1975. The scale of the project was spectacular. It took nine long years to dismantle, catalogue, photograph, clean, treat and reassemble a total of 1,300,232 stone blocks. Each stone had to be individually inspected, scrubbed and chemically treated before being replaced. In addition, a new infrastructure of reinforced concrete, tar, asphalt, epoxy and tin was constructed to support the entire monument, and a system of drainage pipes installed to prevent further seepage.

In the end, the work was completed at a cost of US$25 million, more than three times the original estimate. It is unlikely that the full import of Borobudur as a religious monument will ever be known. An estimated 30,000 stonecutters and sculptors, 15,000 labourers and thousands more masons worked to build the original monument. At a time when the entire population of Central Java numbered less than one million, this represented perhaps 10 percent of the available workforce to a single effort.

BOROBUDUR'S SPIRITUAL SIGNIFICANCE

Seen from the air, Borobudur forms a mandala, a geometric aid for meditation. Seen from a distance on the ground, Borobudur is a stupa, a model of the cosmos in three vertical parts: a square base supporting a hemispheric body and a crowning spire. The traditional pilgrimage route approaches from the east, and ascends the terraced monument, circumambulating each terrace clockwise in succession to see how every relief and carving contributes to the whole.

There were originally 10 levels at Borobudur, each falling within one of the three divisions of the Mahayana Buddhist universe: *khamadhatu*, the lower spheres of human life; *rupadhatu*, the middle sphere of 'form';

Traditional batik at the Brahama Tirta Sari Studio in Yogyakarta.

⊘ CULTURAL SYNTHESIS

Yogyakarta takes its name from Ayodhya, mythical Indian birthplace of the Hindu god Rama. That such a name – in full 'Ngayogyakarta Hadiningrat' – was chosen in 1755 for the capital of a state inhabited entirely by Muslims is a clear indication of the continuity between the Hindu-Buddhist and Muslim eras in Java. In fact, Yogyakarta in its late-18th-century heyday represented the culmination of what scholars have termed Java's 'mystic synthesis' of Islam and other cultural elements.

The city is laid out according to ancient Javanese principles along the mystical axis which runs from the summit of Gunung Merapi to the coast, and which intersects at right angles with the qibla alignment to Mecca, indicated by the Masjid Agung alongside the northern royal square.

and *arupadhatu*, the higher sphere of detachment from the world. The lowest gallery of reliefs, now covered, depicts the delights of this world and the damnations of the next.

The next five levels (the processional terrace and four concentric galleries) show in their reliefs (beginning at the eastern staircase and going around each gallery clockwise) the life of Prince Siddhartha on his way to becoming the Buddha, scenes from the Jataka folk tales about his previous incarnations, and the life of the Bodhisattva Sudhana (from the Gandavyuha). These tales are illustrated in stone by a parade of commoners, princes, musicians, dancing girls and saints, with many interesting details of daily life in ancient Java. Placed in niches above the galleries are 432 stone Buddhas, each displaying one of five mudra or hand positions, alternately calling upon the earth as witness and embodying charity, meditation, fearlessness and reason.

Above the square galleries, three circular terraces support 72

Reliefs show scenes from the Buddha's life.

Intricate detail at Borobudur, the work of some 30,000 craftsmen.

perforated *dagoba*s (miniature stupas), which are unique in Buddhist art. Most contain a statue of the meditating *Dhyani* Buddha. Two statues have been left uncovered to gaze over the nearby Menoreh Mountains, where a series of knobs and knolls is said to represent Gunadharma, the temple's divine architect. These three terraces are, in fact, transitional steps leading to the tenth and highest level, the realm of formlessness and abstraction *(arupadhatu)*, embodied in the huge crowning stupa.

Before leaving the park, have a look at two **museums** near the exit gate. One houses stones, Buddha images and other pieces from the original structure. The other houses an outrigger ship built to replicate vessels seen on the reliefs. The ship undertook an expedition to Madagascar in 2003–4, recreating a trade route that might have been used when Borobudur was constructed almost two millennia ago (the Madagascan language is related to the main languages of Indonesia). Every year, thousands of Buddhists arrive from all over Asia to walk in procession from nearby Mendut temple to Borobudur in celebration of Waisak (date changes annually), the holiest day of the year for Buddhists.

PAWON AND MENDUT

Two smaller, subsidiary *candi* lie along a straight line directly east of Borobudur. The closer of the two is tiny **Candi Pawon** (meaning 'kitchen' or 'crematorium'; daily 6am–sunset), situated in a shady clearing 1.7km (1 mile) from Borobudur's main entrance. It is often referred to as Borobudur's 'porch temple' because of its proximity, and may well have been the last stop on a brick-paved pilgrimage route.

Just 1km (0.6 mile) further east, across the confluence of two holy rivers (the Progo and the Elo), lies beautiful **Candi Mendut** (daily 6am–5pm).

Unlike most other central Javanese monuments, which face east, Mendut opens to the northwest.

The walls of the Candi Mendut ante-chamber are decorated with money trees and celestial beings, and contain two beautiful panels of a man and a woman amid swarms of playful children. It is thought that these two panels represent child-eating ogres who converted to Buddhism and became protectors instead of devourers.

Mendut contains three exquisite Buddhist statues: a magnificent 3-metre (10ft) figure of the seated Sakyamuni Buddha, flanked on his left and right by Bodhisattva Vajrapani and Bodhisattva Avalokitesvara, each about 2.5 metres (8ft) high. The central or Sakyamuni statue symbolises the first sermon of the Buddha at the Deer Park near Varanasi, India, as shown by the position of his hands (dharma-cakra mudra) and by the small relief of a wheel between two deer. The two bodhisattva, or buddhas-to-be, have elected to stay behind in the world to help Buddha's followers.

THE DIENG PLATEAU

Around 100km (60 miles) northeast of Borobudur are what are thought to be the oldest temples in Central Java, dating back to the late 7th century. The route to the **Dieng plateau** ⑬ passes through spectacular scenery with fine views of the Sindoro and Sumbing volcanoes on a clear day, and vistas across meticulously terraced mountainside and villages pitched at near-vertical angles. Eight surviving small temples (out of several hundred believed to have originally crowded the plateau) stand on this isolated 2,000-metre (6,500ft) plateau that is often shrouded in mist. The temples are simple, but it is the mysterious location and the close proximity to volcanic activity, brightly coloured sulphur springs and bubbling mud-holes that are of interest. There is an eerie quality to this site, which retains a reputation for supernatural power in local folklore.

The main temples are named after the heroes of the *Mahabharata* (see page 93) and all are Hindu in design. To the east of Candi Bima is the **Telaga**

Candi Pawon.

Borobudur lay hidden in the jungle for centuries.

⊘ THE MYTH OF THE 'LOST' TEMPLE

A popular myth has it that Borobudur was 'lost' for many centuries, concealed beneath layers of volcanic ash, before being 'rediscovered' by Thomas Stamford Raffles in 1814. In fact the monument's existence was always well-known in the region – there was a local taboo forbidding Javanese princes from visiting the site. It was also visited by Dutch travellers in the 18th century. Raffles himself probably heard of its existence from the Dutch surveyor H.C. Cornelius, who he then employed to survey the site.

Cornelius ordered local villagers to cut back the surrounding foliage, allowing for an unimpeded view of the structure (which, while not 'buried', was sprouting mature trees from its terraces). Raffles' subsequent account of Borobudur was the first to be published in English. He took a number of pieces of its statuary with him when he returned to England in 1816.

Though sporadic Dutch-organised surveying and restoration work went on during the 19th century, so did the plunder of carvings – by villagers for building materials and by colonial and Javanese officials for souvenirs. In 1896, the Dutch gave away eight cartloads of Borobudur statuary to visiting King Chulalongkorn of Siam, including 30 relief panels and five Buddha statues. Eventually the practice of plunder came to a halt. However, various fragments of Borobudur remain scattered around the world in public and private collections, including the British Museum.

⊘ Tip

Rafting on the Progo River, which originates at Jumprit on Gunung Sindoro northwest of Borobudur, is an exhilarating sport in the rainy season. In February, the lower reaches are apt to flood and are extremely dangerous. However, in the dry season, the mighty tiger becomes a kitten and is gentle enough for beginners.

Warna (Coloured Lake), with fluorescent hues caused by sulphur vents. Close by are meditation caves. **Kawah Sikidang**, a few kilometres from the temples, is a spectacular moonscape of fuming sulphur vents and steaming mud pools. There are some excellent day hikes in the area, including that to **Gunung Sikunir** which is a favourite spot for sunrise selfies amongst Indonesian student backpackers.

A visit to the plateau from Jogja makes for a long day trip; it's worth stopping overnight for a proper chance to explore. Guesthouses are available around the plateau with decent mid-range accommodation also available in nearby Wonosobo. Try to visit Dieng early before the afternoon clouds roll in.

East of Dieng plateau in the cool mountain air near the mellow little mountain resort of **Bandungan** are the fascinating **Gedung Songo** ⓮ temples, amongst the most spectacularly situated antiquities in Java. Successors to the *candi* at Dieng Plateau, nine Sivaitic shrines were built by the Sanjaya dynasty in the 8th century and overlook the lofty peaks and verdant valleys of Central Java, but only seven remain, scattered across a steep mountainside. On a clear day three volcanoes and the Dieng massif can be seen from here. The Gedung Songo can be visited as a side-trip from Semarang (see page 178) on the north coast, or as an overnight extension of a journey to Dieng from Jogja. Decent accommodation is available in Bandungan. Also in this area, near Ambarawa, is the wonderful **Museum Kereta Api** (Railway Museum, Jalan Stasiun No. 1, Ambarawa; tel: 024-354 5382), housing 21 German- and Dutch-built cogwheel locomotives and a restored train station. Rides through the scenic countryside are offered on weekends and holidays. Check timetables on arrival.

EAST TO PRAMBANAN AND SURAKARTA (SOLO)

Heading east from Jogja, past the airport, the main Jogja–Solo highway slices across a volcanic plain littered with ancient ruins. In the centre of the plain, 17km (10 miles) from Jogja, lies

Individual dagobas, mini-stupas, at Borobudur.

Prambanan ⓑ (daily 6am–6pm), a Hindu temple complex and a Unesco World Heritage Site. Completed sometime around AD 856 to commemorate a major battle victory, it was deserted within a few years of its completion and eventually collapsed. Preparations for the restoration of the central temple began in 1918, work started in 1937, and it was completed in 1953. Over time, other disasters have brought it harm – including a 5.9-magnitude earthquake in 2006 which damaged 30–40 percent of the complex. A lengthy restoration project is mostly complete, but the upkeep of Prambanan is an ongoing project and further restoration work is usually going on somewhere in the wider complex.

PRAMBANAN COMPLEX

The central courtyard of the main complex contains eight buildings. The three largest are arrayed north to south: the magnificent 47-metre (155ft) tall main **Candi Siva Mahadeva** is flanked on either side by the slightly smaller shrines **Candi Vishnu** (to the north) and **Candi Brahma** (to the south). Standing opposite these, to the east, are three smaller temples that once contained the 'vehicles' of each god: Siva's bull (nandi), Brahma's gander (hamsa) and Vishnu's sun-bird (garuda). Of these, only nandi remains. By the northern and southern gates of the central compound are two identical court temples, standing 16 metres (50ft) high.

Candi Siva Mahadeva, the largest of the temples and dedicated to Siva, is also known as **Roro Jonggrang** (often incorrectly spelled Loro), a folk name sometimes given to the temple complex as a whole. Local legend has it that Roro Jonggrang was a princess wooed by an unwanted suitor. She commanded the man to build a temple in one night, and then frustrated his nearly successful effort by pounding the rice mortar prematurely, announcing the dawn. Enraged, he turned the maiden to stone, and according to the

tale, she remains here in the northern chamber of the temple as a statue of Siva's consort, Durga. In the other three chambers are statues of Agastya, the Divine Teacher' (facing south); Ganesha, Siva's elephant-headed son (facing west); and a 3-metre (10ft) Siva (central chamber, facing east).

One aspect of Roro Jonggrang's appeal is its symmetry and graceful proportions. Another is its wealth of sculptural detail. On the inner walls of the balustrade, beginning from the eastern gate and proceeding clockwise, the wonderfully vital and engrossing tale of the *Ramayana* is told in bas-relief (and is completed on the balustrade of the Brahma temple).

Prambanan's beauty and variety demand more than a single visit. One of the most romantic ways to view the temple is by moonlight, during an open-air performance of the *Ramayana Ballet*, staged over four nights each month around the full moon between May and October. During the rest of the year, abridged performances of the epic are held in the adjacent **Trimurti Theatre**.

Temples at Prambanan.

Buddha at Candi Mendut.

Hindu deities in stone at Prambanan.

Within the same complex as Prambanan itself – and covered by the same entry ticket – is the sprawling Buddhist sanctuary known as **Candi Sewu**. Numerous other ancient structures dot the surrounding landscape. The Kraton Ratu Boko is a ruined palace and temple complex located on a high ridge south of the main highway. A little further afield are seldom-visited temples such as Candi Banyunibo and Candi Ijo. Private transport is needed to reach these places, set in tranquil countryside.

SURAKARTA (SOLO)

Located just 60km (40 miles) northeast of Jogja on the same highway as Prambanan is noble **Surakarta** ⓰, also known as **Solo**, only an hour away by car or train. Start early for a one-day visit or, if time permits, stay longer and enjoy a batik course, gamelan lesson or join one of the many meditation centres on nearby Gunung Lawu. Solo can also be reached by air from Jakarta and Bali. Although larger than Jogja, Solo is more sedate.

Borobudur and Gunung Merapi at sunrise.

SOLO'S KERATON KASUNANAN

On the banks of the mighty Bengawan Solo, Java's longest river, stands the **Keraton Kasunanan** (Sat–Thu 9am–2pm), constructed between 1743 and 1746. As with the Yogyakarta palace, Surakarta's Keraton defines the centre of the town and the kingdom as well as, metaphysically, the hub of the cosmos. Indeed, the similarities between the two courts, built within 10 years of each other, are striking. Both have a thick outer wall enclosing a network of narrow lanes and smaller compounds, two large squares, a mosque and a central or inner royal residential complex. Perhaps the major difference is that Surakarta has no north–south processional boulevard or pleasure palace.

Enter the Keraton at the east gate and pay a small fee for a guided tour of the museum and the inner sanctum. Here, shaded by groves of leafy trees, between which flit the bare-shouldered *abdidalem*, or female attendants, is the large throne hall of the Susuhunan, a titular Muslim

prince. The inner columns supporting the roof are richly carved and gilded. Crystal chandeliers hang from the rafters, and marble statues, cast-iron columns and Chinese blue-and-white vases line the walkways. Remove your shoes and refrain from taking photographs. Notice the royal meditation tower to one side where the Susuhunan is said to commune with Kanjeng Ratu Kidul, the mythical Goddess of the Southern Ocean.

The Keraton museum was established in 1963 and contains ancient Hindu-Javanese bronzes, traditional Javanese weapons and three marvellous coaches. The oldest coach – a lumbering, deep-bodied carriage built around 1740 – was a gift from the Dutch East India Company to Pakubuwono II. The museum also displays some remarkable figureheads from the old royal barges, including Kyai Rajamala, a giant of surpassing ugliness, who once adorned the bow of the Susuhunan's private boat and is said even now to emit a fishy odour when daily offerings are not forthcoming.

DANCE AND MUSIC AS HIGH ART

After visiting the Keraton, stroll through the narrow lanes outside, and be sure to pay a visit to nearby **Sasana Mulya**, the music and dance pavilion of the **Indonesian Arts High School** (STSI), located just to the west of the main (north) palace gate. This is an art school with an illustrious history: it was here that the first musical notation for gamelan was devised at the turn of the 20th century. Visitors are welcome to listen and observe as long as they do it unobtrusively.

PURO MANGKUNEGARAN

About 1km (0.6 mile) to the west and north of the main Keraton Kasunanan is a smaller, more intimate palace of Surakarta's secondary royal line, the Mangkunegaran. Begun by Mangkunegara II at the end of the 18th century and completed in 1866, the **Puro Mangkunegaran** is open to the public (Mon–Sat 8.30am–2pm, Sun 8.30am–1pm).

The Mangkunegaran's outer *pendopo* (audience pavilion) is said to be the

A gamelan musician plays a saron metallaphone.

Ancient temples on the cool heights of the Dieng plateau.

Surakarta street scene.

largest in Java – built of solid teakwood, and jointed and fitted in the traditional manner without nails. Note the brightly painted ceiling with the eight mystical Javanese colours in the centre, highlighted by a flame motif and bordered by symbols of the Javanese zodiac. The gamelan set in the southwest corner of the *pendopo* is known as Kyai Kanyut Mesem ('Kyai Kanyut Smiles'). Try to visit the palace on Wednesday mornings at 10am, when it is used to accompany informal dance rehearsals.

The museum is in the ceremonial hall of the palace, directly behind the *pendopo*, and it mainly houses the private collections of Mangkunegara IV: dance ornaments, *topeng* (masks), jewellery (including two silver chastity belts), ancient Javanese and Chinese coins, bronze figures and a superb set of *keris*.

SOLO'S ANTIQUES AND BATIK

Solo, with its sizeable 'antique industry', is where many dealers collect and restore old European, Javanese and Chinese furniture and bric-a-brac. The

Prambanan, a Unesco World Heritage Site.

starting point for any treasure hunt is **Pasar Triwindu**, just south of the Mangkunegaran palace. Solo is also the home of Indonesia's largest batik manufacturers, most of which have showrooms in town with reasonable fixed prices for superb fabrics, shirts and dresses. For cheaper pieces, visit the huge **Klewer** textile market beside the Grand Mosque and near the Keraton. Just be sure to know what you are doing if making a purchase here – fair batik prices vary widely, depending on the process and the quality of the dyes and materials.

As with Jogja, Solo is renowned as a centre for traditional Javanese performing arts. It is one of the best places to see an evening *wayang orang* dance performance or *wayang kulit* shadow play, or listen to live gamelan music. Ornately carved leather puppets, contorted wooden masks and even monstrous bronze gongs sold here make highly distinctive gifts. Solo is also a major centre for meditation, and there are a few places that hold yoga courses for foreigners.

SYMBOLIC KERIS

The richly embellished dagger is not only a form of high art, but a symbol of masculinity and an essential accessory for every Javanese man.

Neatly tucked into the waistband of the traditional Javanese male attire is the ceremonial dagger, or *keris*. No longer a weapon of defence, this ornate blade is rather an indication of social ranking and a source of cultural pride. An old Javanese proverb states: 'Happy is the man who is the owner of a horse, wife, bird and keris.' Traditionally, the *keris* was considered to be the most important item a man could own.

The traditional *keris* is a lightweight elongated dagger with a blade that is either straight or wavy, resembling a flame or serpent, coupled with a hilt and sheath. Originally worn for protection and used as a thrusting weapon, it remains an essential part of a groom's wedding and other ceremonial Javanese attire. So revered is the dagger that a man's *keris* can be a substitute in his absence at his own wedding.

Thought to possess a life of its own and endowed with magical powers, the *keris* is treated with great respect and reverence. There are many *keris* legends, including stories about wilful and bloodthirsty daggers that are capable of flying, turning into snakes, fathering children and taking human lives.

Stored in a place of honour, treated with perfumed oils and wrapped in silk and velvet, *keris* are passed down as sacred family heirlooms. Every year on the first day of the Javanese calendar, the Yogyakarta palace *pusaka* (heirlooms with spiritual powers), which include an assortment of sacred *keris*, are cleansed with scented water. Believing the objects to be magically endowed, crowds wait outside for the chance of receiving just a drop of the holy water used in the cleaning ritual, while the *keris* is carried from the palace in a coach.

CRAFTING THE *KERIS*

The *keris* were (and still are) crafted by *empu* (master craftsmen), esteemed ironworkers imbued with divine status and who were so revered that they once came under the patronage of the court and were often considered members of the royal household.

Before beginning his work, the *empu* makes offerings, fasts, meditates and asks for divine inspiration. The blade is forged from several layers of nickel and meteoric iron, using a damascening technique, which in turn produces the desired shades of light and dark patterns on the blade, the *pamor*. This pattern becomes visible after the blade has been polished and treated with citrus juice and arsenic. Each pattern has a name and meaning. *Wos wutah* (scattered rice grains), for example, represents prosperity.

Keris are distinguished by the number of curves (always uneven) they support. One wave represents god and king, while three, fire and passion. Each of these qualities is believed to have an effect on the life of the owner. If a man is not suitably matched to his *keris*, it can affect his life in a negative way. The hilt can be plain or carved with a mythical figure – believed to be capable of warding off evil spirits – in wood, bone or ivory and inlaid with precious metals and stones. The scabbard is usually wooden and encased in richly embossed brass, silver or gold.

A keris dagger.

Java Man skull.

The tympanum of Puro Mangkunagaran palace, Surakarta.

GUNUNG LAWU AND BEYOND

The 3,265-metre (10,712 ft) **Gunung Lawu** rises due east of Solo, straddling the border between Central Java and East Java provinces. This is another of Java's mystical mountains. Trekkers and pilgrims make their way up the challenging trail which begins at a pass above the pleasant mountain resort of **Tawangmangu** to the summit, where there are a number of sacred sites. Rituals connected with the Surakarta court are sometimes held here. The whole mountain is steeped in historical and folkloric significance. According to legend, the last Hindu king of Majapahit fled here after his realm fell to the ascendant Muslims of Demak, eventually dematerialising to become the mythical guardian spirit, Sunan Lawu. There are several enigmatic 15th-century temples – amongst the very last to be built in Java – on the slopes. Their style is far removed from the precise refinement of Prambanan and Borobudur, and certain elements – realistic phalluses and multiple images of turtles – suggest an emergence of esoteric folk cults as Java's Hindu-Buddhist culture declined. The best known of these temples, both accessible on a single daytrip from Solo, are **Candi Suku**, featuring a unique pyramid structure and many lurid carvings, and the extensively restored and spectacularly located **Candi Ceto**, accessed via a winding lane through tea plantations. The settlement just below **Candi Ceto** has some very basic homestays. This village, unusually in Java, is mainly Hindu. Despite stories told by guides and locals, however, the community is not a centuries-old survival of pre-Islamic Java; it is the result of mass conversion during the religious and political turmoil of the mid-1960s.

SANGIRAN

Eighteen km (11 miles) north of Solo is **Sangiran** (Sragen) **⑰**, where the remains of the 1.5 million-year-old Java Man were first unearthed in 1891 (see page 125). A Unesco World Heritage Site, the small Museum Trinil (Mon–Sat 9am–6pm) in nearby Krikilan village unfortunately only holds

replicas of Java Man's skull fragments and jawbone, but there are also mastodon tusks, artefacts from prehistoric settlements and fossils, some of them over a million years old. New discoveries in this area are frequent.

THE NORTH COAST

Java's northern coastal ports were once the busiest and richest towns on the island; they served as exporters of agricultural produce from the fertile Javanese hinterland, as builders and outfitters of large spice trading fleets, and as trading entrepôts frequented by merchants from all corners of the globe. Between the 15th and 17th centuries, when Islam was a new and growing force in the archipelago, these ports flourished as political and religious centres.

Beginning to the west, **Cirebon** ⓲ is an intriguing potpourri of Sundanese, Javanese, Chinese, Islamic and European influences. With a small harbour and a sizeable fishing industry, most sites are within walking distance, though a nice way to get around is by *becak* (pedicab).

Cirebon's two major palaces were both built in 1678, giving each of two princes his own court. The **Keraton Kesepuhan** (belonging to the elder brother) sits on the site of the 15th-century Pakungwati Palace of Cirebon's earlier Hindu rulers. Javanese in design with a Romanesque archway framed by mystical Chinese rocks, it is a spacious, pillared *pendopo* furnished with French period pieces. The walls of the Dalem Ageng (ceremonial chamber) behind are inlaid with blue-and-white tiles exhibiting biblical scenes. The adjoining museum has a coach in the shape of a winged and horned elephant grasping a trident in its trunk – a glorious fusion of Javanese, Hindu, Islamic, Persian, Greek and Chinese mythological elements.

Next to the Kesepuhan Palace stands the **Masjid Agung** (Grand Mosque), constructed around AD 1500. Its two-tiered meru roof rests on elaborate wooden scaffolding, and the interior contains imported sandstone portals and a teakwood *kala*-head pulpit. Together with the Demak and

⊙ Tip

The Karimunjawa Marine National Park is 80km (50 miles) off the north coast of Central Java. Dive resorts and lodgings occupy some of the islands, but it remains a serene, little-developed place with crystal clear waters. Access is by light aircraft from Semarang, or by boat from Jepara or Semarang.

Creating batik.

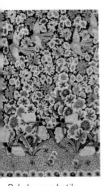

Pekalongan batik shows Japanese influences.

Banten mosques, it is one of the oldest remaining landmarks of Islam on Java.

The **Keraton Kanoman** (palace of the younger brother) is nearby, reached via a busy marketplace. Large banyan trees shade the peaceful courtyard within, and as at Kesepuhan, the furnishings are European and the walls are studded with tiles and porcelain from Holland and China. The museum has a collection of stakes still used to pierce the flesh of Muslim believers on Mohammed's birthday (seni debus), as well as relics from Cirebon's past.

Taman Arum Sunyaragi, about 4km (2.5 miles) out of town on the southwestern bypass, was originally built as a fortress in 1702 and used as a base for resistance against the Dutch. It was cast in its present form in 1852 by a Chinese architect to serve as a pleasure palace for Cirebon's sultans. About 5km (3 miles) north of the city along the main north coast highway sits the hilltop **Tomb of Sunan Gunung Jati**, a 16th-century Cirebon ruler and one of the *Wali Songo*, the 'nine saints' who, according to legend, propagated Islam in Java.

Cirebon's Keraton Kesepuhan.

EAST TO SEMARANG

About 220km (140 miles), a 4-hour drive, east of Cirebon is **Pekalongan** ⑲, which announces itself on roadside pillars as **Kota Batik** (Batik City). The town justifies this sobriquet by producing some of the finest and most highly prized batik on Java. The Pekalongan style, like Cirebon's, is distinctive – a blending of Islamic, Javanese, Chinese and European motifs.

Another 90km (55 miles) and 2 hours to the east, **Semarang** ⑳ rises out across a narrow coastal plain and up onto steep foothills. Known during Islamic times for its skilled shipwrights and abundant supplies of hardwood, it is today the commercial hub and provincial capital of Central Java. The Dutch church, **Gereja Blenduk**, on Jalan Suprapto downtown, with its copper-clad dome and Greek cross-floor plan, was consecrated in 1753 and stands at the centre of the 18th-century European commercial district.

Semarang's most interesting district is its **Kampung Cina** (Chinatown) – a grid of narrow lanes tucked away in

the city centre, reached by walking due south from the old church from Jalan Suari to Jalan Pekojan. Some old townhouses here retain the distinctive Nanyang style of elaborately carved doors and shutters and delicately wrought iron balustrades.

Half a dozen colourful Chinese temples and clan houses cluster in the space of a few blocks, the largest and oldest of which is on tiny Gang Lombok (turn right by the bridge from Jalan Pekojan). This is the **Thay Kak Sie temple**, built in 1772, which houses more than a dozen major deities. Those with time and an interest in things Chinese should visit **Gedung Batu**, Ming Admiral Cheng Ho's grotto on the western outskirts of town. Cheng Ho arrived in Java in 1405 and is credited with helping to spread Islam.

DEMAK AND THE TEAKWOOD TOWNS

From Semarang, there are several towns to the east that may be visited as day trips. During the early 16th century, a kingdom centred on **Demak ㉑**

dominated much of Java as its first major Muslim state. Now, only the mosque remains. The city has become a place of pilgrimage – according to traditionalist Javanese Muslims, seven visits here is equal to a single pilgrimage to Mecca. The grave of Sunan Kalijaga, a member of the *Wali Songo* and spiritual adviser to the Demak royal court, lies 2km (1.25 miles) southeast of the city. Another focal point is Demak's **Masjid Besar** (Grand Mosque), considered the oldest and holiest mosque in Java. Built in 1466, its architecture combines Hindu and Arabic elements.

Neighbouring **Kudus** is renowned for beautiful hand-carved teakwood houses that grace the narrow lanes of the Kauman area with its early 16th-century mosque. Kudus is also known as 'Kota Kretek', or clove cigarette city, as several *kretek* companies are based here.

Jepara, 35km (20 miles) north of Kudus, has long been known for its teakwood carvings, catering to strong demand for finely detailed panels depicting scenes from the *Ramayana* and other Hindu-Javanese tales.

A market in Semarang.

Gunung Semeru smoulders behind the caldera rim of Gunung Bromo.

EAST JAVA

East Java is wilder, earthier, less densely populated and even more dramatically volcanic than Central Java, but it comes similarly steeped in history.

Geographically and historically, East Java (Jawa Timur) may be divided into three regions: the north coast (including Madura island) with its old Islamic trading ports, the Brantas River Valley with its ancient monuments and colonial hill stations, and the eastern salient (known to history as Blambangan) with its spectacular volcanoes, secluded nature reserves and unparalleled scenic beauty nearly everywhere. The broad **Sungai Brantas** traces a circular path through the ancient and fertile rice lands of eastern Central Java, and around several adjacent peaks – Arjuna, Kawi and Kelud. For five centuries after AD 930, this valley was the undisputed locus of power and civilisation on the island. The great kingdoms of this period – Kediri, Singhasari and Majapahit – bequeathed a rich heritage of art, literature and music.

With the arrival of Islam as a political force in the 16th century, and with the great fluorescence of the spice and textile trade, a struggle arose between the rice-growing kingdoms of the interior and the new Islamic trading powers of the coast. Muslim forces conquered the Brantas Valley around 1530, though Blambangan remained mainly Hindu until the early 18th century, and parts of the Bromo-Tengger uplands remain non-Muslim today.

In Surabaya's Arab quarter.

SURABAYA

East Java's provincial capital, **Surabaya** **㉒**, is known as the 'City of Heroes' because of the momentous first battle of the Indonesian revolution which took place here in November 1945 (see page 182).

Surabaya first emerged as a harbour town attached to the Hindu-Buddhist kingdoms of East Java, later establishing itself as a successful independent port. It was eventually conquered by the powerful Mataram rulers of Central Java in 1625, but only after Sultan

⊘ Main attractions

⊙ Map on page 150

Service at the Majaphit Hotel.

Agung's armies had devastated its rice lands and diverted its mighty river.

The Dutch took over in the mid-18th century, and Surabaya developed into the greatest commercial city of the Indies. Today it is Indonesia's second largest city, home to around 3 million people, and though it is predictably hectic, enlightened local governance in recent years has made it far more pleasant and manageable than some other large urban centres, with clean, tree-shaded streets in the centre, good public transport and relatively orderly traffic. The crumbling older quarters towards the port area are far less gentrified, but contain much of historical interest.

ARAB AND CHINESE QUARTERS

The most interesting areas of Surabaya are the old Arab, Chinese and colonial neighbourhoods in the north of the city. The richly atmospheric Arab quarter, generally known simply as Ampel, is centred on the mosque and tomb of Sunan Ampel, one of the legendary saints said to have spread

Arab quarter bazaar in Surabaya.

Islam in Java. The mosque compound is approached via a narrow covered bazaar with a decidedly Middle Eastern ambiance.

Further south, amidst crumbling colonial-era shop-houses, the vast Pasar Pabean market is a warren of stalls and alleys. From late afternoon until early morning the western part of the market turns into an emporium for freshly caught fish.

Beyond the market the original Chinese quarter begins, home to old temples such as **Hong Tik Hian** and Surabaya's oldest Chinese shrine, the 18th-century **Hok An Kiong**. The temple's central deity is the goddess Ma Co, the protector of waterlogged sailors. From the Chinese quarter, walk westwards along Jalan Kembang Jepun to cross the famous **Red Bridge** over the Kali Mas River. Nearby is **House of Sampoerna**, an excellent small museum attached to a factory which makes traditional hand-rolled clove *kretek* (clove cigarettes). There is a good café on site. 'Surabaya Heritage Track' is a free sightseeing bus

⊘ THE BATTLE OF SURABAYA

The Battle of Surabaya remains the most iconic event of Indonesia's bloody struggle for independence. In the aftermath of World War II, British forces were tasked with retaking Java from the defeated Japanese, ahead of an eventual Dutch return. They found themselves stepping into a revolution.

The conditions were particularly tense in Surabaya, where Japanese weapons had fallen into local hands. The situation was beyond the control of senior Indonesian politicians in Jakarta, and was badly handled by senior British officers. When the British commander, Brigadier Mallaby, was killed during unrest in the north of the city, open warfare erupted. It took a month of vicious fighting and aerial bombardment before the British could claim control of Surabaya. But for the defeated revolutionaries it had been a bloody rite of passage which served as a potent emblem for their eventually successful struggle.

Among the most unlikely bit-players in the Battle of Surabaya was a Scottish-American woman who styled herself 'K'tut Tantri'. Born Muriel Pearson in 1908, she had run a hotel in Bali before the war, then signed up as a radio propagandist for the independence movement in its aftermath. Her anti-colonialist radio broadcasts during the 1945 hostilities earned her the nickname 'Surabaya Sue'. She later published a self-aggrandising and wildly unreliable – though entertaining – memoir, Revolt in Paradise.

tour of the city's many historical sites run by House of Sampoerna. Departing the museum three times daily Tuesday to Sunday, it is an excellent way to see the city.

Climb into a taxi and travel south from here, parallel to the river, past the **Heroes Monument**, to see how Surabaya has expanded in recent times. On Jalan Tunjungan is the old-world **Majapahit Hotel** (Jalan Tunjungan, No.65; tel: 031-5454 333; www.hotel-majapahit.com), built in 1910 by the famous Sarkies brothers and wonderfully refurbished. From Jalan Tunjungan, the main shopping street with several shopping centres including the vast Tunjungan Plaza, turn left down Jalan Pemuda to the former **Dutch Governor's Mansion**. Constructed after the turn of the 20th century, this stood at what was then the new centre of colonial Surabaya, now a major hotel district. **Joko Dolog**, a centuries-old statue of King Kertanagara, the last king of the Singasari dynasty (who died in 1292), is enshrined in a small, hidden park directly opposite.

In the southern suburbs, best reached by taxi, stands the magnificent Masjid al Akbar (Great Mosque), better known locally as Masjid Agung, one of the finest pieces of modern Islamic architecture in Southeast Asia, with a vast blue-green-tiled dome. Outside of prayer time appropriately dressed visitors are welcome to tour the mosque and to ascend the free-standing minaret for spectacular views.

MADURA

Madura ㉓ island is now accessible via Suramadu Bridge, the longest in Southeast Asia, in about 15 minutes. Though the bridge has brought increasing development to the west of the island, most of Madura is overwhelmingly rural and deeply traditional. The far east, centred on the sleepy former royal town of Sumenep, is particularly attractive. Sumenep is home to a small palace museum, some interesting royal tombs, and a strikingly attractive mosque, Masjid Agung. There are some fine beaches and unspoilt countryside nearby.

☉ Kids

West of the highway from Surabaya and Malang are resort areas in the northeast foothills of Mt Arjuna that include recreational facilities such as Splash The Waterpark, The Pines Mountain and Forest Adventure facility, and Kakek Bodu Recreational Forest. Heavily involved in conservation and breeding, Taman Safari Park II (www.tamansafari2.com) houses 150 rare species.

Bull races on Madura.

The Madurese have long enjoyed a reputation for toughness, and Madura's dry limestone terrain may account for this. The island's major industries here are fishing, tobacco-growing, salt-panning and batik, but thousands of Madurese migrants have fanned out across Indonesia in search of better economic prospects – bringing their trademark sate (miniature kebabs) and soto (spicy soup) with them.

Madura is also famed for its traditional bull racing (karapan sapi). According to the Madurese, the races began long ago when plough team was pitted against plough team over the length of a rice field. Today's racing bulls are never used for ploughing, but are specially bred; they represent a considerable source of local and regional pride. District and regency heats are held all over Madura and East Java from July, building up to the finale in November in Pamekasan, the island's capital.

MOUNTAIN RETREAT

Tretes ㉔, just 55km (35 miles) south of Surabaya, is a delightful mountain

Garuda close up at Candi Panataran.

resort offering fresh air, cool nights and superb scenery. Walk or ride on horseback in the morning to one of three valley waterfalls in the vicinity. Though it can get busy at weekends, it is peaceful mid-week, and makes a good base for exploring the stunningly beautiful local countryside, which has rice-terrace scenery every bit as extensive, and often more impressive, than that of Bali.

More active souls will perhaps want to hike up **Gunung Arjuna** (3,339 metres/10,950ft), located behind Tretes, through lush montane casuarina forests, or across the Lalijiwa plateau along a well-worn path to neighbouring **Gunung Welirang**, where sulphur is collected by villagers from hissing fumaroles. The area is also studded with ancient monuments, beginning with **Candi Jawi**, just by the main road 7km (4 miles) below Tretes. This slender Hindu-Buddhist shrine was completed around 1300, and is one of several funerary temples dedicated to King Kertanegara of the Singasari dynasty.

Candi Jawi overlooks **Gunung Penanggungan** to the north – a perfect cone surrounded by smaller peaks, and regarded, because of its shape, as a replica of the holy mountain Mahameru. Penanggungan is littered with dozens of terraced sanctuaries, meditation grottoes and sacred pools – about 80 sites in all, most of which are on the mountain's northern and western faces. The most accessible and charming of these are **Belahan**, a bathing pool situated at Penanggungan's eastern foot, and the atmospheric Jolotundo to the west, beyond which a steep trail leads to the summit.

TRACES OF THE PAST

From Tretes or Surabaya, it is about an hour to **Trowulan village** ㉕, near Mojokerto, once the seat of Java's greatest empire, 14th-century Majapahit. Unfortunately, most of Majapahit's monuments were built of wood and soft red brick, so that only the foundations and a few gateways remain. The Trowulan **Museum** by the main road nevertheless has a fascinating collection of terracotta figures and fragments and a useful table-top map of the area. From here, seek out nearby ruins: Candi Tikus (a royal bathing complex), Candi Bajang Ratu (a tall, brick entryway) and Wringin Lawang (a palace gate). Also visit the cemetery at **Tralaya**, 2km (1.25 miles) south of Trowulan, site of the oldest Muslim graves on Java.

MALANG AND ENVIRONS

Malang ❷ is a pleasant, though increasingly busy, highland town, with a cool climate, a two-hour drive south of Surabaya. It makes a good base for exploring the surrounding highlands, and has some excellent accommodation. A superb collection of Javanese and Chinese antiques and art is displayed in **Hotel Tugu Malang**. Even if not staying at this beguiling hotel, it's worth dropping by for a visit (Jl. Tugu No.3; www.tuguhotels.com; tel: 034-1363 891).

There are three interesting temples outside Malang. **Candi Singosari** is on the west side of the main highway from Surabaya, at Singosari. From Blimbing village, north of Malang, take the road to Tumpang, about 20km (12 miles) away. Just before the Tumpang market, a small road to the left leads to **Candi Jago**, begun in 1268 as a memorial to the Singhasari king, Wisnuwardhana. All around the terraces are reliefs in the distinctive *wayang* style of scenes from the *Mahabharata*, and a frightening procession of underworld demons.

East Java's only sizeable temple complex is **Candi Panataran**, located 80km (50 miles) west of Malang (best reached by taking the longer but more scenic route over the mountains via Kediri). This was apparently Majapahit's state temple, assembled over a period of some 250 years between 1197 and 1454. A series of shrines and pavilions arranged before a broad platform, it is assumed that the pavilions were originally roofed with wood and thatch, as was the body of the main temple.

Near Panataran is Blitar, an attractive provincial town with an easy-going atmosphere. It is home to **Sukarno's mausoleum**, the final resting place of the 'father of Indonesian independence' who died in 1970. And on the way to or from Blitar via the scenic Malang–Kediri high road, make a detour north from Batu to Selekta mountain resort – interesting for its colonial bungalows, swimming pools and apple orchards.

GUNUNG BROMO AND THE TENGGER HIGHLANDS

The steep slopes of the active volcanoes Gunung Semeru and Gunung Bromo in **Bromo-Tengger-Semeru National Park** ❷ are home to one of the few remaining pockets of Hinduism on Java. When most of Java converted to Islam in the 16th century,

The tortured lavascape at Gunung Bromo.

Majahapit ruins. Candi Bajang Ratu at Trowulan.

Volcanic activity at Gunung Bromo has been on the increase in recent years.

a few particularly remote regions retained their earlier religious traditions – which generally owed much more to indigenous folk beliefs than to the classical Hindu-Buddhism of the royal courts. Today, the Tenggerese people maintain their uniquely local traditions – though external influence has prompted shifts towards more orthodox Balinese-style Hinduism, as well as some conversions to Islam. The region is a major vegetable-growing area, and the spectacular gardens and high-altitude pine trees are a lovely sight. But the main attraction of the area is a visit to the rim of Bromo's smouldering crater at sunrise.

Gunung Bromo (Mount Bromo) is an ancient caldera 10km (6 miles) across, with four smaller peaks rising in the centre, ranging between 300 and 400 metres (1,000–1,300ft). Surrounding these peaks on the crater floor is sand and lush vegetation; every few years cinder and ash pour forth in eruptions to carpet the countryside with nutrient-rich deposits.

There are two ways to take in the view: either from the crater's edge or a panorama of the entire caldera from afar (if time permits, watch the sunrise from both vistas). For the first, start from **Cemara Lawang** at 2–3am to catch an incredible sunrise at the peak. Make the trek across the sand-sea floor, either by pony or by foot, and once at the base of the crater, climb up an incline of 250 steps. At the top is a narrow lip from where you can look into the belly of the belching sulphurous centre of the crater and take in the 360-degree view of the entire caldera and the majestic **Gunung Semeru** Temperatures can drop to freezing before dawn, so be sure to dress warmly and take a torch.

For the panoramic view, hire a jeep to **Gunung Penanjakan**, 400 metres above Gunung Bromo and about 3km (2 miles) to the west; then it is a short hike along a paved road to the summit. The view here is spectacular. All arrangements need to be made the night before. Both walks can be done in the pre-dawn period; if time is limited

enjoy sunrise at Gunung Penanjakan and after breakfast take a pony ride for the view of Bromo's navel. June–October, during the dry season, is the best time to visit.

Every year thousands of Hindu Tenggerese participate in a midnight procession to toss offerings into Gunung Bromo's caldera in a festival called Kasodo. Their offerings to the spirits of Gunung Bromo are meant to assure blessings for the coming year.

There are several ways to reach the Tengger highlands, and transport can be arranged in Surabaya, Malang or even Bali. Public buses and the train go as far as Probolinggo; from here, there are tour companies with minivans to take you the rest of the way. There is modest accommodation in both Ngadisari and Cemara Lawang (closer to the rim), and the better rooms come with hot water. As Gunung Bromo is inside a national park, a small charge is payable.

THE FAR EAST

East of Bromo-Tengger-Semeru National Park are four other national parks that can be visited on the way to or from Bali (by the Ketapang–Gilimanuk ferry). The most accessible of these is the **Baluran National Park ㉘** at Java's northeastern tip. The park is spread over 50,000 hectares (124,000 acres) inside an eroded volcano cone. This is a chance to observe dry-terrain wildlife not seen in other areas of Java, such as *banteng* oxen, *ajag*, a rare Javanese wild dog, and 150 bird species.

Southwest of Baluran is **Ijen ㉙**. This is a beautiful and peaceful upland massive, with extensive coffee plantations filling a huge caldera ringed by steep ridges and active volcanoes. Plantation visits are possible, and there are a few basic accommodation options. The main attraction here is Kawah Ijen – an active crater where sulphur is mined from steaming vents by hardy local men. An hour-long trek from the road at

Pos Paltuding leads to the crater rim. It is possible to descend into the base to watch the miners at work, but the fumes can be dangerous at times so be sure to take local advice. In recent years there has been much hype about Ijen's "blue fire" – a phenomenon caused by the flaring sulphur after dark. As a consequence many visitors are now encouraged to visit the crater at night. Be warned that actual nocturnal conditions are almost never as impressive as the photos, and cloud often obscures things entirely. Sunrise is a more reliably interesting and attractive time to visit, when you'll also get to see the miners at work.

At Java's southeastern tip is **Alas Purwo National Park ㉚**. There is a watchtower for views of grazing *banteng*, wild boars, peacocks and some of the best surfing in Java at G-Land.

Meru Betiri National Park ㉛ on the southern coast is a sea turtle conservation area surrounded by coffee and cacao plantations. Watch for splendid hornbills, Java warty pigs and giant owls as you trek to the beach to see the turtle nursery.

Sulphur mining is a profitable livelihood at Kawah Ijen.

Horse trekking to the Bromo crater.

The verdant landscape in the mountains near Danau Toba.

Minangkabau wedding.

SUMATRA

The extraordinary wealth of natural resources, flora and fauna and unique cultures makes Sumatra one of Indonesia's most rewarding islands to visit.

Batak architecture.

Exotic Sumatra is one of the world's last frontiers – an island of lush tropical rainforests, extraordinary flora and fauna, and active volcanoes. Home to Sumatran tigers, rhinos and elephants and a host of dynamic ethnic groups, it is the third-largest island in Indonesia and the fifth-largest in the world (roughly the size of Sweden). It is vastly rich in natural resources: over half of the country's exports come from the treasure-trove of Sumatra's bounty of oil, natural gas, hardwoods, rubber, palm oil, coffee and sugar.

Situated at the western rim in the archipelago along the Strait of Malacca, for centuries the region was the gateway for maritime trade through Southeast Asia, receiving merchants from China, India, the Middle East and Europe. The early coastal seaport kingdoms were the entry points for the influx of foreign influence that left a lasting imprint on the very fibre of Indonesia's culture. The first wave started in the 2nd century with Indian Hindu-Buddhist culture; later, in the 13th century, Islam entered with traders.

Sumatra is a tapestry of ethnic groups mostly living in rural communities: in the north are the independent and devout Muslim people of Aceh; in the northern highlands, the proud Christian Batak; and in the west, the matrilineal Minangkabau. The Kubu and Rimbu in the south are the last remaining forest-dwellers, while the Orang Laut (sea people) traditionally lived aboard boats and continue to ply the seas among the hundreds of islands off the east coast.

Batak homes.

Sumatra is a travel haven for nature-lovers, with surfing beaches and 11 national parks sheltering tigers, elephants and orang-utans. There is also memorable Danau Toba, Southeast Asia's largest lake, along with impressive architecture, and ancient megaliths. Allowing enough time is the challenge. The thorns in the island's side are the west coast's susceptibility to earthquakes and tsunamis, and forest destruction. The best time to visit is the dry season in the months of June and July. For the intrepid traveller, the rewards are worthwhile, while an added bonus is the warmth and friendliness of the Sumatran people.

GAM freedom fighter in Banda Aceh addressing a crowd.

NORTH SUMATRA

This engrossing region is known for its great cultures – especially the Acehnese and the Batak – and magnificent landscapes, as well as for its wildlife and rainforests.

North Sumatra has historically been the Indonesian archipelago's first point of contact with external influences from as early as the 2nd century, when Hinduism and Buddhism were introduced by Indian traders. Later, Islam reached its shores through Arab and Indian Muslims in the 13th century.

Early north coast kingdoms took advantage of sea trade passing through the nearby straits. During the Golden Age under Sultan Iskandar Muda (1604–37), the Aceh kingdom expanded to include all the major ports of eastern Sumatra and several on the Malay peninsula. The Dutch declared war on Aceh in 1873, and it took more than 10,000 troops – the largest miliary force the Dutch ever mustered in the East Indies – before the eventual defeat of the sultanate in 1878. Guerilla activities then spread inland to Gayo territories, where the rebel-controlled pepper trade financed the purchase and smuggling of arms from the British. Seemingly insurmountable guerrilla resistance to external government continued, even after Indonesia's independence.

On 26 December 2004, tidal waves crashed into the coastal areas of North Sumatra, including part of the capital, Banda Aceh, causing devastation and loss of life on an unprecedented scale. It did, however, finally bring an end to the decades of armed separatism in Aceh, with an enduring peace process tied to the reconstruction efforts. Today, travellers come to North Sumatra for sojourns to scenic Lake Toba to relax and experience its flamboyant Batak culture, and a few venture as far north as staunchly Muslim Aceh. Trekking in the ancient rainforests of Gunung Leuser National Park in search of orangutans is another significant draw.

Main attractions

Banda Aceh
Medan's historical
buildings
Gunung Leuser National
Park
Bohorok Orangutan
Centre
Berastagi
Samosir island

**Maps on pages
195, 198**

Hotel Carolina on Samosir Island, Danau Toba.

⊙ Fact

Aceh is Indonesia's only province ruled by Islamic Sharia law. Although only Muslim citizens – not foreigners or locals of other faiths – are subject to its harsh punishments, visitors should respect Islamic mores in dress and behaviour. Despite its conservative reputation, Aceh is a very friendly place, and visitor's generally enjoy a warm reception.

Banda Aceh's Moghul-inspired Mesjid Raya Baiturrahman.

BANDA ACEH

For nearly 30 years a separatist group, Free Aceh Movement (GAM), railed against the Indonesian government, seeking independence from the republic. The resulting bloody conflict divided the Acehnese and drew international attention. Following the near-total destruction of Banda Aceh in the 2004 Indian Ocean tsunami, it became apparent that the provincial capital could only be rebuilt with the cooperation of all its citizens, and a radical transformation in the central government helped to create an environment that was favourable to peace talks. In August 2005, President Susilo Bambang Yudhoyono signed a landmark peace accord with GAM in Helsinki – for which he was awarded the Nobel Peace Prize – and GAM renounced its demand for full independence in exchange for political and economic autonomy for the province.

Banda Aceh ❶, capital of Nangroe Aceh Darussalam province, is located along the shores of two rivers, Sungai Krong Aceh and Sungai Krong Daroy.

The original fortress and palace of the Aceh sultanate were destroyed along with the great mosque when the Dutch invaded in 1874, but vestiges of Aceh's glorious past can still be found around Jalan Teuku Umar. The **Gunongan** i a royal water pleasure garden buil by Sultan Iskandar Muda in the 17th century for his Malay princess wife Opposite this is the Pintu (door) Aceh used only by the royal family, to enter the palace.

On Jalan Keraton are the tombs of 15th- and 16th-century Aceh sultans while another series of royal tombs on Jalan Mansur Sjah includes that of Sultan Iskandar Muda, the heroic 12th sultan of Aceh. They in turn surround the **Museum Negeri Aceh** (Aceh State Museum; Tue–Sun 8am–5pm). Inside ceramics, weapons, clothes, jewellery and cooking equipment are on display, but the museum's pride is a large bell that was a gift from a Ming dynasty emperor to the Aceh sultan in the 15th century.

Aceh's centrepiece is the beautiful **Masjid Raya Baiturrahman**, located

north of the museum. Designed by an Italian architect in the Moghul Indian style, it was built by the Dutch between 1879–81 to replace the destroyed Grand Mosque. At night, the huge white structure and its black domes are illuminated. The marble interior may be visited by non-Muslims, except during prayer times.

Heading southwest, there is a Christian cemetery on Jalan Iskandar Muda where many of the Dutchmen killed in the Aceh War, including generals and other senior officers, are buried. The entrance, through wrought-iron Art Nouveau gates, stands between two marble plates on which are engraved the names of all the soldiers.

In Lam Pisang, 6km (4 miles) north of Banda Aceh, is **Museum Tjut Nyak Dhein**, dedicated to the Acehnese heroine of the same name who took part in the struggle for independence from the Dutch in 1875. Her original home was burned to the ground by the Dutch, and this replica is now a museum.

The nearby village, **Kampung Kuala Aceh**, is a place of pilgrimage. Here lies the grave of Teungku Sheikh Shaj Kuala (1615–93), a holy man who translated the Koran into Malay. Aceh's university bears his name.

Medan skyline.

Sumatra

Young orangutan.

Banda Aceh itself is not Indonesia's Land's End. That distinction belongs to remote **Pulau Weh** (Weh island), reached by a one-hour ferry ride from Banda Aceh. The island's main town, **Sabang**, flourished throughout the 1970s as a duty-free port linked to Calcutta, Malacca, Penang and Singapore. The quiet islands offer beautiful white-sand beaches with aquamarine water, excellent for snorkelling and scuba diving.

GAYO HIGHLANDS

In the highlands south of Banda Aceh a scenic Japanese-built track constructed by slave labour during World War II connects Blangkejeren to **Takengon**, the Gayo capital that lies 1,100 metres (3,600ft) above sea level. Takengon is built on the banks of **Danau Laut Tawar** (literally 'Lake Freshwater Sea'). The water is clean, cool and refreshing, though many locals do not swim in it. Fearing they may be pulled into the underwater realm of a seductive fairy, they opt instead for the hot springs at **Kampung Balik**. A paved road follows the west side of the lake, affording spectacular views of rice paddies and pine-clad mountain slopes. **Bireuen** is the chief marketplace for Gayo coffee, cinnamon, cloves and tobacco.

On the coast east of Banda Aceh is **Sigli**, known as Padri when it was the principal port from which Acehnese haji (pilgrims) departed to Mecca. The tragic Padri War started here in 1804; the Dutch took the town and completely destroyed it in the process. Remains of the *padri kraton* (fortress) can be seen on the outskirts of town, along the road to Banda Aceh. At nearby Kampong Kibet is the grave of Sultan Ali Mughayat Syah, the first Muslim ruler of Aceh, who died in 1511. Some 60km (40 miles) south along the coast and a short distance inland is **Lamno** village. A few of its inhabitants, said to be descended from Portuguese stranded here three centuries ago after a shipwreck, do indeed have green eyes and faces that are recognisably Iberian.

A becak taxi, Medan.

MEDAN

Most visitors enter North Sumatra via **Medan ❷**, a sprawling and crowded city with one of the strongest economic growth rates and highest per capita incomes in Indonesia. Once the marshy suburb of a small court centre, Medan developed into a commercial city after the Dutch overran the Deli sultanate in 1872, and 14 years later, became the regional capital.

Though crowded and congested, Medan has retained some architectural gems from its colonial days. The largest concentration of such examples is found along Jalan Jendral A. Yani and around Merdeka Square. Chinese shops line Jalan A. Yani, which is also home to the Tjong A Fie **Mansion** (tel: 081-3751 6003; daily 9am–4.30pm), former home of the eponymous Tjong A. Fie who arrived in Sumatra as a poor migrant from China in the 1870s, but had become a fabulously wealthy tycoon by the time of his death in 1921. The mansion, built in traditional Chinese style, has been beautifully restored and is one of the highlights of Medan.

At the southern end of Medan's longest street, Jalan Sisingamangaraja, stands the magnificent **Istana Maimoon**, constructed by an Italian architect in rococo style in 1888. It is still the official residence of the sultan's descendants and may be visited during the day. One block east of the palace is the imposing **Mesjid Raya** (Grand Mosque). Built in 1906 to complement the palace's architectural style, it is the city's largest mosque.

Across the Sungai Deli, on the west side of Medan, lies the old European plantation town. Its wide avenues, flanked by huge colonial villas, are planted with flowering trees. The Art Deco **Immanuel Protestant Church**, erected in 1921, is on Jalan Diponegoro, while on Jalan Hang Tuah is **Vihara Gunung Timur**, one of Indonesia's largest Chinese temples. It is said to be such a powerful place that photographs taken within will remain unexposed. A Hindu temple, **Sri Mariaman**, off Jalan Arifin, is the

Devastation from the 2004 tsunami.

spiritual centre for Medan's sizeable Indian community.

In south Medan, the **Taman Margasatwa** zoo (daily) nurtures a varied collection of native Sumatran wildlife, including Sumatran tigers. The **Plaza Medan Fair** has permanent cultural and agricultural exhibits, as well as an amusement park. Rare Buddhist and Hindu statues, Islamic gravestones and Batak artefacts are on show at the **Museum Sumatera Utara** on Jalan Joni (Tue–Sun 9am–3pm).

DEEP FOREST: GUNUNG LEUSER NATIONAL PARK

Northwest from Medan, some three hours by road, a narrow road winds up the Alas River Valley to **Gunung Leuser National Park ❸**, an 8,000-sq km (5,000-sq mile) park covered in dense jungle that is home to elephants, rhinos, sun bears, tigers, 500 bird species and orangutans. The park is both a Unesco World Heritage and a World Network of Biosphere Reserves Site. Surrounding sputtering **Gunung Leuser**, 3,404 metres (11,167ft) high and Sumatra's second-highest peak, the park reaches all the way to the west coast and is probably one of the most accessible in Indonesia.

On the eastern edge of the Gunung Leuser reserve is **Bukit Lawang** where the **Bohorok Orangutan Centre** is located. Although it no longer rehabilitates the red great apes, visitors are welcome. A one-hour hike through the jungle brings you to the platforms used for early-morning and afternoon feeding of wild and semi-wild orangutans. Permits are required from the PHKA office (take a photocopy of your passport with you). The well-run Bukit Lawang station provides comfortable lodging, decent food, and a superb visitor centre complete with slide shows and information concerning local wildlife. The centre also arranges treks to Gunung Leuser, ranging from a couple of hours to several days. This type of trekking through jungle is not for the uninitiated: leeches, malaria and protection from dampness are major concerns.

Batak architecture overlooking Danau Toba.

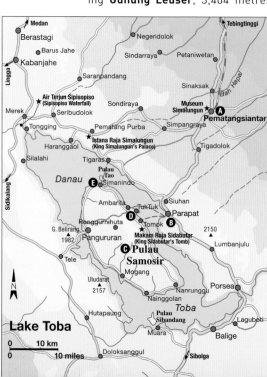

The park's centre in **Kutacane**, situated in the heart of the Alas Valley, a 3–4-day hike north, is the jumping-off point for white-water rafting on the Sungai Alas and the base camp for other activities in the national park (Kutacane is a 6- to 8-hour journey from Medan). **Ketambe**, a 30-minute drive from Kutacane, is a research station for primates, elephants and Sumatran tigers. Friendship Guest House here offers trekking for 1–6 days around Gunung Leuser and to the top of neighbouring Gunung Kemiri.

Located in the Gunung Leuser National Park buffer zone, and encompassing Namo Sialand and Sei Seidang villages, is Tangkahan, a community-based ecotourism project. Among its activities are jungle trekking, elephant safaris and river cruises to observe the wildlife such as gibbons, orangutans, sun bears and many bird species. For adventurous travellers, Kalong cave is waiting to be explored.

MEDAN TO DANAU TOBA

The main route from Medan to **Danau Toba** ❹ (Lake Toba) runs southeast along the coast through the market town of Tebingtinggi and inland to Pematangsiantar. Side roads along the first 50km (30 miles) offer access to fine beaches such as Cermin and Sialangbuah, renowned for its mudskippers that swim like fish and climb trees.

Pematangsiantar ❹, 130km (80 miles) south of Medan, is the second-largest city in North Sumatra. This cool highland rubber and palm-oil centre is notable for its **Museum Simalungun** (daily) on Jalan Ahmand Yani, which contains an excellent display of Batak artefacts including *pustaha laklak*, bark-leafed books containing sacred formulas in Batak script used by ancient shamans. From here, continue west to Parapat and Lake Toba.

A longer, more westerly Medan–Parapat route runs through **Berastagi**, a hill resort and market town with Dutch-built villas and a cool climate, and the Karo Batak highlands. Located between two volcanoes – Sibayak and Sinabung – Berastagi produces fresh vegetables such as carrots, cabbages and tomatoes and is known for its passion fruit, usually made into syrup. A two-hour drive heading south leads to **Sidikalang**, popular for its coffee.

Only a short bus trip from **Kabanjahe**, north of Sidikalang, is a spectacular viewpoint near the northern tip of Danau Toba that overlooks the remote Tongging Valley and Sipisopiso Waterfall. In the surrounding area are **Barus Jahe**, a traditional Karo Batak village, and **Lingga**, with its massive, pyramid-roofed *rumah adat* (traditional clan houses), some over 250 years old. A lucky visitor might stumble across a Karo Batak wedding or rice harvest festival. From here, the road skirts Toba's eastern shore, passes through the

Canoe on Danau Toba.

Gunung Leuser National Park.

Monday-market village Haranggaol, and continues to Parapat.

The Bataks, one of the great highland peoples of Sumatra, inhabit a fertile volcanic plateau south of Medan that covers much of northern Central Sumatra. In the middle lies the lovely **Danau Toba**, a vast crater lake containing the lush Samosir island (nearly the size of Singapore). Danau Toba, the result of a great prehistoric eruption, is today one of the highest (900 metres/2,900ft) and deepest (450 metres/1,480ft) lakes on earth.

More than 3 million members of six distinct Batak tribes make their homes in the high country, which stretches 500km (300 miles) north–south and 150km (90 miles) east–west around Lake Toba. Each of these groups – the Toba, Karo, Pakpak, Simalungun, Angkola and Mandailing Batak – has its own dialect, customs and architectural style.

SAMOSIR ISLAND

Around 170km (110 miles) from Medan, on the eastern shore of Danau Toba

is **Parapat ⓑ**. A tourist resort since colonial times, today it offers deluxe hotels, golf courses, water sports and a refreshingly brisk climate. Parapat is nestled on the lake's eastern shore, and is a favourite weekend getaway for Medan residents. For most visitors, Batak sights are the main attractions.

The best place to experience Danau Toba's spell is **Samosir ⓒ**, a 1,000-sq km (380-sq mile) island in the lake. Samosir is regarded as the original home of the Bataks in Sumatra, and the Toba Batak, the 'purest' Batak tribe. Boats depart from Parapat for Samosir daily. The main entry point is **Tomok**, a 30-minute ride across quiet water. The carved boat-like tomb of King Sidabutar is here. In an enclosure opposite the tomb are ritual statues of a buffalo sacrifice. At the end of an avenue of souvenir booths leading from the jetty are dozens of stands selling *kain ulos* (hand-woven fabric), two-stringed mandolins, ornate woodcarvings, Batak calendars and many other items of cultural interest. Other boats from Parapat will take visitors directly to the dozens of attractive, waterfront guesthouses scattered in Tomok, Ambarita and on the Tuk-Tuk peninsula.

Tuk-Tuk ⓓ is a tourist village composed largely of small hotels. On the peninsula is a community hall for Batak dances and a few traditional houses, as well as inexpensive accommodation. With the arrival of Christianity on Samosir in 1848, Toba Batak took enthusiastically to Lutheran hymnals. Sunday church services are fine entertainment, though there are many other opportunities to hear *ture ture* (tribal ballads) in village *warungs*.

Ambarita, an hour's walk from Tuk-Tuk, has three megalithic complexes. The first is just up from the jetty and is notable for its 300-year-old stone seats and the tomb of Laga Siallagan, the first *raja* of Ambarita. If an enemy was captured in Ambarita, neighbouring

Ambarita village was once the scene of grisly beheadings.

rajas were invited to this first hilltop complex for an initial conference before moving on to the second, a cluster of stone chairs where the fate of the prisoner was decided. The third complex is located south of Ambarita and includes a unique breakfast table. Here, the prisoner was reportedly beaten to death, decapitated and chopped up on a flat stone, cooked with buffalo meat, and eaten.

Simanindo , at Samosir's northern tip and a half-day walk from Tuk-Tuk, is 16km (10 miles) from Ambarita. Ferries run to Simanindo from Tigaras on the eastern shore north of Parapat. The village has a huge former king's house, which has been restored and is now a Batak **museum**. Look for the buffalo horns in front, one for each generation. A 10-minute boat ride off Simanindo is little **Tao island**, where a few tiny bungalows offer escape to those who find even Samosir hectic.

Although **Pangururan**, on Samosir's west coast, can be reached in half a day by the coastal path from Simanindo, a hike across the island's forested central plateau offers unforgettable views. From Tomok, the climb past the king's tomb to the plateau above takes about three hours. Pangururan is another 13km (8 miles) beyond and can be reached in less than 10 hours. Stay the night at one of the villages before pressing on to Ronggurnihuta and its swimming lake. It may frequently be necessary to ask directions from locals. In the wet season, this climb is extremely muddy and slippery. It is easier to take a ferry to Pangururan and then hike back to Tuk-Tuk.

Pangururan lies near the Sumatran mainland and is connected by a short stone bridge. Its main attraction is an hour's walk away – the *air panas*, or hot springs, halfway up the hill command a fine view of the lake. Every Sunday, a round-island cruise lasting most of the day departs from several villages, stopping at many of the islands and villages. Or take a stroll along the island's only road and listen to the glorious hymns at the many churches, an uplifting way to spend the morning.

A ferry crosses every hour from Parapat to Samosir Island.

Batak dance performance.

☉ THE BATAK

Wedged between fervently Muslim peoples, the Minangkabau and the Acehnese, the Batak somehow retained their traditional beliefs until the middle of the 19th century, when German and Dutch missionaries converted many to a mystical sort of Christianity. But traditional *adat* and bygone customs are still practised. Cemeteries display stone sculptures of dead ancestors, shamans communicate with spirits, and priests consult astrological tables to make decisions for their clans.

When first encountered by the Dutch, the Batak were viewed as primitive cannibals isolated for centuries from the rest of the world. They seemed to be constantly warring with their neighbours; headhunting and cannibalism were features of local culture. But the Batak were anything but primitive. In fact, they were sophisticated and settled agriculturalists, possessing elaborate crafts, calendars and cosmological texts written in an Indic alphabet.

A Batak *marga* (clan) consists of several *huta* (communities) tracing descent from a single male ancestor. Kinship and clan loyalties are especially strong – in some cases fiercely defended – and weddings and funerals can draw kinsfolk in the thousands. Genealogies, some of which go back five centuries, are carefully kept as they determine status in personal relations and formal ceremonies.

Surfing off the coast of Nias.

WEST SUMATRA

Rugged West Sumatra is home to beautiful upland scenery, proud Minangkabau culture with its fiery cuisine, fabulous surfing and a string of fascinating offshore islands.

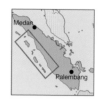

West Sumatra's terrain, with its fertile valleys, lush rainforests and majestic peaks, offers some of the most memorable landscapes in all of Indonesia. Bukit Barisan Selatan National Park, home of the few remaining two-horned Sumatran rhinoceros, the country's largest national park, Kerinci Seblat, and Bukit Tigapuluh National Park are all here. The region is also graced with two large crater lakes, the larger and more stunning of which is Maninjau just west of Bukittinggi, with smaller Singkarak to its southeast.

The highest peak in West Sumatra is Gunung Kerinci in the rugged, little-visited Kerinci Seblat National Park. Indonesia's second-highest mountain, it attracts climbers who like a challenge. Conservation groups there have trained local guides to take the adventurous on treks through the forest.

Just off the west coast lies a string of islands that lure visitors of entirely different sorts. The spectacular breaks at Nias have beckoned surfers for the last decade or two, some of whom have become volunteers in health care, community empowerment and disaster relief through SurfAid International, which has weathered the many upheavals of nature over recent years. The other islands, the Mentawais, draw extreme trekkers who relish visiting the friendly Siberut people, who live in

the forests and happily tell the stories that their tattoos represent.

While the attractions in this region are limitless, the number one destination remains the Minang highlands, home to the Minangkabau people who, despite their staunchly Muslim identity, make up the largest matrilineal society on Earth (see page 211). Property and wealth are inherited through the female line, and both men and women trace their lineage through their mothers and retain loyalty to the clan houses of their grandmothers. Their

Main attractions
Bukittinggi
Nias
Siberut
Bukit Tigapuluh National Park
Bukit Barisan Selatan National Park
Kerinci Seblat National Park

Maps on pages 195, 205

A Minangkabau matriarch.

distinctive traditional *rumah gadang* (clan houses) dot the countryside of the highlands, with elaborately carved exteriors and upturned rooflines that resemble the horns of a water buffalo.

PADANG

The capital of and gateway to West Sumatra is **Padang ❺**, a thriving commercial centre. It is the island's third-largest city, and 90 percent of its population are ethnic Minangkabau. Home to the largest seaport on the western coast, **Teluk Bayur** is 6km (4 miles) south of the city centre. The harbour came into existence in the 18th century after the discovery of gold in the highlands and to accommodate the lucrative pepper trade. At one time, Sumatra supplied over half of the world's pepper needs. Today, the busy seaport loads ships with cargoes of coffee, tea, cinnamon, coal and wood.

Most travellers regard Padang as a stopover en route to the Minang Highlands or west coast islands. But the city does have some semblance of old-world charm, in the Dutch-built colonial homes and the shophouses lining the wide avenues in the area around **Kampung Cina** (Chinatown) and the **Pasar Raya** (Central Market) area. Best explored by walking or by horse-drawn cart, the route starts at Jalan Hiligoo and continues south along Jalan Pondak and onto Jalan Niaga to the old colonial waterfront. Here, both banks of the Sungai Muara are filled with hand-painted fishing boats and ferries. Cross over for a view of the Chinese cemetery before proceeding 4km (2.5 miles) south to **Air Manis** fishing village.

Padang offers few sights other than the **Museum Adityawarman** (Tue–Sun 8am–4pm) which houses Minangkabau artefacts in a traditional *rumah gadang* (clan house). Regularly scheduled cultural dance performances take place nearby. (Check the programme with the tourist office or museum.) In the evening, head to the waterfront for a spicy Padang meal, cool ocean breezes and a view of the sunset over the Indian Ocean.

BUKITTINGGI

A two-hour drive from Padang north through the lush tropical Anai Valley delivers you to picturesque hilltop **Bukittinggi ❻**, the heart of Minangkabau culture. Blessed with friendly people, a relaxed atmosphere and cool mountain air, Bukittinggi is the best base for visiting the surrounding Minang Highlands.

Bukittinggi, which means 'Tall Hill', stands at 930 metres (3,050ft) and is surrounded by the Gunung Agam, Gunung Singgalang and Gunung Merapi volcanic peaks. It is a pleasant town to stroll through. The well-educated townsfolk, who have the highest literacy rate in the nation, are friendly and eager to practise their English. The cool mountain air also enhances touring on foot. In the centre of town, a clock tower with a stylised roof stands

Fishing boats at Padang.

as the city's landmark; nearby is the busy Pasar Raya (Central Market).

Taman Bundo Kanduang  (Rumah Adat Baandjuang Museum; daily 7.30am–5pm), a 140-year-old *rumah gadang*, marks the city's highest point. Exhibits include wedding and dance costumes, musical instruments, weaponry and other cultural artefacts.

Crossing a footbridge takes you to the remains of Benteng de Kock, built by the Dutch in 1825. The fortress itself does not hold much interest, but it provides a good vantage point to view farmland and the smouldering **Gunung Merapi** (2,891 metres/9,484ft) and **Ngarai Sianok Canyon** Ⓑ.

Better views of the spectacular canyon, sometimes referred to as the Grand Canyon of Indonesia, can be had at the lookout point in Panorama Park, a favourite leisure spot for locals. A pleasant hike through the 4km (2.5 mile) canyon is possible along a footpath that starts in rice fields. At the halfway point is a bridge; head up a flight of steps (slippery in the rainy season) to the silversmith village **Koto**

Gadang Ⓒ. Here, delicate silver filigree jewellery and hand-embroidered shawls (based on Flemish laces) are made. From here, you can take public transport back to Bukittinggi.

NORTH OF BUKITTINGGI

An easy 12km (7.5 mile) drive north of Bukittinggi is the 3,100-hectare (750-acre) Rimba Panti Nature Reserve, which contains the **Rafflesia Sanctuary** Ⓓ, named after the world's largest flower, which can grow up to a metre (3ft) in diameter. The foul-smelling *Rafflesia arnoldii* only blooms between August and September. It may be necessary to hike over muddy paths in search of the bloom.

Continuing north another 15km (9 miles) is **Ngalau Kamang**, a limestone cave with stalactites and stalagmites. It also houses a small lake. Payakumbuh, 40km (25 miles) east, is the gateway to the cliffs and waterfalls at **Harau Canyon** Ⓔ, a lush reserve surrounded by 100-metre (330ft) high granite walls and home to various species of monkey and deer, as well as sun

A grey langur at Bukittinggi.

A Dutch colonial dwelling in the countryside outside Bukittinggi.

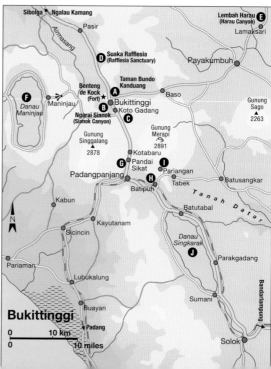

bears, leopards and even a few tigers. To get there from the main highway, head north past Payakumbuh for 10km (6 miles) to Lamaksari village. Turn left and proceed for another 3km (2 miles). Permits are sold at the entrance.

WEST AND SOUTH OF BUKITTINGGI

Heading west from Bukittinggi is the deep crater lake **Danau Maninjau** **F**, renowned for its serenity and beauty. There is a wide range of accommodation and eateries there, along with canoes and motorboats for hire. For a day trip, the lake can be reached within two hours by bus from Bukittinggi. Even better, spend a few days relaxing and swimming in the cool, clear water. From the Embun Pagi lookout point, the road winds and zigzags an amazing 44 turns before arriving at the lake.

Just 12km (7.5 miles) south of Bukittinggi is the weavers' village **Pandai Sikat** **G**. Weaving has been a major business since the late 18th century, and women and girls here create by hand *kain songket* (cotton or silk

base worked through with heavy gold or silver threads), which are popular with Jakarta women for formal events. Excellent-quality sarongs can be expensive and are sometimes just rented for the evening.

Continue southeast to the plains at **Tanah Datar**, where the ancient Minangkabau kingdom existed for half a millennium before succumbing in the Padri wars of the early 1800s. The area has the finest examples of traditional Minangkabau architecture *rumah gadang* with roofs turned up to resemble the horns of a water buffalo. The first stop in **Batipuh** **H** village is the traditional *surau*, or men's house, built entirely of wood in the Koto Piliang style.

A side road from here, heading east for 5km (3 miles) and skirting Gunung Merapi, goes to **Pariangan** **I**, believed to be the original Minangkabau village. Set in a beautiful valley, steps lead to the traditional clan houses and a royal tomb. Take a leisurely stroll here and see one of the last *surau* of its kind still in use. Back on the main road, **Tabek**

Rice fields.

⊘ BATANG GADIS

Lacking sufficient infrastructure to attract more than a few intrepid trekkers, the entry point to obscure **Batang Gadis National Park** is Panyabungan village, north of Padang. In addition to protecting strange and wonderful creatures such as Malayan tapirs and porcupines, Sumatran serows, tigers and elephants, and many varieties of rare cats, the park has 242 bird species and the huge, smelly Rafflesia flower. Also within park boundaries are natural and Japanese caves and Sorik Marapi volcano.

When Batang Gadis was established in 2004 it was unique in that it was Indonesia's first national park to be founded based on the requests of the local people, who were concerned about the illegal logging that was destroying their forests.

village has fine examples of traditional clan houses and the oldest building in West Sumatra.

Continuing east, the area between Bukittinggi and Batusangkar is arguably among the most scenic. Fertile lands grow many varieties of fruits and vegetables, as well as irrigated highland rice. Some 20km (12 miles) east of Padangpanjang, **Batusangkar** was once a residence of the Minangkabau kings. The main attraction, the royal palace Istana Pagaruyung, was destroyed by fire in 2007, and a new palace has been built.

South from Batipuh is the lovely **Danau Singkarak ❾**, larger than Danau Maninjau and easily accessible by road, though not as developed. Beyond the lake is **Solok**, a mountain town known for its picturesque highroofed houses and woodcarvings.

WEST COAST ISLANDS

Running parallel to Sumatra's west coast, about 100km (60 miles) offshore, is a string of ancient islands – peaks of an undersea non-volcanic ridge

separated from mainland Sumatra by a deep trench. Simeulue, Nias, the Mentawai group and Enggano were first 'discovered' in the 17th century by the Dutch. In the 19th century, missionaries arrived, and today 80 percent of the islanders are Christians, but they still retain some strong traditional beliefs. The most visited island, Nias, is known for its stone-jumping rituals. Travelling overland from Medan or Padang will require an overnight stay in **Sibolga**. From here take a ferry to Gunung Sitoli on Nias, or go by one of the daily flights from Medan.

NIAS ISLAND

The main points of interest on **Nias ❼** – the traditional villages and surfing beaches – are located in the south, a 4–7-hour journey on decent roads thanks to tsunami aid programmes.

The largest of the west coast islands, Nias is 100km (60 miles) long by 50km (30 miles) wide, and is home to one of Southeast Asia's most unusual ancient cultures, which revolves around stone: in architectural style, sculptures

A fisherman on Danau Maninjau.

A stone-leaping Nias tribesman.

Surfing off Nias island is top-class.

and rituals. In its most memorable traditional dance, *Fahombo*, Niasan tribesmen leap feet first over stone columns several metres high. *Tutotolo* is a warrior dance performed by young men leaping in combat.

Niasan villages are veritable fortresses, with great stone-paved central 'runways'. Stilt houses stand in parallel rows on hillsides, shielded by a thorny bamboo barricade from foreign attack. Northern Nias, raided by Acehnese slave traders for centuries, has few cultural remnants, although the capital, **Gunung Sitoli**, is found here. The remote centre of the island holds cultural interest, however. Amid jungle are the ruins of abandoned villages with huge single standing stones.

SOUTHERN VILLAGES OF NIAS

All of the major tourist attractions are located in southern Nias. **Telukdalam** is the largest town. Most visitors head for the beautiful white-sand beaches and aquamarine waves at **Lagundri**, proclaimed to be one of the best surf spots in the world. Simple and more upscale accommodation options are available here.

Bawömataluwo, 15km (9 miles) from Telukdalam, is a village turned touristy because of its easy accessibility. Built more than 100 years ago on a summit for protection from Dutch attacks, it is reachable by a wide stone staircase of 480 steps along an alley between two rows of houses. The central 'square' is the venue for stone-jumping performances and nearby is the ornate chief's house. There are stone statues and around 300 megaliths.

Hillisimaetano is a quiet village built in the past 70 years, where raising chickens and pigs – the main livelihood – goes on at a traditional pace. All 140 houses in the village face the chief's house located in the centre. **Gomo Lahusa**, 40km (24 miles) northeast of Telukdalam, and **Gomo** are both worth a visit to see fine old *menhir* stones.

SIBERUT ISLAND

South of Nias, **Siberut** ❽ is the largest and most visited of the Mentawai

archipelago and is covered in dense tropical rainforest with isolated farming settlements. The indigenous inhabitants are forest-dwellers, though almost all now live a settled lifestyle.

Siberut island measures about 110km by 50km (70 miles by 30 miles), and the port of entry is in the south at Muara Siberut, reached by ferry from Padang. As throughout the Mentawai's the only upscale accommodation is in isolated surf resorts; those who come to explore the interior generally stay in basic homestays arranged by their guides. The main attraction is the trek inland to visit remote villages where people live in traditional longhouses. **Rodok**, a 4–5-hour boat ride away, is a government village, and another two hours' journey leads to **Madobat**. Both are ideal locations from which to begin a trek inland.

The people of the interior live in small villages or in *uma* (longhouses). They are well known for the tattoos they incise over large sections of their bodies, and for their *puliajiat* rituals: these go on for several weeks to purify houses, in order to ensure harmony and reunite the souls of individuals with their bodies.

A Unesco Biosphere Reserve, **Siberut National Park** is home to a unique collection of flora and fauna due to its separation from any other landmass for over 500,000 years. Most notable are its endemic monkeys: primitive black gibbons *(Hylobates klossii)*, Mentawai macaques, and two langurs, *Presbytis potenziani* and pig-tailed.

NATIONAL PARKS

Back on the mainland, east of Padang the **Bukit Tigapuluh National Park** is under tremendous threat from logging and palm-oil plantations, with two-thirds of the park already logged. With the park housing at least 10 critically endangered species, these operations have drawn the attention of wildlife conservation organisations worldwide. On the upside, orangutan reintroduction has worked well here, and the World Wildlife Fund caught several rare Sumatran tigers on film using

Nias warrior in ceremonial garb.

camera traps in mid-2011, intensifying the campaigns of several groups against further logging.

Along Sumatra's entire west coast, stretching from the northern to the southern tips, is the Barisan mountain range, and **Bukit Barisan Selatan National Park** encompasses 3,568 sq km (1,378 sq miles) of these heavily forested hills. This park joins Gunung Leuser and Kerinci Sebalat National Parks as a single Unesco World Heritage Site, and is home to three important Sumatran species – elephant, rhino and tiger – and has the only population of Sumatran striped rabbit ever recorded. The threat to this conservation area is not logging, but encroaching coffee plantations.

Two hours south of Padang is the northern border of Indonesia's largest reserve, **Kerinci Seblat National Park**, which covers an amazing 14,000-sq km (5,400-sq mile) stretch of jungle and mountains. Most visitors begin their explorations in the Kerinci district dominated by the active volcano **Gunung Kerinci**, which rises 3,800 metres (12,480ft), making it Indonesia's second-highest peak after Gunung Puncak Jaya in Papua.

Rare wildlife in this Unesco World Heritage Site park includes Sumatran tigers and elephants, clouded leopards, Malayan sun bears and tapirs, over 375 species of birds, and the world's largest and tallest flowers. There are no orangutans, but this is the reputed homeland of the mysterious *orang pendek*, Sumatra's miniature answer to the yeti, and the mythical *cigau*, half-lion and half-tiger.

The national park office in Sungaipenuh (Mon–Fri) has a good visitor centre and some English-speaking staff. There are a number of simple hotels and a colourful market there. Homestays and trekking operators are available in Kersik Tuo, a tea plantation village at the foot of Gunung Kerinci, where treks start. From the south of Kerinci, trek on forest paths (2 days) to Renah Kenumu, a traditional village with many megaliths, hot springs and good wildlife-spotting.

Sumatran tiger.

THE MATRILINEAL MINANGKABAU

They may be Muslims, but intriguingly in Minangkabau culture it is the women who hold the key to social rights, identity and inheritance.

The fertile highlands of West Sumatra are home to one of Indonesia's most interesting ethnic groups, the Minangkabau. With a reputation for being intellectuals, Minangkabau men feature prominently in the national government and are known for their keen business sense. Throughout Indonesia there are restaurants run by Minangkabau men who serve up spicy Padang food.

What makes the Minangkabau so interesting is that while they are devout Muslims, they also belong to a matrilineal society, tracing social identity and inheritance through the female line. In fact, the Minangkabau are one of the few remaining matrilineal societies that still exist in the modern world.

Minangkabau can trace their descent to a *rumah gadang* (clan house), to which they pledge allegiance and maintain a social obligation throughout their lives. Each rumah gadang has descendants who can be traced back to a single grandmother.

All valuable property, land and house are owned in common by the clan, led by the grandmother and including all her female heirs and her eldest brother, and cannot be sold without group consent. The men are involved in the management of the communal property, but it is the women who maintain the rights of use, including landownership. Minangkabau women thus have a high economic status in society.

ROLES FOR MINANGKABAU MEN

Men spend most of their time in the fields, and at night young boys go to the *surau*, the Islamic study hall. Young men are encouraged to *merantau* (literally 'to go into non-Minangkabau lands'), to emigrate and seek their fortunes and experience the world. When the seasoned wayfarer returns home with his wealth, he is deemed ready for marriage.

When a woman marries, she pays a groom price to her husband's female family members. After the wedding, the man goes to 'visit' his wife in her home, but in the morning, he returns to his mother's house to work the crops and to raise his sisters' children. His nieces and nephews are his responsibility; his own children are in turn raised by his wife's brothers.

Households are the domain of the women, who are actively involved in daily affairs, while husbands and brothers live elsewhere. The men travel, but remain in close touch with the village, sending money home for ceremonies, the building of mosques and for the maintenance of the family's *rumah gadang*, a source of cultural pride.

The *rumah gadang* has a roof that resembles buffalo horns, and elaborately carved exterior panels are the pride of local woodcarvers. Other examples of the tribe's excellent craftsmanship are beautiful hand-woven *kain songket* textiles, fine silver filigree jewellery, lively music and a *silat* dance combining martial arts movements with dance.

Tradition has it that the Minangkabau derived their name – *minang* (victory) and *kabau* (buffalo) – from an ancient battle. In an effort to avoid bloodshed they proposed a contest between two water buffaloes. The Javanese brought to the arena a strong buffalo bull, while the Sumatrans entered a nursing calf that had been starved for days and had spikes affixed to its horns. The small calf quickly went in search of milk only to impale the underside of the bull, killing it. The Javanese returned home and left the Minangkabau in peace.

A Minangkabau woman in distinctive costume.

An aerial view of the East Sumatran plains, characterised by slow, meandering rivers and large tracts of forest and swamp.

SOUTH AND EAST SUMATRA

Very few travellers make it to the southernmost regions of Sumatra, but the region is home to interesting towns, fine jungle and mountain landscapes, and excellent surf.

Southern and easternmost Sumatra has long been far from the beaten tourist track, thanks in part to vast distance and poor transport infrastructure. The modern domestic flight network and improved road conditions have made matters easier, however, and for those with time to spare this is a fascinating region to explore.

In the east, broad alluvial lowlands no more than 30 metres (100ft) above sea level are drained by numerous meandering rivers, including the Sungai Batanghari, navigable for nearly 500km (300 miles) inland, and the Musi, Sumatra's longest river. In contrast, the west coast is mountainous, rising to volcanic peaks of more than 3,000 metres (10,000ft) before dropping sharply to the Indian Ocean at the former Dutch and British colonial outpost, Bengkulu. South of Bengkulu is Krui, one of Sumatra's popular surfing beaches.

Sitting off the eastern coast are Bintan, Batam, Bangka and Belitung islands, the former two part of a 'golden triangle' project between Indonesia, Singapore and Malaysia. Bintan's northern beach is a sprawling complex of resorts and golf courses, while Batam is primarily industrial. Bangka and Belitung were formerly major sources of tin for

global markets, though today they are better known as emerging beach holiday destinations for domestic tourists and backpackers.

BENGKULU

The small, sleepy seaside city of **Bengkulu ❾** was founded in 1685 by the British. Its fort, **Benteng Marlborough**, was constructed in 1713–19 and restored in the late 1970s. Old gravestones with English inscriptions can be seen in the gatehouse. Sir Thomas Stamford Raffles was governor of

❂ Main attractions
Bengkulu
Pasemah Highlands
Way Kambas National
Park
Bintan and Batam islands
Belitung
Muaro Jambi

Map on page 195

The elusive Sumatran rhino can be seen at Way Kambas National Park.

Bengkulu from 1818 to 1823. During his time in Sumatra local guides showed him and the botanist Joseph Arnold the vast parasitic flower known locally as padma raksasa or kerubut. Although the plant had previously been identified by a French traveller, Raffles' account was the first made public in Europe, and today its scientific name is Rafflesia arnoldii. Examples can be found at the **Dendam Tak Sudah Botanical Gardens** near the lake of the same name 8km (5 miles) southeast of Bengkulu.

South of Bengkulu is Krui beach, known among surfers for its brilliant waves. There are several other good beaches here and a choice of accommodation.

Inland is the beautiful upland Pasemah region, centred on the small town of Pagaralam. Dotting the surrounding mountain plateau are carved megaliths, tombs, pillars and other stone ruins thought to date from about AD 100. Oddly shaped rocks have been fashioned into figures of armed warriors riding elephants, wrestling buffaloes or fighting snakes. The area is dominated by volcanic **Gunung Dempo**, which can be climbed by hardy trekkers. Further south along the same mountain chain is the remote Danau Ranau, one of the remotest of all Sumatra's upland lakes. It is a tranquil spot with some basic lakeside accommodation.

BANDAR LAMPUNG

Arriving from West Java, the Sumatran port of entry is Bakauhuni harbour near **Bandar Lampung** ⓫. The ferry passes within view of Anak Krakatau, which sits on the site of the former enormous Krakatau volcano that erupted in 1883 (see page 150). The **Lampung Provincial Museum** (Tue–Sun; 9am–4.30pm) on Jalan Teuku Umar displays Chinese ceramics, Dongson bronze kettledrums, kain tapis (hand-woven ceremonial cloths) and archaeological finds from Labuan Meringgai.

There are hot sulphur springs at **Kalianda**, 38km (23 miles) north of the ferry terminal, where there are

A poster for Laskar Pelangi. The film has helped to establish the fine local beaches on the tourist trail.

hotels and restaurants. Nearby are the remains of an old Dutch fort.

On Sumatra's southeast coast, **Way Kambas National Park** ⓫ comprises estuaries, marshes and open grassland and is the home of the **Sumatra Rhino Sanctuary**. Recommended is the four-hour (one-way) boat trip through rainforests from Labuhan Meringgi, 12km (7 miles) south of the reserve, to the Way Kambas estuary, an excellent way to look for wild elephants, tigers and boars that come to the river's edge to drink. Birdwatching is also spectacular, with resident kingfishers, lesser adjutants, woolly-necked storks and pelicans. The park also houses an **Elephant Conservation Centre**, where the pachyderms are bred and trained to perform heavy work and to patrol park boundaries.

PALEMBANG

Going north along the east coast, **Palembang** ⓬, a booming oil town, is Sumatra's second-largest city and sits on the banks of the mighty Sungai Musi. A major port for well over 1,200 years, Palembang was the capital of the Srivijaya kingdom around AD 600 and a spiritual centre where Mahayana Buddhist monks from as far away as China studied and translated texts.

Palembang had unhappy experiences of European interference during the colonial era, beginning in 1811–12 when British meddling culminated in a bloody incursion to unseat the then sultan and to seize the valuable offshore island of **Bangka**. The following two decades saw frequent forced changes at the head of the sultanate and frequent hostilities before the Dutch eventually assumed outright control.

Palembang's ornately carved traditional houses and shops are raised on piles above the Musi, where river merchants ply their trade from boats. The region produces fine woven fabrics

and has its own dances, including the *gending srivijaya*, dating from the 7th century. The **Museum Rumah Bari** (Tue–Sat 8am–4pm, Sun 8am–noon), occupying several buildings, contains important megalithic statuary, Hindu and Buddhist sculptures, primitive ethnic crafts, weaponry and Chinese porcelain. An old Dutch fort is still used by the Indonesian army.

West of Bangka, on the east coast of the mainland, is **Sembilang National Park**, reached by motorboat from Palembang in about four hours. Its lack of easy access has prevented large-scale tourism development, which could be a good thing for the tigers, elephants, tapirs, giant tortoises, freshwater dolphins and otters that live there. This park is also excellent for birdwatching, as it is a habitat for migrating birds that come from as far away as Siberia.

At Sembilang's northern boundary, **Berbak National Park** is a Ramsar protected wetlands site. It owes its importance to its large, undisturbed swamp forests, criss-crossed by muddy rivers.

⊙ Tip
Boats can be hired in Canti village, near Bandar Lampung, to make the choppy 3-hour crossing to Anak Krakatau volcano. Krakatau can also be accessed from West Java.

Sumatran elephants.

Skewered meat is a street-food staple.

A swanky pool at the Angsana Resort & Spa, Bintan island.

JAMBI

Further north, **Jambi** , the site of the ancient Melayu kingdom, is today a modern city, its growing economy based on palm oil, logging, rubber, coffee and tea exports. The surrounding forests are still home to a handful of Kubu people, the original hunter-gatherer inhabitants of the area, though most are now settled in modern communities.

Exploration of the city starts along the river, where a large number of people live on floating rafts or in houses built on stilts over the Sungai Batanghari. You can walk or ride on a *dokar* (horse-drawn cart), and visit the Pasar Raya (Central Market).

The Hindu temple complex **Muaro Jambi**, 25km (15 miles) northeast of the city, is an hour by car or 30 minutes by speedboat. Accessible by four-wheel-drive along the Sungai Sengering are the 10 stalactite **Tiangko Caves**.

Relatively small **Bukit Duabelas National Park** is in Jambi province and consists of lowland tropical rainforest in the northern part, while in the south, the secondary forest is a result of logging. This park is the home of the Rimbu people, hunter-gatherers who live in small groups and are governed by traditional laws.

RIAU PROVINCE

Between the swampy shores of Sumatra and the Malay Peninsula lies a chain of more than 3,000 small islands. These and the eastern mainland Sumatran lowlands comprise **Riau** province, one of the fastest-growing parts of Indonesia in terms of economics, population and tourist expansion.

Pekanbaru , the provincial capital and the largest city in mainland Riau, is a thriving oil-production centre. This friendly oil town, with a large foreign population, is a good base for exploring nearby jungle abodes of the durian-loving Sumatran rhinoceros, as well as tigers, elephants and birds. At **Siak Sri Indrapura** village, four hours downriver, stands a palace that was built in 1723.

Muara Takus, a temple near the hydroelectric plant, dates from the 9th century AD. It is believed to have been built when the power of the South Sumatra-based Sriwijaya Empire was at its peak.

In this area at the **Tesso Nilo National Park**, the World Wildlife Fund and Indonesian forestry department operate a Sumatran tiger conservation unit. In a successful community empowerment programme, mahouts are selected from villages and trained to patrol the park on elephant-back. Called the Flying Squad, these groups herd wild elephants that threaten villages and crops back into the park.

BATAM AND BINTAN ISLANDS

Once part of a maritime sultanate, the islands of the Riau Archipelago are now a zone of major economic activity. **Batam** ⑮ has been developed into a major industrial satellite of Singapore and is popular with weekend visitors from there, who come for its golf courses, beaches, duty-free shopping and seafood. Ferries and hydrofoils ply the waters to and from Singapore almost hourly, from sunrise to sundown.

Bintan ⑯ is the largest of all the Riau islands, and its northern shore is a string of high-end resorts catering to well-heeled Singaporeans and Indonesians.

The energetic **Tanjungpinang** port town, situated on the island's southeastern coast, is a quick one-hour ferry ride from Singapore, and is also a jumping-off spot to nearby tiny islands and the Lingga archipelago. Attractions include the small but interesting **Museum Riau** situated on Jalan Brigjen Katamso in the eastern suburbs. You can catch a speedboat to **Senggarang**, a Chinese village on the far side of the Sungai Riau. Its four shrines include the Banyan Tree temple, a 300-year-old clan house suspended in a giant banyan tree.

Just across from Tanjungpinang is **Penyengat**, the historical home base of the Riau sultans, their lavish court and royal city that encompassed nearly 10,000 citizens. A book entitled *Bustanul Katibin*, the first Malay grammar text, was published on Penyengat in 1857, laying the foundation for Bahasa Indonesia, the lingua franca of the entire country.

Spanning 14km (9 miles) along the north coast is **Pasir Panjang** beach, a sprawling complex of deluxe hotels, golf courses, spas and condos and the reason most tourists go to Bintan. A self-contained resort area, every water sport imaginable is available. From here, excursions can be arranged for trekking up Gunung Bintan; enjoying the cool breezes amid lush greenery at Lagoi Park and Reservoir; boating up the Sebung River for an eco-tour of the mangrove forests; interacting with bottlenose dolphins at Dolphin Lodge; and riding an elephant at Bintan Elephant Park.

⊙ Tip

Both Batam and Bintan islands are easily accessible from Singapore. High-speed catamarans can whisk you to the resort islands in under an hour, and numerous travel agents in Singapore sell room-and-ferry packages.

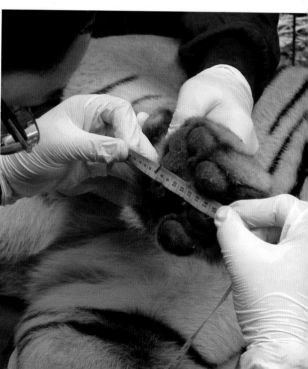

Measuring a Sumatran tiger being tracked at Sembilang National Park. The paw size is a good indicator of the animal's age and health.

The entrance to Taman Kemuda Saraswati temple in Ubud, Bali.

Legong dance performance.

BALI

Bali has been on the tourist radar for a century, but despite the crowds it retains a unique cultural charm, and beyond the seething southern resorts the 'real Bali' endures.

The name Bali evokes visions of mystical landscapes, mysterious temples and hospitable islanders. It's an image that has lured travellers for decades, but despite the rampant commercialism in some areas, its culture and landscapes remain as captivating as ever.

Coconut and flower offerings at a Balinese temple.

Despite its small size, there are always new facets of Bali to explore. Regional autonomy, giving each district control over its own destiny – and revenues – has stirred the creative juices of hitherto little-visited areas. The southern coastline of West Bali, for example, is filling up fast with new resorts. The difference here is that instead of luxury five-star international chain hotels, the accommodation is more of the boutique variety, with many places managed by Balinese who favour taking guests on scenic drives through the 'cultural landscape of Bali' – designated by Unesco as a World Heritage Site – to villages to soak in the local culture rather than staging in-house 'shows'. Trained, English-speaking trekking guides at West Bali National Park are chosen from local communities and are a part of village empowerment programmes. Resorts near the park help to patrol its boundaries and lead environmentally smart activities for local children. At nearby Pemuteran, resorts and dive shops teach and employ villagers to restore and protect reefs.

Pura Tirtha Empul, Ubud.

The north coast beaches are sprouting healing, wellbeing and yoga centres. Lovina has morphed from a sleepy alternative beach destination to a springboard for exploring the highlands to its south. Newly built family-run resorts now dot the highlands, bases for the activities that cool mountain air-seekers can enjoy.

On the east coast, Amed is spawning bungalows and villas that are ideal for a combination of beachside relaxation, underwater adventures and inland exploration. Offshore, Nusa Lembongan still draws the crowds, but it is its long-overlooked neighbour, Nusa Penida, that has become the most talked about new destination in Bali, for its rugged limestone landscapes and picture-perfect beaches.

South Bali remains as busy – and enjoyable – as ever, but resorts are being developed further west to appeal to a more exclusive clientele, eventually flowing into expensive villa-mansions as far afield as Tanah Lot.

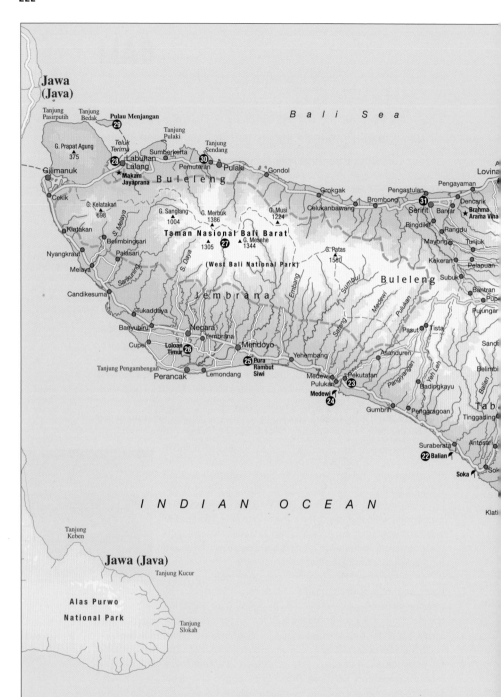

**Jawa
(Java)**

Tanjung
Pasirputih

Tanjung
Bedak

Pulau Menjangan

㉙

B a l i   S e a

Tanjung
Pulaki

G. Prapat Agung
▲
375

*Teluk
Terima*

Tanjung
Sendang

Sumberkerta

㉘ Labuhan
Lalang

㉚

Gilimanuk

★ Makam
Jayaprana

Pemuteran

Pulaki

Gondol

B u l e l e n g

Lovina

A

Cekik

G. Kelatakan
▲
698

G. Sanglang
▲
1004

G. Merbuk
▲
1386

Grokgak

G. Musi
1224
▲

Celukanbawang

Pengastulan

Brombong

Seririt

Pengayaman

㉛

Dencarik

Banjar

★ Brahma
Arama Viha

Klatakan

Belimbingsari

Palasari

Taman Nasional Bali Barat

G. Mesehe
1305 ㉗ ▲ 1344

Ringdikih

Rangdu

Nyangkraut

S. Melaya

S. Daya

(West Bali National Park)

G. Patas
▲
1580

Mayong

Tunjuk

Kakeran

Pelapuan

Melaya

Sankuning

Embang

B u l e l e n g

Subuk

Candikesuma

J e m b r a n a

Sumbul

Medewi

Pulukan

Bantran

Pup

Tukaddaya

Banyubiru

Negara

Yembrana

Cupel

Loloan
Timur

㉖

Mendoyo

Satang

Pasut

Tista

Pujungar

Sand

Perancak

Tanjung Pengambengan

㉕ Pura
Rambut
Siwi

Lemondang

Yehembang

Medewi

Pulukan

㉓ Pekutatan

Asahduren

Pangyangan

Yeh Leh

Balian

Belimbi

Badingkayu

Medewi ⚓
㉔

Gumbrih

Pengaragoan

T a b

Tinggading

I N D I A N   O C E A N

Suraberata

㉒ Balian ⚓

Soka ⚓

Antosari

Sok

Klati

Tanjung
Keben

Jawa (Java)

Tanjung Kucur

Alas Purwo

National Park

Tanjung
Slokah

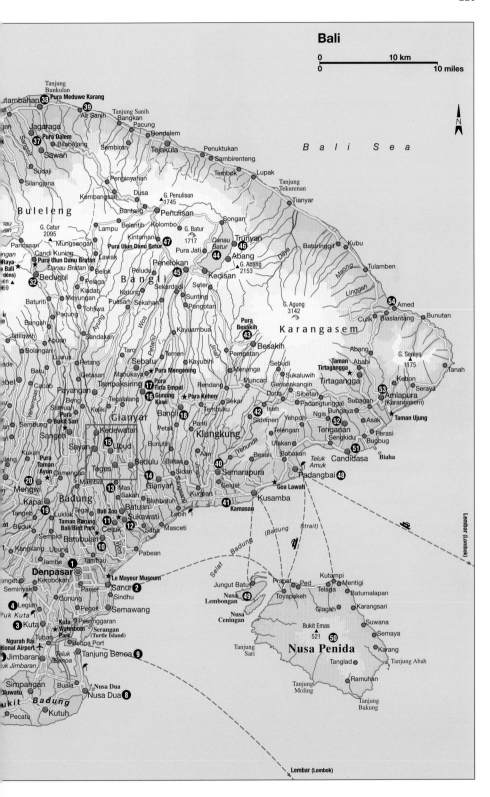

Bali

0   10 km
0   10 miles

SOUTH BALI

The busy south is the heartland of tourism, business and governance in Bali – though it still offers superb beaches, epic sunsets and pockets of tranquillity and sophistication.

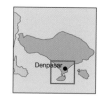
Denpasar

Today, southern Bali is overwhelmingly urban, with the capital, Denpasar, merging seamlessly with the busy resort areas to the east, west and south. The region's saving grace is its long coastline, from the vast west coast beaches to the craggy limestone cliffs of the Bukit Peninsula.

Throughout the island's history, southern Bali has been the first to welcome or repel outsiders. The first recorded Balinese ruler, Sri Kesari Warmadewa – possibly an invader from Java – left an inscribed pillar at Sanur in AD 914. In later times, important Javanese priests trod these shores. Empu Kuturan came to Bali in the 10th century and introduced the *meru*, or multi-tiered roofed shrine. At the turn of the 20th century, south Bali's encounters with European colonialism were shockingly violent, but in the decades that followed the region's reputation as a tourist paradise emerged. The first hotel on Kuta beach was built by an American couple in 1936. Mid-20th-century political turmoil stalled development for a time, but since the late 1960s South Bali has seen never-ending tourism expansion, with the industry as deeply embedded in local lifestyles and culture as rice farming once was. Today, the mix of old established tourist demographics with visitors from emerging markets,

especially China, a large and diverse expat population, and huge numbers of domestic tourists, create an air of manic cosmopolitanism, which, while repelling some visitors, is for others southern Bali's main attraction.

Though the area is now a single conurbation, the different areas of southern Bali maintain distinct characters. Kuta remains the hub of budget tourism, bolstered by the booming domestic market, while Tuban, closer to the airport, is marginally more upmarket and particularly popular with middle

Main attractions
Museum Negeri Propinsi
  Bali, Denpasar
Taman Werdi Budaya,
  Denpasar
Sanur
Kuta
Pura Tanah Lot
Bukit beaches
Pura Luhur Uluwatu
Nusa Dua
Tanjung Benoa

Map on page 222

The kecak dance.

Shadow puppets.

class visitors from Indonesia's big cities. North of Kuta, Legian harbours those who want to be part of the Kuta scene, but prefer to sleep somewhere quieter. To the northwest, exclusivity comes in the form of beaches in Seminyak and Petitinget, giving way to more diffuse development in Kerobokan and Canggu, dominated by villas. On the opposite coast, Sanur enjoys a much slower pace, as a mixed resort area catering to most tastes and budgets.

Further south, Jimbaran and the rugged cliffs of the Bukit Peninsula create an entirely different atmosphere, with a number of ultra-exclusive resorts and extensive villa complexes. Nusa Dua continues to draw those who seek total, luxurious escape, isolated from the rest of the world, while Tanjung Benoa captivates a less staid crowd of sun- and sea sports-lovers.

DENPASAR

Denpasar ❶ is a traffic-clogged government and financial centre incorporating winding alleys, illogical one-way streets and pungent smells. If your mind has been unwinding on the beach, it may well be wound back up on an excursion into Denpasar. Once a parking spot is located, most of the city's main sights are within walking distance from each other.

Central to the city is **Taman Puputan** (Puputan Park), a large, grassy open space commemorating the battle between the *raja* of the Badung Empire and the Dutch militia in 1906. Rather than being conquered by the Dutch, thousands of Balinese warriors, dressed in their finest regalia and armed only with *keris* daggers and spears, hurled themselves into battle in a heroic sacrifice, dying either by their own hands or by Dutch bullets in ritual suicide known as *puputan* (literally, 'end'). Today, the slaughter of the estimated 600 to 2,000 is memorialised by a bronze statue. North of the square is the former Dutch governor's residence, where the *raja*'s palace once stood.

Catur Mukha, the great statue with four faces and eight arms at Denpasar's main intersection (at the northwestern corner of Taman Puputan), represents the Hindu god of the four directions.

MUSEUM NEGERI PROPINSI BALI

East of the square is **Museum Negeri Propinsi Bali** (Bali Museum; Sat–Thu 8am–3.30pm, Fri 8am–12.30pm). Built in 1932 by the Dutch, it presents a comprehensive history of Bali's social and cultural development from prehistoric times to the early 20th century. Items are well presented, although no specific dates of origin are given, but knowledgeable English-speaking guides are on hand. The museum is notable for its fine architecture, combining the two principal edifices of Balinese temples (*pura*) and palaces (*puri*): split gate with outer and inner courtyards, and the *kulkul* (wooden signal drum) tower.

The museum is representative of the entire island. The main building, with its wide-pillared verandah, resembles the Karangasem palaces of East Bali, with a porch used by officials in audience with the *raja*. The windowless building to its north reflects the Tabanan palace style of West Bali. The brick building, **Gedung Buleleng**, belongs to the northern palace style of Singaraja; inside are beautiful examples of wedding costumes and items used in religious rituals.

Next to the museum is the modern state temple, **Pura Jagatnata**, dedicated to Sanghyang Widi Wasa, the supreme god (manifested in Bali's numerous local deities and ancestral spirits). Elaborate ceremonies are held here every full and new moon. The tall *padmasana* (lotus throne), made of white coral, symbolises universal order. The turtle Bedawang Nala and two *naga* serpents represent the foundations of the world, while the throne signifies the cosmic mountain.

Denpasar means 'north of the market'. **Pasar Badung** (daily 24 hours), on Jalan Gajah Mada is a four-storey building housing Bali's largest traditional market. Locals shop for fruit and vegetables, meat and seafood, clothing, spices, baskets, ritual paraphernalia and everything else. Women wait outside offering market tours for a negotiable fee, with stops at shops where they earn a commission. Politely

The Museum Negiri Propinsi Bali.

decline their assistance and stroll on your own. Across the Tukad Badung canal is **Pasar Kumbasari** (daily 8am–5pm), offering the same items as Pasar Badung plus handicrafts and art.

Nightlife in Denpasar revolves around the three huge colourful *pasar malam* (local night markets) that operate at Pasar Kumbasari; Pasar Kereneng, near the bus station off Jalan Kamboja; and the Pekambingan (Goat Penis) area just off Jalan Diponegoro. Here, an array of temporary stalls offer all kinds of cooked food, while hawkers push more unusual items like snake oil and charms as well as the ubiquitous T-shirts and sandals.

Pura Maospahit (daily during daylight hours; donation), on Jalan Sutomo, is the oldest temple in the city. It dates from the 14th century, when Majapahit Empire emissaries arrived from Java. Extensive earthquake damage in 1917 resulted in much of the temple being rebuilt; the section at the back is the only part that has remained unaltered for 600 years.

DENPASAR'S ARTS

A permanent exhibition of traditional and contemporary Balinese visual arts is at the **Taman Werdi Budaya** (popularly called the **Art Centre**; daily 8am–3.30pm), 2km (1.25 miles) east of downtown, on Jalan Nusa Indah. Bali's numerous art disciplines are represented at this large complex, including painting, woodcarving, shadow puppetry, silverwork, weaving, dance costumes and even ivory carving. Works by Bali's foreign artists are displayed in the museum.

The Art Centre was established in 1973 to showcase Balinese art and culture and includes teaching facilities, a restaurant, craft shop and an outdoor arena for traditional dances. The grounds are also home to the annual Bali Art Festival (mid-June–mid-July).

Next to the centre is **Sekolah Tinggi Seni Indonesia** (STSI; Mon–Fri 8am–2pm), the Indonesia Institute of the Arts, founded in 1967. Students study traditional dance, music and puppetry, and classical and contemporary choreography.

An exhibit at Denpasar's Art Centre.

For serious study, the **Pusat Doku-mentasi** (Documentation Centre) in Renon offers a collection of works in all languages on Balinese life and culture. Documents may not be removed, but can be photocopied on the premises. A lovely tree-lined 'suburb' southeast of Denpasar, **Renon** is also the location of most foreign consulates and the respected Udayana University.

SANUR

Local tradition maintained that shipwrecks held bounty from Baruna, god of the sea, and thus anyone had rights to them. The Dutch had a different viewpoint. In 1904, a Chinese schooner was wrecked off the shores of **Sanur ❷**. Pillaging by the local people breached a treaty between the Balinese and the Dutch, and this incident was just the excuse the Dutch needed to wage war against the Badung *raja*. The result was the *puputan* massacre commemorated in Denpasar's Taman Puputan.

Sanur became an enclave for artists around the world in the 1930s. By the 1950s, the first cluster of bungalows in Sanur was built, attracting international travellers. The high-rise Bali Beach Hotel opened in 1966, built with Japanese reparation money after World War II. Subsequently introduced bylaws restricting building heights mean that it remains the only true high-rise in southern Bali, an unmissable landmark (now operating as the Inna Grand Bali Beach Hotel) towering over the surrounding low-rise resorts.

Today, Sanur has all levels of accommodation, with access roads lined with shops and restaurants. Amid the development and tourism frenzy, Sanur has managed, remarkably, to retain much of its quaint heritage as a Brahman-dominated village, where trance performances are still staged during local temple festivals. Sanur's seas are calm and shallow, disappearing altogether at low tide, leaving little more than great swathes of sandy mud and coral stretching for hundreds of metres out along the reef. When the tides are high, however, Sanur offers windsurfing and sailing.

One of the few historical sites in Sanur is the home of Belgian painter

Museum Le Mayeur.

Beach volleyball at Sanur.

An artist at work in Legian.

Eating out, Seminyak.

Jean Le Mayeur de Mepres. He moved to Bali in 1932, where he lived until his death in 1958. **Museum Le Mayeur** (Sat–Thu 8.30am–3pm, Fri 8.30am–12.30pm), just north of Inna Grand Bali Beach Hotel, has gardens full of statues, luxuriant gold-and-crimson carvings, and Le Mayeur's own paintings, mostly of his late wife, Ni Polok, a renowned *legong* dancer.

At the southern end of Sanur is the **Pura Belanjong** (daily during daylight hours; donation), notable for the island's oldest example of writing, the Prasasti Belanjong, an inscribed pillar dating from AD 913 and discovered in the early 1930s. The 177cm (70in) tall stone column is not much to look at, but close inspection reveals two forms of writing, ancient Balinese and Sanskrit.

KUTA, TUBAN AND LEGIAN

In former times **Kuta ❸** was a leper colony and slave station with poor soil; its original villagers were farmers, fishermen and metalsmiths. At the outset of mass tourism, they looked askance at foreigners frolicking along the ocean, a spiritually hostile zone in Balinese worldviews. But they soon saw there were profits to be made and invited travellers into their homes for clean, simple and cheap accommodation.

Today Kuta is the ultimate manifestation of contemporary Bali's transformation by tourism, as the brashest and most congested of all its resort areas. Beneath the surface, however, a traditional community endures; locals continue to leave *canang* – little offering trays – at the high-tide mark each day to pacify the spirits. The surf at Kuta surf break is among the best for learners, but the undertow is fierce, so be sure to swim in places marked by flags. The sunset here is usually glorious.

Inland from the beach, **Kuta** is packed with a dazzling array of pubs, bars, souvenir shops, tattoo parlours, travel offices, accommodation and handicraft kiosks. Nestled in between are temples, somehow retaining their dignity. Beach and street hawkers can be an annoyance. Kuta's nightlife scene is the most raucous in Bali, with some darker undercurrents of drug-dealing,

rostitution and organised crime, though by day the area remains popular with families, from both other parts of Indonesia and overseas. South of Kuta, down Jalan Dewi Sartika, quieter **Tuban** is a midrange resort area. **Waterbom Park** (daily 9am–6pm) has water slides, restaurants and spa treatments. There are lifeguards on duty, but adults must accompany children under 12 years old. It can get crowded later in the day and especially at weekends, with long queues, but is well worth the wait.

Just opposite Waterbom Park and next to Discovery Kartika Plaza Hotel is the modern Discovery Shopping Mall – right on the beach – with an array of shops and the Centro and Sogo department stores.

In memory of the victims of the 2002 Bali bombings, a permanent memorial was built on the site of the destroyed Paddy's Pub on Legian Street. The memorial is made of intricately carved stone, set with a large marble plaque, with names and nationalities of each of those killed, and is illuminated at night.

A new bar, 'Paddy's Reloaded', was reopened further along Legian Street.

Legian ❹ is more sedate than Kuta and is preferred by Bali's young expatriate population. Their influence can be seen throughout the area in boutiques and a number of excellent restaurants, cafés and bars.

SEMINYAK, KEROBOKAN, PETITENGET AND CANGGU

Further north, the decidedly hip **Seminyak** is home to exclusive hotels, designer boutiques, spas, trendy beachside restaurants and nightclubs, which are crammed into every available space. This is expat heaven, and expensive private and rental villas have replaced much of what once was the village.

Seminyak has the same wide sandy beach and thundering surf as Kuta, but without the heaving crowds. **Jalan Kayu Aya** at its northern boundary and **Jalan Abimanyu** at its southern end have also made a name for themselves: the former has a clutch of hip restaurants and the latter some equally trendy bars and clubs.

Pura Tanah Lot.

Northeast of Seminyak is **Kerobokan.** Without a beach to lure travellers, it is popular with longer-stay visitors, with a large number of rental villas the key draw. Along Jalan Raya Kerobokan are furniture shops and galleries catering to exporters.

Northwest of Seminyak is **Petitenget.** Formerly known to tourists only as a part of Seminyak (the dividing line is the north side of Jalan Kayu Aya), it is now establishing its own identity as upmarket, like its neighbour, but removed from the horrendous traffic further south.

Continuing northwest towards Tanah Lot, the coastline is an enormous construction zone. This is **Canggu**, once a rural area only known to locals surfers, but now dominated by vast villas. A few patches of farmland still survive, but Canggu has largely been incorporated in Bali's urban sprawl.

PURA TANAH LOT

Continuing northwest from Canggu will bring you to one of Bali's most noted sites, **Pura Tanah Lot ❺** (daily, daylight hours). From the Kerobokan junction, turn west towards Canggu and follow the signs.

Set apart from the land on a stone pedestal carved by incoming tides, Tanah Lot's solitary black towers and tufts of foliage spilling over the cliffs recall the delicacy of a Chinese painting, although the gauntlet of souvenir stalls and hawkers on the temple approach may diminish this image. In caves surrounding the temple dwell striped sacred snakes, discreetly left undisturbed by Balinese. Only worshippers are allowed inside the temple, but visitors get a dramatic view from the adjacent hill, especially at sunset.

Tanah Lot is attributed to the 16th-century priest Danghyang Nirartha. During his travels, Nirartha saw a bright light emanating from a point on the west coast and came to this spot to meditate. The disciple of a local spiritual leader became fascinated by Nirartha and began to study with him. This angered the local priest who, filled with jealousy, challenged Nirartha. The unflappable Nirartha simply moved his meditation spot into the ocean, and this point became known as Tanah Lot, or 'Land in the Sea.'

JIMBARAN AND BUKIT PENINSULA

An exclusive resort area is found along the coast south of **Jimbaran ❻**, housing hotel bigwigs such as Four Seasons and InterContinental. All of them face the sea within easy reach of Jimbaran village and its justly celebrated beachside seafood restaurants.

Connected to the mainland by a low, narrow isthmus, the limestone tableland of the **Bukit Peninsula** (also known as Bukit Badung, or simply 'the Bukit'), rising to 200 metres (660ft) above sea level, is a striking contrast to the lush Bali mainland. Vantage spots along the road that crosses the hill afford breathtaking northern vistas rising to the peaks of distant volcanoes;

Uluwatu lace shop, Seminyak.

n ideal place to catch beautiful sunsets. Various exclusive resorts – including the ultra-luxurious Bvlgari – are scattered across the Bukit, amidst every-multiplying villa complexes.

PURA LUHUR ULUWATU AND THE BUKIT BEACHES

At the western tip of Bukit Badung, where rocky precipices drop almost 100 metres (330ft) to the ocean, is Pura Luhur Uluwatu ❼ (daily, daylight hours), 70 metres (230ft) up on a dramatic promontory. Originally dating from around the 16th century, it is one of the Sad Kahyangan, or Six Temples of the World, revered by all Balinese. The holy Javanese priest Danghyang Nirartha established this temple, and it is said he achieved enlightenment here. The innermost sanctuary, *jeroan*, is off-limits to non-worshippers but can be viewed from the side. South of the temple and car park, a panoramic short path leads along the cliff top. Uluwatu is famous among tourists for its spectacularly located nightly performance of the *Kecak* dance. Most visit on organised excursions, but tickets are also available at the gate.

The Bukit is prime surfing territory, with a string of fabled reef breaks along the southern and western coast. These places are explicitly not for beginners, but the Cliffside cafes at **Suluban** (also known as Uluwatu among the surf fraternity for the nearby temple) provide an excellent vantage point. There are some stunning beaches along the coast heading back north from Uluwatu, including easily accessible **Padang Padang**, the massively developed Dreamland area, and Bingin and Balangan further south.

NUSA DUA AND TANJUNG BENOA

Nusa Dua ❽, on the east coast of Bukit Peninsula, is a slightly sterile paradise. A purpose-built, luxury hotel enclave, sprawling in the middle of a coconut grove and alongside a white-sand beach, Nusa Dua caters decidedly to the upmarket traveller. Luxury hotels wrap around the beach, among which are several international chains. Water sports available here include spectacular parasailing, and jet-skiing. The well-regarded **Bali Golf & Country Club** has a championship golf course, with nine holes heading towards the sea and nine holes inland. At least seven temples are within Nusa Dua's bounds.

For many years, **Tanjung Benoa** ❾, a fishing village north of Nusa Dua on a long peninsula, was long overlooked by hotel developers, but the peninsula is now lined with four- and five-star hotels, as well as lower-end accommodation and restaurants. Benoa offers an attractive stretch of white-sand beach, which, like Sanur, is susceptible to the tides. A walk north up the peninsula reveals a bustling morning market and a multicultural community, evolved from decades as a trading centre, reflected in Chinese and Muslim cemeteries, and Chinese, Muslim and Hindu temples.

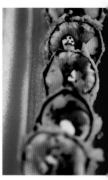

Seminyak sushi bar.

⊘ THE CREMATION CEREMONY

Balinese Hindus believe a soul borrows a physical human body, so upon death this body is returned to the five elements – wind, earth, fire, water and ether – to release the soul and enable it to reincarnate on earth or unite with the divine Supreme Being. No weeping or grief is openly displayed, as this makes the soul unwilling to leave.

Cremation ceremonies are so costly that a family often waits years to share expenses in a joint ceremony. In the meantime, the body is purified and buried in the village cemetery. Once a cremation date is set, ritual specialists, priests, friends and neighbours help mobilise the communal spirit. If a body has been buried, the bones are exhumed or the body is placed in a sarcophagus inside a colourful cremation tower.

A noisy procession leads the way as dozens of men carry the tower on their shoulders to a field where the cremation will take place, spinning it at crossroads to confuse the soul so that it cannot find its way home to disturb the living.

After the corpse is reduced to ashes, the family gathers and pulverises the charred bone fragments, and puts them in a yellow coconut that they cast into the sea. Purification ceremonies for the community who participated in the cremation are held three days later.

Topeng show in Ubud.

CENTRAL BALI

Beyond the tourist centres lie rice terrace panoramas, ancient temples, and a series of craft villages where art is an authentic part of everyday life.

Denpasar

Central Bali is best known for Ubud, the island's artistic centre, and many visitors perch there and are content to wander its narrow streets on extensive shopping expeditions or relax in its healing centres, perhaps taking in a dance performance in the evenings. Situated in the hills north of Denpasar and only accessible by narrow, winding, often traffic-laden roads, Ubud is the epitome of Bali for many travellers.

Beyond the now overcrowded town, much of the rich history of Balinese culture lies peacefully hidden in the surrounding countryside and can be enjoyed on day trips of scenic drives taking in memorable vistas of rice fields and deep river gorges. Antiquities dating from the 11th century abound in the outlying areas west, north and east of Ubud, with one rare artefact dating back to Indonesia's Bronze Age. And along with these treasures are glimpses into the deep-rooted traditions that remain very strong within Balinese society.

THE ROAD TO UBUD

The road from Denpasar to Ubud is now developed along most of its route, but it still passes through a series of distinct communities. The first 'village' outside Denpasar is **Batubulan** ⑩, stretching for about 2km (1.2 miles) and distinguished by stone-carving shops lining

the roadside. Soft *paras* stone, found in nearby ravines, is used to create deities and demons for temples, households and, now, tourists. Males carve in groups at roadside 'factories', reproducing designs formed by their ancestors and, increasingly, those which appeal to visitors.

Batubulan holds daily performances of the Barong dance on a stage near Pura Puseh temple. The drama depicts the age-old struggle between good and righteousness – the path of *dharma*, or right-doing – and the negative forces which seek to destroy them.

○ **Main attractions**
Batubulan
Celuk
Sukawati
Ubud
Goa Gajah, Bedulu
Moon of Pejeng, Pejeng
Tampaksiring temples

◉ **Maps on pages
222, 239**

Batabulan stone carving village.

Craftsman at work, Batubalan.

Gamelan music is essential for ceremonies.

Taman Burung Bali Bird Park (daily 9am–5pm), just to the north of Batubalan, houses over 1,000 specimens of 250 exotic bird species in a well-designed aviary and is dedicated to the conservation of rare and endangered birds from Indonesia and elsewhere. Paved paths lead through 2 hectares (5 acres) of gardens representing deserts, rainforests and marshlands.

Continuing along the road to Ubud, numerous wood- and stone-carving shops are interspersed among the houses of **Singapadu**, but the village is more famous for producing some of Bali's talented musicians and dancers. There are also a number of mask workshops, where you can watch a chunk of wood evolve into a beautiful work of art, and also browse collections of finished pieces.

CELUK TO GIANYAR

At the main junction before the bird park, the route turns eastwards to Gianyar. **Celuk** ⓫, some 4km (2.5 miles) from Batubulan, beckons visitors. Here local smiths create sterling silver and gold brooches, gem-studded bracelets and earrings of all descriptions using simple hand tools. Don't miss the shops on the road north and perpendicular to the main road, as many fine jewellers dwell off the beaten track.

Across the Wos River, **Sukawati** ⓬ anchored an extremely powerful kingdom in the 18th century. The town now sports an art market and is home to some of the best *dalang* (puppeteers) on Bali. *Wayang kulit* – shadow puppetry – is a difficult art. Aside from manipulating different puppet characters, memorising hundreds of stories, singing, cueing the musicians, and creating a variety of voices, a *dalang* must be clean in mind, body and soul. He is akin to a priest in many respects and can even make the holy water necessary for Balinese rituals (an honour usually reserved for Brahman priests). *Wayang kulit* stories are imbued with innuendo and impart the values of daily life to the audience.

Many *dalangs* make their own puppets, delicately carved out of buffalo hide and then painted. A number of

dalangs live in the *banjar* behind the Sukawati market, where visitors can watch them work. In Puaya village, north of Sukawati, cowhide also is made into dance accoutrements, such as traditional costumes with ornamented filigree leather headdresses, colourful gilded clothes and beaded epaulets.

Sukawati's **Pasar Seni** (Art Market; daily 8am–7pm) is a two-storey building filled with woodcarvings, clothing and knick-knacks, ceremonial umbrellas, statues, bamboo flutes and basketry. If passing Sukawati early in the morning, look through the *pasar pagi* or morning market, about a block behind the Pasar Seni. In this steaming, packed, warehouse-like barn is every trinket that is on sale in Kuta, but for half the price. The market closes mid-morning.

The family-friendly **Bali Zoo** (tel: 0361-294 357; daily 9am–6pm; night zoo daily 6am–9.30pm) in Sukawati is a 4.6-hectare (12-acre) landscaped zoo that houses many species of exotic birds and other rare creatures such as lesser ape *siamangs*, crocodiles and Komodo dragons.

The **Pura Desa** (village temple; daily during daylight hours; donation) in **Batuan** dates from the 11th century, with fine examples of temple carvings. Head west at the bend in the road. The temple is located directly across from an open-air pavilion.

Mas ⓱ (north of the 'Fat Baby Statue' T-junction to Sakah) is best known for its intricate woodcarvings and masks. Along the main road is Ida Bagus Anom's studio, an artist renowned for new designs in masks. On the west side of the main road is Njana Tilem Gallery.

Many of the inhabitants of Mas are *brahmana* who trace their roots to the great Brahman sage Danghyang Nirartha, the founder of **Pura Taman Pule** (daily during daylight hours; donation), which is just behind the football field.

At the gamelan factory in Banjar Babakan, **Blahbatuh**, barefoot men pump bellows to stir up the heat for forging. They squat with large hammers, bending bronze alloys into the desired shape for the metallophones and knobbed kettles used in gamelan. After

Making shadow puppets.

they are cooled, the master adjusts the instruments' tuning with a bamboo tuning fork. Gamelan casings are assembled and painted here, and instruments for entire ensembles (worth well over US$10,000) may be purchased.

On the back road, 1km (0.6 mile) east from Blahbatuh, is **Belega** village, where bamboo furniture of all sorts is produced. Another 1.5km (1 mile) northeast is **Bona**, which specialises in products woven from dried fan palm leaves. Bona is also the place where the dramatic *kecak* dance was born.

GIANYAR

The richly cultural Gianyar region is part of the old kingdom of the same name, and extends from Central Bali to the southern coast. With bountiful fields and harvests, the people here have had ample time to cultivate artistic talents, resulting in an ideology where aesthetic excellence takes place in everything – carving, painting, weaving, music and dance.

The main town of **Gianyar ⑭** is a fairly quiet administrative centre.

During Dutch confrontations, the Gianyar regency was sympathetic to the colonists and thus suffered considerably less violence than other southern kingdoms. The last *raja* maintained his figurehead position until his death in 1999. The former palace, Puri Agung Gianyar, opposite Gianyar field, is not open to visitors.

The speciality of the area is woven *kain endek* (weft ikat cloth) used in traditional wear. Numerous factories conduct informal tours, where visitors can watch the dyeing and weaving process.

UBUD

Northwest of Gianyar is **Ubud ⑮**. Named after *ubad*, or medicine, it refers to the healing properties of plants growing on the Campuhan River at the western end of town. Ubud was also the seat of a 19th-century aristocratic family, whose descendants continue to command great respect among the locals.

The first few foreigners to settle here, from Europe in the 1920s, were artists seeking inspiration within their surroundings. The masses that followed in subsequent decades brought

Batuan mask makers.

commercialisation, which in turn benefited growth of the arts.

Ubud's tourism foundation, **Yayasan Bina Wisata** (west of the main market, daily 8am–8pm) unifies the needs of both travellers and citizens. Visitors are asked to respect local ceremonies, wear traditional clothing when appropriate and learn about the area's people. The foundation's staff helps to answer questions and plot journeys, and a message board carries details of area festivals, ceremonies and cremations.

THE ARTS QUARTER

West of the Ubud market on Jalan Raya Ubud is **Museum Puri Lukisan A** (daily 9am–6pm). Founded in 1953, the excellent collection showcases the richness of traditional and modern Balinese art. The main building exhibits older works, a second displays paintings by the spirited Young Artists of the 1960s, and a third houses temporary exhibits. Further west is the **Blanco Renaissance Museum** (daily 9am–5pm), which sits at the top of a steep driveway, just past Campuhan Bridge. The ornately

decorated museum displays the works of the late self-professed Spanish-Filipino 'maestro' – mainly erotic paintings of his favourite models: his Balinese wife and their daughter.

To understand Balinese art better, a visit to **Neka Art Museum B** (Mon–Sat 9am–5pm, Sun noon–5pm) beyond Campuhan is essential. This wonderful display of paintings was assembled by former schoolteacher Suteja Neka, one of Bali's foremost art connoisseurs. Nearly 400 artworks are chronologically displayed and well documented with descriptive labels in English and Japanese, providing an excellent background to the development of Balinese painting. The multilingual staff are both friendly and knowledgeable. The museum also has an extensive research library, well-stocked bookstore and souvenir shop, and a café with spectacular panoramic views. For works for sale, visit **Neka Art Gallery** (tel: 0316-975 034; daily 9am–5pm) on Jalan Raya Ubud.

Further east along the same street is **Seniwati Gallery of Art by Women** (Tue–Sun 9am–5pm), established

Door detail, Neka Art Museum.

Schoolgirls, Ubud.

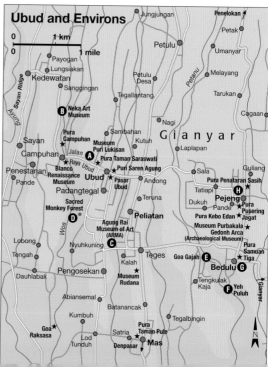

⊘ Tip

Ubud's Threads of Life Indonesian Textiles Arts Centre (Jalan Kajeng 24; www.threadsoflife.com) sells beautiful handmade textiles from throughout Indonesia. Ask about its tours to Balinese villages that specialise in ikat and *songket* weaving.

in 1991 by British expatriate Mary Northmore. The gallery represents female artists from Bali and other parts of Indonesia, as well as foreigners.

South of Ubud, in the direction of Pengosekan village, lies **Agung Rai Museum of Art (ARMA)** ⊙ (daily 9am–6pm), showing an extensive collection of works by Balinese, Indonesian and foreign artists. A side room features a small painting attributed to German artist Walter Spies. Works are titled in English, Indonesian and Japanese. ARMA also promotes Balinese performing arts and has a bookshop and library.

Continue south on the main road towards Denpasar to **Museum Rudana** (daily 9am–5pm). Its massive building shows works in the Kamasan, Ubud and Batuan styles, paintings by well-known contemporary Indonesian artists, and exquisite wooden sculptures.

CENTRAL UBUD

Pasar Ubud (daily 7am–5pm), at the junction of Jalan Raya Ubud and Monkey Forest Road, has a warren of cheap souvenir stalls in its upper levels. The lower levels remain a local produce market – especially lively first thing in the morning, when 'traditional Bali' briefly holds sway before the modern tourism commerce kicks in for the rest of the day. Across the road from the market, on the northeast corner of the intersection, is **Puri Saren Agung**, from where Ubud was ruled from the late 1800s until World War II. The buildings were erected following a devastating earthquake in 1917. Evenings here see traditional dance performances.

Take a stroll down shop- and hotel-lined Monkey Forest Road to Ubud's **Sacred Monkey Forest** ⊙ (8.30am–6pm), for a walk through beautiful and dense tropical jungle. Like all 'monkey forests' in Bali, the experience is punctuated by roving gangs of mischievous annoying and fearless macaques, which ostensibly protect the temple. They are amusing up to a point, usually breached when one of them pinches keys, sunglasses or any other shiny object, and runs off with it. This walk is best done in the cooler early morning or late afternoon. A temple in the forest, **Pura**

Ubud market.

⊘ OFFERINGS AND INCENSE

Consecrated offerings of food, flowers and palm-leaf figures are essential to the religious rituals of Bali. The island's Hindu-Dharma religion is a fusion of Hinduism and indigenous traditions. Ancestors and deities of fertility and nature are worshipped along with the Hindu Trinity – Brahma, Vishnu and Shiva – and the Buddha.

The supreme god is Sanghyang Widi Wasa, and all gods are considered mere manifestations of him. Hindu-Dharma is founded on the Balinese system of cosmology that strives to maintain the harmony between the cosmos, its divine principles and human existence. Gods and demons are worshipped equally, and daily rituals are performed to maintain this balance. Religious life revolves around sacrifices, offerings and purification ceremonies.

The common daily offering, *canang*, is a small palm-leaf tray of flowers and cooked rice, sprinkled with holy water and anointed with incense. Offerings presented to the gods are made from gifts of nature and left to decay naturally or, if containing food, are later taken home to be eaten by the family who made them. Offerings made to demons or evil spirits are left on the ground, while those to gods are put on high altars, with incense used to carry the essence of it upwards to heaven.

Dalem Agung Padangtegal, is dedicated to Durga, the goddess of death, who often takes the form of Rangda, the queen of the underworld.

AROUND UBUD

West from downtown beyond Campuhan, the road turns north to **Kedewatan**, a village blessed with outstanding views. South from Kedewatan is **Sayan**, a small Ubud 'suburb' that teeters on the edge of the beautiful Sayan ridge, with the Sungai Ayung tumbling down below. The entire ridge from Sayan to Kedewatan and north to **Payangan** is now an enclave of villas and super-deluxe resorts. The Ayung is a popular spot for white-water rafting trips. The two-hour journey floats through 25 Class II rapids, giving an adrenalin rush without too much danger.

Penestanan, between Sayan and Ubud, grew from obscurity when Dutch-born Arie Smit, who lived and worked here as a respected artist, established a small art group during the early 1960s. With Smit's encouragement and enormous freedom of subject matter and style of expression, young painters produced imaginative, Naïve-style scenes of village life and rituals that became known as the Young Artists style.

East of Ubud, **Peliatan** gained fame in the 1950s for its *legong* dancers, who took New York and Paris by storm while on tour. Today, their descendants continue the tradition. One of the few all-female gamelan troupes (gamelan *wanita*) in Bali rehearses in Peliatan.

BEYOND UBUD

Northwest of Ubud is another noted monkey forest. Sangeh's legendary history can be traced to the Hindu *Ramayana* epic, in which the monkey-general Hanuman went to search for magical healing herbs that grew on a mountain. Unable to find the plants, he broke off the peak, but part of the mountain fell to the earth in **Sangeh**, along with a group of monkeys from his army, whose descendants remain there to this day to pester travellers. A moss-covered 17th-century temple, **Pura Bukit Sari**, lies in the heart of the woods.

Feeding the wildlife at Ubud's Monkey Forest.

Pura Taman Pule Hindu temple on Koningan Day, a major Balinese festival during which the ancestors' souls are revered.

Waiting to Dance by Abdul Aziz, Nekka Art Gallery.

An 'elephant cave' lies off the Ubud–Gianyar road, east of Peliatan in Bedulu. **Goa Gajah** Ⓔ (daily 9am–5pm) is mentioned in the 1365 *lontar* (palm-leaf) manuscript of a Javanese court poem as a Balinese place called Lwa Gajah (Elephant River), a Buddhist priest's dwelling, which may refer to the Petanu River, near the cave. Goa Gajah, dating from at least the 11th century, was excavated in 1923.

The entrance is actually a carved head of a monster with a gaping mouth and hands that look as if they are trying to pull apart an opening for people to enter. All around the entrance are fantastically carved leaves, animals, waves and humans. Inside is a 13-metre (43ft) long passage stopping at a T-junction 15 metres (50ft) wide. At one end of the passage is a four-armed statue of elephant-headed Hindu deity Ganesha. At the opposite end is a set of three *lingga* (phalluses). Sleeping niches and Buddhist ruins outside the cave suggest religious syncretism. To the side of the entrance is a 1,000-year-old statue of Hariti, a

Buddhist demoness-cum-goddess. Large male and female figures spout water from their stomachs in a bathing place in front of the cave.

Continue down the road and turn south at a statue to see 14th-century reliefs at **Yeh Puluh** Ⓕ (daily during daylight hours). This 25-metre (80ft) long, 2-metre (7ft) high rock wall is carved in high relief. Aside from Ganesha, there are no religious themes, only scenes from daily life. The sequence begins with a *kakayonan*, the cosmic tree of life used in *wayang kulit* performances.

BEDULU AND NORTHWARDS

Bedulu Ⓖ village was once the site of the early Mahayana Buddhist Warmadewa dynasty dating from the 5th century. By the late 10th century, Balinese religion lacked cohesion due to conflicts between the different sects. Several holy men gathered with the king at **Pura Samuan Tiga** (Temple of the Tripartite Meeting; daily during daylight hours). Out of this exceptional meeting emerged the fusion of Balinese religion

as practised today, with the three elements of animism-ancestor worship, Buddhism and Shivaism.

North of Bedulu is the archaeology museum, **Museum Purbakala** (Mon–Thu 8am–3pm, Fri 8am–noon), with four buildings displaying megalithic and Bronze Age artefacts from throughout Bali.

The **Pejeng** ❼ area has a cluster of important old shrines and sacred springs. Across the road in the rice fields is **Pelinggih Arjuna Metapa** (Shrine of the Meditating Arjuna). Loincloth-clad statues of Arjuna, warrior-hero from the Hindu *Mahabharata* epic, along with two servants, are displayed in a small pavilion with a few other relics.

Just up the road on the same side is **Pura Kebo Edan** (Crazy Water Buffalo Temple; daily during daylight hours; donation). The site is remarkable for its more than 3-metre (11ft) tall statue called the Pejeng Giant, showing a masked male figure dancing upon a wide-eyed figure, perhaps a corpse. Scholars believe that the figure

symbolises Bhairava, a Tantric manifestation of the Hindu god Shiva.

Still further north is **Pura Pusering Jagat** (Navel of the World Temple; daily during daylight hours; donation). It has a shrine with large and unusually realistic stone figures of a *lingga* and *yoni*. Childless couples bring offerings, pray and touch the shrine to ask for offspring. The temple also houses the Pejeng Vessel, Naragiri (Mountain of Men), a cylindrical vessel carved with a scene of the gods and demons churning the ocean of milk to produce the elixir of immortality.

One of the most impressive antiquities in this area – in all of Indonesia, for that matter – is the **Moon of Pejeng** at **Pura Penataran Sasih** (daily during daylight hours), on the main road to the north of Bedulu. This temple was probably the religious centre of the old Pejeng-Bedulu kingdom.

A large 190cm (75in) bronze kettledrum, the Moon of Pejeng, dates back to Indonesia's Bronze Age, which began in 300 BC. It is said to be the largest metal drum in the world cast as a

Making an offering at Pura Kehen.

Pura Kehen.

single piece. Shaped like an hourglass, the rare drum is decorated with eight stylised faces displaying wide-open eyes and earlobes distended by big rings. Other ornamentation suggests that it probably originated in northern Vietnam during the Dong Son era.

Legend says that the drum was a moon (or the wheel of a chariot) that fell from the heavens one night and landed in a tree. The brilliant light disturbed a nocturnal thief, so he climbed up the tree and urinated on it. The moon exploded and killed him, cracking and losing its shine as a result (thus explaining its present condition). Today, no one dares touch the drum, not even the temple priests.

TAMPAKSIRING TEMPLES

Continuing north to **Gunung Kawi** ⓰ (daily during daylight hours), a complex of rock-hewn temples and monks' meditation niches overlooks the Pakerisan River in a valley near **Tampaksiring**. There are 10 temple facades here. Legend says that Kebo Iwa, powerful prime minister of Bedulu, used

magic to carve the monuments, using his fingernails, in just one night. This 11th-century 'Mountain of Poets Temple' complex is remarkably preserved. Mistakenly called tombs, research indicates that the temple facades are monuments commemorating the Warmadewa dynasty. Royal funeral cults in which kings, queens and consorts were deified after death began in Bali around this time.

Up the road is **Pura Mengening** (Clear Water Temple; daily during daylight hours; donation). In a reconstructed temple on a hillside is a freestanding structure, similar in form to those hewn from rock at Gunung Kawi. This temple has a spring of pure water, as indicated by its name, and feeds into the Pakerisan River. It might be the commemorative temple of the Warmadewa king Udayana.

Just to the east, the Balinese believe the sacred **Pura Tirta Empul** ⓱ (Bubbling Water Temple; daily during daylight hours) spring at Tampaksiring was created by the god Indra when he pierced the earth to create the elixir

The Moon of Pejeng, the largest single-cast bronze kettledrum in the world.

of immortality to revive his fallen warriors. The bathing place was built in the 10th century and its waters are said to have curative powers. Balinese from all over the island come to purify themselves here. After presenting a small offering to the spring's deity, men and women go to different sides to bathe. The waters have a common source, but each spout has a different ritual function.

PURA KEHAN

As you climb the slopes of the volcano, the weather turns cooler. Bamboo forests line the roads, and plots abound with sweet potatoes, peanuts, corn and spices on the way to **Bangli** ⑱, capital of an 18th-century kingdom of rulers descended from the Klungkung royal house. The largest and most sacred temple of the district is **Pura Kehen** (daily during daylight hours; donation), an ancient terraced mountain sanctuary and state temple of Bangli.

Below the foot of the stairway is an old temple that houses a collection of bronze plate inscriptions. Statues of

mythological figures line the first terrace to Pura Kehen, from which steps lead to a magnificent gate that the locals call 'the great exit'. Above the gate is the frightening face and splayed hands of Bhoma, the demonic son of the earth who prevents harmful spirits from entering the temple. On both sides of the opening are figures of villagers gesturing in welcome.

An enormous banyan with a *kulkul* (warning drum) nestled in its branches shades the first courtyard, where the upper walls are inlaid with Chinese porcelain plates. An 11-tiered *meru* (pagoda) dedicated to the god Shiva dominates the inner sanctuary. In the northeast corner of the courtyard is a high throne with three compartments for the Hindu Trinity of Brahma, Vishnu and Shiva.

Just 3km (2 miles) west of Bangli is a road to **Bukit Demulih**. It is well worth climbing this 'Hill of No Return' for superb views of Central Bali on a clear day. To reach the volcanoes Batur and Agung, continue north from either Bangli or Tampaksiring.

> **⊙ Fact**
>
> On the full moon of the fourth Balinese month (Sept–Oct), villagers bring a sacred stone for ritual cleansing at Pura Tirta Empul. Dated AD 962, the inscription on the stone – deciphered in the early 1900s and which describes the bathing of the stone – was something the villagers had unwittingly been carrying out for over 1,000 years.

Gunung Kawi, Ubud.

⊙ LIFESTYLE CENTRE

Amid the designer fashion and jewellery boutiques, five-star resorts, and some of the best dining on the island, Ubud is more or less returning to its ethnic roots as a healthy lifestyle centre.

Healing centres such as Como Shambhala and Fivelements Puri Ahimsa specialise in short- and long-term wellness programmes, and The Yoga Barn (www.theyogabarn.com) and Intuitive Flow Sanctuary for Yoga and Healing (www.intuitiveflow.com) include yoga and meditation. Others, such as Bali Botanica Day Spa (www.balibotanica.com), focus on massage.

The Ubud Organic Farmer's Market (www.indonesiaorganic.com) supports local farmers by selling their produce at the ARMA Museum on Wednesday mornings. Bali Buddha Café (www.balibuda.com) serves and sells organic food and health products.

📷 BALINESE CEREMONIES AND FESTIVALS

The frequency of Balinese ceremonies and festivals means that most visitors will be able to attend at least one celebration during their stay.

Balinese Hinduism views a person's life on earth as just one stage in their continued existence as part of an ongoing cycle. As part of these beliefs, a person's life is marked by rites of passage that are celebrated by the whole community.

The first important ritual is performed at birth, when the baby's placenta is buried in a coconut shell near the entrance to the family house. Babies are regarded as being the reincarnation of ancestors. They are therefore thought of as being holy and are treated with reverence. At puberty the tooth-filing ceremony takes place, although to save money this expensive custom is often delayed until marriage.

The final and most important rite in the cycle of life is cremation. Cremation rituals are seen by the Balinese as joyous occasions, as they release the soul from the body of the departed.

TEMPLE FESTIVALS

An odalan takes place every 210 days or once a year, during a particular full moon, to mark the 'birthday' or dedication of a temple. It can be a brief one-day affair or an elaborate event that goes on for weeks and involves months of preparation.

The most important of Balinese festivals is Galungan. During this time, the deified ancestors descend from heaven and take up residence in their family temples, where they are worshipped by their descendants for five days. As part of the festivities, all over the island streets are lined with penjor, tall bamboo poles decorated with palm-leaf ornaments, fruits and biscuits.

In the days before the end of the lunar-solar year, which varies according to the Balinese calendar, villagers take their temple artefacts to the sea for ritual cleansing. The new year begins with Nyepi, the 'Day of Silence' when no one is allowed outside. Fires and lights are extinguished and noise is forbidden so that evil forces leave in the belief that the island is deserted.

A wedding takes place after the groom's family sends a delegation to the bride's home to officially ask for her hand. The couple dress in their finest garments for the ceremony.

Canan sari petal tray offering, Air Panas Banjar.

Days of honour

Tumpek are days set aside to honour physical things that make life possible. On Tumpek Landep, keris (daggers) are ritually cleansed and presented with offerings to fortify their protective powers. Other metal objects, especially cars and motorcycles, are also treated with respect.

Small packets of rice cake are tied around trees on Tumpek Wariga, or Uduh, to thank them for their fruits, flowers and wood. Songbirds and gamelan instruments are honoured on Tumpek Krulut because of the beautiful sounds that they make. Domesticated animals such as cattle, water buffaloes and pigs are fed better food on the special days set aside for them, called Tumpek Uye or Kandang.

Sacred masks and dance costumes along with wayang kulit (leather puppets) used for ceremonies are presented with offerings on Tumpek Wayang. A special day honours Betari Dewi Saraswati, goddess of learning and knowledge. Offerings are given to lontar (palm-leaf manuscripts) and books. No reading or writing is allowed, and students pray to Saraswati to ask for her blessings.

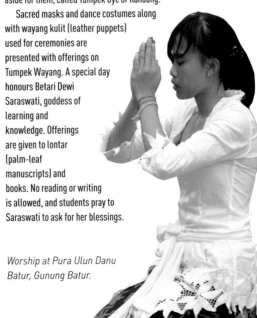

Worship at Pura Ulun Danu Batur, Gunung Batur.

st Balinese Hindus make ritual pilgrimages to Besakih mple to obtain holy water during an odalan or at full moon.

Villages celebrating their odalan temple festival, seseh, Tabanan.

WEST AND NORTH BALI

For a slower pace and more intimate encounter with this magical island, head to the shores and mountains of the west or explore the cool highlands in the north.

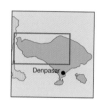
Denpasar

The cool central mountains, the wild western shorelines, and the sleepy beaches of the far north are worlds apart from the hectic resort areas of southern Bali. In the west the landscape is much drier, and off the coastal highway that leads from Pura Tanah Lot to Gilimanuk, the beaches have experienced low-key development in recent years. Once only remote surfing areas, their newly built resorts and villas are good bases for taking in the refreshing sea air and for scenic mountain drives to the north. Menjangan island in West Bali National Park is Bali's premier dive destination, with the north coast's Pemuteran a close second.

The north coast highway grips the shore, passing through Lovina, an excellent starting point for exploring the scenic Bedugal highlands to the south. Also along this road are even more developments: villas and resorts catering to wellbeing, yoga, meditation and healing that continue east of bustling Singaraja.

WEST BALI

North of Pura Tanah Lot, Tabanan regency is one of Bali's most prolific rice-growing areas. It has also long been home to some of the island's most admired gamelan orchestras and dancers. New tourist resorts are

springing up throughout the region, particularly on the coast, which is popular with surfers. At the end of every side road from the main highway leading to the shore are long, often black-sand beaches with surf that sometimes breaks over 3 metres (10ft) high. Be aware that the undertow and currents are treacherous.

MENGWI AND TABANAN

Northwest of Denpasar, at the start of the highway that goes on to hug the southern coastline, **Kapal** ⑲ shelters

○ **Main attractions**
Balian Beach
Medewi Beach
West Bali National Park
Pulau Menjangan
Pemuteran
Bedugul highlands
Lovina
Singaraja

Map on page 222

Flowers at Tabanan.

the most important temple in the area, Pura Sada (daily during daylight hours; donation), an ancestral sanctuary honouring the deified spirit of Ratu Sakti Jayaningrat, whose identity remains uncertain. The temple's original foundations may be as old as the 12th century, but the temple itself was rebuilt during the 17th century. The oldest of the Mengwi state shrines, Pura Sada was destroyed in the great earthquake of 1917 and restored in 1949.

Mengwi 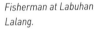 principality, 6km (4 miles) north of Kapal, was, until 1891, the centre of a powerful kingdom dating from the Gelgel dynasty. Pura Taman Ayun (daily during daylight hours), built in the 18th century, has a surrounding moat, giving the impression of a garden sanctuary, explaining the name *taman*, or garden. From the bustling nearby town of **Tabanan** a scenic road heads north to Pura Luhur Batukau (see page 255).

Dipping down off the main road to a southern bypass, in **Kerambitan** ㉑ the Tabanan royal family has two palaces – **Puri Anyar** and **Puri Agung** – where they showcase their *tektekan* gamelan ensemble of bamboo drums and wooden cow bells. For a fee, anyone can book a 'royal' evening, including either a *joget* (flirtation dance accompanied by a bamboo gamelan) or a *Calonarang* (trance performance), complete with a dinner. If it is just the surroundings you are interested in, there is a guesthouse in Puri Anyar.

BALIAN BEACH

Continuing west along the southern Trans-Bali highway, the environment begins to change and the landscape becomes increasingly dry. About 10km (6 miles) west of Antosari, a side road through Lalang Linggha village leads to the crashing surf at **Balian beach** ㉒. Formerly a low-budget surfers' hangout, served by a few basic guesthouses, an array of more upscale accommodations and eateries have sprouted here. It's by no means overrun, however, and the beach that makes a wonderful stopover for a bite to eat while taking in the enormity of the sea.

Fisherman at Labuhan Lalang.

☉ SUBAK

Unesco awarded the 'Cultural Landscape of Bali' the status of World Heritage Site in 2012. With its origins in the *Tri Hita Karana* philosophy that developed on Bali with influence from India more than 2,000 years ago, subak is Bali's traditional system of irrigation, and has shaped the island's landscape to how it looks today. Working in harmony between man, nature and God, *subak* was first introduced in the 9th century. There are five areas on Bali with rice terraces and water temples that have made use of the water available in an efficient, sustainable and harmonious way, as well as producing very productive paddy fields that supply rice for the relatively high density of people on Bali.

MEDEWI TO GILIMANUK

At **Pekutatan** ㉓, a side road heads north over the mountain and descends to the northern coast at Pengastulan. This narrow, paved road is among Bali's most beautiful routes, its 10km (6 miles) passing through exquisite rainforest and coffee, cocoa and clove plantations. The destination is a giant old *bunut* tree that is so large that its aerial roots descend on both sides of the road, which passes through the tree. A holy site for Balinese Hindus, there is a shrine on one side of the tree, and many motorists stop there to ask the spirits for permission to continue their journeys by making a small offering.

For several decades, surfers and locals kept the eastern reaches of **Medewi** ㉔ to themselves, staying in basic lodgings and picking their way across the rocky shore to reach the good waves. Now, upmarket resorts have appeared along this stretch of coast, where black-sand beaches far removed from their crowded counterparts in South Bali are luring an increasing number of travellers. Almost all the resorts still cater mainly to surfers, but instead of the nomadic hard-core dudes who dominated Medewi in the past, there is a new generation of novices who are eager to learn the sport in safer environments and with the benefit of babysitting services, spas, restaurants and cultural tours for those times when the sun gets too hot.

Near Medewi stands the tranquil **Pura Rambut Siwi** ㉕ (Lock of Hair Temple; daily during daylight hours; donation), founded by High Priest Danghyang Nirartha in the 16th century. Perched on a cliff overlooking the sea, the pavilions west of the temple offer panoramic views over rice fields and the ocean. It is said that Nirartha's stopover here relieved the village of a devastating epidemic, and before moving on, he presented the people with a lock of his hair, explaining the temple's name. His hair and some of his personal belongings are enshrined in the inner courtyard of the main temple.

Belimbing rice terraces, Tabanan.

⊘ Tip

The endangered Bali starling is rarely spotted in the wild at West Bali National Park, as their numbers are so few. See them instead on Nusa Penida, off the southeast coast, where a breeding-and-release programme has proved over-whelmingly successful.

West of Pura Rambut Siwi is **Negara**, the provincial capital. There is little to see here, except that every year between July and October the town's prized buffalo take part in annual racing competitions, which are fun to watch. Wearing colourful banners, their horns decorated and with wooden bells tied around their necks, they race along the 4km (2.5-mile) track at speeds of up to 50kph (30mph). The daredevil charioteers twist the bulls' tails to give them extra motivation. Rehearsals are held every second Sunday and the competitions are staged in August, around Independence Day, and in October.

One kilometre (0.6 mile) south of Negara is **Loloan Timur** ㉖. Its residents are Muslim Buginese who originated from Sulawesi, and they continue to build their homes in the Bugis style on stilts. The bamboo musical instruments they play, gamelan *jegog*, which accompany traditional dances, sound like thunder. Today there are nearly 50 ensembles, mostly located in the Sangkar Agung area.

Further south, along the coastline near Perancak, villages run a sea turtle conservation programme. Small donations to tour the area and an adopt-a-nest scheme help to fund the hatchery. While in Perancak, look for the fishing boats painted in bright colours that line the shore.

The north and southwest coast roads meet at **Cekik**, where a short spur road continues a few kilometres north to **Gilimanuk**, the access point for a 30-minute ferry journey (but much longer wait), operating 24 hours a day across the Bali–Java Strait. Accommodation in Gilimanuk is limited to homestays. The Bali–Java Strait is just 3km (2 miles) wide, but its waters are treacherous.

WEST BALI NATIONAL PARK

In order to visit **West Bali National Park** ㉗ (Taman Nasional Bali Barat; park headquarters Mon–Thu 8am–3.30pm, Fri 8am–1pm), first obtain a hiking permit and ticket from the visitor centre in **Labuhan Lalang** ㉘ (tel: 0361-61060; daily 7am–5pm) on Teluk

Medewi beach.

⊘ SCENIC DRIVES

For spectacular scenery, take the winding road from Antosari, west of Balian beach, north to Belimbing and Sanda, where rice terraces are carved from hillsides on either side of the road as far as the eye can see. Continuing north in the direction of Pujungan, a track on the right leads to a scenic waterfall. From this point onwards, clove and coffee plantations are interspersed with rice fields until the road reaches Pupuan.

From Pupuan, there are two options: head north across the hills for 12km (7.5 miles) to Mayong and on to the coast at Seririt, or continue south, descending by twisting road via Tista, Manggissari and Asahduren villages to Pekutatan in West Bali, from where you can rejoin the main highway to Gilimanuk.

Terima (Reception Bay). You can also book tours and treks at the centre.

Official guides, who usually speak English, are a requirement for trekking within the park, and are part of a community empowerment programme. The 760-sq km (300-sq mile) conservation area, much of which is off-limits, is home to deer, civets, monkeys, rare wild Javan buffalo and the nearly extinct Bali starling or Rothschild's mynah *(Leucopsar rothschildi)*, a small white-crested bird with brilliant blue streaks around its eyes and black-tipped wings. Many wild birds live on the gentle slopes of **Gunung Prapat Agung**, which anchors Bali's western tip. There are several trails from which to choose, designed to suit different interests and capabilities. Short and medium treks (1–3 hours) focus on mangrove and mountain forests and savannahs for birdwatchers. Longer treks (6–7 hours) can be customised. All guided tours must be booked in advance.

The park is known for its spectacular diving and snorkelling off **Pulau**

Menjangan  (Deer Island), about 10km (6 miles) offshore. One of Bali's best dive sites, it is surrounded by deep waters, coral reefs, sandy slopes and walls housing a wide variety of large and small marine life. There are eight dive sites, and at Pos 2 a shallow reef attracts snorkellers. Walking around the perimeter of the uninhabited island takes about 45 minutes, and there are some stunning panoramic views of volcanoes and mountains on Java from here.

Boats to the island can be hired at Labuan Lalang and at a second pier at Banyumandi, near Mimpi resort. On Menjangan there is an ancient temple, Puri Gili, and Balinese-Hindus often depart from Banyumandi to make offerings here. There is a modest canteen, and showers and changing rooms are available for a small charge. Wait until other divers appear and share the cost of the boat. Overnighting on the island is forbidden.

There are four upmarket resorts in the area; for cheaper accommodation most people stay at nearby Pemuteran,

The reef at Pemuteran is one of the most colourful on the Bali coast.

Negara bull races.

The Reef Seen Dive Centre runs trips out to the reef at Pemuteran.

Puru Ulun Danu, Bratan.

where transport to and from Menjangan can be arranged.

Near Labuan Lalang and still within the park is **Makam Jayaprana**, a local hero's tomb and temple, which is worth the hike for the view.

NORTH BALI

A rather sleepy fishing village, **Pemuteran ㉚** is the nearest place to the West Bali National Park and has a wide range of low- to medium-priced bungalows and hotels, and some exquisite luxury villas, all catering to divers, snorkellers and nature-lovers. For many years, Pemuteran was only a place to sleep and eat, but it has earned a good reputation for diving and snorkelling in its own right thanks to the Reef Seen Aquatics Dive Center and Taman Sari Bali Resort, which pioneered reef restoration here. Now joined by other dive shops and local businesses, an effort that began simply has blossomed considerably.

A community project called Reef Gardeners teaches local people the importance of environmentally sound fishing practices and that keeping the reefs healthy is an economic plus. Village divers who have been trained by the co-op patrol reefs regularly looking for signs of lawbreakers and plagues that may devastate the corals. They also operate a sea turtle egg rescue centre, hatchery and release programme, Proyek Penyu, which can be visited. Donations for tours are welcome and keep the programme running.

Using local divers and products, the project has also created an astonishing submarine wonderland by sinking several traditional boats, some at great depths and one only five metres (16ft) from the surface at low tide. The main attraction is the Taman Pura (Temple Garden), a re-creation of a Balinese Hindu temple complex under the sea comprising 25 carved sandstone statues.

THE CENTRAL MOUNTAIN REGION

A road leads south at **Pengastulan-Seririt ㉛**, climbing over the mountains and through rice fields and clove

plantations before eventually descending to the coast in South Bali. Several scenic routes are possible, among which is a beautiful but meandering drive that goes through Ringdikit and Rangdu villages. Just south of Rangdu, a turn eastwards at Mayong continues to Lakes Tamblingan and Buyun, nestled in hillside coffee plantations, and Bratan in the **Bedugul highlands**.

Bedugul ❷, 1,300 metres (4,300ft) above sea level, is a mountain-lake resort area favoured by Indonesians for weekend retreats. In the not-so-distant past, tourists limited their visit there to a day trip from Ubud or Lovina to see **Danau Bratan**, a lake filling the long-extinct, often mist-veiled Gunung Catur crater, and its temple, **Pura Ulun Danu Bratan** (daily during daylight hours), sitting on a small promontory and one of the most photographed sites on the island. The lake is an essential water source for surrounding farmlands, and Bedugul people honour Dewi Danu, the lake goddess, here.

To the west of Danau Bratan, a scenic backroad passes two further lakes

at Buyan and Tamblingan to reach Munduk, which has emerged in recent decades as a popular upland accommodation centre, with a number of spectacularly located small resorts and guesthouses, and fabulous views over the ridges to the west.

North of Bedugul proper is Bukit Munggu market, popularly called **Candi Kuning**, where wild orchids and colourful flowers are sold alongside vegetables. Nearby is **Kebun Raya Eka Karya Bali** (Bali Botanical Gardens; daily 8am–6pm). This refreshing 1.5-sq km (370-acre) park is sliced by hiking trails through towering forests, and the sprawling grounds are home to more than 2,000 plant species, focusing on orchids, medicinal and ceremonial plants, roses and cacti. There is a library and café, and guides are available for a nominal additional cost.

Southwest of the Bedugal highlands, along the winding artery skirting the mountains, is one of Bali's most venerated temples, **Pura Luhur Batukau** ❸ (daily during daylight hours), situated near Batukau on the slopes of

Dolphin-watching at Lovina.

Singajara.

⊘ CHRISTIAN VILLAGES

From Cekik on the far western coast, travel 15km (9 miles) south to Melaya and turn inland to Belimbingsari village. Home to Bali's largest Protestant community, its impressive church has distinctly Balinese design elements and a *kulkul* (warning drum) instead of a bell to signal the start of Sunday services, which begin at 9am.

A short drive to the south is the 1,500-strong Catholic community in Palasari. Like Belimbingsari, the early converts settled in remote West Bali by choice after being shunned by the Hindu Balinese. The cathedral, built in 1958, is adorned with Balinese touches, and is a stunning piece of architecture in the middle of nowhere. Friday mass at 5.30pm and Sunday mass at 6.30am are good times to visit.

⊙ Tip

Dolphin-watching, a popular activity in Lovina, is increasingly controversial. Convoys of early-morning boats carrying dolphin-seeking tourists go on a chase, which very likely disturbs the dolphins' morning reveries.

Gunung Batukau (2,276 metres/7,467ft high). The western Batukau highlands are famed for magnificent landscapes, and the view from **Jatiluwih** village takes in the whole landscape of southern Bali. Nearby, **Yeh Panas** surges hot water from the riverbank, graced by a small temple for prayers and offerings. The springs are part of a modest resort and are open to visitors for a fee.

PENGASTULAN-SERIRIT TO SINGAJARA

Back to the north coast highway, from Pengastulan-Seririt heading east there are pockets of resorts away from the main highway on the north shore dedicated to healing, meditation and yoga. Set almost alongside these is an astonishing number of private villas, many of them for rent. The road is lined with vineyards that feed Bali's blossoming wine industry.

Further east is a 12km (7.5-mile) long stretch of black-sand beach encompassing Pemaron, Tukad Mungga, Anturan, Kalibukbuk,

Air Panas Banjar.

Kalisasem and Temukus villages, collectively called **Lovina** ㉞. In the 1970s and 1980s, Lovina was the escape of choice for crowd-weary former Kuta enthusiasts, but as development continued it was transformed from quiet fishing village to a Kuta clone, minus the bars. After a slump, when it became threadbare and musty, it has taken on new life; modern resorts and renovations abound, but it is no longer the quiet haven it once was. The diving has never been spectacular here – the biggest attraction is early-morning dolphin-watching boat trips – and today's travellers use it primarily as a base for exploring North Bali and the highlands with sand and surf on the side rather than the other way around.

The next stop is Singaraja, formerly Bali's capital city. In contrast to the south, citrus fruit orchards, tomatoes, vanilla, coffee, cacao, grapes and cloves replace the familiar rice paddies. About 10km (6 miles) south of Singaraja, the **Air Terjun Gitgit** (daily during daylight hours) waterfalls flow vigorously during the rainy season. The soft pink sandstone that gives North Bali's temples their distinctive character was quarried near here.

Singaraja ㉟ has a cosmopolitan flavour, derived from centuries as an important trading port until 1953 when shipping was moved to the more convenient Benoa Harbour in the south. Bali's second-largest city after Denpasar, it is home to long-established Arab and Chinese communities, as well as other settlers from all over Indonesia. The **Gedong Kirtya** historical library (Mon–Thu 7.30am–3.30pm, Fri 7am–12.30pm) on Jalan Veteran is a repository of old books and Balinese manuscripts established by the Dutch in 1928. It has a fine collection of *lontar* manuscripts – books inscribed on palm leaf strips and preserved between two pieces of wood or bamboo. The ancient volumes cover subjects such as literature, mythology, history and religion.

There are some Dutch-era buildings hidden behind clutter on Jalan Ahmad Yani, and across a small bridge, a gift from the queen of Holland, is the old harbour. Just over the bridge is **Ling Gwan Kion** Chinese temple, an interesting structure dating back to 1873, with beautifully manicured gardens. Someone will be happy to show you around and tell you about the historic accoutrements that remain here. Some of the old waterfront buildings are being restored and the restaurants on stilts make an excellent lunch stop, serving grilled fish amid cool ocean breezes. From Singaraja, a major north–south highway goes to Denpasar.

SINGARAJA TO AIR SANIH

East from Singaraja, the land becomes increasingly dry as the road winds around the east coast, eventually passing an area devastated by the 1963 Gunung Agung eruption north of Tulamben. Deep, black gashes in the earth caused by lava flows replace all forms of agricultural life here.

In **Sangsit** ㊱ an unusual 15th-century *subak* (irrigation cooperative) temple, **Pura Beji** (daily during daylight hours; donation), dedicated to rice goddess Dewi Sri, is garnished with many *naga* – serpents that symbolise water and fertility. The road from nearby Kubutambahan going south leads to Danau Batur and Kintamani.

About 15km (10 miles) southeast of Singaraja at **Jagaraga** is **Pura Dalem** ㊲ (Temple of the Dead; daily during daylight hours; donation). Interesting reliefs portray life before and after the arrival of the Dutch, including scenes such as two Europeans in a Model T Ford attacked by armed bandits and a Dutch steamer under siege by a sea monster. Southwards is **Sawan**, a village

with gamelan makers and a talented gamelan *angklung* orchestra.

Further east on the coast road, **Pura Meduwe Karang** ㊳ (daily during daylight hours; donation), is a dry-land agriculture temple. Just as *subak* temples ensure irrigated crop harvests, this 1890 temple gives 'blessings' for plants grown on non-irrigated land. It has many fertility themes, including numerous portrayals of erotic acts. Carvings in this 'Temple of the Landowner' show ghouls, domestics, lovers, noblemen and even a bicycle-riding Westerner, believed to be Dutchman W.O.J. Nieuwenkamp, who travelled all over Bali by bicycle at the beginning of the 20th century.

Further east, 17km (11 miles) from Singaraja, at **Air Sanih** ㊴ (Yeh Sanih; daily during daylight hours; donation) travellers, for a small fee, can dip in a cool, spring-fed swimming pool. Facilities include luxury villas and spas as well as budget lodgings and restaurants. Continuing east, the road and villages become simpler, the land grows more arid and the number of tourists dwindles.

⊙ Tip

West of Lovina, turn left at Dencarik and continue for about 3km (2 miles) to **Brahma Arama Vihara** (daily 8am–6pm) in Banjar. The striking Thai-style Theravada Buddhist temple, with its bright orange roof and colourful statues of Buddha and other figures, was founded in 1958 by a Balinese monk and rebuilt in this location in 1971. The views down the coast are stunning, and visitors are welcome as long as they dress modestly, lower their voices and walk quietly barefooted.

Pura Beji features numerous naga serpent sculptures.

Scenes from the Mahabharata adorn a ceiling at Taman Gili's Kerta Gosa pavilion (bale), Semarapura.

EAST BALI

The east, with its unspoilt rural landscapes, tall mountains and rugged coastline is what many visitors have in mind when they imagine 'the real Bali'.

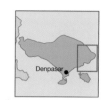

East is the most auspicious of compass points in the Balinese worldview, and an excursion among the temples, palace ruins, crater lakes and black-sand beaches of this area reveals why. Less developed and simpler than the island's south, eastern Bali has a different ambience defined by lava-strewn landscapes, ancient kingdoms and good diving and snorkelling, far removed from the urban centres of the south. Partly hidden by the eastern coastal ranges is the colossal **Gunung Agung**, Bali's tallest peak at 3,142 metres (10,308ft), which on clear days can be seen soaring above the countryside.

Eastern Bali has a number of attractive accommodation centres. The long-established resort area at Candidasa, the sleepy harbour town of Padangbai, and the more recently emerged coastal destination of Amed all make good bases for explorations here, while inland in Sidemen an array of charming guesthouses and small resorts are immersed in some of Bali's finest scenery. Offshore, meanwhile, Nusa Lembongan is a well-established island playground, and its much larger neighbour, Nusa Penida has emerged in recent years as a new frontier for tourism in Bali, with spectacular limestone landscapes, and a burgeoning accommodation scene.

Statues outside Taman Gili's Kerta Gosa pavilion.

SEMARAPURA (KLUNGKUNG)

As the seat of the Dewa Agung (the title of the reigning king), **Semarapura** ⑩ (also called Klungkung) holds a special place in the island's history and culture. The palaces of Klungkung's *raja* and noblemen have supported and developed the styles of music, drama and the arts that flourish today in Bali.

The kingdom's capital was moved to Semarapura from nearby Gelgel in 1710 and a new palace was built here. The great gate is all that remains of the Puri Semarapura palace, razed in a *puputan*

○ **Main attractions**
Semarapura (Klungkung)
Sidemen
Pura Besakih and Gunung Agung
Danau Batur
Padangbai
Nusa Penida
Tenganan
Amed

Map on page 222

Carvings at Pura Besakih.

Weaving double ikat fabric.

battle with the Dutch in 1908. It stands within the grounds of **Taman Gili** (daily 8am–5pm), a compound housing the remains of Bali's most powerful kingdom, at the town's main intersection.

One of the two focal points of the park is **Kerta Gosa** (Pavilion of Peace and Prosperity), an open *bale* (pavilion) beautifully decorated with exquisite examples of Kamasan paintings and Klungkung architecture. Eighteenth-century ceiling murals depict scenes from the *Mahabharata*, including punishments and rewards of deeds, either in the present lifetime or the next.

Next to Kerta Gosa is **Bale Kambang** (Floating Pavilion), surrounded by a moat, which is similarly decorated and was used by the royal family as a place to rest and be entertained. Also in the compound are a small museum and a tourist information office, and across the street is Puri Agung, the home of the current *raja*.

Kamasan lies 2km (1.2 miles) south and is a pleasant place to stroll around and see the artists at work. Using natural pigments, they illustrate episodes from Javanese classic literature, and the figures look like *wayang kulit* shadow puppets. Although Kamasan-style paintings are sold all over Bali, cheaper and better-quality works are found here. Stop by I Nyoman Mandra's painting school (ask for directions), where young artists imitate the master's strokes.

SIDEMEN

From Klungkung, turn north, passing through Bukit Jambul's astonishing landscapes. In **Sidemen** , many households are engaged in some aspect of textile weaving. This is one of the centres of *endek* (weft-ikat cloth) weaving, and the clack-clack-clack of the looms can be heard from the road. *Songket* cloth – cotton or silk with an overweft of silver or gold threads – is also produced here. Sidemen is exceptionally beautiful – a deep, intricately terraced valley stretching north towards Gunung Agung, and closely resembling stylised artistic images of old-time Bali. West of the main village, various attractive guesthouses and small resorts are

⊘ A NEW ERA OF KINGS

When Indonesia declared independence in 1945, all the *rajas* and sultans throughout the archipelago (except in Yogyakarta see page 158) relinquished their powers and pledged allegiance to the new republic, ending a centuries-long era of often-warring fiefdoms and empires.

This stance started to change in 1989 with the crowning of the king of Pemecutan, one of Denpasar's three royal houses, and again in 2005 when Tabanan reinstated the title. In 2010, Semarapura followed suit, naming the son of the last colonial-era Klungking *raja* their new king amid great pomp and ceremony, incorporating elaborate Bali-Hindu rituals and sacred dances.

While the new kings have no official authority, some analysts see this symbolic gesture as a return to traditional values.

scattered across the slopes, surrounded by rice fields and forest. It is a rewarding area to explore on foot.

PURA BESAKIH AND GUNUNG AGUNG

Folklore has it that when the deities made mountains for their thrones, they set the highest peak in East Bali. In every temple a shrine is dedicated to the spirit of **Gunung Agung**. The tapering form of cremation towers, *meru* (pagodas) and even temple offerings bear the shape of a mountain, mirroring reverence for this holy volcano.

On the slopes of Agung lies **Pura Besakih** ⓭, the Mother Temple (daily during daylight hours; camera fee). Easily accessed from Besakih village, the temple houses ancestral shrines for all Hindu Balinese, who regard the complex as the pinnacle of sanctity. Besakih originated in the 8th century as a terraced sanctuary honouring Gunung Agung's gods. Over a period of more than 1,000 years it was enlarged, and today it comprises 30 public temples with hundreds of shrines. Non-worshippers are not allowed into the inner temple unless they wish to pray, but the layout can quite easily be seen from the open gates. Do not enter the grounds unless invited, and be sure to be dressed in *sarong* and a temple sash.

Pura Penataran Agung is the paramount sanctuary in the Besakih complex. Steps ascend in a long perspective to split gates. Inside the main courtyard is a triple-throned shrine for three aspects of god: Siwa, as creator; Pramasiwa, god without form; and Sadasiwa, god as half male and half female. Others interpret this trinity to be Vishnu, Brahma and Shiva. Only worshippers may enter, but visitors can circle the outer walls for a view of the courtyard.

During festivals, the shrines are wrapped in coloured cloths in three sacred colours: red, symbolising the earth as lava and associated with Brahma; white, as light, associated with Shiva; and black, as both water and heaven, and associated with Vishnu. Yellow cloth – a colour symbolising compassion – is also used to cover the shrines during festivals.

GUNUNG BATUR

The road north from Besakih leads to the crater lake **Danau Batur** ⓮. Bali's largest lake, Danau Batur is cradled within the **Gunung Batur** caldera, an active volcano. At 1,717 metres (5,635ft) above sea level, it is considered to be the female counterpart to Gunung Agung's male. The crater itself is 11km (7 miles) in diameter and 200 metres (660ft) deep. Try to arrive in the early morning, before the mist descends.

Penelokan ⓯, at 1,450 metres (4,800ft) above sea level, is a spectacular point to take in views of Gunung Batur and the lake. The cliff is lined with tourist restaurants with large glass windows, and can be a nice coffee stop to enjoy the panorama protected from the cold and mist. A steep, winding road descends to lakeside **Kedisan**. On the volcano's flank at

A temple festival at Besakih.

Prayer, Pura Ulun Danu Batur.

Pura Ulun Danu Batur.

Toya Bungkah, hot springs are reputed to have medicinal qualities. Travellers who climb Batur use Toya Bungkah as a staging point.

Trunyan ㊻, a village across the lake, is inhabited by the so-called Bali Aga – isolated mountain communities who largely rejected Javanese-influenced Hinduism, and whose customs probably closely resemble the indigenous religion that once held sway across Bali. The villagers practise unusual burial customs with the dead left under a sacred tree in the open air for nature to decompose, covered only by a cloth. The name Trunyan comes from the *taru menyan* (fragrant tree) that grows in the cemetery. Trunyan has a somewhat negative reputation for hostility and aggressive begging – greatly exacerbated by the number of tourists who visit – though in recent years things have improved as local residents have been given more say in tourism management.

Gunung Batur intermittently spews lava, ash and steam, but nothing drastic has occurred since 1926. Treks across the barren landscape resulting from the eruption – where there is an active reforestation programme – can be arranged through the trekking guides' association office at Toya Bungka, which has a reputation as something of a cartel, making it difficult for guides from other parts of Bali to operate here.

'HEAD OF THE LAKE' TEMPLE

Back on the main road from Penelokan heading towards Kintamani is Bali's second-most important temple after Besakih, **Pura Ulun Danu Batur** ㊼ (daily during daylight hours). As it is a major *subak* (irrigation) temple, rituals here are linked with the veneration of the Goddess of the Lake, Dewi Danu.

Inscriptions from the 10th century indicate that nearby **Kintamani** – a mountainous area taking its name from the windy town at 1,500 metres (4,920ft) up – was one of Bali's earliest kingdoms. A paved road at Sukawana leads to Pinggan on the crater's north side, with a flight of 300 steps rising to the mountain sanctuary, **Pura Tegeh Koripan** (daily during daylight hours), the highest temple in Bali

at 1,745 metres (5,725ft). From Kintamani the road leads north to Kubutambahan, east of north coast Singaraja.

THE EAST COAST

Back to the east coast road, **Gelgel** is the former capital of the Klungkung dynasty. In the 1400s and 1500s, Gelgel's Dewa Agung held immense power, but the dynasty's influence declined in the 17th century as it lost battles and allegiances. This misfortune was attributed to a curse that had fallen on the palace. Consequently, the palace was moved to Klungkung, but there was no improvement in fortune. Small conflicts and jealousies broke out among the kings, and the result was the creation of numerous minor kingdoms.

Exquisite hand-woven *songket* and *endek* are made in many homes in Gelgel. To the east is **Pura Dasar** (daily during daylight hours; donation). During the full moon in October, dozens of villagers come here to take part in a very colourful temple ceremony.

Eastwards, a perfectly shaped bay is cradled by the hills at **Padangbai** ⓭. This is the main harbour for public ferries to Lombok and Nusa Penida, as well as the most popular departure point for speedboat transfers to the Gilis off Lombok. But despite its function as a port, it is also one of the most attractive of Bali's coastal communities, with some attractive budget and midrange accommodation, good eateries, and a well-preserved village atmosphere back from the waterfront.

The village area lies north of the ferry port, with pleasant cafés serving fresh seafood lining the shore. The beach here, while attractive, is crowded with fishing boats so not ideal for swimming, but two other beaches lie a short walk away, either north or south. Over the northern headland – crowned by an important local temple – Blue Lagoon has a small strip of sand and decent snorkelling. To the south, where the forest is gradually masking an abandoned

resort development, is the beautiful little Bias Tugel, with good swimming and some simple wood-and-thatch eateries.

There is excellent offshore diving in this area, and Padangbai is home to several dive centres.

NUSA LEMBONGAN AND NUSA PENIDA

The tiny island of **Nusa Lembongan** ⓭ is a popular water-sports area, with a plethora of accommodation options lining the beaches on the western side of the island. The best surfing is off the south and west coasts, and good diving can be found off the west and east coasts. Be careful of dangerous undertows. Many boating companies in South Bali offer day trips here; some include lunch at a resort and jet-skiing and other water activities.

East of Lembongan is the much larger **Nusa Penida** ⓭, a dry, sparsely cultivated island. Until very recently, Nusa Penida was one of the few regions of Bali almost completely untouched by tourism, with only a couple of very basic accommodation options. Then young travellers

Puri Agung Karangasem, Amlapura.

– both foreign and Indonesian – spotted its highly photogenic landscapes, with white sand beaches at the foot of towering limestone cliffs, and Nusa Penida became the Instagram-worthy viral destination of the moment. By general Balinese standards it remains undeveloped, with rough roads in the interior. But there is now plentiful accommodation, and much improved transport links from Sanur and Padangbai.

Highlights of Nusa Penida include the spectacular cave temple, Goa Giri Putri, the much-photographed beach at Pantai Atuh at the easternmost tip of the island, and the delightful Crystal Bay beach in the west, with excellent snorkelling just offshore. Most accommodation is on the north coast, especially around Ped where fast boat transfers arrive, but various standalone resorts are popping up elsewhere.

CANDIDASA AND ENVIRONS

Back on the east coast road, the next destination is **Candidasa** ❺, first passing through Manggis, where there are two luxury resorts overlooking the sea on Balina beach. Unfortunately Candidasa's shores are blighted by jetties protruding into the water, intended to stop the erosion, making it impossible to walk more than 50 metres (160ft) on the beach, which is only visible at low tide. Nevertheless, Candidasa has a good range of hotels and restaurants, so is a convenient base to explore East Bali.

TENGANAN

West of Candidasa is a turn-off northwards to **Tenganan** ❺ (daily during daylight hours), a Bali Aga village. Within its bastions, all houses are arranged in identical rows on either side of wide, stone-paved lanes running the length of the village. There is evidence the Tengananese originated from Bedulu, but some accounts say they came from East Java.

Tenganan communally owns large tracts of well-cultivated land and is one of the richest villages in the area. Traditionally, the men do not work in the fields. The aristocratic Tenganan people instead rent out their land to neighbouring villagers and spend their time inscribing dried palm leaves to make illustrated *lontar* manuscripts or crafting an especially fine quality of basketry.

The women still weave the incredible *kain geringsing*, a cloth believed to have the power to immunise the wearer against evil and sickness. Only the finest *geringsing* pieces are worn as ceremonial dress by the Tenganan people; imperfect ones are sold, and even these fetch high prices on the market.

AMLAPURA (KARANGASEM)

Amlapura ❺, further east, is the capital of Karangasem regency. The former kingdom, founded while the Gelgel dynasty waned in the late 1600s, turned into the most powerful state in Bali during the late 18th and early 19th centuries

Puri Agung Karangasem (daily 9am–5pm) long served as the residence of these kings, who extended their domain across the eastern straits

Crystal Bay on Nusa Penida.

to Lombok. During the Dutch conflict at the turn of the 20th century, the raja of Karangasem cooperated with the conquering army and was allowed to retain his title and powers. The palace where the last *raja* was born is a 20th-century amalgam of European and Asian architecture. The main building, **Bale Maskerdam**, contains furniture gifted by the Dutch royal family. Opposite is the ornate **Bale Pemandesan**, used for tooth-filing ceremonies and embellished with Chinese features.

The kings of Karangasem created delightful water gardens to escape the heat of East Bali. Some 8km (5 miles) south, near the beach, lies **Taman Ujung** (daily 8am–5pm), a vast complex of pools and pavilions built in 1921. Destroyed by an earthquake in 1979, it was renovated and reopened in 2004, and is indeed a heavenly garden worthy of a visit once again.

Taman Tirtagangga (Water of the Ganges Park; daily 8am–5pm), 6km (4 miles) north on the road to Culik, is another royal water park with beautiful gardens. Locals flock here just before sunset to bathe in pools fed by natural springs gushing out from animal fountains and statues, believing the waters to have healing properties. There is an upmarket resort and excellent restaurant overlooking the bathing pools owned by descendants of the royal family.

EAST COAST BEACHES

At Culik, continue east to **Amed** ⑬, where guesthouses and resorts line a stunning shoreline. Actually a compilation of seven villages and beaches all collectively called Amed, this is an ideal choice for dropping out for a little while. The snorkelling is good at high tide, with coral reefs just off the beach, and there are dive spots further afield. From here, dives at **Tulamben**, where the well-known World War II *Liberty* cargo shipwreck lies, can be easily done in a day trip, as can visits to Tirtagangga, when you've had enough sun and surf.

From Amed, the road north runs close to the coast all the way to Singaraja (see page 256). Village life in this area is simple and rustic, and there are occasional views of the ocean.

Nusa Lembongan.

An idyllic stretch of beach near Senggigi.

The spice market, Mataram.

NUSA TENGGARA

Nusa Tenggara's scattered islands vary widely – in culture, character and landscape. And though there are pockets of emerging tourism, most of the region remains deliciously distant from the beaten track.

Gili Trawangan beach.

This sparsely inhabited archipelago extending eastwards from Lombok to Timor is formed by the protruding peaks of a giant submarine mountain range that stretches all the way to Sumatra. Sandalwood rather than spices was the treasure that foreign merchants sought in this southern corner of the East Indies, always something of a backwater in Indonesian history. Nusa Tenggara translates as 'Southeastern Islands' in Javanese.

The first Portuguese ships reached the area in 1512, and by the end of the century they had hijacked the Timorese sandalwood trade and established fortresses on Flores and Solor. The Dutch wrested much of the spice trade away from their rivals in the 17th century, but what remained of the area's sandalwood was largely depleted by then.

Songket-weaving.

One of Indonesia's poorest and least fertile regions, most of its 10 million inhabitants are subsistence farmers or fishermen, and strong currents of traditional belief are intertwined with Islam or Christianity here. There are unexpected pockets of development and prosperity, however – not least around the vast gold reserves of western Sumbawa, and the tourist honeypot of Labuanbajo, gateway to the Komodo National Park – home of the eponymous dragons.

Lombok has long picked up the overflow traffic from neighbouring Bali's ever-booming tourism industry. And visitor numbers to Komodo have rocketed in recent years, thanks to better air links to the gateway town of Labuanbajo. But beyond this, true adventure is still a ready possibility amongst the many attractions: the myriad fine hand-woven ikat textiles produced in traditional villages; excellent water sports; or the splendid nature of the national parks and reserves. Surfers have frequented the south-coast villages for decades, and the superb marine life attracts divers to Alor. But as elsewhere in Indonesia, it is the people of Nusa Tenggara, with all their cultural differences, who give the region its greatest appeal.

Infrastructure is slowly improving, but roads remain rough, flights and ferries unreliable, and journey times long – though that can all be part of the adventure.

The beach at Gili Air.

LOMBOK

Bali's eastern neighbour offers a quieter and more laid-back island experience. Lombok has lovely beaches fringed by beautiful coral reefs, fabulous surfing and a spectacular volcano.

Kupang

Lombok has long been overshadowed by its better-known western neighbour, Bali. In the 19th century it was dominated by the Balinese kingdom of Karangasem, and in the modern era its modest tourism industry has operated almost entirely in Bali's slipstream. It deserves to be a destination in its own right, however, with stunning landscapes and a unique culture.

Most inhabitants of Lombok are the indigenous Sasak, though there are significant ethnic Balinese populations, especially in the west, as well as settlers from other parts of Indonesia. Today the overwhelming majority of Sasaks are orthodox Muslims (sometimes known colloquially in Lombok as *Islam Waktu Lima*, 'Five Times Islam' after the requisite number of daily prayers). A few communities on the slopes of Gunung Rinjani still maintain elements of an old syncretic belief system, combining elements of Islam with unique local practices, known as *Islam Wetu Telu*, and there are also some tiny Sasak Buddhist communities.

Most of western Lombok is green and lush, but to the east and south the island becomes increasingly arid. Along the west coast are some of the snowiest-white beaches imaginable, and while **Senggigi beach** has been its main calling card in the past, its five-star resorts are beginning to take a back seat to Mangsit

and other beaches further north, which offer hip boutique hotels.

The three small 'Gilis' – Trawangan, Meno and Air – once only popular with budget divers and snorkellers now attract more mature travellers as well, with more upmarket hotels and villas being built to accommodate them. Other dive resorts have sprung up on Lombok's southwestern peninsula, and with an influx of foreign investment, the southern beach, Kuta (also spelled Kute), has developed considerably. Mataram, the island's main city, is

⊙ Main attractions
Pura Lingsar
Senggigi beach
The Gilis
Bayan and Senaru
Tetebatu
Gunung Rinjani trekking
Kuta
Mawun beach

Map on page 273

Sasak villagers at Sade.

The coral reefs off the Gili Islands offer superb snorkelling.

Pura Meru.

the provincial seat of West Nusa Tenggara, which includes its eastern neighbour, Sumbawa. Inland, the mighty volcano of **Gunung Rinjani** – at 3,726 metres (12,224ft) the third-highest peak in Indonesia – offers challenging and exhilarating trekking conditions.

While Lombok does not have the overwhelming commercialism of Bali and its cultural experience is more restrained, the flipside is that it possesses a greater sense of adventure.

WESTERN LOMBOK

Three main towns in western Lombok – Ampenan, Mataram and Cakranegara – meld together to create what is, for Lombok, an urban sprawl. **Mataram** ❶ is the administrative centre of political and cultural life, with provincial government offices, banks, mosques, bookstores, the General Post Office and Mataram University.

In Mataram, the **Museum Nusa Tenggara Barat** (Jalan Panji Tilar Negara No.6; tel: 0370-632 159; Tue–Thu and Sat–Sun 8am–2pm, Fri 8–11am) houses artefacts from Lombok and Sumbawa, and occasionally hosts special exhibitions. Displays include exhibits on geology, history and culture. The **Taman Budaya** cultural centre on Jalan Majapahit presents traditional music and dance nightly. The provincial tourist office is on Jalan Langko.

The **Gunung Pengsong Temple** (daily 8am–5pm; donation), 9km (5.5 miles) south of Mataram, sits atop a peak with vistas of rice fields, Gunung Rinjani and the sea. Populated with monkeys, this is the hill the Balinese had aimed for in the mythical account of their initial arrival in western Lombok. Today, it is an area populated by a significant community of Balinese Hindus. In March or April, a buffalo is sacrificed here to ensure a rich harvest. At that time of the year, houses are repainted and the entire village spruced up to honour the rice goddess Dewi Sri.

Merging into Mataram on its west side is **Ampenan**. With its numerous shops, cheap hotels, dusty roads, plentiful horse-drawn carts called *cidomo*, Islamic bookstores and an Arab quarter, it is easily the island's most colourful

town. Early Arab traders were drawn to Ampenan when it was the only harbour for incoming and outgoing ships. Nowadays, it is used only for fishing and shipping cattle. On special holidays, the beach is a venue for performances of the *gandrung* social dance or for the *wayang Sasak* shadow play.

MARKET TOWN

Cakranegara ❷, abutting Mataram at its eastern boundary, is Lombok's main market centre. It is also home to many Chinese and Balinese, who make up more than 50 percent of the town's population. Many weaving and basketry industries are located in Cakranegara – items of which are sold in Bali at many times the Lombok price.

Several important Balinese temples occupy Cakranegara and the surrounding area. **Pura Meru** (daily 8am–5pm; donation), built in 1720 by Balinese prince Anak Agung Made Karang, is the island's largest temple. Its giant *meru* (pagoda) for the Hindu Trinity – Siwa (Shiva), Wisnu (Vishnu) and Brahma – is the 'centre of the universe' for the

Balinese here, and its annual festival, held over five days during the September or October full moon, is the largest Balinese Hindu event on Lombok. The outer courtyard hall has drums that call the devout to ceremonies and festivals. Two buildings with raised offering platforms are in the centre courtyard, while the interior enclosure holds 33 shrines and three multi-tiered *meru*.

Across the street stands the Mayura Water Place and its **Pura Mayura** (daily 8am–5pm; donation), built in 1744 as the court temple of the last Balinese kingdom in Lombok. A large artificial lake holds a *bale kambang* (floating pavilion) that was once used as a platform where justice was dispensed and meetings held. Today the gardens are a playground for children and a pasture for grazing cattle. The temple sits behind sedate water gardens.

The structures and pool at **Taman Narmada** (daily 8am–5pm; donation), 10km (6 miles) east of Cakranegara, were reportedly built in 1805 as a replica of Gunung Rinjani and Segara Anak, the lake within Rinjani's caldera.

> **⊙ Tip**
>
> Although many people arrange treks on Gunung Rinjani from the Gilis or Bali, arrangements are best made on Lombok itself, especially via the reputable local agencies based in Senaru. The standard trek takes three days and two nights, beginning in the Sembalun valley, summiting the following morning, and then skirting the caldera and finishing at Senaru.

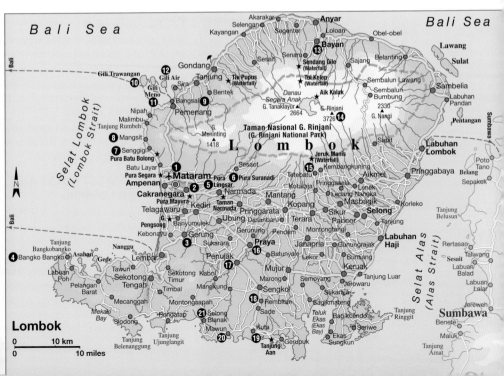

When the elderly king Anak Ngurah Gede Karangasem of Mataram could no longer make the trek to Segara Anak, he built Taman Narmada. The annual pilgrimage and offering at Rinjani's crater lake continue today, and the festival at **Pura Kalasa** coincides with them during the full moon of either October or November. The Narmada gardens are splendid, with traditional dances performed on special occasions. Some of the pools are open to swimmers and are popular with local children.

THE SOUTHWEST PENINSULA

Most of the goods shipped to Lombok today arrive at **Gerung ❸**, near **Labuan Lembar**, to be distributed. Gerung is the village of the *cepung*, a men's social dance in which they read and sing from the *lontar monyet* (monkey manuscript), drink *tuak* (palm wine), dance and imitate *gamelan* instruments vocally. The road southwards continues to the westernmost point of the island – a sheer cliff standing above Bangko Bangko beach. Turning on the road to

Monkeys are a common sight at Lombok temples.

Sekotong south of Lembar, you will eventually skirt the coastline and witness beautiful scenery of turquoise sea and blindingly white beaches. There are cottages and fine snorkelling at **Gili Nanggu**, accessible by boat from either Lembar or Tawun. The snorkelling is good at Palangan beach, and this is the place to catch boats to Gili Gede, Gili Ashan and others. The route ends at **Bangko Bangko ❹**, with a stunning forest and a white-sand beach surrounding Lombok's best surfing area, Desert Point.

EXPLORING CENTRAL LOMBOK

East of Cakranegara in **Lingsar ❺** is **Pura Lingsar** temple complex (daily 8am–5pm; donation). Originally built in 1714, this is one of the most important Hindu temples of Lombok. It was also traditionally a focus of worship for syncretic Wetu Telu Muslims, and some local Buddhists and Christians occasionally pray here for prosperity, rain, fertility, health and general success.

Located a few kilometres northeast of Narmada in **Suranadi** is the oldest and holiest of the Balinese temples in Lombok, **Pura Suranadi ❻** (daily 8am–5pm; donation), a complex of three temples founded by a Javanese priest, Danghyang Nirartha. Chilly spring water bubbles up into restored baths, which are open to swimmers. Beyond Suranadi is **Hutan Wisata Suranadi** (daily 8am–5pm). Stroll through the botanical garden, where specimens are labelled, to see birds, monkeys and butterflies.

THE NORTHWEST COAST AND NORTHERN LOMBOK

Heading north from Ampenan is **Pura Segara**, where, following cremations, the Balinese who live on Lombok come to scatter the ashes of their loved ones into the sea. En route to Senggigi, the road passes **Batu Layar**, an important *makam* (ancestral grave) where Sasak Muslims come to picnic and to pray for health and success. Nearby is **Pura**

Batu Bolong (daily 8am–5pm; donation), an interesting Hindu temple on a cliff facing Bali. It sits beside a large rock with a hole, from which the temple takes its name. This is a great sunset point with fantastic vistas of Bali.

About 10km (6 miles) north of Ampenan is beautiful **Senggigi** ❼, with glorious beaches, picturesque views of Bali's Gunung Agung to the west, good coral for snorkelling and diving, and millions of dollars invested for tourism. Senggigi is an attractive place to stay, with several deluxe hotels as well as budget accommodation.

While Senggigi has always had the lion's share of visitors to itself, there is now competition from sheltered **Mangsit** ❽ beach to its north. Taking the place of international chain hotels here are villas and stylish boutique hotels offering a friendly, personalised service.

North of Mangsit along the scenic and hilly coastal road, there is a variety of terrain and villages. First is **Pemenang**, followed westwards by **Bangsal** ❾, which has an attractive beach. Boats depart from here for the three islands fondly called 'The Gilis': Gili Air, Gili Meno and Gili Trawangan. For decades they have attracted visitors from around the world for their pristine waters, great diving and snorkelling and their laidback charm.

Gili Trawangan ❿, the largest and most distant of the three islands, has two types of visitors: partygoers, who flock to the southwest side of the island to enjoy gorgeous white-sand beaches, cheap (and not so cheap) accommodation, and of course, parties. North coast visitors spend their days in quiet relaxation, sunbathing and diving. **Gili Meno** ⓫ is the least developed of the three islands. Its attractions are uncrowded beaches, Meno Wall off the west coast, popular with divers, and quiet walks under the stars. **Gili Air** ⓬, closest to the mainland, has the largest local population and a range of dive shops that service all the needs of divers. It has basic as well as moderately priced accommodation.

There is no fresh water on the Gili islands, which means saltwater showers and the absence of lush gardens.

⊘ **Where**

Though isolated, Lombok's southwest peninsula is undergoing slow but steady tourism development. Four islets off Sekotong – Gili Kedis, Bili Tangkong, Gili Nanggu and Gili Sudak – have been dubbed 'honeymoon islands' because of their peacefulness and solitude.

The crater lake at Gunung Rinjani.

Sunset from Gili Trawangan.

Most water is shipped from the mainland, so there is a need to conserve it. Drink only bottled water, eat only cooked food, and choose accommodation with mosquito nets.

Back on the mainland, the south-facing beach at **Sira**, along the peninsula north of Bangsal, is a good launch spot for snorkelling on the offshore coral reef. This is also the site for the **Kosaido Country Club**, an 18-hole course with magnificent sea views. Around the point, in Medana Bay, is the luxury Oberoi resort.

Northeast of **Gondang**, along the coast, is **Tiu Pupas** waterfall, a 20-minute walk beyond the end of a poorly marked, rocky road. While the spring-fed falls may be disappointing during the dry season, they flow into a deep pool suitable for swimming. Trekking through a traditional Sasak village, **Kerurak**, makes the effort worthwhile. Dusty **Segenter** village, 20km (16 miles) from Gondang and inland at Sukadana, provides a glimpse into the harsh reality of life on the island's dry side. The 300 villagers in this northern

Pura Lingsar.

interior village eke out a living growing corn and beans, yet they welcome visitors with smiles.

Bayan is one of the last strongholds of Wetu Telu traditions – though locals generally consider themselves 'proper' Muslims and insist that Wetu Telu is simply a form of complementary adat ('custom'). The ancient wooden mosque here hosts important Wetu Telu ceremonies and there are a number of secretive shrines in the nearby forests. In nearby **Sedang Gile**, the waterfalls are among the island's most spectacular and are worth the effort of descending 200 vertical steps to view them.

Start planning the ascent to **Gunung Rinjani** with a visit to Rinjani Trekking Center (Jalan Pariwista Senaru, Kec. Bayan; tel: 62 370 631 932; www.rinjanitrekkingcenter.com; daily 7am–5pm) or the Rinjani Trekking Club (www.rinjanitrekking.com) in **Senaru**. Both offer a series of programmes for climbing the volcano and for trekking in the Gunung Rinjani National Park, all of which involve the local communities.

Inside the Gunung Rinjani caldera is a crater lake, **Danau Segara Anak** (Child of the Sea), with a second steaming volcano growing at the edge. It is a difficult climb; go with an authorised local guide and wear warm clothing.

EASTERN AND CENTRAL LOMBOK

South of the north coast road are **Sembalun Bumbung** and neighbouring **Sembalun Lawang**, located in a valley on the slopes of Gunung Rinjani. Both villages are alternative points for climbing Gunung Rinjani, and there are a number of tourist agencies that organise treks in the region, as well as several homestays. Be warned that climbing Rinjani is not for amateurs. What starts out easily enough becomes a steep winding path to the ridge. The final ascent to the summit is over loose gravel, rising steeply, and there's also the cold, wind and low oxygen levels to contend with. Gunung Rinjani National Park is officially closed to climbers and trekkers in the rainy season, which is roughly December to March.

Southeast of Gunang Rinjani, **Lenek** is well known as a source of traditional Sasak music and dance, including *tari pakon*, a medicinal trance dance. A local cultural patron of the arts has established an organisation to reinvigorate the performing arts, and visitors are welcomed for a rustic stay here. To the west is **Pringgasela**, a village steeped in tradition and a major centre for *ikat*-weaving. Visit the small houses and shops here to purchase hand-woven fabrics.

Tetebatu 🟦, at the southern foot of Gunung Rinjani, is a cool mountain retreat with views of beautiful rice terraces. The area is wet and misty during the rainy season. About an hour's trek north of Tetebatu through a monkey-filled forest is **Jeruk Manis waterfall**. (Be advised to stay well away from the mischievous monkeys, who are known to nip tourists, and steal food, bags and jewellery.) **Bonjeruk**, in central Lombok, is a village of *dalang*, or puppeteers, for the *wayang Sasak* shadow play; many of the puppets are made here. Near **Lendang**

⊙ **Tip**

Traditionally most visitors reached the Gilis via Lombok itself. However, if you are short on time or not looking to explore the rest of Lombok, they are now best reached on a direct speedboat transfer from Bali, avoiding the long journey via Lombok's airport or main ferry port.

Penujak pottery village.

The women of Penujak and neighbouring villages have been making pottery since the early 16th century.

Nangka is Jojang spring, with great vistas and a forest inhabited by black monkeys. In August, Sasak boxing takes place in the village.

TO THE SOUTH

Praya ⑯ is a crossroads and the hub of the south. Home of the Saturday market, it is central to many of the area's handicrafts villages. Southwest of Praya is **Penujak ⑰**, one of three traditional pottery-making villages sponsored by the New Zealand government. The other two are **Banyumulek**, south of Mataram, and **Masbagik** Timur, in East Lombok.

The women of all three villages have been making pottery since the early 16th century, with skills being passed from one generation to the other. Visitors can watch as a greyish-brown clay that comes from local riverbeds is manipulated into shape by hand, sometimes using a wooden paddle. Instead of a potter's wheel, the women walk around the jar, building up and scraping the walls as they go. After drying in the sun, the earthenware is baked in pits where the clay turns a rich reddish-brown in the process.

On the road leading south from Praya, which skirts Lombok's modern, though isolated international airport, are two traditional Sasak villages sandwiched between the main road and rice fields. On the west side of the road is **Rembitan ⑱**, an authentic hilltop village with the oldest mosque in Lombok, **Masjid Kuno**. Only Muslims may enter this thatched-roof house of worship. An interesting walk through the village is encouraged by residents, who act as guides for a small fee. On the east side of the road is **Sade**, a village with clusters of thatched *lumbung* or rice barns, which is open to tourists.

Kuta ⑲, 45km (28 miles) southeast of Cakranegara, is fronted by an expansive and beautiful white-sand beach. There are various upscale resorts and budget guesthouses here. Kuta's market (early on Wednesday and Sunday mornings) is a lively cacophony of chickens and local chatter and is brightened by colourful fruits and woven baskets. Tourism development has proceeded in stop-start fashion for decades, but the 2011 opening of the long-delayed international airport nearby has finally led to more sustained expansion. Compared to Kuta's Balinese namesake, however, the area remains thoroughly low-key.

Mandalika beach is also the site of the annual Bau Nyale festival commemorating the legend of the beautiful Putri (Princess) Mandalika, who long ago was sought as the bride of every Lombok *raja*. When she could not choose between the suitors, she threw herself into the sea from a headland, saying, '*Kuta*', or 'Wait for me here'. When she jumped, hundreds of *nyale* sea worms floated to the surface. Thus, every year on the anniversary of her fateful demise, the *nyale* worms return to the site. Thousands of residents – including young people who flirt and strut while watching the sea

⊘ ALFRED RUSSEL WALLACE

Although 19th-century British biologist Alfred Russel Wallace developed the theory of evolution at the same time as Charles Darwin, he is better known today for identifying the great ecological frontier that runs through the middle of the Indonesian archipelago, popularly known as the Wallace Line.

Sponsored by the Royal Geographical Society, Wallace spent eight years travelling through the region, from Singapore to Papua, collecting over 125,000 insect, bird and mammal specimens. During that time he noticed a marked difference between the flora and fauna of the western and eastern parts of the archipelago. Those to the west were recognisably Asian, while in the east there appeared to be more in common with Australia, with marsupials and parakeets among other species.

Wallace originally theorised an absolute dividing line between the two spheres, but modern scientists have established that there is in fact a hazy transition zone, known as Wallacea, spanning the middle regions of Indonesia. In places, however, elements of Wallace's original hard line can be identified. The strait between Bali and Lombok is one such place, so deep that it never dried out even during the ice ages when sea levels fell. Bali was as far east as large Asian animals, such as tigers, were ever able to colonise without human assistance. Wallace's book, *The Malay Archipelago* remains a classic.

worms spawn – gather for the festival. Associated with fertility, the *nyale* are ground up, and the resulting mixture is either placed in irrigation channels to ensure farmers will have a good harvest, or fried and eaten in the manner of a love potion.

ASTONISHING LANDSCAPE

West of Kuta village, the beach at **Mawun** ⑳ runs the length of a perfect half-moon bay, flanked by massive headlands. This deserted spot off the beaten track is barren of trees, which accentuates the spectacular scenery and the sound of the sea. Apart from the occasional fisherman or young girls selling sarongs, it is possible to have this fine beach all to yourself. It can also be reached by bicycle from Kuta, although the road is a bit steep.

A picturesque little fishing village lies on the fringe of the wide, sweeping **Selong Blanak** ㉑ beach, west of Mawun. Colourful, small fishing *prahu* (boats) rock in gentle waves at the eastern end of the bay. What sets this site apart from other beaches is the scale of the surrounding landscape, which is of continental, not island, proportions. The sand, sea and distant hills are painted in an astonishing palate of colours, making this an ideal place to bask in nature's beauty.

East of Kuta lies a series of beautiful, untouched beaches. **Tanjung Aan** has spectacular scenery off the peninsula, just a few vendor shacks and a virtually undisturbed beach. Another 3km (2 miles) east is **Gerupuk**, well known as a surf location and also ideal for windsurfing and kite-surfing. Local fishermen harvest seaweed in the nearby bay.

Further east, beyond **Batu Nampar**, is the infrequently visited **Batu Rintang**. With its traditional thatched-rice barns and huts, this village offers a realistic look at local life. Outside Batu Nampar are salt works and floating seaweed frames, farmed by migrants from South Sulawesi and Madura. South and east, respectively, are found the coastal settlements of **Ekas** and **Tanjung Luar**, inhabited by Bugis fishermen from Sulawesi, who arrived here during the early 1600s.

Kuta beach on the south coast of Lombok.

Diwu Mbai waterfall on Moyo Island.

SUMBAWA

Some of the best surf in the world can be found off the coast of Sumbawa. Non-surfers can trek through forests, snorkel off the south coast of Pulau Moyo or view ancient stone sarcophagi.

Larger than Bali and Lombok combined, Sumbawa's contorted form is the result of violent volcanic explosions. It was Gunung Tambora that isolated the people of the west from the Bimanese for centuries. So separate are they that the native language of the Sumbawanese is more akin to those of the Balinese and the Lombok Sasaks, while the Bima language is more like those of Flores and Sumba. When islanders say 'Sumbawa', they mean the western part of the island. The east is simply called 'Bima'. The influence of Javanese culture and Hindu_Buddhism was only ever limited here, and today most Sumbawans are fairly conservative Muslims: visitors should wear respectful attire away from the beaches.

Until fairly recently, there were only two reasons to visit this little-known island: to hire a boat from Sape in the east heading for Komodo National Park or to catch a big wave on its west or southeast coasts. Improved air service to Labuanbajo, Flores, from where the sail to Komodo is much easier and prettier, has negated the first reason, leaving surfing as the island's biggest tourism attraction. The breaks at **Hu'u** attract surfers from around the world, and sunsets from the beaches on clear evenings are absolutely stunning.

There are other things to do and see in Sumbawa besides the surf. The rich and famous use part of Pulau Moyo, off the

north coast, as a remote luxury getaway. Moyo is also a nature reserve protecting forest and wildlife, and there are two waterfalls presenting rugged trekking opportunities. The mighty Gunung Tambora provides off-the-beaten-track trekking, and there are megaliths believed to be related to those in Sumba.

WEST SUMBAWA

Ferries from Lombok arrive at Poto Tano in West Sumbawa, where buses await passengers bound for the surfing beaches or Sumbawa Besar.

Map on page 282

⊘ Main attractions
Hu'u Beach
Batu Tering
Palau Moyo
Gunung Tambora
Bima

White sands and stones on Sekongkang Beach.

On the west coast from Taliwang south to Sekongkang beach (familiarly called Yo-Yo's), the scenic coastline has superb white-sand beaches. There is prime surfing at Scar Reef near **Jereweh**, at Supersucks near Maluk, and at Yo-Yo's on the south coast. **Maluk** ❶ and neighbouring **Benete** are bustling centres of goods and services to satisfy the needs of the copper- and gold-mine employees who work near Maluk. Budget hotels, bars and restaurants cater for surfers.

On the north coast at **Sumbawa Besar** ❷ is the **Dalam Loka**, the former sultan's palace. Made entirely of wood, it is raised on 99 stilts to remind followers of the 99 names given to their god. It is now a museum used for cultural activities. The late sultan's heirlooms are kept in nearby Balai Kuning (Yellow House) where his daughter lives, and can only been seen by appointment.

The hills east of Sumbawa Besar contain large stone sarcophagi, carved in low relief with human forms and crocodiles. **Batu Tering** ❸, about 29km (18 miles) south of Sumbawa Besar, has megaliths said to be the royal

tombs of ancient chiefs of a Neolithic culture that thrived about 2,000 years ago. About 2km (1.25 miles) beyond is Liang Petang (Dark Cave), with stalactites and stalagmites resembling humans and weaving looms.

Travelling west from Sumbawa Besar brings you to **Pulau Moyo** ❹. Two-thirds of the island is a game reserve to protect the island's deer, *banteng* wild ox, 21 bat species and wild boars. The flora here ranges from savannah to dense jungle containing teak, tamarind and banyan trees. There are two waterfalls; the one near Labuan Aji village is an easier trek. South of the island the water is crystal clear and the reefs undisturbed, ideal for snorkellers and divers, with a white-sand beach opposite the island at Tanjung Manis.

Moyo is accessible in about 45 minutes by speedboat from Sumbawa Besar. Alternatively, fishing boats can be hired from Ai Bari. Simple accommodation is available at Tanjung Pasir on the mainland. The luxurious Amanwana resort, with modified villas using canvas tent toppings, is also on Moyo.

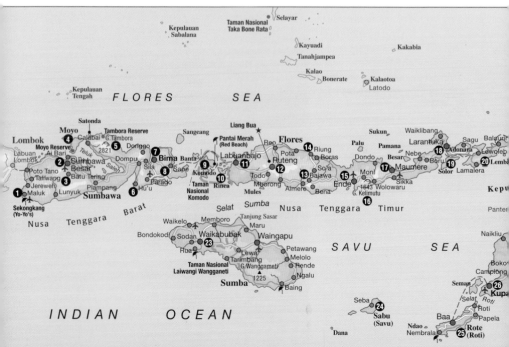

It's totally isolated, and bookings have to be made in advance.

EAST SUMBAWA

Heading east from Sumbawa Besar, the land narrows connecting West with East Sumbawa. From here, fertile river valleys with shimmering velvet-green rice fields are replaced by the monotony of rolling scorched brown hills. Picturesque bays and harbours shelter *bagan* (fishing platforms). Along the coasts, families line the shores damming up sea water to make salt.

Serious trekkers may want to ascend **Gunung Tambora** ❺. In 1815, some 100 cu km (25 cu miles) of debris were ejected into the atmosphere with a force equivalent to that of several hydrogen bombs, creating 'the year without summer' in 1816. Located on the northern peninsula of Sumbawa, the gaping, 2,821-metre (9,250ft) high caldera offers spectacular views on a clear day. The ascent begins at **Calabai**, a small logging town on the coast. It is a very difficult three-day climb and a guide is essential.

Due south of Dompu is **Hu'u** ❻. Better known amongst surfers as 'Lakeys', it offers superlative waves on the outlying reefs at Periscopes, Nangas, Lakey Peak, Lakey Pipe and Cobblestones. The main beach in front of the Lakey Peak surf-break has beautiful white sand, and at low tide there is good reef-walking. Swimming and snorkelling is possible in small inlets.

At **Bima** ❼, if there is a festival going on, you may catch *pencak silat* (martial arts) and other dance performances at the sultan's palace. At the *pasar* (local market), you'll see women wearing colourful headscarves that are unique to this region; unmarried women must cover everything except their eyes.

There are several traditional villages in the hills east of Bima, where traces of pre-Islamic belief systems endure. **Donggo** is the main settlement. Women here still weave indigo cloth, from which they make their traditional clothing.

The road that connects Bima and **Sape** ❽ is hilly and winding. Look for rice storage barns near Maria village and plantations of little purple shallots.

Sumbawa is famous for its surf.

A bicolour blenny on the coral reef south of Pulau Moyo.

Komodo island.

KOMODO AND RINCA

The main attractions of these inhospitable islands are the remarkable Komodo dragons, the largest lizards in the world, and some of the best diving in the region.

A Unesco World Heritage Site, **Komodo National Park** lies in the strait between Sumbawa and Flores and is the habitat of the world's largest lizard, *Varanus komodoensis*, the Komodo dragon.

Although there are dragons on two other nearby islands, in order to protect wild populations visitors are only allowed on Komodo and Rinca (pronounced *rin-cha*). Most visitors couple Komodo dragon-spotting with snorkelling and diving while in the park. At Pantai Merah (Red Beach), near Komodo, reefs teeming with colourful fish are very near the shoreline.

Komodo island is home to several human settlements, including its largest village, Kampung Komodo (population about 1,300), located only a few kilometres west of Loh Liang ranger station. Over the centuries the islands have been settled by a mix of seafaring Bugis and Bajo people, as well as convicts exiled from the Bima sultanate. Today the mostly Muslim villagers mainly make their living from fishing. Modestly dressed visitors are welcomed.

KOMODO

The highlight of a visit to the national park is seeing the dragons in their natural habitat. On **Komodo** ❾, the most popular trek is a 2km (1.2 mile) walk to **Banunggulung**. With prior arrangement, those who wish to see more of the elusive reptiles away from the tourist crowds can continue past Banunggulung to **Poreng**, in the northeastern part of the island, or as far as **Sebita** on the coast. Shorter walks are also possible from the ranger station at **Loh Liang** (where basic tourist accommodation is available) to Kampung Komodo to the southwest. Trekkers on both islands must be accompanied by a park ranger. Keep your distance from all wild animals, and remember that the dragons can move very quickly if disturbed, that they are dangerous creatures and that medical attention is far away.

⊙ Main attractions
Komodo
Pantai Merah
Rinca
Padar
Diving and snorkelling

Map on page 282

A reminder of the age of the dinosaurs.

There are several other longer trails to choose from. The most frequented long-haul trek is to **Gunung Ara** (730 metres/2,390ft), one of a chain of mountains that extends along the northern part of Komodo. It is a one- or two-day excursion, and from the summit you can take in great panoramas of the islands, their craggy peaks, sandy bays and the sparkling turquoise sea. Similar views can be enjoyed from **Gunung Satalibo**, at 740 metres (2,420ft) high, the island's tallest peak. The trails are those used by foraging animals, bordered by tall grasses concealing large stones, so sturdy walking shoes and trousers are recommended.

Scuba diving and snorkelling in the park waters are among Indonesia's best. There are 260 species of reef-building corals, sheer-drop walls and around 1,000 species of fish and marine mammals, including manta rays, sharks, sea turtles, dolphins and whales. The waters to the south of the park are cooler than those to the north, creating an ideal habitat for corals and reef fish, while to the north, rich plankton and nutrients attract a wide variety of temperate marine life. For snorkellers, **Pantai Merah** (Red Beach) offers butterfly, parrot and triggerfish, giant clams and colourful corals at close range. The gorgeous beach is pink due to an abundance of red coral in the region.

As Komodo National Park is in the transition zone described by 19th-century naturalist Sir Alfred Russel Wallace (see page 278), birdwatchers will find a mixture of Asian and Australian species. Squawking cockatoos and noisy friarbirds flock in tropical kapok and gnarled tamarind trees, disturbing green Imperial pigeons, black-naped orioles, sunbirds and flowerpeckers. On the forest floor there are jungle fowl, the forebears of domesticated chickens, quails scratching for insects and mound-building megapodes.

RINCA

Not having received the same publicity as Komodo, **Rinca** ⑩ island is not as crowded as its more famous neighbour in the high season (July and August), and provides a far more natural experience.

On Rinca, there are two moderately easy treks (2–3 hours each) from the

The visitor centre at Komodo National Park.

nger station at **Loh Buaya**, which also has limited basic accommodation. ne, to the east of the compound, is p and across a ridge where there is a reathtaking view of the Komodo group f islands, with Flores rising from the ea at one point. Watch for herds of wild orses, which are absent from Komodo. he other trail goes in the opposite irection through monsoon forest, here wild buffaloes wallow in streams. is best to leave on expeditions early the mornings so you can see the ani- als at their most active, and you can void the extreme midday heat.

ISITING KOMODO ATIONAL PARK

sitor numbers to Komodo have creased exponentially in the last ecade, thanks to the major upgrad- g of Labuanbajo's airport which now as regular flights from Jakarta and her major Indonesian cities, and n upsurge in domestic tourism. As consequence, the national park has me under enormous pressure and cal authorities are struggling to work out how to mitigate the impact while continuing to reap the economic ben- efits in what was previously a seriously impoverished region. Suggestions of prohibitively expensive new entry fees to reduce visitor numbers, or even a temporary shut-down of the entire park, have been made, so it's important to check the current situation before travelling. Make sure that any boats you charter use sound anchoring practices to avoid damaging coral at snorkelling sites, and check that all litter is taken out of the park.

The vast majority of people visit via Labuanbajo, which is now a major tour- ist resort with excellent services and air connections. Daytrips and overnight visits can be arranged from here, and there are also various low-key resorts on small islands within the park, accessed from Labuanbajo. Few peo- ple these days visit directly from Sum- bawa, but it is still possible to charter boats for overnight trips in Sape. Other visitors arrive on longer sea voyages – aboard organised cruises, typically originating in Bali.

⊘ **Tip**

The small island of Padar in the channel between Komodo and Rinca has become incredibly popular with visitors in recent years – in large part for the iconic panorama from its main peak, which is now badly eroded as a consequence. Padar also has beautiful beaches, though there are no resident dragons.

The saliva produced by Komodo dragons is highly septic.

⊘ THE DRAGONS OF KOMODO AND RINCA

There are about 6,000 Komodo dragons on Komodo, Rinca, Gili Montang, Flores and Nusa Kode. According to the International Union for Conservation of Nature's list of threatened species, the Komodo dragon is not endan- gered, but is considered vulnerable. The greatest threat to the monitors is from deer poachers, who kill off the animals on which they feed.

Male dragons can reach three metres (10ft) or more in length and weigh an average of 70kg (154lbs). Females usually attain only two- thirds of this size and lay up to 30 eggs at a time.

The reptiles are carnivores, favouring rotting meat, which they track by flicking their forked tongues into the air to identify odours. However, they can hunt when there is no carrion available; by lifting their massive bodies up on muscular legs they can sprint briefly at 20kph (12mph). Stealth predators, they lie in wait to ambush using claws and tails to knock vic- tims senseless. When preying on large animals such as buffalo and deer, Komodo dragons do not usually achieve an outright kill in the first attack, but if they manage to bite their victim the creature will usually die from septicaemia due to the toxic bacteria in the dragon's saliva. The dragons patiently track the dying animal by scent, sometimes over many days.

During the mating season (July to August) Komodo dragons prefer to attend to the business at hand in seclusion, making them more difficult to spot.

Ikat weaving on a hand loom near Maumere.

FLORES

Green, mountainous Flores is home to some of the most beautiful landscapes and most intriguing cultures in Nusa Tenggara.

Flores extends a long arm east from Komodo towards the Solor archipelago, its highland landscape punctuated by volcanic cones, its coastal waters fringed with nature reserves and a marine park. Diverse cultures with ancient traditions have survived in the isolated villages of the interior.

A 750km (470-mile) highway runs the length of Flores in a series of curves and switchbacks from Labuan-bajo in the west to Larantuka in the east and is plagued by landslides in the rainy season. For the hardy, a trip across the Trans-Flores highway offers a look at many facets of one of Indonesia's most interesting islands. Despite the dominance of Catholicism here, a great deal of cultural diversity remains, with many intriguing traditional villages.

By breaking the journey up into overnight stops, on one day travellers can be awed by the patterned rice fields near Ruteng, revel in the cool mountain air at Bajawa or snorkel at the marine national park in Riung. The next day could include Ende, and Kelimutu's three crater lakes at Moni, passing cocoa, vanilla, coffee and pineapple plantations along the way. The third leg of the journey leaves the volcanoes behind and dips down to a gorgeous azure sea and enters former

Gunung Kelimutu.

Portuguese strongholds at Maumere and Larantuka.

Named Cabo das Flores (Cape of Flowers) by the Portuguese in the 16th century, Flores was already a vital link in inter-island trade with the 15th-century Javanese Majapahit Empire and later with South Sulawesi's Gowa kingdom, which began converting coastal communities to Islam. The Portuguese built a fort on Solor island, to the east, to protect their trading interests in malaria- and cholera-ridden Timor and established a Catholic mission at Larantuka.

◎ Main attractions
Labuanbajo
Ruteng
Riung
Bajawa's traditional
  villages
Gunung Kelimutu
Larantuka

Map on page 282

A cacao plantation near Labuanbajo.

The Dutch acquired the Portuguese settlements on Flores in 1859 in exchange for Portuguese holdings in eastern Timor with a proviso that Catholicism be encouraged. They also bombarded Muslim Ende twice and exercised increasing authority here, but fully controlled the island only after subduing a bloody rebellion in 1907–8. Thereafter, Catholic missionaries flooded Flores, sparking a new wave of conversions.

WESTERN FLORES: MANGGARAI

The western third of Flores is called **Manggarai**. Primarily Muslim, Manggarai is self-sufficient in rice, and exports fine coffee and livestock. **Labuanbajo** ⑪ sits on a beautiful bay filled with the outriggers of local fishermen. This has always been the main gateway to the Komodo National Park, as well as the port for interisland ferry traffic from Sumbawa, but Labuanbajo has undergone dramatic transformation in recent years. No longer a sleepy harbour town, it is now the main tourist centre east of Lombok, with a plethora of accommodation and dining options, and regular flights from Bali and Jakarta. The fabulous sunsets remain.

Batu Cermin (Mirror Rock) is a series of caves and canyons about 5km (3 miles) from Labuanbajo by car, and from there on foot. A large grotto contains stalactites and stalagmites, and while some of the caves are narrow and dark, others receive sunlight from above.

A three-hour drive southeast of Labuanbajo (83km/52 miles) brings you to the volcanic Lake Sano Nggoang region and the 15,000-hectare (37,000-acre) **Mbeliling Forest Nature Reserve**, which has been developed as a community-based ecotourism destination. A two-day trek includes birdwatching for prevalent swamp species, hiking to Savanna Peak for panoramic views, and visits to healing sulphuric hot springs and an old wooden church and parish houses.

Continuing east from Labuanbajo, the road winds up to **Ruteng** ⑫, a pleasantly cool town situated up in the western hills. Watch for the traditional *lingko*, spider's web-shaped rice fields near **Cancar**, before reaching Ruteng.

Ruteng is primarily a government centre and a good stopping-off place to break up the overland trip. The top of **Golo Curu** (Welcome Mountain) has great sunset views and an old Dutch church (five minutes by *bemo* or a 45-minute walk). Rainforest-covered **Gunung Ranaka** (2,400 metres/7,874ft) looms over Ruteng – it is a four-hour walk to the summit – and is a good venue for birdwatching.

Kampung Ruteng, just outside Ruteng, features a stone ancestral altar. **Todo** village, 21km (13 miles) from Ruteng, is known for its megalithic stones and a drum whose head is reputedly covered by a woman's skin. From Todo, drive to Denge village via Dintor and make a four-hour mountain trek up to **Waerebo**, 1,000 metres (3,280ft) above sea level. This is the only remaining village in Manggarai where traditional houses still exist. Built on five levels, with high-pitched straw roofs, the living areas are at the bottom and the top four levels are used for storage. With the assistance of BirdLife Indonesia, the 35-member Waerebo Tourism Body was formed to improve the local economy through environmental conservation and low-impact tourism. A local travel agency can arrange an overnight stay in one of the houses, which is inhabited by eight families.

About 12km (7.5 miles) north of Ruteng is **Liang Bua**, where the fossils of *Homo floresiensis* were found by a joint Indonesia-Australia team. The tiny skeletons, nicknamed 'Hobbits', are believed to be a new human species that existed alongside modern humans as recently as 12,000 years ago, yet may have descended from *Homo erectus*, which arose some 2 million years ago.

CENTRAL FLORES: NGADA

The next stop is **Bajawa** ⑬, whose attractions are its cool mountain air, exquisite yellow-on-black supplementary warp *sarongs* and traditional villages. More than any other area of Flores, the Ngada region has retained its traditions and rituals alongside Catholicism. Bena, Luba, Langa, Gurusina and Nage villages offer examples of Ngada's ancient culture. All have *ngadhu* shrines, with carved tree-trunk bases, and *bhaga* – miniature houses – in the village centre. The *ngadhu* and *bhaga* symbolise male and female tribal ancestors who are said to live in the shrines. Interesting megalithic stones are easiest to find at **Bena** and at nearby **Wogo Tua** (Old Wogo). The week-long Reba festival begins in Bena in late December, then moves to other villages according to dates selected by their *adat* (local

customs) leaders. Wearing traditional ikats, the people dance around the village and sing to reconcile humans and nature.

A deer hunt in **So'a** is a fertility ritual associated with puberty rites: circumcision for the boys and tooth filing for the girls. Strong taboos against sex are enforced throughout the hunt, including a prohibition against the consummation of recent marriages. After the hunt, young women dip their hands into the blood of slain deer to enhance their fertility.

Langa and Bena lie in the shadow of a perfectly coned volcano, **Gunung Inerie** (2,227 metres/7,306ft). It can be climbed in 3–5 hours, depending on your level of physical fitness. **Gunung Ebulobo**, one of Flores's most magnificent volcanoes, can be climbed from Mulakoli village, off the main road to Ende.

From Bajawa, it is a three-hour drive to the northern coastal village of **Riung** ⑭, an excellent side trip for those with time to spare and who are interested in snorkelling in the

This Ngadhu shrine in Langa features a human figure on its rooftop.

Wae Rebo Village.

Seventeen Islands Nature Reserve. Riung is also one of the few sites inhabited by Komodo dragons outside Komodo National Park.

EASTERN FLORES: ENDE TO THE EAST COAST

On the main road east from Bajawa, it is 125km (80 miles) and about four hours to **Ende** ⑮, one of Flores's two major towns. In contrast to the other, Maumere, Ende has a distinctly Islamic flavour; it was an important Islamic trading port from the late 17th century to the 19th century. During the Japanese Occupation, the city was the regional capital for the eastern archipelago. Sukarno was exiled here in 1933, and Ende was later bombed by the Allies.

A couple of hours' drive northeast of Ende are three adjacent volcanic crater lakes on **Gunung Kelimutu** ⑯, a spectacular sight, surrounded by lush countryside. The lakes, at an altitude of 1,640 metres (5,380ft), are separated only by low ridges and, curiously, are of different colours.

The misty descent from Gunung Kelimutu.

Like chameleons, their colours have been constantly changing since Gunung Iye in Ende erupted in 1969. Theories for the changes in colours range from imbalances in bacterial and microorganisms to dissolving minerals as the water eats through the rock. Village elders say the colours remain constant, but optical illusions make them appear to be different. The best time for viewing is at sunrise. The trip up to the lakes can be arranged at your lodgings in Ende or in **Moni** at the base of the mountain where there are guesthouses and simple eateries.

Around Ende is the beginning of the ikat-weaving area, producing exquisitely woven cloths in which intricate designs are tie-dyed on to the threads before weaving begins. In Ende ikats the designs are of a solid colour, usually reddish brown. Some 12km (7.5 miles) east of Kelimutu, at Wolowaru, turn south to **Nggela** coastal village to see superb textiles being woven. From Ende to Maumere, the road cuts diagonally across the island towards

⊘ ANCIENT TRADITIONS

Catholicism claims about 95 percent of Flores's 2 million inhabitants. The church has put heavy emphasis on improving living conditions through its schools, health services and agricultural programmes. And although the clergy in Flores are well aware of the continued existence of many traditional beliefs and customs, they make no systematic efforts to eliminate them.

The ancient traditions that have survived are many and varied. Some islanders still worship their ancestral spirits. They also believe in Dewa, a god who lives in the sky, and Nitu, a goddess who lives beneath the earth, in the water, in large trees and in the ocean. Pythons were once worshipped in Flores, lending the island another former name, Snake Island.

the north coast. The distance is 150km (90 miles), but the winding, scenic drive can take seven hours.

Maumere ⑰ was the main entry point to Flores before the upgrade of Labuanbajo's airport, and it is still a hub for regional air connections. Visit Maumere's market to see local women with swept-up hairdos dressed in traditional weavings, bright green or yellow blouses and heirloom ivory bracelets. While made in the same manner as Ende's, the ikat cloths of Maumere have a greater variety of colours. Watch weavers at work in nearby villages Watublapi, Sikka or Nita. Maumere itself is not particularly attractive, but there are a number of excellent beachside accommodation options nearby, especially at Waiara to the east of town which has good snorkelling just offshore.

Ledalero Museum on the outskirts of Maumere has an interesting collection of regional ethnological objects. The little museum is run by Ledalero Catholic Seminary, where many of Indonesia's priests study and are ordained. It is attached to the church, and visitors are welcome – ask at the church for the museum to be opened.

A SLICE OF IBERIA

A 140km (87-mile) road journey takes you to **Larantuka** ⑱ on the eastern tip of Flores. For about 300 years it was a Portuguese colony, and the Catholic rituals reflect that Iberian influence. Men dressed in white hoods carry the coffin of Jesus through the streets during Good Friday processions, stopping along the way for prayers and hymns in a version of the *Via Dolorosa*. But local beliefs creep in. A statue of the Virgin Mary is bathed in holy water. The statue is said to have been found on the beach by a local man, who reported to the king that he met a beautiful lady. But when the king reached the beach, the lady was not there. Instead, they found a statue and a message in the sand that said: *Renha Rosari* (Queen of the Rosary). Larantuka is a departure point for excursions to the small islands to the east.

The coloured lakes of Kelimutu.

ELSEWHERE IN NUSA TENGGARA

This remote region is way off the tourist trail, but there is a great deal of interest in the traditional cultures of Alor and Sumba, as well as Rote's world-class surfing.

Few tourists make it to the far-flung islands that are scattered south and east of Flores. Yet for anyone with an interest in traditional culture, these outposts are richly rewarding. The inhabitants' ancient belief systems, their megalithic tombs and symbolic architecture have long attracted researchers, while collectors worldwide are drawn by the hand-woven ikat cloth in an astonishingly wide variety of colours and motifs for such a small area.

Eastern Nusa Tenggara's biggest draw these days is its waters. Surfers have long sought out the great breaks on Rote, Sumba and Sabu. But the ocean, now acknowledged to be one of the world's most varied marine biodiversity areas, also attracts divers from near and far. Part of the Coral Triangle, which reaches north to the Philippines, a large sweep of the Savu Sea is a Marine Protected Area.

At the far eastern end of the archipelago is Timor. The provincial capital, Kupang, is the main gateway to the region for those travelling by air, with good links to big cities in western Indonesia. It's also the hub for local air and sea transport.

SOLOR ARCHIPELAGO

East of Flores lies the Solor archipelago, which includes Solor, Adonara and Lembata. Larantuka is the gateway, and boats frequently ply the waters between these islands.

Solor ⑲ is guarded by a Portuguese fort, constructed in 1566, and still in good shape. The entrance is covered by an impressive arch and, in one corner, rusting cannons have survived and stand to attention over approaches from the sea. But it is the traditional weaving that visitors come here to see. Unique among all other *ikat* cloths of the region, Solor's fabrics have a brilliant red background instead of the dark indigo used elsewhere. Neighbouring Adonara, dominated by the Ile Boleng

Weaving ikat cloth on Sumba.

volcano, has some beautiful beaches and intriguing village cultures, plus very basic guesthouse accommodation.

To the east, the women of **Lembata** ⑳ are known for producing ceremonial ikat cloths. A good 'bride's wealth' weaving sells for hundreds of dollars due to its importance as part of the wedding arrangements. Top-quality cloths are given to the groom's family, who in turn give the bride's family a gift of equal value – heirloom ivory tusks, first brought to the area in the 14th century. The island is also noted for its traditional whaling industry, conducted with tiny open boats and hand-thrown harpoons, centred in **Lamalera**, a favourite of anthropologists and documentary-makers, with homestay accommodation available.

Towering over Lembata is **Gunung Ile Ape** (also called Lewotolo), which has major significance in local traditional beliefs. Ile Api can be climbed from its northern slope in four hours of fairly easy walking, but take a guide and go early, before the clouds cover the sulphurous crater.

ALOR ARCHIPELAGO

East of the Solor islands lies the Alor archipelago: Pantar and Alor, best reached by flight or ferry from Kupang. At **Pantar** ㉑, Gunung Sirung awaits climbing for views of the yellow crater and the aroma of sulphurous fumes.

Alor ㉒ has always been known for its bronze kettledrums, *moko*, replicas of those from the 2,000-year-old Dong Son era of northern Vietnam. Hundreds and perhaps thousands of the drums are kept as heirlooms and are an essential part of the bride price here. Although the *moko* found on Alor were cast in either Java or China, how they ended up on this island, which was not part of traditional trade routes, remains unknown.

Today, however, it is the spectacular diving that attracts visitors. Renowned worldwide as one of Indonesia's top three dive destinations, Alor's rich reefs

and diverse marine life are equalled by excellent visibility. Sunfish (*mola-mola*), whales, mantas, whale sharks and migrating orcas are just some of the highlights, as well as muck diving.

A short drive from the major town, **Kalabahi**, is Takpala, perched atop a mountainside giving spectacular views of Maimol Bay on the northern coastline. Traditional dances can be prearranged here.

SUMBA

South of Flores, **Sumba** is barren throughout the long dry season, but it teems with remnants of an ancient ancestor-worshiping culture. In past centuries it was a source of sandalwood, horses and slaves, but today Sumba's attraction is its sculptured megalithic tombs, war game rituals (*Pasola*) and intricate *hinggi* ikat textiles.

West Sumba is lush and green during the rainy season, and its people live in distinctive houses with high-peaked roofs. Ancestral and land worship are still strong here. Traditional villages with elaborate megalithic tombs are

A bronze moko drum on Alor.

A Sumba market.

Picturesque Nemberala Beach, Rote Island.

scattered throughout the district: near **Waikabubak** there are a number of ancient mausoleums, and even within the confines of the town there are hilltop communities featuring traditional tombs and houses decorated with buffalo horns. **Sodan**, 25km (16 miles) southwest of Waikabubak, is perhaps the most interesting of the traditional villages.

In West Sumba's exciting *Pasola* ritual, scores of colourfully arrayed horsemen on bareback charge one another in a dramatic mock war. Held in several villages, the event begins after the full moon during an annual migration of *nyale* sea worms.

East Sumba is dry, rocky and inhospitable. Most of its people live near or on the coast, and an extensive handloom industry has flourished here for several centuries, producing distinctive *hinggi* ikats known for their bold designs. To see the process, set out for **Prailiu**, just outside of **Waingapu**. Some 70km (40 miles) southeast of Waingapu is **Rende**, which is known for good ikats as well as for megalithic tombs with unusual carvings. In the vicinity of **Ngalu** and **Baing**, 125km (80 miles) south of Waingapu, whole villages produce the fabulous *kombu* woven cloths – bargaining is expected.

ROTE AND SABU

Rote and Sabu are two seldom-visited islands off the west coast of Timor. With little rainfall to encourage rice growing, both learned centuries ago to rely on a sturdy drought-resistant palm, the *lontar (Borassus sundaicus)*, for sustenance when there was no other food available. The liquid taken from the inflorescence from two or three trees is enough to support a family during times of drought by reducing it to treacle and storing it in clay pots. Often farmed plantation-style, parts of the palm are also used for building materials and household tools.

Sabu (also spelled Sawu and Savu) is extremely remote, and visited mainly by protestant missionaries and intrepid surfers. Although overwhelmingly Christian, it has some fascinating traditional villages such as Namata where traces of the local Jingi Tiu belief system survive. The southern coast is

wild and rocky, while the more sheltered northern shore features long, deserted beaches. Equally beautiful are the island's ikat weavings, which are far more elegant than others nearby.

Rote ㉕ (also spelt Roti), a land of dazzling white-sand beaches and rolling plains, shelters 18 different ethnic groups, each of which was formerly ruled by its own *raja*. Rotenese men are known for their debating skills, and historically the island produced many successful attorneys. The island's south coast is a paradise for surfers.

Ikat cloths produced by the Rotenese are far more colourful than those of their neighbours, containing a good deal of red, white and black. Unique to the island is the *sasando*, a mandolin-like instrument made of *lontar* leaves. Also sought after here is silver jewellery from neighbouring **Ndao** island.

TIMOR

For many centuries, **Timor** was known as a source of fragrant sandalwood, a draw for foreign traders. The Portuguese and the Dutch later fought to control the trade and subsequently divided the island into Dutch West Timor and Portuguese East Timor. Indonesia invaded East Timor in 1975 after the Portuguese pulled out, but after an unhappy quarter-century of Indonesian rule, ending in bloody violence, it became independent as Timor-Leste, which officially gained independence in 2002 after a period of UN administration. West Timor remains a part of Indonesia.

The capital of East Nusa Tenggara province, **Kupang** ㉖ has regular air and ferry services to and from the rest of Indonesia. Kupang's attractions include the town market and the **Museum Negeri Kupang** (Museum of East Nusa Tenggara).

Timor also offers good cave diving and snorkelling and a great variety of fine textiles. On the main road between Kupang and Dili (Timor Leste), **So'e** is a bustling little town with a cool, pleasant climate. There are some fascinating traditional communities in the surrounding hills, particularly Boti, which welcomes visitors and is still ruled by a hereditary 'king'.

An Alor tribal elder takes aim.

Orangutans at Tanjung Putting
National Park.

Floating accommodation at Tanjung Puting National Park.

KALIMANTAN

This vast, wild territory used to be known for its head-hunters. Today orangutans head the list of attractions.

Chillies at Samarinda market.

Kalimantan is Indonesia's name for its two-thirds share of Borneo, the world's fourth-largest island (after Australia, Greenland and New Guinea). Borneo's north coast comprises Malaysia's Sarawak and Sabah and the tiny independent oil-rich Brunei sultanate. Kalimantan, with an area of 540,000 sq km (200,000 sq miles), represents nearly 30 percent of Indonesia's land area, but is occupied by barely six percent of the population.

Although the name Kalimantan may be unfamiliar, many of us have notions about Borneo: impenetrable jungles concealing Dayaks – the former head-hunting tribes with long earlobes – and dangerous wild animals may leap to the minds of romantics; the plight of endangered orangutans evokes passionate conversation among animal-lovers; and forest degradation catches the attention of global warming-watchers.

From Kalimantan's hinterland of low-altitude mountain ranges, great rivers cascade, traditionally serving as crucial channels of communication between the people of the interior and those on the coast. Today vastly improved road and air transport networks have largely superseded the traditional commercial river traffic, but the rivers now attract tourists who seek to travel deep inland to visit surviving forests and Dayak communities.

Dayak longhouses.

Few tourists visit South Kalimantan, but its capital, Banjarmasin, is one of the island's most colourful towns. West Kalimantan is the most unexplored of all of Indonesia's Bornean territories, though upgraded infrastructure makes inland journeys here increasingly straightforward, with welcoming Dayak longhouse settlements and national parks the reward.

Tanjung Puting National Park's orangutans are Kalimantan's biggest tourist draw. They were first brought to the world's attention by Birute Kaldikas, who started studying them at Camp Leakey in the 1970s; this is the most accessible area for wildlife-viewing, and as the nature-loving world continues efforts to protect some of the planet's oldest forests, interest in the furry red apes is not likely to wane.

A Dayak boy in festival finery.

EAST, SOUTH AND NORTH KALIMANTAN

Though environmental pressures and economic progress have changed the character of eastern Kalimantan, river journeys here still give access to enduring cultures and extraordinary wildlife.

Kalimantan Timur (East Kalimantan), or Kaltim for short, is the destination of choice for many 'soft' adventurers happy to travel by air-conditioned houseboat up Sungai Mahakam (Mahakam River) to see Dayak settlements, while doing a bit of wildlife spotting en route. For extreme trekkers, however, the possibilities are endless, with the only limitations being time, money and stamina.

Covering an area about the size of England and Scotland combined, the Mahakam River and its tributaries criss-cross Kaltim, serving as 'roads' for a scant 2 million inhabitants. Inland areas are mainly inhabited by Dayak peoples, some of whom maintain elements of their traditional lifestyles, particularly communal longhouse dwelling, while on the coast remnants exist of two rival kingdoms that ruled from the 13th century until the last surviving sultan relinquished his authority to the Indonesian government in 1960.

Much smaller and far more densely populated, Kalimantan Selatan (South Kalimantan), or Kalsel, is separated from its two neighbouring provinces by the densely forested Meratus Mountain Range, with the Barito and Martapura rivers servicing the hinterland. Dayak tribes live upriver; on the coast, fringed by vast mangrove forests, are the primarily Muslim Banjar people, whose

ancestors include Malays, Javanese, Arabs, Chinese, Buginese and Dayaks, as befits the people of an important trading port.

The northernmost province, Kalimantan Utara (North Kalimantan) only came into being in 2012. Wild and remote, it contains large areas of national park – well preserved, but difficult to access.

EAST KALIMANTAN

The usual port of entry to East Kalimantan is **Balikpapan ❶**, a busy oil

Main attractions
Mahakam River
Kersik Luwai Nature
  Reserve
Apokayan
Kayan Mentarang National
  Park
Kutai National Park
Banjarmasin
Sungai Amandit

Map on page 305

Bamboo rafting in Kandangan.

A totem on a Dayak longhouse.

and timber town with a population of 600,000. It's not a place that holds great interest for travellers, who generally head straight to Samarinda by air or via the 115km (70-mile) paved road to begin their journeys up the mighty Mahakam.

Samarinda ② a similar-sized city, is the jumping-off point for visits to Dayak country and is the capital of Kaltim province. There is not much to see here apart from waterfront activity: freighters loading or discharging, coal barges being shoved around, rafts of logs under tow to nearby lumber mills. Half a day is enough in Samarinda, giving you time to check out timetables for planes or boats heading inland.

MAHAKAM RIVER TRIPS

The Mahakam is the main 'highway' into the hinterlands. Its source is in the Muller Mountain Range and from there it rushes, meanders, twists and turns downstream. Along the river are Dayak settlements, which are the major attraction for visitors. Also in the area are four lakes harbouring strange

Dayak boy outside their village longhouse.

and wonderful animals, such as freshwater dolphins and Siamese crocodiles (*Crocodylus siamensis*).

Tour packages, arranged in Samarinda, are the best way to traverse the Mahakam, with some offering overnight stays either on houseboats or in longhouses set up for visitors. For all riverboats, the first major stop out of Samarinda is **Tenggarong ③**, the former sultan's capital, about 2–2.5 hours away. En route, watch for sawmills and barges laden with coal – evidence of two of Kaltim's major industries – and daily activities in riverside villages. There is a **museum** housing Ming-dynasty ceramics and Dayak handicrafts that is worth a visit.

Alternatively, a new toll road links Samarinda to Tenggarong. The drive takes about 30 minutes, and the tour allows travellers to visit Tenggarong's museum and then join a cruise boat for short trips on the Mahakam or longer trips upriver. Tenggarong is also home to the Erau festival, held every 22–28 September, celebrating the town's founding and honouring former royalty.

⊘ CRUISING THE MAHAKAM RIVER

The most popular way to reach Dayak country is by houseboat up the **Mahakam River**. Many tour operators offer packages, and they are more or less the same with a few basic differences. The first is the size of the boats: large ones for groups and smaller ones for individuals. Most are fully air-conditioned with Western toilets and hot-water showers, and they have two decks. Downstairs is a kitchen, where cruise meals are prepared, and a salon for dining and relaxing. Upstairs on the smaller boats is a sleeping room and a terrace, the larger boats have 10 cabins.

The main destinations of nearly all Mahakam cruises are Tenggarong, Muara Muntai, Danau Jempang, Tanjung Isuy, Mancong and the Melak area (Eheng and Kersik National Park). Nowadays houseboats cannot travel further upriver than Tering in mid-Mahakam.

One Samarinda tour operator, De'gigant Tours, includes Muara Pahu in its cruises due to the excellent wildlife spotting on the Bolongan River, with freshwater dolphins as the highlight. Stops at Dayak villages and watching life along the river are also attractions, as well as the changes of the river from vast and wide to narrow channels, while small hinterland villages are replaced by towns, and rather solitary travel becomes crowded with ships of all sizes getting ready to haul cargo through the Makassar Strait.

Dayaks come from miles away to perform traditional dances and recreate traditional rituals such as funeral ceremonies, contrasting greatly with the more sedate dances of the Kutai Muslims, who don their best ceremonial costumes for the occasion.

The next major stop, **Kota Bangun ❹**, lies six hours upstream from Tenggarong and is the last chance for accommodation with modern conveniences. From here, travellers can hire a motorised canoe into the upstream hinterland.

Riverside **Muara Muntai**, 2–3 hours from Kota Bangun, is home to both Kutai Dayak and transmigrants. It is also the departure point for exploring the mid-Mahakam lakes region, the beginning of Dayak country. Small motorised canoes can be rented here for the two-hour run to **Tanjung Isuy ❺**, a Dayak village on **Danau Jempang** (Jempang Lake), sometimes called Green Lake due to massive amounts of a rampant water weed. Welcome rituals and dances are often performed for tourists here, the most popular destination in the Kaltim area.

At **Mancong** village, a rebuilt *lamin* (longhouse) with 24 doors – the only two-storey longhouse in Kalimantan – gives an idea of past splendours. There has been a communal house on this site for more than 300 years.

Danau Semayang, one of the two other lakes in the region, harbours freshwater dolphins and several bird species, such as lesser adjutants and egrets. Connected to Semayang is Danau Melintang, whose forested shores include leaf and unusual proboscis monkeys and at least 298 bird species. Siamese crocodiles are also found in this area.

DAYAK COUNTRY

Melak ❻, the district capital, is a busy little town, and is home to the Tanjung Dayaks. There are lodgings and a modest restaurant, and local handicrafts are for sale. Downriver from Melak is the **RASI Freshwater Dolphin Information Centre**, located at the Bolongan River Delta at Muara Pahu. The centre supplies information about spotting freshwater dolphins.

The Mahakam River, a transport artery for eastern Kalimantan.

There is a local road system out of Melak with transport (jeeps or motorcycles) for visiting the **Kersik Luwai Nature Reserve**, 10km (6.25 miles) to the south. The 5,000-hectare (12,355-acre) reserve is ideal for trekking, sheltering 100-plus species of orchids, including the famous 'black' variety, *Coelogyne pandurata*, which blooms April through December. Nearby Dayak villages Pepas Eheng and Ombau Asa have lived-in longhouses. Pepas Eheng can be reached in one hour by car from Melak. There's a beautiful waterfall, Jentur Gemuruh, at Ombau Asa. Ask around if you wish to witness a funeral ceremony in progress; the rituals feature the sacrifice of a water buffalo performed with spears.

Upriver from Melak is **Barong Tongkok**, where the nearest authentic longhouses are located. Beneath the T-shirts and shorts worn by most villagers in the area beat the hearts of followers of the traditional religion, Kaharingan (meaning 'life'). Influenced by Hinduism, Kaharingan focuses on the supernatural world, and involves ritual

practices such as shamanic curing. A nice place to overnight, Barong Tongkok has lodgings, shops and motorcycles to take visitors to other Dayak villages. Between Barong Tongkok and Tering is an ancient megalithic site reachable by trekking 40km (25 miles).

Six hours upstream from Melak, year-round river navigation stops at **Long Iram**, more than 400km (250 miles) from the coast. Some of the larger passenger boats make the Samarinda–Long Iram run in about 36 hours, have bunks and mattresses for a small surcharge, and kitchens serving simple meals. Several larger riverside towns offer basic accommodation, and their restaurants serve rice-based meals. Beyond Long Iram, there is only the hospitality of the Dayaks or government officials. Many of the Dayaks in this area, and also further upstream, belong to the Roman Catholic Church, which tolerates and even encourages some traditional rituals.

If the river level is not too low, boats can reach **Long Bagun** in 4–6 hours from Long Iram. Several Dayak groups

The Islamic Centre at Samarinda.

are settled along this stretch of the Mahakam, including the Kenyah, who are known for their huge sculptures and paintings in communal buildings.

Beyond Long Bagun, logistics are a problem because a series of rapids choke off most river travel, with only an occasional powerful twin-outboard longboat roaring through. Chartering a boat may entail a long wait. It is a great experience, but unless you have plenty of time, the best way to reach the uppermost areas of the Mahakam is to fly from Samarinda to **Data Dawai**, a landing strip near Long Lunuk village. From Data Dawai, charter a boat to go upriver to Long Apari, the last village on the Mahakam.

KUTAI NATIONAL PARK

On Kaltim's east coast, the principal attraction at **Kutai National Park** ❼ is orangutans. There are another 60 mammal species and 300 species of birds here, including proboscis monkeys, clouded leopards, tarsiers and hornbills, as well as monitor lizards, crocodiles and pythons.

To reach the park, travel from Balikpapan either by road (about 300km/186 miles, 6–7 hours), by bus to Sangatta village (1–1.5 days), or fly from Balikpapan to **Bontang**, the site of a natural gas plant on the coast. At Bontang, report to the park office for a permit before beginning your journey. From Bontang, take a motorised canoe to riverside Sangatta for the best wildlife viewing. Park facilities are limited to two basic rooms. Nearby is excellent birdwatching, the only place in Kalimantan where eight hornbill species can be spotted.

DERAWAN ARCHIPELAGO

North of Bontang, **Tanjung Redeb** (Berau) is the entry point to the **Derawan archipelago** ❽, which is growing in popularity as a dive destination. The town itself is nothing to brag about, but there is a replica of the Gunung Tabur palace across the river, now a museum, which was damaged by Japanese bombs during World War II.

The archipelago consists of several islands, and the sea gardens here are

A bead panel from a Kayan baby carrier.

Freshwater dolphins in the Belongan River.

spectacular, with several hundred species of reef fishes and corals, dugongs, lobsters and endangered sea turtles. Several varieties of dolphins are also prolific here, and humpback and other whales frequent deeper waters.

At **Derawan** itself there is a WWF-sponsored sea turtle sanctuary. To reach it, fly from Balikpapan into Tanjung Redep and go overland to Tanjung Batu (about two hours). From here it is 30 minutes by speedboat to Derawan, where there is a dive resort.

Palm-fringed **Nabucco** Island, with white-sand beaches, also has a dive resort. A 30-minute boat ride takes you to Big Fish Country, inhabited by barracuda, sharks, rays, groupers and bumphead parrotfish. Water-skiing and wakeboarding are also available here. **Maratua** is home to the archipelago's new airport, with daily flights from Balikpapan promising increased development in the coming years.

Sangalaki island's main diving draw is manta rays, which feed on plankton north of the islands. The reefs here are 4–40 metres (13–130ft) deep and there

is a shipwreck, attracting scorpionfish, jawfish, frogfish and ribbon eels. A local foundation that protects green turtles allows visits to the hatchery and to the beach to see turtles laying eggs at night.

Nearby is **Wehea**, a Dayak community that set up a small ecotourism business with money received in settlement from a logging company dispute. There is a lodge and campsite, and canoes are available for wildlife spotting and village visits. At least 600 orangutans inhabit the forest here.

NORTH KALIMANTAN

Near the border with Sarawak, the forested highlands of the **Apokayan region** ➒ are relatively undeveloped. The isolated Kenyah residents are some of the most traditional Dayaks in Kalimantan. Travel to this area is not for the casual tourist, but for adventurers it offers a glimpse of one of Indonesia's most remote regions.

Currently air travel is the only means of access, other than weeks of trekking. Be warned that flights are often

Local community on the Derawan Islands.

delayed or cancelled, and it is advisable to avoid this scenario if time schedules are tight. On the bright side, roads to Apokayan are improving, and in time the area will be more accessible.

Located on the uppermost reaches of the Sungai Kayan, a dozen villages are strung out on either side of the landing strip at **Long Ampung**. Due to its isolation and difficulty in obtaining essentials, most Apokayan inhabitants have migrated to more accessible locations. Those who remain usually live in longhouses, and the prolific artwork of the Kenyah is still in evidence. There are good trails for trekking, and distances between villages can be covered in a few hours or by boat on small rivers.

Among the highlights is **Long Uro**, a two-hour walk from Long Ampung, where there are Dayak carvings in front of the village and a cemetery. An easy hour's walk away is **Long Lindung Payau**, with ancient stone relics.

The last human settlement on the Sungai Kenyah, **Long Sungai Barang**, is a demanding four-hour walk over hills and through jungle. On a lake surrounded by mountains, Long Sungai Barang is an excellent place to rest for a few days and gather strength for the trip back to 'civilisation'.

KAYAN MENTARANG NATIONAL PARK

In the heart of the Apokayan region is **Kayan Mentarang National Park**, 13,605 sq km (5,253 sq miles) of untouched rainforest, the largest block of its kind on Borneo. The park protects a wealth of flora and fauna, many species of which are endemic. Much of the park is lowland and hill forest populated by *Dipterocarp* trees, while the remainder is cloud forest.

Wildlife, including pangolins, proboscis monkeys, slow lorises and tarsiers, three hornbill species and Bulwer's pheasants, may be difficult to spot due to hunting by the several thousand Dayak people who live here. The WWF has five regional field offices and a research station at Long Alango that can help with information.

Inside the park are the **Krayan Mountains**, near Long Bawan. Krayan

Boats are an important form of transport in Kalimantan.

An orangutan at Kutai.

⊘ **Tip**

The term Dayak is actually a catch-all encompassing a huge array of different ethnic groups. Few Dayak languages are mutually comprehensible, and until the 20th century few Dayaks would have had much sense of their own 'Dayakness', which was mainly a construction of outsiders. In modern Indonesia and Malaysia, however, strong ideas of pan-Dayak pride and identity have emerged.

forms a plateau 1,700 metres (5,570ft) above sea level where ancient, impenetrable cloud forest with dense undergrowth and sandstone valleys dominates. Further east, **Sebuku Sembakung** is a protected area where rarely seen pygmy elephants reside.

Access to the area is difficult due to its remote location, and trips are expensive. It is essential to make arrangements with a local tour operator. Small aircraft do fly into the area, but they require booking one month prior to departure.

SOUTH KALIMANTAN

Kalimantan Selatan (Kalsel), often called the 'Land of a Thousand Rivers', is a small, swampy province on the southeast coast. There are frequent flights to the capital city, **Banjarmasin ⓾**, interesting for its colourful floating markets and bustling canals. The majority of Kalsel's people are Banjarese. Largely Muslim, with a sprinkling of Protestants and Catholics, the Banjarese are strict adherents to their religion, with thousands

making the pilgrimage to Mecca each year. Modest dress is required while travelling in the region.

Criss-crossed by rivers and tributaries, Banjarmasin teeters at the brink of sea level, dipping below that when the tide is in. Perched on the banks of the intersection of the Martapura and Barito rivers, floating houses line the waterways, water taxis ply the riverine 'highways', and *jukung* (dugout canoes) replace street-side shops.

There are a couple of places (under the Yani Bridge and at Kuin Pertamina) to rent a *klotok* (motorised canoe) to tour the Sungai Barito. Start early to visit one of the charming floating markets. **Pasar Terapung**, 30 minutes from town, is the most famous and has been bobbing along the Sungai Kuin for 400 years. It gets under way before dawn and the activity peters out a couple of hours after sunrise. Female vendors glide through the canals in canoes selling fruit, vegetables and fish or light refreshments to housewives whose front (or back) doors open onto the water.

A floating market near Banjarmarsin.

Closer to town, the Martapura or the Barito are good places to experience riverside life at its bustling best. Take a *klotok* or a *bis air* (water bus) up a branch of the Sungai Martapura just beyond the Trisakti docks – which are for large ships – to see a modern lumber mill, where cranes lift enormous felled trees out of the river. A short way up the Martapura, open-fronted stores sell brightly coloured plastic items to water-borne shoppers. Housewives gossip and exchange pleasantries as they handle laundry chores, while naked children bathe.

A bit further on, graceful Bugis-style schooners *(pinisis)* are constructed from sturdy ironwood along the riverbank. Just beyond, there is an all-night fish market and a red-light district. Sunsets on the rivers can be bewitching.

The ultra-modern **Masjid Raya Sabilal Muhtadin** (Grand Mosque) rests on land formerly occupied by a Dutch fortress and is one of Asia's largest places of worship. Its metallic flying saucer-shaped dome is clearly visible from the river. Inside, beautifully finished stone panels with copper inlaid inscriptions from the Koran line an open space for praying. Doors and windows are decorated with reliefs taken from traditional Banjarese designs. As when visiting any mosque, dress modestly (women should have their knees, midriffs and arms covered), and remove footwear before entering.

GEMSTONES AND GOLD PANNING

At **Cempaka**, about 45km (28 miles) from Banjarmasin, workers dig shafts 10–15 metres (33–49ft) deep, shored up with bamboo scaffolding and fitted with steps, where men wait downhole to pass baskets of soil, clay and gravel to the surface. The search is for gems, and they hope to duplicate the 1965 find of the 100-plus-carat Trisakti Diamond. Attentive women puddle the dirt, sift it through a screen, then pan it, watching with experienced eyes for even the smallest diamonds, sapphires, amethysts, garnets and gold. In nearby **Martapura**, the gems are cut and polished. Some stones purchased

The Derawan islands off the east coast are rich in coral reefs, turtles and fish.

A green turtle.

in this area have been appraised in the West at a higher value than that which was paid. Shopping with reputable dealers is advised, paying particular attention to quality.

For another look at mining, 65km (40 miles) southeast of Banjarmasin in **Pelaihari** is a gold-mining region started by Chinese settlers at the request of the Banjar sultan six centuries ago.

SUNGAI AMANDIT

Itineraries on the **Sungai Amandit** range from half- to two-day trips poling downriver by bamboo raft from Loksado through white-water rapids past scenic mountains. The river originates in Gunung Meratus, flows through Loksado and meets the Barito further downstream. Treks at Meratus can also be arranged.

The Amandit can be navigated in two segments: from Loksado to **Muara Hatip**, near Kandagan (Class 1–2.5 rapids), including a night's stay at a simple lodge at Muara Hatip. Stage two is from Muara Hatip to

Rafting in Loksado.

Batu Laki, where the rapids increase to Class 3 at the mouth of the Sungai Muara Harang.

Getting to **Loksado**, 40km (25 miles) east of Kandangan, and Dayak country, is a somewhat rough ride. Twenty-four kilometres (15 miles) east of Kandangan is Lumpangi, which can be reached by bus in about two hours. Cramped pickup trucks run sporadically from here to Loksado through mountainous country in about 1.5 hours. Loksado itself is a charming little town, with some accommodation available.

There are about 20 longhouses around Loksado, but they do not have the long verandas seen in other parts of Kalimantan although the concept is the same. They can house 10 families or as many as 120 people. Aruh Ganal, a tribal ceremony, is held during the harvest season. The reward for the arduous journey is seeing nature at its best, with 500 bird species, 150 snake species, and many other reptiles, amphibians and several hundred varieties of freshwater fish.

ORANGUTANS: THE FIGHT FOR SURVIVAL

At orangutan rehabilitation centres across Kalimantan, the race is on to protect the apes' habitat from deforestation and to educate the community.

Orangutans have grabbed world headlines not only for their endangered status but also because their numbers have dropped dramatically over the last few decades. With five distinct subspecies, two in Sumatra and three in Borneo, scientists and activists have latched on to the cause with great vigour, drawing attention to Indonesia's poor forest-management practices in the process. In the past, poaching was the greatest threat due to the high prices their cute young faces and intelligence commanded from private individuals, zoos and theme parks. Today, the larger culprit, as for most protected species, is dwindling habitat caused by fires, logging and forest-clearing for commercial plantations.

In the wild, an infant orangutan stays with its mother for the first seven to eight years of its life. During this time, it learns to distribute its weight while moving through the trees, to build a fresh sleeping nest each night, and to identify edible forest foods.

Indonesia's first rehabilitation centre was established in Sumatra in 1971, and since then several others have been created as surrounding release sites reached capacity. The best known of these centres is Camp Leakey in Tanjung Puting National Park, Central Kalimantan. The centres' jobs are to teach the orangutans basic skills so they can survive in their jungle habitats, and to release them back into the wild.

Whether or not orangutan rehabilitation programmes are successful is debatable, but through their work they attract global attention to the problem, thereby forcing state and local officials to take action. Nowadays, in addition to orangutans, most centres focus on protecting remaining forests and replanting which, in turn, helps to secure the futures of hundreds of other species that play vital roles in forest ecosystems. Efforts also include community development: providing jobs – thus financial stability – and environmental education.

BORNEO ORANGUTAN SURVIVAL FOUNDATION

One especially noteworthy project is at Samboja Lestari, 40 minutes from Balikpapan, East Kalimantan, an area severely devastated by drilling for oil, logging and forest fires. Operated by award-winning Borneo Orangutan Survival Foundation (BOS), in addition to reforestation, rehabilitation and community involvement, they operate a Sun Bear Sanctuary. Sun bears are hunted for their gall bladders, claws, teeth, skins, skulls and paws.

BOS also manages several other forest and wildlife reserves in Kalimantan, a primate conservation education programme in Jakarta and a satellite monitoring centre that keeps track of deforestation, commercial plantations and illegal logging. Visitors are welcome at its Samboja Lodge – all revenues go to BOS conservation projects – which also offers trekking excursions into virgin rainforest in search of wild orangutans, to orangutan 'islands' and into nearby Dayak tribal villages. There are also volunteer opportunities aplenty for those who want to be more deeply involved. For further information, visit www.sambojalodge.com.

Seeing orangutans in the wild is a highlight of any trip to Indonesia.

A basic rainforest path in central Kalimantan.

CENTRAL AND WEST KALIMANTAN

Less visited than the eastern half, the west and centre of Kalimantan is home to large wilderness areas and multicultural coastal towns.

Central and West Kalimantan are both huge provinces that are rarely visited by tourists due to poor infrastructure and lack of promotional effort by the tourist industry. Although Pontianak, the capital of West Kalimantan, is a busy trading centre, its equivalent in Central Kalimantan, Palangkaraya, isn't much more than a small government administrative town. For both provinces the major industries involve deforestation – logging, palm oil and mining – placing them under the watchful eye of a carbon emissions-oriented world.

However, for adventurous souls, both areas hold many attractions. Six national parks protect remaining habitats, with orangutans bringing the most international attention. But there are many other endangered species to search for, such as the proboscis monkey, sun bears, tapirs, clouded leopards and a wide variety of gibbons. Crocodiles and false gharials swim the rivers that criss-cross both regions, while pythons sun themselves in trees and hornbills soar above forest canopies.

Dayak communities, who have their own deep-seated cultural heritage, also attract tourists. The Ngaju of Central Kalimantan, for example, held so fiercely to their religion, *Kaharingan*, that they fought the Indonesian government and won the right to have it acknowledged as a form of Hinduism,

one of the country's officially recognised faiths. So strong is the Dayak influence in Central Kalimantan that the province also recognises their traditional laws. In West Kalimantan, many Dayaks live in the upper reaches of the Kapuas River and deep within the isolated national parks.

CENTRAL KALIMANTAN

Kalimantan Tengah (Central Kalimantan), or Kalteng, is the Dayak province par excellence. For centuries dominated by the Muslim Banjarmasin, the

Main attractions

Tanjung Puting National Park
Pontianak
Singkawang
Longhouses near Putussibau
Danau Sentarum National Park

Map on page 305

Dayak festival masks.

local Dayak fought a short guerrilla conflict to obtain separate provincial status, which was granted to them by former president Sukarno in 1957. The Ngaju Dayak predominate among the province's several groups. Many were converted to the Protestant faith by German missionaries in the late 19th century, with this clear distinction from the Muslims of the coast aiding the emergence of a powerful Dayak identity beyond individual ethnic and linguistic groups.

PALANGKARAYA

The capital of Kalteng, **Palangkaraya ⓫**, has a population of around 200,000. Most of the commercial and business activities are concentrated in the Pahan-dut district, where a village once existed on the Sungai Kahayan before the place was selected as the provincial capital.

There are two docks on the river: Rambang, the lower one, serves boats heading downriver. Flamboyant is for upstream passengers. While in Palangkaraya, see Dayak artefacts at **Museum Negeri Propinsi Kalimantan**

Tengeh Balanga (Museum Balanga; Sat–Thu 9am–4pm, Fri 9–11.30am). It is located near the Pasar Kahayan market at the 2.5km mark, just off the paved road running parallel to the river.

Dayak country is found up the Sungai Kahayan. There are daily passenger boats heading upriver as far as **Tewah**. Speedboats that allow stops along the way can also be chartered. From Tewah, where regular river traffic usually stops, hire a motorised canoe to **Tumbang Mire** and beyond, to the traditional Ot Danum Dayak land with longhouses and funerary structures. Travel here depends essentially on water levels. Try to reach Tumbang Korik, on a tributary, or **Tumbang Maharoi**, the last village on the river.

Alternatively, let a tour operator do all the logistical work, something that is difficult without a basic knowledge of the Indonesian language. Otherwise, from Palangkaraya you can arrange boats on the Katigan (Rangkan) River for two full days, camping or staying overnight in village homes in **Tumbang Samba** and **Penda Tangaring**. It is a three-hour hike from Penda Tangaring to a Dayak longhouse built in 1870 by a member of the Kahayan Dayak tribe. In front of the longhouse is a mausoleum where the bones of ancestors were placed following the customary *tiwah* funerary ceremony. *Sepundu* poles, carved to represent humans, were used in days gone by to tie up sacrificial animals (and slaves) awaiting their fate.

The Borneo Orangutan Survival Foundation has a rehabilitation centre at Nyaru Menteng, 28km (17.5 miles) north of Palangkaraya, which can only be visited with a permit acquired in advance. Visitors are not allowed to come in close contact with the orangutans, but the information centre is open to the public on Sundays, and many local people enjoy strolling through the forest.

South of Palangkaraya, **Sebanggau National Park** is centred on a river by

The forest at Tumbang Samba.

the same name, which is black from decaying plant material. The park is an important research area for its large population of orangutans and agile gibbons, but it is difficult to reach with virtually no infrastructure to facilitate tourism.

TANJUNG PUTING NATIONAL PARK

Orangutan-watching in **Tanjung Puting National Park** ⑫ is the province's major attraction. The starting point is **Pangkalanbun**, which is accessible by air. Scheduled arrivals and departures ply routes to and from Pontianak, Ketapang, Banjarmasin, Jakarta, Semarang and Surabaya.

Once in Pangkalanbun, it is necessary to obtain an entry permit at the park office. From there, hire a taxi for the 20-minute drive to **Kumai**, a riverside village that is the entry point to the park, a Unesco Biosphere Reserve. At the harbour, either hire a klotok (local motorised boat) or a speedboat to go upriver. While speedboats are faster, the noise they generate may nullify

whatever chances there are for birdwatching or quiet enjoyment of the nipah and mangrove ecosystems along the muddy jungle river.

There is one lodge and a homestay on the river, both with basic amenities and food service, or serious adventurers can elect to sleep aboard the klotok. If choosing the latter, buy supplies in Kumai (include enough for a two-man boat crew), and one of the crew will prepare simple meals.

Friends of the National Parks Foundation (FNPF) runs a small guest house at the Tanjung Harapan post and can also arrange upriver expeditions. All money received helps support FNPF's conservation and village projects.

The highlight of the Tanjung Puting National Park experience is the orangutan feeding sessions (check times upon arrival) at one of the three park outposts. The first, **Tanjung Harapan** – directly opposite the Sekonyer River Ecolodge – cares for orphaned infants and new arrivals and has a visitor information centre. By far the most famous of the three, **Camp Leakey**

> **⊙ Fact**
>
> Camp Leakey was established by Birute Galdikas in 1971 for her research into orangutan behaviour. A disciple of Louis Leakey, whose life's work was to establish a link between humans and apes, Galdikas was the only scientist among his protégés, who also included Jane Goodall and Dian Fossey. For 20 years Galdikas continued her research here, and although she no longer works in the camp, her presence brought it international renown.

The visitor notice at Camp Leakey.

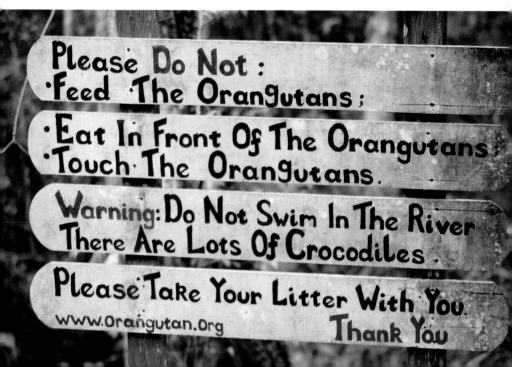

can be somewhat of a circus during high season (June–August), with visitors who are less conservation-oriented clamouring to walk down jungle paths to see the red apes in action. Older orangutans, sometimes with their offspring, can be found at **Pondok Tanggui**. During the feeding sessions at Camp Leakey and Pondok Tanggui, orangutans that hover near the stations are offered bananas and milk to supplement seasonal lack of food in the forest. Allowing tourists the experience achieves an additional benefit: raising awareness of the plight of orangutans and the shrinking forests. It is a joy to sit quietly and watch as semi-habituated orangutans, lumbering hand over heavy hand through the trees, arrive at the feeding platforms. Their gregarious antics can be amusing.

BEST WILDLIFE VIEWING

The best wildlife viewing is possible from the river. At sunrise, proboscis monkeys begin their day's foraging. Occasionally, one will belly-flop

into the river, his lightly webbed toe enabling him to swim against the currents. During these times, the bird are particularly active. Azure-hue kingfishers, greater coucals and thre species of hornbills are among the 22 species recorded in the park. Alon the riverbanks, watch for mudskip pers and archerfish, pythons sunnin themselves on branches, and estua rine crocodiles. In the late afternoon the groups of proboscis monkeys, on male and his female harem per tree settle in for the night and are easy t spot, with their long straight tails hang ing down from their branch roosts. Fo a sublime jungle river experience, as the boatman to stop the engine for while to allow the boat to drift quietl Sunsets can be spectacular.

WEST KALIMANTAN

Kalimantan Barat (West Kalimantan or Kalbar, covers another huge area enveloping essentially the Sungai Kap uas Basin. In the 1600s, diamond field attracted the attention of the Dutch and these were quickly depleted. In th

Children in Pontianak.

1700s, the sultan of Sambas imported Chinese coolies to work alluvial gold deposits, which continued until the beginning of the 19th century. The 18th century also saw Pontianak established as the resistance headquarters for Dutch efforts to stave off advances from Englishman James Brooke, the 'White Raja', who ruled the neighbouring territory now known as Sarawak.

Dominated by the Kapuas, Indonesia's longest river, Kalbar's transport, communications and economy revolve around its waterways.

The provincial capital, **Pontianak** ⓭, lies near the sea at the junction of branches of the Kapuas and Landak rivers, their bridges giving views of riverborne markets, floating houses and a working port. Pontianak is an unusual name. In Malay folklore a pontianak (also known as kuntianak) is the vampire ghost of a woman who died during childbirth. Legend has it that the town was once the haunt of many such vampires.

While the city's **Museum Negeri** (State Museum; Tue–Sun 8am–3pm),

housing prehistoric and historic artefacts as well as ceramics, is worth a visit if there is time, the old wooden **Keraton Kadriah** or Istana Qadriah (Sultan's Palace) on the far side of the Kapuas from downtown, is excellent and a must-see. The main entrance to the palace is in the shape of a Portuguese gate. The *istana* belongs to the descendants of Syarif Abdul Rahman, an Arab rover who founded the city in the late 18th century with Dutch backing.

Located bang on the equator, the coastal road heading north 3km (2 miles) from Pontianak towards the Pinyuh River passes a strange-looking monument called **Tugu Khatulistiwa** (Equator Monument). Having become somewhat symbolic of Pontianak, miniatures of the monument are available in local shops. About 120km (75 miles) northwest of Pontianak on the road to Singkawang is **Kampung Saham**, a Kendayan longhouse settlement with a beauty all its own. At **Mempawah** is the **Amantubillah Palace**, built in 1780, and the **Juang Mandor Cemetery** commemorating the 21,000 people killed

Siamese crocodiles.

in Japanese skirmishes and buried in mass graves.

Just outside **Singkawang** ⓮ are a couple of huge ceramic kilns turning out vases and jars. The large Chinese population in this area descended from the miners who arrived here to work during the gold rush at the beginning of the 19th century. There are several striking Buddhist temples in the area.

Near Singkawang, **Pasir Panjang** beach is ideal for swimming. Also in the vicinity, the **Gunung Poteng** hill resort is a great place for nature-lovers with its cool, fresh air. Raya Pasi is home to a variety of flora and fauna, including the parasitic Rafflesia, the largest flower in the world. Sing-kawang is also near the Lo Fat Fun, Niyut and Prinsen nature reserves.

North of Pontianak (5 hours by car) is **Sambas**, a former sultanate and pirate's lair. There is not a lot to see in Sambas, and the town is a centre for the production of *kaim sambas*, a fine textile interwoven with gold and silver threads. Similar to the Malay *songket* and those from Palembang (Sumatra),

the cloth is sold at a much lower pric by the weavers in their homes tha in Pontianak shops. The **Istana Sam bas**, a palace remnant of the forme kingdom, is still in good condition an houses many antiques.

DEEP INTO DAYAK LAND

These days trips inland along th course of the Kapuas River are gener ally made by land or air. Improved roa conditions have largely done awa with old, slow public river transpor Though short hops by boat are sti possible, and charters for longer trip can be arranged.

East of Pontianak, on the way t Sintang is **Sanggau**, which has a abundance of hot springs, lakes waterfalls, caves and forests for jun gle trekking. There are basic over night facilities in Sanggau.

Sintang ⓯, the home of some o West Kalimantan's most traditiona Dayak groups, is situated in the middl portion of the Kapuas Basin. There is small museum in Sintang that is wort a visit, and it is possible to visit some o the area's longhouses.

Nearby, **Gunung Kelam** (Dark Moun tain) looms over the countryside. Thi superb, sheer-walled rock is a chal lenge for even the best climbers. Fo traditional Dayak country, head up th Sungai Melawi, which flows into th Kapuas at Sintang. Take either th Sungai Kayan, a tributary of the Mel awi close to Sintang, or else go up th main stream of the Melawi, past **Nang Pinoh** and to Gunung Schwaner. In th far upriver villages, there are carve funerary structures.

Putussibau ⓰ is the last town i West Kalimantan on the Sungai Kap uas. It is a pleasant, surprising! sophisticated town with a lively mar ket and an array of accommodatio options. There are many impressiv longhouse communities, easily accessi ble from a good road running upstrea from the town along the Kapuas. Thi

⊘ THE DAYAKS OF KALIMANTAN

The term 'Dayak' is an amorphous one. Although its origin is unclear, 'Dayak' distinguishes the 200 or more ethnic groups living in the inte-rior of Kalimantan from the coastal-dwelling Malays. While Malays make their living through trade, sea fishing and farming settled areas, the Dayak prefer to fish the rivers, hunt and gather forest produce.

The Dayak were romanticised in the past – and with good reason. They were noted head-hunting jungle warriors, lived in massive long-houses and practised strange rituals. One of the more novel practices of Dayak men was the *palung*, the practice of inserting objects into the foreskin of the penis as sexual enhancers. One British explorer wrote of this practice in the 19th century: 'One lively range of objects can be so employed – from pigs' bristles and bamboo shavings to pieces of metal, seeds and beads...'

While the *palung* – mostly used by the Kenyah and Kayan – never hurt a man's chances with women, there was, however, the bride price to come up with. Back in the old days, no suitor needed to apply to marry the chief's daughter unless he could produce several freshly severed heads. These heads were believed to be essential for the spir-itual and material welfare of the village. Thankfully, for most, head-hunting is now outlawed.

road is gradually being extended and will eventually connect West Kalimantan with the upper reaches of the Mahakam in East Kalimantan. For now, the fabled 'Cross-Borneo Trek' passes this way. There are further attractive longhouses off another road that runs north from Putussibau to the Malaysian border, most of which accept guests for overnight stays. The upgraded border crossing at Badau provides a useful backdoor to Malaysian Borneo, with onward transport available to Kuching.

LITTLE-VISITED NATIONAL PARKS

There are several remote conservation areas in West Kalimantan. Travel to these regions on a budget via public transport is arduous and time-consuming, and the alternative – going by chartered vehicles and boats – is expensive. For extreme adventurers the rewards include going where few travellers dare to venture, encountering local communities and viewing wildlife that includes orangutans and many other endangered species of flora and fauna.

On the border of East and Central Kalimantan, **Bukit Baka-Bukit Raya** contains part of the Schwaner Mountains. Bukit Raya (2,278 metres/7,474ft) is its highest point and also the habitat of sun bears, clouded leopards, agile gibbons, slow lorises and proboscis monkeys.

From Putussibau it is possible to visit two other parks. Seldom visited by tourists, but relatively accessible, **Danau Sentarum National Park** is a vast matrix of freshwater swamp forest, peat swamp forest and open water. Lying west of Putussibau near the Sarawak border, the main access point is the village of Lanjak where boats can be chartered to visit the remote ranger station at Bukit Tekenang where basic accommodation is available. Bukit Tekenang is itself an island. A walkway from the jetty leads through its dense forest and offers chances to spot monkeys and hornbills, and there are stunning views over the park from the hilltop.

Betung Kerihun National Park, north of Putussibau, is also near the Malaysian border and contains both lowland and montane rainforests harbouring orangutans, Muller's Bornean gibbons, lorises, tarsiers and surilis. Smelly Rafflesia also grow here. Many outdoor experiences await the adventurous in this park: climbing Gunungs Lawit and Kerihun, exploring ancient caves and shooting class IV and V rapids.

South of Pontianak is **Sukadana**, gateway to **Gunung Palung National Park 🕖**. There are homestays at Buntok and Lubak Baji. The park is a vital conservation area because of its diversity of habitats that include many ecosystems, from mangroves and swamp forests to montane forest. Thought to be the world's largest population, orangutans are the flagship species here, but there are also sun bears, red-leaf monkeys, crocodiles and cobras.

Tarsiers are nocturnal primates found in the depths of the Borneo jungle.

Evening light in a south Sulawesi village.

Burial caves at Lemo, Tana Toraja, with effigies of the dead.

SULAWESI

This strangely shaped island with unusual jagged contours contains an astonishing variety of life within its jungles and offshore reefs, as well as fascinating indigenous cultures.

Tapping rubber on a plantation.

It is little wonder that nature-lovers regard Sulawesi as paradise on earth: its terrestrial fauna is a mosaic of Asian and Australian animals that has produced new species found nowhere else on the planet. The mountainous regions of the central highlands are separated by deep gorges and fast-flowing rivers, and are dotted with highland lakes. In the lush rainforests – such as in Lore Lindu National Park – live an astonishing array of mostly endemic fauna, including babirusa pig-deer, anoa dwarf buffalo, eccentric maleo birds, saucer-eyed tarsiers and scores of fabulous butterflies. A Neolithic settlement, cave stencils, megaliths, sarcophagi and other artefacts have also been found here.

The waters surrounding the island are equally compelling, teeming with an incredible abundance of marine life, rich coral reefs, underwater valleys and vertical drop-offs. Long known to the international diving community is Bunaken Marine National Park on the far northeastern tip of the island. Further northeast, more islands are being developed for marine tourism. Together with Wakatobi Marine National Park – located in the Coral Triangle in the southeastern quadrant – they may soon replace Bunaken in popularity. The Togian Islands Marine National Park between the northern 'arms' of the islands is also attracting increasing attention, as is the Taka Bone Rate National Park off the southwest coast.

The livestock market in Rantepau.

The population of nearly 18.5 million is also diverse, made up of peoples who speak more than 40 languages. Sulawesi, meaning Island *(sula)* of Iron *(wesi)*, is aptly named for its rich deposits of nickel-iron, copper and gold. Its best-known ethnic groups are the coastal Bugis, Indonesia's primary shipbuilders and seafarers, and the Torajans, whose arc-roofed houses and effigy-guarded burial caves decorate breathtakingly scenic valleys in the southwestern part of the island. But there are also the Makassarese of the area surrounding the capital city, historical rivals of the Bugis for maritime mastery, and the proudly Christian Minahasan in the northeast, famed for their spicy cuisine.

Distinctive Toraja architecture.

SOUTH SULAWESI AND TANA TORAJA

The coast of South Sulawesi is the homeland of the Bugis, who once dominated.

Striking landscapes and remarkable people are the hallmarks of **Sulawesi Selatan** (South Sulawesi). Makassar, its capital, is the largest city in eastern Indonesia and is a vibrant conglomerate of government offices, businesses and trade.

The coastal and lowland regions of South Sulawesi are inhabited mainly by the Bugis. These renowned seafarers have arguably played a more important role in the history of the archipelago than any other group besides the Javanese. Also on the coasts are the Mandarese, renowned throughout the archipelago for their shipbuilding and expert sailing skills.

It is Tana Toraja, however, that visitors come here to see. In the highlands, towards the north of the peninsula is a verdant, mountainous region whose people retain ancient traditions and take pride in their crescent-roofed homes.

BUGIS HISTORY

The Bugis have always been great seafarers and shipbuilders. During the Hindu period they returned from sojourns abroad – as far away as Australia – with foreign goods and treasures from the sea, and with new beliefs and practices as well. These influences lasted for many centuries, elevating Bugis kingdoms to power between the 12th and 15th centuries. After 1500,

trade relations with sultanates on Java's north coast were strong, eventually converting the Bugis to Islam.

Though later subdued and dominated by the Dutch, even in the 18th and 19th centuries Bugis groups continued to found new sultanates on the Malay peninsula and in the Riau archipelago. Today, there is hardly a bay or estuary without a Bugis settlement on it.

The Bugis courtly heritage is not well preserved. Cultural performances seem to be limited to displays of fire-breathing and *takraw* ball manoeuvres.

Main attractions
Benteng Rotterdam
Pelabuhan Paotere
Tana Beru
Tana Toraja
Batutumonga
Mamasa
Taka Bonerate National Park

Map on page 328

Traditional boat building at Bira.

Most tourists are wont to bypass the Bugis homelands en route to Toraja in the north, although there is much history and natural beauty in the south.

MAKASSAR

Makassar ❶ is a big modern city of about 1.7 million people – the business centre for eastern Indonesia and the capital of South Sulawesi province. The city (which was officially known as Ujung Pandang until 1999, before reverting to its original name) flourished as the port and trading centre for Gowa. The old fort (*benteng*) was one of the 11 Gowanese strongholds

when it was first erected in 1545. The Dutch conquered and reconstructed it in 1667, renaming it **Benteng Rotterdam**. With its interior church and trading offices, it stands as an excellent example of 17th-century Dutch fortress architecture. The fort now houses the **Museum Provincial Makassar** (Tue–Sun 8am–2pm), with displays of old ceramics, manuscripts, coins, musical instruments and ethnic costumes. In the southwest corner of the fort is a dungeon where one of Indonesia's national heroes, Prince Diponegoro of Yogyakarta (1785–1855), was imprisoned for 27 years after defying

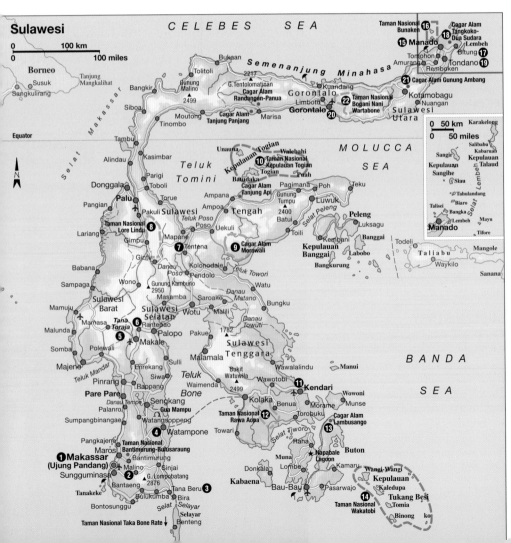

both the Dutch and his own family by leading a series of popular uprisings in Central Java between 1825 and 1830. The **Tomb of Diponegoro** is located in the middle of town on a street which carries his name.

In the late afternoon, **Pelabuhan Paotere** in the northern part of Makassar makes a pleasant place to stroll and watch the activity aboard the many *pinisi* schooners. **Pantai Losari**, a sand-free seafront promenade and cruising strip, is a popular sunset gathering place. Also on Pantai Losari is Trans Studio Theme Park, a three-hectare (7.5-acre) indoor recreational centre with entertainment, safaris and rides inspired by children's programming on the owners' two television stations. A nearby getaway, **Samalona** island, offers good snorkelling and sandy beaches.

Just south of Makassar lies **Sungguminasa**, the former capital of the Tallo sultanate. Today, the wooden palace houses the **Museum Ballalompoa** and contains many weapons, royal costumes and a gem-studded gold crown weighing 15.4kg (34lbs) that may be viewed on request. Near Sungguminassa are tombs of the Gowa kings, of whom Sultan Hasanuddin (1629–70) is the most famous for his brave leadership in the struggle against the Dutch. Just outside the cemetery, a small fenced-off plot holds **Batu Tomanurung**, the stone upon which the kings of Gowa were once crowned. On a side road nearby lies the tomb of Arung Palakka, the king of Bone and arch-enemy of Sultan Hasanuddin.

SOUTHERN ROUND-TRIP

To escape the lowland heat of Makassar, travel 70km (45 miles) to **Malino ❷**, lying on the slopes of Gunung Bawakaraeng, about 760 metres (2,500ft) above sea level. This cool, quiet pine-forest resort area is noted for its *markisa* (passion fruit) orchards. The seedy fruit produces a refreshing drink. The lovely **Takapala Waterfall** is an easy 4km (6-mile) walk south of the town.

A road from Malino leads east to **Sinjai** on the southern coast of the peninsula. From there, a coastal road – breathtaking for its steep precipices and spectacular views – leads east to **Tana Beru ❸**, heart of the Bugis shipbuilding industry. Round-bellied *pinisi* (schooners) are still fashioned here with simple hand tools and without the use of metal or nails. Teak cords are hewn into planks, then fastened with wooden pegs according to an ancient design retained in the communal memory. Sails were once made of plaited banana and pineapple fibres, then later of woven cotton and silk. Rituals are employed in all phases of construction, from the selection of the tree to the final launching, to ensure that the craft will be seaworthy. The finished 200-tonne *pinisi* or a lighter vessel called *bago* appear to be unstable until fully loaded with copra or timber – then they are among the best cargo ships afloat today.

Further down the southeast tip of the peninsula lies **Bira**, a relaxed white-sand

The 17th-century Dutch fortress at Benteng Rotterdam.

beach resort area featuring caves, reefs for snorkelling and diving, boat-building and traditional weaving crafts. Turning westwards along the southern **Bulukumba Coast**, the road returns to Makassar through small towns like Bantaeng, Jeneponto and Takalar, names found in a Chinese text six centuries ago.

ANCIENT CAVES

A mountainous 180km (110-mile) road heads northeast from Makassar towards Watampone, the former capital and port city of the Bugis kingdom Bone. En route, it passes a series of gushing waterfalls at **Bantimurung**. **Bantimurung-Bulusaraung National Park** encompasses the second-largest karst mountain range in the world. Out of the 250 butterfly species Alfred Russel Wallace discovered in the valleys near waterfalls here, only about 100 remain. Nearby are **Gua Leang-Leang** caves, which contain 5,000-year-old red-henna hand stencils. To the east is the brisk mountain resort **Camba**, where the views are superb and there are many mysterious caves.

The once-bustling port town of **Watampone** ❹ (or Bone) is quiet now, but retains its former dignity. The **Museum Lapawawoi** houses the regalia of the kings of Bone, as well as a copy of the 1667 Treaty of Bonggaya that ended the Dutch economic dominance over the area; both may be seen on request. Watampone's harbour is still a centre for inter-island shipping, and a ferry leaves here for Kolaka in Southeast Sulawesi. Boat-building and fishing are the principal industries, although beautiful cotton and silk *sarongs* are still woven here, as well as unusual orchid-fibre plaiting. South Sulawesi's largest cave system, **Gua Mampu**, is about 30km (20 miles) away. Stalactites and stalagmites here resemble animals and humans, and give rise to local legends.

On the mountain plateau northwest of Watampone, nestled on the shores of Danau Tempe, lies **Sengkang**, seat of another feudal kingdom of old. It is best known today for its hand-loomed silk weavings. South of Sengkang in the hill country is the town's twin-court centre, **Watangsoppeng**.

From Watangsoppeng, a road leads northwest to **Pare Pare** on the coast. This was once the site of the powerful Supa trading kingdom that connected Makassar to the highlands and the ports of the Mandar kingdom. In the days of *pinisi* and Portuguese galleons, Pare Pare's deep natural harbour was favoured over Makassar's. Further to the north and west, the Mandar kingdom once stretched all along the coast of what is now Mandar Bay. The Mandarese are distinct from the Bugis, yet, as they are also great sailors they are often confused with them. Their shipbuilding tradition still rivals that of their southern neighbours and is centred on **Balangnipa**, between Polewali and Majene. On the eastern coast lies the Bugis Luwu kingdom, its harbour, **Palopo**, deemed the oldest of all Bugis kingdoms, and today, an important gateway to South Sulawesi.

Traditional houses in Lemo.

TANA TORAJA

Tucked amid the rugged peaks and fertile plateaus of inland South Sulawesi live many isolated groups known collectively as the Torajan. According to traditional accounts, the Torajan left Pongko island, located to the southwest, some 25 generations ago and crossed the ocean in canoes *(lembang)*. Arriving in Sulawesi, they made their way up the Sungai Sa'dan, which now cuts diagonally across **Tana Toraja ⑤**, and settled on its banks.

During the course of the 20th century virtually all Torajans converted to Christianity. However, they have successfully maintained key elements of the older Aluk Todolo belief system – particularly the dramatic funeral customs – alongside their firm Christian faith. The area is notably prosperous by rural Indonesian standards, thanks to productive agricultural conditions, tourism and remittances from successful Torajans working in big cities.

The Torajan traditionally live in small settlements perched on hilltops surrounded by stone walls. Several extended families inhabit a series of *tongkonan* houses in each village, which are arranged in a circle around an open field. In the middle stands a sacred stone or banyan tree used for ritual offerings. Granaries *(lumbung)* face the dwellings. The roofs of *tongkonan* rise at both ends like the bow and stern of a boat; ritual chants compare these dwellings to the vessels that carried their ancestors here. House panels are exquisitely carved with symbolic geometric and animal motifs executed in the sacred colours of white, red, yellow and black. The roof represents the heavens, and the house – representing the universe – is always oriented northeast to southwest, the directions of the two ancestral realms according to Torajan cosmology.

In 1905, many Torajan villages were brought under direct Dutch control. To facilitate their administration, they were ordered to move from their hilltop perches and settle in more accessible valleys and plateaus. Instead of stone walls, hedges now ring these villages.

The winding mountain road from Makassar to Tana Toraja, which even at

Playing on Pantai Bira beach.

⊘ TAKA BONERATE

Another of Sulawesi's difficult-to-reach locations, **Taka Bonerate National Park** appears to be in the middle of nowhere in the Flores Sea, some 30km (20 miles) offshore. Taka Bonerate (a Bugis name meaning 'coral piled up on sand') was Indonesia's most recent addition to the Unesco 'Man and Biosphere Programme' in June 2015. The islands are surrounded by table reefs, making the marine park a paradise for snorkellers and divers, who can spot four species of endangered sea turtles, jackfish, eels, groupers and giant clams. Underwater visibility is usually excellent, while above water the bird life is also of interest. The problem is getting there. The journey takes at least 14 hours from Makassar on a series of bus and boat rides, and the only accommodation on the islands is in villagers' homes.

> **Tip**

Visitors are welcome at Torajan funerals – which often resemble communal festivals. Despite what freelance guides touting for business in Rantepao will tell you, a guide is not essential, but it will certainly help you make sense of what is going on. July and August are the prime months for funerals, but they do take place throughout the year.

local drivers' breakneck speeds takes a minimum of seven hours, passes Pare Pare and inland Enrekang. From here, the road enters a land of steep terraced slopes, tall bamboo forests and high mountain peaks. Across the Sungai Sa'dan from Salubarani, there is a large boat-shaped arch, marking the entrance to Tana Toraja. The road continues through Bambapuang Valley and past the shapely Buntu Kabobong (Erotic Hills).

Some 18km (11 miles) past Makale lies **Rantepao** ❻, the centre of the Toraja tourist trade. In nearby *tongkonan* villages, Torajans practise weaving and woodcarving. Interspersing rice paddies are several cave tombs *(liang)* where rows of wooden effigies *(tau tau)* stare eerily from suspended balconies like sentries of their stony graves. The best-known gravesite is at **Londa**, about 2km (1.2 miles) off the main road connecting Makale with Rantepao. Here, the effigies are those of noblemen and other high-ranking community leaders. Similar tombs can be seen at **Lemo**, where the burial chambers are carved

out of a sheer rock face. On a hillside behind **Ke'te**, coffins are guarded by life-sized statues.

Especially beautiful *tongkonan* grace **Palawa**, a village on a small hill about 9km (5.5 miles) from Rantepao. Other traditional villages are located north and east of Rantepao. A journey from Makale northeast to Sangalla is worth the effort, as older *tongkonan* houses here provide a more traditional atmosphere.

An essential daytrip destination – and an attractive overnight alternative to bustling Rantepao – is the elevated area around Bututumonga, to the north, high on the slopes of Gunung Sesean. Views across Toraja from here are stupendous, especially at dawn.

WEST TORAJA

If time is abundant and legs are strong, the 80km (50-mile) route connecting Toraja to neighbouring **Mamasa** offers an excellent introduction to rural life. The entire route is now just about passable by jeep, but the section between Bittuang and Mamasa town is best traversed on foot. The journey takes two to three days, with accommodation in village homestays along the way.

Few travellers visit Mamasa, also known as West Toraja. As well as the mountain jeep/trekking route, it can be approached from Makassar – a hard 10–12 hours, and the road up from the coast west of Pare Pare. Mamasa's spectacular villages rest on rugged tracks, but several are accessible with a jeep and a guide. From Polewali at Mandar Bay, it is a 98km (61-mile) journey, taking four–five hours via an equally bad road.

The best way to see Mamasa is on foot in order to capture the fabulous views en route of traditional houses, tombs and villages. Guided treks taking three–four days can be arranged with prior notice. This is the only place in Sulawesi where copper is worked and a dazzling array of jewellery with unique designs produced.

Distinctive Torajan tongkonan dwellings are a feature of the region.

FEASTS FOR THE DEAD

In Torajan culture a death merits an enormous banquet, after which the body is laid to rest under the watchful eyes of life-sized effigies.

The Torajan are perhaps best known for their elaborate funerary feasts, offered to ensure that souls of the dead will pass to the after-world *(puya)* in a manner appropriate to their living status. Only when the rites have been performed, it is believed, will the ancestors bestow their blessings upon the living, thus maintaining the fragile balance between the various realms of the cosmos.

The week-long feasts require an enormous outlay of material wealth – kin groups save and work for many years to ensure a suitably elaborate funeral is held between July and September, following harvest. A person is considered dead only when his or her funeral feast has been held. Before that, the deceased is regarded as merely 'sick', and the body is embalmed and kept in the southwest end of the *tongkonan*, where it is fed and visited as if still alive, for weeks, sometimes months or even years.

When enough money has been saved, under the guidance of a *tomebalun* (death specialist), the ceremonies begin. Family members and friends return to the village from cities where they have gone to work bringing gifts of buffaloes, pigs, betel nut, fruit, cigarettes and *tuak* (palm wine). The body is placed in a tongkonan-shaped coffin, then placed on an open platform in the village ceremonial field *(rante)*.

Feasting, chanting and dancing continue all night, with buffalo fights and boxing matches during the day. The rites culminate in the slaughter of as many as 100 buffalo and pigs, depending on the wealth and status of the deceased. The blood is collected, cooked with the meat, and distributed among the guests. On the last day of the feast, the coffin is lowered from the platform and carried to the village gravesite. From here, the soul of the deceased ascends to the realm of the deified ancestors *(deata)*.

TERRIFYING TAU TAU

Each village has its own burial site, some in cliff faces, others carved out of large rocks scattered in verdant rice fields. Only the very wealthy in certain villages are buried in caves carved into the cliff face where they are guarded by *tau tau* – life-sized wooden effigies of the dead. The coffins of lesser members of the community are placed on overhanging rocks close to the burial caves; bones and skulls from decayed caskets litter the ground below.

As the *tau tau* are exposed to the elements, they become weatherbeaten and faded over time. Statues are repaired once every 25 years, and in a ceremony known as *ma'nene*, the clothing of the *tau tau* is replaced. Over the years, many burial sites have been plundered by grave robbers, as genuine *tau tau* effigies are highly prized by collectors in the West.

Cliff burials, Londa, Tana Toraja.

WEIRD WILDLIFE

Thanks to its diverse ecological zones, Indonesia has a range of fauna and marine life that is quite unlike anything else seen on the planet.

The Indonesian islands have intrigued naturalists for hundreds of years because of their enormous number of endemic species and incredible range of animals of both Asian and Australian origin. To the west of the biological divide popularly known as the Wallace Line (see page 278) is Sundaland – Sumatra, Java, Bali and Kalimantan – where tapirs and sun bears dwell among Asian rhinos, tigers, elephants and orangutans. To the east is Papua, home to Australasian species such as tree kangaroos, wallabies, echidnas and large, flightless cassowaries. Sulawesi and the islands of Maluku and Nusa Tenggara sit within the transition zone known as Wallacea and have a unique mixture of both Asian and Australasian species.

JEWELS OF LAND AND SEA

Due to the islands' separation from any mainland for 200 million years, an unusually large number of endemics have evolved here. More than 125 of Wallacea's 220-plus mammal species are found nowhere else in the world. Sulawesi is home to the anoa (dwarf buffalo), babirusa (pig-deer), at least five species of tiny nocturnal tarsiers, and the odd mound-building maleo bird. Perhaps Indonesia's most famous species is the Komodo dragon (see page 287) of Nusa Tenggara. There are also nearly 50 frog species living on the Indonesian islands, of which 30 are unique to this region.

The marine life is equally diverse. Warm, clean, plankton-rich seas are an ideal environment for some of the most biologically diverse coral reefs in the world, where a kaleidoscope of fish species thrive and new discoveries are not unusual.

Alfred Russel Wallace originally came to the Indonesian archipelago in search of magnificent birds of paradise, which were first seen in Europe adorning ladies' hats. Many of the 26 species found in Papua, such as the male lesser bird of paradise (Paradisaea minor), perform spectacular displays to attract mates.

The dwarf cuscus is the smallest of the two Sulawesi species. Its relative, the bear cuscus, is twice its size. In Papua, the spotted cuscus is prevalent and ranges to northern Australia. All are marsupials and are the largest of the world's possums.

The babirusa is a unique species. Endemic to Sulawesi, its name translates as 'pig-deer', although there is no genetic link to deer and the animal is only distantly related to pigs.

The rare coelacanth.

The oldest fish in the world

In 1998, shark net fishermen from Manado Tua, North Sulawesi, shocked the scientific world with their catch of a living coelacanth. This extremely rare and endangered fish was assumed extinct for 70 million years until a fishing trawler accidentally dragged one up in South Africa in 1938. Since then, a small population of the prehistoric fish, dating back 400 million years, was thought to exist exclusively off an isolated island group in eastern Africa.

Coelacanths inhabit underwater lava caves between 20 and 600 metres (66–1,968ft) deep during the day and drift-hunt during the night. Their fleshy, lobed fins resemble legs, which places them at the base of four-legged animal evolution.

The Manado Tua coelacanth, hailed as a new species, *Latimeria menadoensis*, was found an amazing 10,000km (6,200 miles) from its African counterparts. The specimen is preserved in the Museum Zoologicum Bogoriense in Cibinong, Java.

prehistoric times, orangutans ranged throughout Asia om China to Java. Nowadays, however they are found nly in parts of Borneo and Sumatra.

The warty frogfish is one of nine frogfish species found in the Lembah Strait north of Sulawesi. Although frogfish have been recorded throughout the Indo-Pacific region, Indonesia has the highest concentration. Pictured here are an orange adult and juvenile.

A hornbill.

SOUTHEAST AND CENTRAL SULAWESI

The castaway lifestyle of the isolated Togian Islands is the big draw here, but elsewhere there are charming lakeside towns, enigmatic megaliths and pristine national parks.

Sulawesi's out-of-the-way Central and Southeastern provinces have some of the lowest densities of people in all of Indonesia. They also have some very sizeable tracts of wilderness in their national parks and nature reserves, as well as some superb diving and snorkelling in their marine national parks. In addition to nature opportunities, Central Sulawesi also has some cultural and historical points of interest, such as the megaliths in the valleys of Lore Lindu National Park.

In the past, both provinces were largely ignored by travellers due to transport challenges. However, with the growing popularity of diving and snorkelling in the Togian islands and at Wakatobi, access to these remote areas is improving.

CENTRAL SULAWESI

Central Sulawesi is the largest province in Sulawesi, with about 60 percent of its terrain swathed in rainforest. The majority of the province's 2.6 million people live along the coastlines, while the remainder inhabit rifts and valleys of the mountainous landscape. Extensive mountain ranges have proved formidable barriers to migration and many of the inland dwellers are still relatively isolated. Twelve

ethnic groups and 24 languages are officially recognised.

Palu, its capital, was devastated by a tsunami in 2018, but is slowly recovering and is still a major transport hub. The major attractions lie elsewhere however. The lakeside town of **Tentena** ⓐ on the shores of Danau Poso has re-emerged as a charming stopover on the long overland route between Toraja and the Togians. It's a sleepy place with a refreshing climate. There are fine freshwater beaches and dramatic waterfalls nearby, and

Main attractions
Tentena
Lore Lindu National Park
Togian Islands
Rawa Aopa National Park
Wakatobi Marine National Park

Map on page 328

Tonkean macaques at Lore Lindu National Park.

Tomini Bay offers superb diving, with great visibility and a rich variety of marine life.

A coconut crab at Wakatobi.

overnight excursions to Lore Lindu can be arranged.

LORE LINDU AND MORAWALI

Arguably one of the country's most important biological refuges, **Lore Lindu National Park** ❽, a Unesco Biosphere Reserve, hosts incredibly diverse plant and animal life within its rugged geography. Seventy-seven bird species endemic to Sulawesi and eye-catching butterflies abound, and three of the island's strangest and most elusive mammals, *anoa* (dwarf buffalo), *babirusa* (pig-deer) and nocturnal Sulawesi palm civets, reside in the park.

More than 400 megalithic statues, estimated between 700 and 5,000 years old, dot Napu, Besoa and Bada valleys in Lore Lindu. The origin of these carvings is unknown, although they almost certainly related to ancestor worship. While the smaller stones are just 50cm (20ins) high, the decidedly phallic-inspired stone images of humans are up to 4 metres (13ft) high.

Further along the eastern peninsula, the land becomes increasingly infertile and isolated, but no less captivating. The administrative centre, Poso, is the usual entry point for the **Morawali Nature Reserve** ❾ via Kolonodale, a tiny town on spectacular Teluk Towori. Transport and guides can be arranged in Kolonodale to visit the Wana people, who still hunt wild boar and other Sulawesi fauna with poisoned-dart rattan pipes.

KEPULAUAN TOGIAN MARINE NATIONAL PARK

Towards the north, the remote forest-capped **Togian Islands Marine National Park** ❿ consists of 56 islands clustered in the huge, calm, azure Tomini Bay. Sheer limestone cliffs, secluded white-sand beaches, and wonderful snorkelling and diving can be found here. Species to spot are hawksbill and green turtles, coconut crabs and dugongs. The beautiful setting and relaxed pace often lull travellers into extending their stay to include trekking in the forests for many of Sulawesi's unique birds and mammals. The Togians have a mixed population, though many villages are occupied by Bajau, the so-called 'sea gypsies' who once lived largely on boats and now dwell in stilt villages over the water.

Isolated resorts are scattered across the Togians, with a small clutch located close together on Pulau Kadidiri a short hop from the main settlement and ferry port at Wakai. All resorts run daily boat trips to visit snorkelling and dive sites and local villages. Excursions to trek on the isolated volcanic island of Una Una can be arranged. Ampana is the most popular entry point to the Togians, via either daily public ferry or chartered speedboat. There are also several public ferries a week from Gorontalo – useful for those travelling to or from northern Sulawesi.

SOUTHEAST SULAWESI

Southeast Sulawesi is a rugged province with impassable mountains to the north, savannah to the east and a chain of fragmented islands to the south. Although isolated from the rest of the island by land, air and sea links are quite good. The majority of the 2.2-million population lives in the south.

The capital of Southeast Sulawesi is **Kendari** ⓫, a port town whose craftsmen are renowned for their intricate silver filigree work. Outside the town, fine beaches and snorkelling are located at Hari island. In nearby Morame, spectacular seven-tiered waterfalls canopied under lush foliage are wonderful to visit for a day of soaking and swimming. **Rawa Aopa National Park** ⓬, about 70km (44 miles) west of Kendari, has a number of ecological habitats to explore with the assistance of guides arranged by the Kendari tourist office. *Babirusa* and both species of *anoa* live in the park's sub-montane and coastal forests, and a paddle in a dugout along mangrove forests and peat swamps is a good way to catch sight of many of the 155 bird species, of which 37 are endemic.

MUNA AND BUTON ISLANDS

On the larger islands south of the mainland, the area around Raha on Muna Island attracts tourists who come to see the red-ochre cave depictions at Goa Mabolu, but the highlight is the incredible scenic beauty of **Napabale Lagoon**.

Although Muna is largely deforested, neighbouring **Buton** – Sulawesi's largest island and former seat of the powerful Wolio sultanate – is still cloaked in impenetrable virgin rainforest. The more accessible secondary rainforest in **Lambusango Nature Reserve** ⓭, about a 2-hour drive from Bau-Bau, offers a good chance to see macaques, tarsiers and hornbills. Operation Wallacea (www.opwall.com) has a research site here. Benteng Keraton in **Bau-Bau**, Buton's main settlement, was a fortress and palace protected by a 3km (2-mile) stone wall overlooking the Buton Strait. During the 17th-century Dutch era, Bau-Bau was an important stop between Makassar and the Maluku Spice Islands to the east.

Southeast Sulawesi's biggest attraction is **Wakatobi Marine National Park** ⓮, its name derived from the first two letters of its four biggest islands: Wangi-Wangi, Kaledupa, Tomia and Binongka. The park is significant for its position in the Coral Triangle containing a high biodiversity of corals and marine life, thus offering spectacular diving.

There is a Marine Biology Research Base on Hoga island near Kaledupa that is visited by top European and North American marine biologists and students every July and August, where Operation Wallacea also runs research and training expeditions.

Until recently the area was difficult to reach, but now Bau-Bau has an airport with regular flights from Makassar.

The tropical forest at Lore Lindu National Park.

NORTHERN SULAWESI

Fabulous underwater scenery, the primeval beauty of the Minahasan highlands and some of the planet's oddest creatures make their homes in volcanic North Sulawesi.

Map on page 328

Something of an anomaly, Sulawesi Utara (North Sulawesi) is a fertile, snake-like volcanic peninsula outstretched in the middle of the vast Maluku Sea. World-class diving surrounds the province, and a menagerie of exotic wildlife resides in its national parks and reserves.

The full spectrum of diving activities ranges from magnificent coral gardens at Bunaken National Park and Bangka Strait to the underwater volcanoes at the Sangihe-Talaud islands and the unusual and rarely seen critters of Lembeh Strait. Land-based activities focus on rainforest hiking in Tangkoko-Dua Saudara Nature Reserve and Bogani Nani Wartabone National Park, along with volcano-climbing, river-rafting, treks to powerful waterfalls and even golf. Exploring the scenic Tomohon-Tondano highlands area rounds out the choices. The people are genuinely friendly and open.

SEASIDE MANADO

Nearly 2.5 million people make their homes in North Sulawesi, about 10 percent of whom reside in **Manado** ⓯, the provincial capital. The city – unexpectedly cosmopolitan and prosperous in this far-flung corner of Indonesia – lies at the foot of the lovely mountainous Minahasa region, which is dotted with active volcanoes, highland lakes and hot-water springs. Coconut plantations stretch for miles along the coasts (18,000 tonnes of copra are produced in North Sulawesi every month) that teem with fish and coral. Inland there are bountiful clove and coffee plantations, terraced rice fields and vegetable and flower gardens.

Alfred Russel Wallace called Manado 'one of the prettiest towns in the East'. These days, despite its fine setting and excellent local cuisine, it is mainly a congested array of glitzy shopping malls,

Coconuts are a significant part of the local economy.

with a scattering of minor attractions: 19th-century **Ban Hin Kiong** Buddhist temple, the **Museum Negeri Propinsi Sulawesi Utara**, and a 30-metre (98ft) statue of Jesus Christ. The real attractions, however, are the nearby mountains, coral reefs and rainforests.

BUNAKEN MARINE NATIONAL PARK

Manado is an excellent staging point for diving and snorkelling trips to **Bunaken Marine National Park** ⓰, 15km (10 miles) offshore. The coral reefs teem with thousands of species of colourful tropical fish along steep drop-offs that plunge thousands of metres into the abyss. Sea turtles, sharks and pods of dolphins make their way around the park, and there is also a World War II-era wreck to explore.

Further to the north, the 70-odd islands in the **Sangihe-Talaud** chain offer white-sand beaches and equally spectacular diving. Dotted with volcanoes and unusual rock formations, some of the islands are over 1,500 metres (4,920ft) high and are densely covered by coconut palms.

Like most unspoiled areas, the islands are not easy to get to. Divers who are not deterred by the long journey and want to discover the unknown are rewarded with 60-metre (200ft) visibility and 100-year old gigantic sponges. Some of the other highlights include an underwater lava flow and Mahangetang, a submarine volcano that releases silver bubbles into the sea – an unforgettable sight.

A very good road network radiates from Manado. One interesting route runs 55km (35 miles) east to **Bitung** ⓱ on the eastern coast of the peninsula. Bitung is situated along **Lembeh Strait**, which is a divers' mecca for unusual muck-dwelling creatures such as hairy frogfish and mimic octopus. Along the way, the road passes through Airmadidi (Boiling Water), and the main road continues east to the

coastal Kema, populated by *burghers* (Minahasan-Dutch settlers), who all have Dutch surnames. South of Kema there is a stretch of coastline ideal for water sports, with coral gardens, around Nona island.

TANGKOKO-BATUANGAS NATURE RESERVE

From Bitung, a fairly bumpy northern road winds through to the **Tangkoko-Batuangas Nature Reserve** ⓲, one of the most important places for terrestrial nature conservation in Minahasa. There are few places in the world where such a wide variety of habitats, plants and animals are crammed into one small forest (8,890 hectares/21,990 acres). To date, scientists have documented 26 mammal, 18 bird, 15 reptile and over 200 plant species here, including spectral tarsiers – one of the world's smallest primates – troops of endangered crested black macaques, marsupial cuscus, endemic red-knobbed hornbills and eight species of kingfishers. Local guides are available at Batu Putih village at the entrance of the reserve.

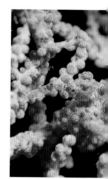
Coral at Bunaken National Park.

Sunset at Bunaken.

⊘ Tip

At Pinawetengan, about a 30-minute drive from Tomohon, there is a small but well-endowed mini-museum as well as a weaving handicraft area. Visitors can watch the weavers at work and purchase their lovely woven handicrafts, which are named after the village.

MINAHASAN HILLS

A road south from Airmadidi winds up through the **Minahasa highlands** to the lovely lake district at **Tondano ⑲**, an attractive town surrounded by rice fields and forested hills. On the way to Tondano there is an open-air museum in **Sawangan** displaying *waruga* – stone sarcophagi hewn from boulders – with engraved depictions of the deceased's prior occupation. Dating from the 12th century, Minahasans once encased their dead in *warugas* in a crouching foetal position to facilitate rebirth, together with their most valued possessions.

On a hill outside Tondano at Kampung Java, a Muslim enclave in a Christian region, lies the mausoleum of Kyai Maja, a Javanese leader who fought with Diponegoro during the Java Wars (1825–30) and was exiled here by the Dutch. There are a number of interesting towns around **Danau Tondano** (Tondano Lake) , including Ranopaso and Pulutan, noted for hot springs and ceramics. At the southern end of the lake is the **Kolongan Kawangkoan**,

site of *kolintang* performances, bullock cart races and Japanese caves. Bukit Temboan Rurukan offers a panoramic vantage point.

West from Tondano, the road cuts through more hills on the way to **Tomohon**, a busy centre for market, education and missionary activities. There are hot springs nearby at Lahendong, amid a clove tree plantation, and several at Langowan. A short walk from Tincep brings you to an impressive waterfall, and construction of made-to-order Minahasan houses can be seen at **Woloan**. An easy hour's hike up a wide path on **Gunung Mahawu** volcano is rewarded by a 360-degree view of Minahasa and the surrounding islands.

TOMOHON

When Alfred Russel Wallace travelled through this region, he wrote of 'fine volcanic peaks 6,000 or 7,000 feet high, forming grand and picturesque backgrounds to the landscape' in the Minahasa highlands. North Sulawesi is the only part of a strangely sprawling island that has volcanoes. Nestled between two of them, is **Tomohon**, meaning 'people who pray'. The town is a bustling place with a pleasant climate. The large traditional market, uphill from the centre, is infamous for its grizzly array of exotic meats – from whole fruit bats to pythons. There are far less gruesome culinary attractions closer to the centre of town where a large array of colourful food-stalls and small roadside eateries operate. Delicious pork *sate* (miniature kebabs) is a local favourite, and there are also some fine baked goods available.

For energetic travellers, a trek to the top of either of Tomohon's adjacent peaks, Lokon or Mahawu, is both challenging and worthwhile for spectacular views. Lokon erupts from time to time; its last episode was in August 2015, causing concern in nearby

A waruga stone sarcophagi.

villages and the town of Tomohon. On a clear morning from the rim of Mahawu's crater there is a bird's-eye view of the whole region, including Manado and Bunaken to the north, and as far as Bitung and Gunung Duasudara to the east.

Amurang, a small harbour town located 80km (50 miles) southwest of Manado, has a thriving trade with East Kalimantan across the Sulawesi Sea. Surrounded by lovely hills, this is the gateway to southern Minahasa and the colonial town Gorontalo, a day's drive west via the Trans-Sulawesi highway.

GORONTALO

Diving has been available for several years in **Gorontalo ⓴**, with the season being November to April. Twenty dive sites include dramatic coral walls, multiple pinnacles, caverns, muck, shallow coral gardens and two wrecks. A particularly important feature is Sulawesi's continental wall, which comes within a few metres of the coastline bringing deep blue water to the shore. Gorontalo has a growing list of new, undescribed and endemic species, as well as some of the most dense and diverse hard coral growth in the Indo-Pacific region. The huge, surreal Salvador Dali sponge can only be found in Gorontalo.

A scenic inland road heads east to the Kotamobagu coffee plantation region. Nearby is **Gunung Ambang Nature Reserve ⓴**, an active nesting site for the unusual mound-building maleo bird. Further west lies **Bogani Nani Wartabone National Park ⓴** (formerly called Dumoga Bone National Park), a vast mountainous rainforest rich in fruit-bearing trees such as durian, nutmeg and figs, and home to a collection of endemic Sulawesi animals including the babirusa (Sulawesi 'pig-deer') and the shy anoa. The New York-based Wildlife Conservation Society, established in 1895, partners with a local conservation group to manage three of the largest communal nesting grounds for the maleo birds in the park. Its southern coast is the last known site of beach nests for this endangered land-bird.

A fishing boat at Gorontalo.

A crocodile festival in the Papuan interior.

A Dani mummy in Papua's
Baliem Valley.

MALUKU AND PAPUA

Papua, Indonesia's last frontier, remains a land apart, while to the west the myriad landfalls of Maluku, former crucible of the spice trade, offer endless island-hopping opportunities.

The scattered islands of Maluku province quietly conceal the influence they had in the shaping of the world as it is today. They were once among the most valuable real estate on earth; many battles were fought over the rights to control the trade of the exotic Spice Islands' produce. Nutmeg, mace and cloves were once worth their weight in gold, and many artefacts from this golden age of the Spice Race can be uncovered when exploring Maluku. The adventurous traveller will be well rewarded with rich experiences here.

Ambon, in central Maluku, is the provincial capital and logistical hub of the region, with Halmahera to the north and Tanimbar to the south. Southeast of Ambon is the Banda archipelago, nine small islands that remain under a sleepy spice-laden spell.

Today the Maluku islands are a destination for international dive tourism and a Mecca for underwater photographers. An array of sites ranges from the pristine coral-encrusted walls of the Banda islands to the photographic opportunities found in Ambon Bay's sheltered critter habitats.

PAPUA

Papua is captivating, diverse and remote. This region occupies the western half of New Guinea, formerly called Irian Jaya, the third-largest island in the world (after Australia and Greenland). The Indonesian half of the island has a population of more than 3.6 million on a landmass almost twice the size of Britain, representing 22 percent of Indonesia's total area.

Until recently, relatively few intrepid travellers visited Papua. Almost all went to meet its indigenous tribespeople – the Dani, Lani and Yali of Baliem Valley and the south coast's Asmat, Amungme and Kamoro – many of whom still maintain strongly traditional lifestyles. These days it is the pristine waters and the incredible biodiversity of the Raja Ampat islands that lure the greatest number of travellers, who come for the outstanding diving. Even non-divers will find many reasons to visit Raja Ampat, as kayaking, birdwatching and other adventure programmes are developed.

Papua's relationship with the rest of Indonesia has long been fraught. Hived off from the rest of their East Indies possessions at a late stage by the Dutch, then kept under colonial control as the rest of Indonesia gained independence, it was only incorporated into the modern republic in the 1960s. From the outset, the region has been restive, with a low-level separatist movement met by forceful government responses. It is always important to check the current security situation before travelling here.

A Naulu man on the island of Seram.

MALUKU

The fabled Spice Islands, once coveted by European powers, are today a sleepy backwater, though for divers and adventurers this is one of Indonesia's most prized regions.

The idea of the fabled 'Spice Islands' – once the world's only source of nutmeg and cloves – tantalised European traders and geographers for centuries, before the archipelago was finally located by the Portuguese in the 1500s.

While Maluku's current production of nutmeg and mace is negligible, for centuries the tiny Banda islands supplied every last ounce of both, their origin a well-kept secret by Arab traders in Venetian markets prior to the arrival of the Portuguese. Control of the spice-producing islands assured vast fortunes, and countless lives were lost in the quest for them. But changing culinary fashions, falling prices and British success in propagating nutmegs and cloves in Sri Lanka was to end the spice wars forever. Today Maluku (formerly known as the Moluccas) is a backwater within Indonesia, though for travellers it is one of the most rewarding – if sometimes challenging – regions to explore.

Scattered across the sea north of Timor and east of Sulawesi like a double-handful of dropped pearls, part of Maluku extends to the Arafura Sea south of Papua. Due to remoteness, Maluku's two national parks bring in few visitors, but its spice trade-era and World War II historic sites are of interest to history buffs. It is the sensational diving, however, that lures most

Local children on Seram Island.

visitors. With so much sea, virtually every type of marine topography can be found here.

FLORA AND FAUNA

With eastern Maluku in the Wallacea transition zone, there are only a dozen or so species of land mammals. Indigenous marsupials include the squirrel-like gliding possum, three kinds of prehensile-tailed cuscus, a tree-climbing kangaroo and the wallaby. There are also over 25 species of bats.

⊙ Main attractions
Ambon's diving
Manusela National Park
The Bandas
The Kai Islands
Ternate
Aketajawa-Lolobata
National Park

Map on page 350

Birdlife, however, is prolific. The 300-odd species of birds include over 40 different kinds of birds of paradise, which are concentrated in the Aru archipelago; a couple of dozen species of parrot, headed by the large, handsome red-crested palm cockatoo; beautiful crimson lories; and strange mound-building megapods. These can be seen in Maluku's two national parks.

AMBON

Ambon ❶ is the metropolitan focus of Maluku. By the 19th century, due to Dutch influence, about half of Ambon's population had converted to Christianity. The newly baptised Ambonese availed themselves of educational opportunities, forming the backbone of the Dutch colonial army. Not even World War II could shake their loyalty to Holland. Maluku was overrun by superior Japanese forces in spite of strong Australian resistance in Ambon, and the area became a central Japanese base. After the war, the Dutch returned to Ambon, where – almost uniquely in an Indonesia by then firmly gripped with anti-colonial fervour – they received a warm welcome. When Indonesia eventually gained its

independence, only Ambon resisted the change; thousands fled to Holland while others fought a guerrilla war against the Indonesian military. Other tensions later emerged – between the finely balanced local Muslim and Christian populations – leading to extensive communal violence at the close of the 20th century, though peace has long since returned to the region.

Ambon city's architecture, functional but nondescript due to bombing in 1944, was almost entirely destroyed during the 1999–2000 upheaval. Fortunately, the entrance to the 18th-century **Benteng Victoria**, Ambon's most worthwhile colonial relic, remains. However, it is difficult to find, and it is forbidden to take photographs unless one has a permit from military security in Jakarta. At the end of Ambon's main street, Jalan Patty, is **Masjid Al Fatah**, the main mosque next to the handsome old **Masjid Jame**.

The **Museum Siwalima** is located on a hill just beyond the urban area. Off the paved road on the way up, see the impressive Japanese shore battery, still protected by its concrete bunker. The museum displays aspects of Maluku's natural history and geology, but the emphasis is on ethnography, with many fine objects, including ancestral carvings from the southern islands. Unlike many museums in Indonesia, most of the interesting showcases have an English description. The summit of **Gunung Nona** has the best view of the bay and Ambon town. Ambon Bay hosts some intriguing dive sites in **The Twilight Zone**, with strange-looking creatures inhabiting slopes beneath the traditional fishing fleet; there's also a Dutch shipwreck.

On the outskirts of town, in the opposite direction from the museum, the large, well-trimmed **Australian War Cemetery** holds the remains of Australian and other Allied troops who died during World War II. Lovingly maintained by the Australian government, many of those buried here were prisoners of war who perished in spite of the heroic aid given to them by the Ambonese.

BEYOND THE CITY

Soya Atas village is less than halfway up the slopes of 950-metre (3,100ft) high **Gunung Sirimau** ❷. There is a fine church there, but be sure also to check out the *baileo* – a ritual meeting place with sacred megaliths. From Soya Atas, a path leads up to a sacred hilltop site with more megaliths and a water container that never dries out. Drinking this water is said to bring health, love and prosperity. Footpaths from Soya Atas descend to some of Ambon's most traditional villages. A guide is recommended. Beware of the local Luhu ghost in the area, the beautiful daughter of a former *raja* with a predilection for handsome foreign men.

A couple of popular beaches lie to the west of town. **Amahusu** is 7km (4 miles) away on the bay side, while **Namalatu**, 16km (10 miles) out, faces

Dried salted fish is a food staple in many remote islands.

A pitcher plant.

the island's southwestern shore. In the other direction, east of Ambon, the beach at **Natsepa** offers protected, shallow water. Beyond Natsepa, the road leads to Tulehu village and on to **Waai ❸**, which has sacred eels living in a spring-fed cave whose waters flow into a crystal-clear pool. Their keeper entices the eels to slither out of the cave by flicking his fingers on the water's surface, then cracking open raw eggs. Near **Honimua** village at Liang, there is a long, deserted beach and a pier from which dolphins and skipjacks can be spotted. The best swimming and snorkelling is off **Pombo island**, accessible by boat from either Tulehu or Honimua.

Rounding the bay out of Ambon city, a paved road cuts across Hitu to the island's north coast. On this road are clove plantations, occasional stands of mace and nutmeg and – with luck – you can see villagers processing sago tree trunks into a starchy paste, the staple diet for many people. On the north coast, the road swings to the west. At **Hila** village is Immanuel

Church and the Masjid Wapauwe, whose foundations were laid in 1414. A short stroll away are the seaside ruins of the majestic but neglected Benteng Amsterdam.

DIVING NEAR AMBON

Ambon's diving is diverse and exciting. In 2008 Maluku Divers discovered a new species of frogfish, *Histiophryne psychedelica*, found only on the slopes of The Twilight Zone. This discovery has generated huge international interest in the destination, which is now extremely popular for underwater photographers. There are several sites off Seram island, too, and the fish-smothered slopes around nearby **Pulau Tiga**.

Among the islands near Ambon, **Saparua ❹**, a two-hour ferry ride from Tulehu, offers several interesting attractions. **Ouw** village produces pottery – simple, elegant and functional – for practical use and for sale in Ambon. Dominating a turquoise bay, **Benteng Duurstede** has been restored and bristles with cannons.

MANUSELA NATIONAL PARK

Seram, the largest and among the least-known islands in Maluku, hovers over Ambon, Saparua and Molana. Seram lies within the Wallacea Transitional Zone and is a key area for global studies on species evolution. The central **Manusela National Park ❺**, which is home to 2,000 species of butterflies and moths and 120 species of birds, covers an area of 189,000 hectares (467,103 acres). **Wahai** village is the northern entrance to the park, and **Sanulo** village, overlooking the Bay of Teluti, is the southern gateway.

Many of Ambon's traditions are said to have originated in Seram, including the division into two sets of customs, the *patasiwa* and the *patalima*, as well as the *pela* alliances between two villages, often located far apart. Seram

The active Gunung Api looms over Banda.

also has a reputation for magic, with many anecdotes of people who can fly and change their shape at will. While the western part of the island has lost its mystery, thanks to a thriving lumber industry, the remote eastern mountains are where the magic is concentrated. **Gesser**, on the eastern tip of Seram, has the exotic Bati hill tribe, known to have exceptional supernatural powers. They remain secluded from civilisation by choice.

Another group of mountain people, the Naulu, live close to **Masohi** ⑥. One of the most deeply traditional of Maluku's many ethnic groups, the men's distinctive red headbands, worn after initiation rituals, distinguish the Naulu from their Malukan neighbours. The initiation requires a five-day trek in the mountains of their ancestral homeland, where they must kill a deer and a boar with a spear and a tree-dwelling cuscus with a single arrow. Explorations further into Naulu lands require hiking (with a guide) inland to the mountainous Manusela National Park.

BANDA

South of Seram and Ambon is the tiny **Banda archipelago** ⑦. Long the world's only source of nutmeg, it was tapped into global trade networks since at least the Roman era, but the locals remained in control of their own economy until the Portuguese arrived in 1512, followed by the Dutch a century later, to set up a spice monopoly. The English, who arrived shortly after the Dutch, attempted to undercut their rivals by shipping nutmeg to Europe from Run – their own toehold in the Bandas. The monopoly was restored when Britain and Holland traded Manhattan for Run, but as spices were increasingly produced elsewhere, the nine Banda islands faded into obscurity.

The Bandas' importance in the English–Dutch struggle to control the spice trade is evidenced in its remaining forts. A military headquarters until 1860, **Benteng Belgica** was restored in the early 20th century and dominates **Bandaneira** ⑧, the major island of the archipelago. Closer to the sea, **Benteng Nassau**, important during

Nutmeg was once worth a fortune.

⊙ BANDA AND THE NUTMEG SAGA

At the heart of wars between European nations and Indonesia from the 14th to the 17th century was a small egg-shaped seed from the nutmeg tree *(Myristica sp.)* and the colourful orange-red membrane surrounding it called mace. For many centuries these treasures only grew in the Banda archipelago and were sold by Arab traders in Venice for a profit of as much as 2,500 percent.

By the time the first Europeans – the Portuguese – arrived in the 16th century, unlike its neighbouring Islamic sultanates, Banda was organised into several village republics. Not only did the Bandanese take great pride in their active role in the shipping of their own goods between Maluku and Java, they had a thriving entrepôt trade in equally precious cloves.

Whereas the sultans of Tidor and Ternate made deals with Portuguese (and later the Dutch and the English) in return for increased power over all of Maluku, the Bandanese remained independent until the VOC arrived. With the consent of the Tidor and Ternate sultans, the VOC drove the Bandanese into slavery, destroyed their plantations and massacred as many as 15,000 inhabitants in 1621 for refusing Dutch control. The VOC eventually resettled the Banda islands with imported labourers.

VOC governor-general Jan Pieterszoon Coen's efforts to control Banda in 1621, crumbles in neglect. The string of forts continues on neighbouring **Banda Besar** island with Benteng Concordia and Benteng Hollandia, built by Coen high on a ridge to command the surrounding seas, and destroyed by earthquake in 1743. Benteng Revingil (Revenge) rises from the ocean on **Ai** island. On both islands, old nutmeg smokehouses line trails through fragrant nutmeg groves, dotted with huge mango and *kanari* (tropical almond) trees, coffee and other exotic plants, as tropical birds fly overhead.

Energetic souls may want to climb **Gunung Api** ⑩, an active volcano directly opposite Bandaneira. The last major eruption was in 1988, but fortunately almost all of the lava and ash fell on the side away from the town. The view from the summit is spectacular. Attempt this with a guide and get an early start to beat the heat of the day. In Bandaneira, the **Museum Rumah Budaya** holds many historical artefacts. Other sites include a church

dating from 1852, its interior stone slab graves inscribed with the names of Dutch colonialists, and the **Mesjid Hatta-Syahrir**. The **Istana Mini**, the old governor's mansion, has the former resident's suicide note carved on one of the window panes. Next door is the former **VOC headquarters**, which has a statue of King Willem III, the great-grandfather of the present Dutch queen. The **Museum Muhammad Hatta** and the **Museum Sjahrir** contain memorabilia of Indonesia's top nationalist leaders who were exiled in Bandaneira in the mid-1930s. The **Museum Captain Cole** was named after the British leader who captured Banda from the Dutch in 1811.

Banda's islands, like the majority of Maluku's fertile waters, offer excellent diving opportunities. Snorkelling is also possible on sites within Banda's huge natural harbour. One special site, **Lava Flow**, situated upon the lava from Gunung Api's 1988 eruption, has been identified as having the world's fastest-growing table corals, with layer upon layer reaching a span of 3 or 4 metres

Banda's underwater life.

(10–13ft). Sharks and pelagic species patrol deeper waters, while a myriad of colourful fish swarm coral-encrusted walls. Banda has a unique mandarin fish; every evening divers can observe and photograph its mating ritual. In April and October, the seas are calm and visibility excellent. The Bandas also have seasonal fishing, primarily for tuna, marlin and snapper.

THE KAI ISLANDS

East and southeast from the Banda islands, travel becomes more difficult. But the isolated islands of Kai (also spelt Kei) are emerging as a destination, thanks to their powdery white sands and slowly improving transport links. The airstrip near Tual was built by the Japanese during World War II. Nearby, in the grounds of the Roman Catholic mission, a relief sculpture depicts the history of Catholicism in the area, starting with the arrival of Jesuits in the late 19th century. During the war, the Japanese invaded the Kai islands, murdering the bishop and 13 foreign priests.

Tual ⓫ on Dullah island is the capital of the Maluku Tenggara (Southeast Maluku) district and the transportation hub for an extensive network of roads and sea lanes. A half-hour ride away is Dullah village, where the Museum Belawang displays a splendid ceremonial canoe, complete with carved decorations. Close to Tual is Pasir Panjang, a powder-white beach that stretches for 3km (2 miles). From Tual, motorised canoes depart for the mountainous Kai Besar island. Occasional boats from Tual also head for Dobo ⓬, Maluku's pearl capital and the largest town of the Kepulauan Aru archipelago. Comprising 25 islands, the coastlines of the Aru islands are mangrove swamps, housing an abundance of pearl oysters, shrimp, lobsters and other fish. Its low-lying palm forest holds unusual butterflies, flocks of several species of birds of paradise

and wallabies. Aru is also significant as a turtle nesting ground. Rare dugongs are still easily spotted in the seagrass beds found throughout Aru.

KEPULAUAN TANIMBAR

South of the Kai islands is the Kepulauan Tanimbar group of islands. This area only went under Dutch control in the first years of the 19th century, during the final phase of Holland's colonial expansion in Indonesia. Saumlaki on Yamdena island was a Japanese air base during World War II. Tanimbar artists carve strange statues of humans with big heads.

At Sangliat Dol ⓭, on northeast Yamdena, there is a megalithic staircase that leads to the village ceremonial ground featuring a huge stone boat with a carved prow. The local people believe that their ancestors arrived in this sacred craft. Near Saumlaki is an island known for its rare species of orchids.

TERNATE AND TIDORE

North of Ambon, the administrative and geographical district of the

A coral reef off Banda.

The Nicobar pigeon feeds on the fruit of the nutmeg tree.

Dried cloves from Ternate.

northern third of Maluku is dominated on maps by Halmahera, but tiny **Ternate** ⓮ island is the real centre of power and communications as it is the capital of North Maluku province. Two-thirds of the island's people live in Ternate town, the business and market centre of the region.

One of the major clove-producing islands of Maluku, Ternate had been trading with Chinese, Arab and Javanese merchants hundreds of years before the first European arrival. The Portuguese were there in the early 1500s, followed by the Dutch at the start of the 17th century. **Benteng Oranje** was built by the Dutch in 1667 and is currently used by the Indonesian police and military. There are many ancient cannons in the large complex. On the outskirts of town, towards the airport, there is a mosque whose foundations date back to the 15th century. Its multi-tiered roof covers an airy space, beautifully designed for prayer and meditation.

A bit further out on the road to the airport, the **Kedaton**, or Sultan's Palace, built in 1796, houses a museum. Prior arrangements can be made through the local tourism office to see the museum's jewel, the magical crown reputed to be a personal gift from Allah to the first sultan who submitted to Islam. Some hair attached to the crown is said to be growing, requiring periodic trimming. A few years ago, when Gunung Gamalama threatened to erupt, the son of the last officially recognised sultan took the crown on a boat ride around Ternate to calm the impending eruption. It worked. Three times a week the crown and the resident spirits receive offerings of flowers, holy water and betel nuts.

A 45km (30-mile) paved road encircles Ternate, never wandering far from the coastline and the volcanic slopes of the 1,720-metre (5,640ft) Gunung Gamalama. At **Dufa-Dufa** village, the Portuguese **Benteng Toloko** fort stands on a seaside cliff, in surprisingly good shape and with a still-legible seal on its main entrance. **Batu Angus** (Burnt Rock) is a former lava flow, now jagged rock, which continues underwater for quite a distance. On the northeast coast, the steep slopes of **Hiri** island pop into view. Nearby, there are two crater lakes, both called **Danau Tolire**.

After rounding the north of Ternate, the crumbling Portuguese **Benteng Kastella** fort comes into view. From here, there is a path to the sacred Akerica royal springs and to the huge old Afo clove tree. Past Kastella and just before Ngade village is **Danau Laguna**. This lake, partially covered with lotus plants, is home to sacred crocodiles who, it is believed, trace their ancestry to a princess. Seeing one of them is said to lead to a lifetime of good luck. A path along one side of the lake rises to give a splendid view of Danau Laguna, with Maitara and Tidore islands in the background. The last stop, **Benteng Kayu Merah** fort, offers a sea-level view of the same islands.

Tidore ⓯ island, a bit larger than Ternate, is for the less energetic, belying its history as a former rival of Ternate's clove production in the 17th century. Frequent boats leave Bastion for **Run**, where there is a weekly market. Tidore is dominated by the volcano Gunung Kiematubu. A paved road encompasses most of the island, but beyond the main town of **Soa Siu**, the surface degenerates considerably.

HALMAHERA AND MOROTAI

At one time governed by the sultanates of Tidore and Ternate, **Halmahera's** 🔟 main town is **Tobelo**, which lies on the eastern shore of the island's northern peninsula. **Daru** village is south of Tobelo, while further south near the bottom of the bay is **Kao**, which hosted some 80,000 Japanese troops during World War II, earning itself the name of Little Tokyo. Prior to landing on Morotai further north, Allied planes bombed the installations here. A few anti-aircraft guns still guard the landing strip, which was built by the Japanese. There are several bunkers near the runway. Offshore, superstructures of Japanese shipwrecks protrude above the surface of the water.

On the northeastern peninsula of Halmahera is **Aketajawe-Lolobata National Park** 🔟, a small (1,673-sq km/646-sq mile) conservation area by Indonesian standards. Out of 51 mammal species found in North Maluku, seven are endemic to Halmahera island. Equally important are the 211 bird species found in the park, of which 24 are endemic.

Morotai island 🔟 was the site of a major battle during World War II. The task force led by General Douglas MacArthur swept ashore after destroying the light Japanese defence there, as well as the concentration of power at Kao Bay. Morotai was vital to MacArthur's island-hopping strategy towards the Philippines and onwards to Japan. Although many of the relics from the war were carted off to a steel mill in Java, there are still remnants of war machinery. In 1973, a Japanese soldier came out of the jungle, nearly three decades after Japan surrendered. And it is rumoured that there may still be Japanese survivors on the island.

⊙ Where

Some 2km (1.2 miles) northeast of central Ambon in Karang Panjang is the statue of Martha Tiahahu, a local heroine who took up arms against the Dutch when her father was captured by the colonial forces. When caught and exiled to Java on a ship in 1818, she starved herself to death.

Fort Kalamata was built by the Portuguese.

Dani inhabit central and western New Guinea.

PAPUA

As one of the world's last great wildernesses, Indonesia's easternmost land offers great promise to explorers, but advance planning is essential. Allow lots of time for any expedition to the region.

Ambon

Papua, the western half of the large island of New Guinea, is Indonesia's final frontier and one of the most extraordinary places on earth. Yet its sheer isolation and the logistical challenges and expense of travel here, have long kept all but the hardiest adventurers away Those who do make the journey return home with rave reviews, and in recent years some of the official restrictions on travel have been lifted, and transport links to key destinations – including the Baliem Valley – have greatly improved. Off the westernmost tip of Papua, meanwhile, the surreal Raja Ampat archipelago has become one of the most highly-prized diving destinations on the planet. Nonetheless, it is always worth checking the current situation before departing for Papua, especially with regards to security and permit requirements in inland areas (where a long-running though low-level separatist movement has been met with severe responses from the Indonesian authorities).

Papua is remarkably culturally rich. Reductive clichés about 'stone age' tribes, 'uncontacted peoples', headhunting and cannibalism abound in popular literature. But the Dani, Lani and Yali people of the breathtakingly beautiful Baliem Valley; the far-famed Asmat artists of the southern lowlands; and countless other groups across the region all preserve distinct

Asaro Mudmen.

and proud cultural identities alongside their sometimes uneasy status as citizens of modern Indonesia.

JAYAPURA AND AROUND

Jayapura ❶ (popularly known to many locals as Port Numbay), the capital of Papua province, lies on Yos Sudarso Bay. Its constricted site along several indented, steep-walled coves is gorgeous. Highly recommended is the splendid view of the city from the base of a communications tower, on a steep hill just at the back of the harbour.

⬙ **Main attractions**
Baliem Valley
Asmat
Wasur National Park
Raja Ampat

Map on page 360

Jayapura and Sentani were little known to the outside world until General MacArthur and the Allies arrived in 1944, turning the area into a giant military base. **Hamadi**, about 4km (3 miles) south of Jayapura, is the spot where the Americans landed in their quest to drive the Japanese out of New Guinea. Jayapura saw the biggest amphibious operation of World War II in the southwestern Pacific, involving 80,000 Allied troops. Rusting tanks and aeroplanes still rest half-buried in the sand. **Tanjung Ria** beach, known as Base G during the war, lies to the west.

While waiting for travel documents to be processed, many elect to go to **Abepura**, between Jayapura and Sentani, to visit the excellent **Museum Loka Budaya** (Mon–Fri 7.30am–4pm), on the Cendrawashih University grounds. It has a good collection of ethnographic pieces, as well as an impressive collection of Asmat art donated by the Rockefeller Foundation. On the same road, the **Museum Negeri** houses an interesting collection of both natural history exhibits and ethnographic pieces.

Danau Sentani is the third-largest lake in Papua and has a very good restaurant for a lunch stop. Boats can be hired here to **Apayo** island, where the residents still produce Sentani bark paintings. A visit can also be made to the island village of **Doyo Lama**, famous for its large woodcarvings and unexplained rock paintings.

At **Gunung Ifar**, 6km (4 miles) outside of Sentani, the remains of General MacArthur's World War II headquarters can be seen. As the hill is on a military base, visitors have to report to the local military office to deposit their passports.

INLAND TO BALIEM VALLEY

The fertile **Baliem Valley** lies in Papua's highlands, a 45-minute flight southwest from Jayapura. At 1,500 metres (4,900ft), the valley is cool, especially at night, but the midday sun can still burn. The area is surrounded by the steep Sudirman Mountain Range which kept it hidden from Western eyes until 1938 when American explorer Richard Archbold flew his seaplane over the mountains and sighted a lush

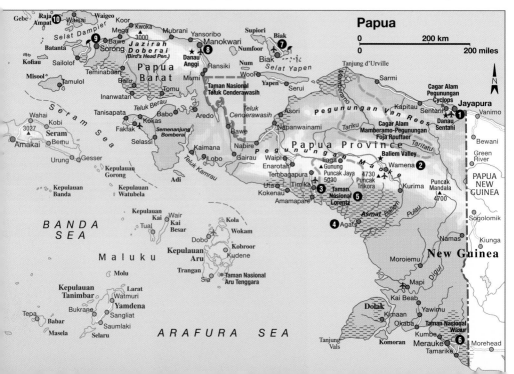

valley dotted with the thatched roofs of Dani huts. The *National Geographic* reported the discovery in its March issue of 1941, but it was not until 1945, when the first missionaries made contact with the estimated 95,000 tribespeople, that the world was made fully aware of the valley and its inhabitants. The creamy-brown Sungai Baliem snakes through a valley that is 55km (34 miles) long and 15km (9 miles) wide, before pouring out through a southern gorge to the Arafura Sea.

The Dutch established **Wamena ②**, the only urban centre in the Baliem Valley, in 1958. It has a bustling, colourful traditional market – Pasar G.B. Wenas – where locals and settlers gather to sell forest and farm products and handicrafts: stone axes, baskets, fibre bags, bows and arrows.

The indigenous people of the Baliem Valley are divided into several groups – the Dani, Lani and Yali. Although they had advanced agricultural techniques, until the 1960s, when steel and other modern materials were introduced, they used only wood, bone and stone

for weapons and tools. Although much changed in the subsequent half-century, Baliem is still a culturally distinct and proud place where tribal laws and time-honoured customs still have considerable importance. Older men still wear *koteka* (penis gourds), while some women wear grass skirts and carry babies, piglets or sweet potatoes in their fibre bags. Disputes, which occur over land, pigs or women, are settled by fines and payment in pigs.

The **Balai Latihan Kerja** is a government-run cooperative designed to teach the Dani and Lani skills in pottery making, rattan weaving and leather working. This facility is located near the police station and visitors are welcome. There is no admission charge.

To visit the small **Museum Wamena** (free, but a donation is welcome), you have to ask for it to be opened for you. It showcases the daily life, traditions and ceremonial items of the Dani, Lani and Yali tribes. Behind the building is a suspension bridge over the Sungai Baliem, leading to a small Dani compound which welcomes visitors. You will be

⊙ Tip

Travel restrictions for interior regions of Papua are always in flux, and it may be necessary to obtain *surat jalan* (travel permits) in advance, particularly for trips to remote areas, from regional police headquarters (see page 378). Tour operators should make arrangements in advance for those on organised trips; independent travellers will have to check current restrictions and make their own arrangements on arrival in Jayapura, Biak or Sorong.

Dani warriors.

In the interior, many waterways are spanned by precarious-looking bridges.

expected to pay to take photographs; 5,000 rupiah per shot should suffice.

TREKKING IN THE BALIEM VALLEY

In addition to unique ethnic groups, the main reason to visit Wamena is for the trekking – suitable for varying levels of capability – through breathtaking landscapes not seen elsewhere in Indonesia. In the highlands south of town, one- or two-day jaunts take hikers into the Baliem Gorge through sweet-potato fields and over stone fences surrounding Dani villages. Walk along the powerful **Baliem River** and cross a suspension bridge to Sogogmo village, surrounded by terraced fields and groves of wild sugar cane, ending at **Kurima**.

On another outing, hike to the top of **Gunang Sekan** for outstanding views of the southern Baliem and the Siepkosi valleys, passing fields of flowers, including orchids, mosses and carnivorous plants. It's an easy walk into the fertile **Pugima Valley** from Siepkosi, the only area where beautiful pottery is made using primitive methods.

Travellers with only a few days usually arrange for a Dani village to perform a mock war and pig feast. **Amomoge** village, a 45-minute drive northwest of Wamena, is the most popular choice. Elderly village warriors will gladly show their arrowhead scars, attesting to wartime bravery.

A 15-minute walk from here is **Jiwika**, famous for its blackened, mummified warrior. In the past, important Dani were preserved with the use of herbs and a process of smoking in a secret ritual known only to a select few. Although the secret is still handed down to one couple in every village each generation, it has not been used for over 250 years. There is also a mummy at **Akima**, a 10-minute drive from Jiwika.

Behind Jiwika in the northern part of the valley is the **Kotilola Cave**, with lush vegetation, and further on is the vibrant market at **Uwosilomo**. From here, drive through a mountain pass surrounded by forest, taking time to study the fauna in the highland woodlands. Heading back to Wamena, there is another mummy at **Meagaima**.

A drive along the western side of Baliem Valley through grassy savannahs and acacia forests reveals a landscape totally different from the fertile, terraced fields elsewhere. Follow the route through **Elagaima** and **Kimbim** (where there are local markets), and on to **Gunung Magi** in the Pyramid region for a view overlooking a western segment of the Baliem River. The white clapboard houses, with chimneys, were built here by American missionaries, perhaps lonely for home, in the early 1950s.

A five-day trek will take those in good shape to **Yali country**, where it is easy to negotiate a night's stay in a traditional hut or a local schoolteacher's house. Or, weather permitting, drive to **Habema Lake** (about three hours; 90km/60 miles), a lake within a swamp surrounded by orchid-producing high mountain forest. On a clear day, you can see **Gunung Trikora** (4,730 metres/15,520ft) from here.

ASMAT TERRITORY

Timika ❸ is dominated by the Grasberg mine, one of the largest copper and gold mines in the world. Officially opened in March 1973 by then-President Suharto, the current operator is Freeport McMoRan. Controversy frequently attaches to the mine, over finances and environmental and human conditions, with the subject entangled in wider debates about Papua's separatist movement.

Timika is also the jumping-off point for travel to **Agats** ❹ (which can also be reached via Merauke), the only town in the **Asmat** region. The Asmat people long had a warlike reputation, but are now fishermen and carvers. They live in the harsh environment of an alluvial swamp on the south coast of Papua, bordered on the north by towering central highlands, making travel and exploration in this area extremely difficult. In 1770, English explorer James Cook stopped in Asmat territory near the Casuarina coast in search of fresh water. As Cook and his men approached the jungle, Asmat warriors appeared. Cook, fearing danger, fired at the group and returned to his ship. In 1913, this place was named **Cook's Bay**.

✿ Tip

To see tribal people proudly performing traditional dances, mock battles and canoe races, try to catch one of the annual festivals at Raja Ampat, Lake Sentani, Baliem Valley or Asmat.

Tribesman in the Wamena region sporting a penis sheath.

✿ ASTONISHING DISCOVERIES

The **Mamberamo-Foja Mountain Nature Reserve**, west of Jayapura, comprises 8 million hectares (nearly 20 million acres), much of which is untouched forest. With little human impact, scientists are discovering numerous previously unknown species each time they conduct research there. Exploration began in the late 1890s when women's hats adorned with feathers from a bird that ornithologists had never seen before arrived in Europe. Subsequent British expeditions to find the origins of the bird failed. Fast-forward one century, when a team led by anthropologist Jared Diamond discovered the golden-fronted bowerbird in the Foja Mountains in 1979.

The region is so remote and bureaucracy so intense (together with local opposition to admitting strangers), that saying that arranging further expeditions has been 'difficult' is an understatement. However, following years of negotiations, a team from the Indonesian Institute of Sciences, Cenderawasih University, the Smithsonian Institution, Conservation International and others was finally allowed to enter in 2005. Results of subsequent explorations are now beginning to be published, the delay caused by the arduous task of determining what species the new discoveries belong to.

The first Asmat carvings were taken to Holland in the early 20th century, thus beginning the art world's interest in these 'primitive' carvers. Although primitive art experts recognised the carvings of the Asmat as unique, the objects had no value to the Indonesian government. The Dutch gave up control of Papua in 1962, and when Indonesian officials arrived in Asmat in 1963, they ordered the destruction of the statues and put an indefinite ban on carving and on feast ceremonies, which were part of the rituals surrounding warfare. The ban proved effective and did indeed bring tribal violence under control.

Five years later the ban was lifted when the Indonesian government, in consultation with the United Nations, decided to open up the Asmat area to outside visitors. Around that time, the mysterious death of Michael Rockefeller, son of American billionaire Nelson Rockefeller, who came to Agats to buy Asmat carvings for museums in the United States, brought the art to world attention.

As the Indonesian government went about systematically destroying the art of the Asmat, Catholic missionaries Bishop Alphonse Sowada and Father F. Trenkenschug bought as many pieces as their funds would allow. Their collection now resides in the **Asmat Museum of Culture and Progress** (Mon–Sat 9am–noon, afternoons by appointment), the finest collection of Asmat art in the world. It is rare to find an old, high-quality piece of Asmat art today. In the past, the tools used by the Asmat were suitable for use only on soft woods. Many of these carvings were intended for a specific ceremony and then discarded. The recent introduction of metal tools now allows the Asmat to use hard woods such as ironwood.

The best way to proceed upon arrival in Agats is to go to one of the two hotels in town and ask around for an Asmat guide who speaks English. There are two villages near Agats – **Syuru Kecil** (small) and **Syuru Besar** (large). Syuru Kecil can be reached by elevated boardwalk, Syuru Besar by longboat. Either of these villages can be 'hired' for several hours to don their traditional dress and perform dances and perhaps even a ceremony. A motorised longboat can provide transport to either upriver or downriver villages more removed from Agats. However, the villages within only a one-day longboat journey are very similar to those near Agats.

On a longer trip, it is often possible to negotiate to spend a night in the *jeu*, or men's house. The Asmat speak their own language, but Bahasa Indonesia is increasingly widely spoken, so the guide can act as translator. An introduction to the chief is the first order of business. The Asmat are usually quite happy to assemble their members in the men's house and answer questions. Having visitors is an exciting time for the Asmat, and they enjoy talking about the past. Often they will conclude such a session with drum-playing and chanting.

Dani tribal chief.

LORENTZ NATIONAL PARK

Between Timika and Agats is **Lorentz National Park ❺**, a Unesco World Heritage Site (permits to visit are required). At 2.5 million hectares (6.2 million acres), it is the largest protected area in Southeast Asia, with the rare feature of incorporating a tropical marine environment, lowland wetlands and a snow-capped mountain, **Gunung Puncak Jaya** (formerly called Gunung Cartenz Pyramid). At 5,030 metres (16,503ft), Puncak Jaya is the tallest peak between the Himalayas and the Andes, and one of only three equatorial glaciers on the planet.

WASUR NATIONAL PARK

Merauke, the easternmost town in Indonesia, is the entry point to southern Papua. It was founded in 1904 by the Dutch in answer to complaints from British citizens concerning Asmat headhunting raids on their side of the border to the east. Today, it is virtually one long street – Jalan Raya Mandala. There is a bank and a police station, where permits to enter Wasur National Park, southeast of Merauke, may be processed.

Wasur National Park ❻ is a 400,000-hectare (990,000-acre) natural treasure trove. A Ramsar wetlands protected site, the park contains several diverse habitats: extensive open-water swamplands (Rawa Biru), vast tidal mudflats, dry savannah grasslands, luxuriant mangroves, lowland forest and eucalyptus woodlands. In the rainy season Rawu Birus overflows its banks and the only access is by canoe. In the dry season, a jeep is required. An English-speaking guide can be found in Merauke if you enquire at your accommodation. The wildlife is more Australian than Indonesian; look for wallabies, bandicoots, cuscus and echidnas. Fabulous birdlife includes cassowaries, lapwings, spoonbills, crowned pigeons and eclectus parrots. The Kanum, Marori, Marind and Yei people who inhabit the park's 14 villages are hunter-gatherers, and they actively participate in discouraging poachers.

NORTH COAST EXPLORATIONS

Boot-shaped **Biak ❼** island, lying one degree off the equator on Papua's

An Asmat armada in the Agats area.

north coast, is the site of an Indonesian naval base, but during World War II it was the location of some of the worst battles fought between the Allies and the Japanese over control of New Guinea. Divers can explore shipwrecks sunk from these battles. The **Japanese Caves** are also of interest. Near the entrance to the caves, on Jalan Sisingamangarja, the **Museum Cenderawasih** contains a collection of war relics – one half for the Allied memorabilia and the other for the Japanese.

Southwest of Biak lies **Teluk Cenderawasih National Park**, encompassing the waters around Mioswaar, Nusrowi, Roon, Rumberpon and Yoop islands. The reef ecosystem here is part of the Coral Triangle region and is rich in many coral varieties, more than 200 fish species, four types of sea turtles, dugongs, blue whales and dolphins.

BIRD'S HEAD PENINSULA

Cave diving in Raja Ampat.

The **Bird's Head peninsula** (Jazirah Doberai), located on the western tip of Papua, is so called because, on the map, it resembles the head of a huge westward-flying bird. **Manokwari** ❸, the capital of West Papua province, and Sorong are the principal towns on the peninsula. Manokwari was the site of the first European settlement and the first permanent Christian mission. Today, it remains a strong missionary centre. **Gereja Koawi**, a monument to the first missionaries, is located just past the hospital and behind the church. A **Japanese War Memorial** is also sited in the town.

Manokwari is host to over 30 separate language groups. The three main ethnic groups in the area are the Wamesa in the south, the Arfak in the Arfak Mountains and the Doreri along the coast. While here, take a side trip to **Danau Anggi** in the Arfak Mountains either by air or hike the distance in four days. The panorama is truly spectacular. The area is home to the endemic Arfak butterfly, famous for its shimmering wings.

The Sougb people make their home in the Anggi region. Although Christian,

⊘ KAROWAI TREE PEOPLE

Papua's Karowai people are often referred to as 'tree people' because their homes can be as high as 45 metres (150ft) above the ground. They live in the dense jungles of eastern Papua, a three-day journey by boat, charter plane and foot from Asmat on the south coast. They may also be reached from the highlands of the Baliem Valley. An extended family or two small families might share a treehouse consisting of one large room with no room dividers, but with separate male and female areas. (Intimate relations are never allowed inside.) Hunting dogs and baby pigs live alongside.

The Karowai women spend their days caring for the children, cooking and sometimes making a foray into the jungle to collect their staple food, sago, and sago worms, the larvae of the scarab beetle. The men make bows and arrows, discuss the next hunt and clear land for growing sago palms. They also organise ceremonies, such as the yearly sago worm ceremony.

The Karowai are well connected with the outside world; however, a related group, the Karowai Batu, rejects most contact with outsiders. Papua is home to a number of other such groups. Often romanticised by outsiders as 'uncontacted peoples', these groups are generally well aware of the outside world, and deliberately choose to maintain their distance.

The Sougb still retain traditional beliefs. The men wear red, the women black, and they have retained their traditional huts and customs.

Sorong ⑨, the other large town in this area, has good beaches and reefs and attracts dive charters. The town has two World War II memorials to the Japanese who died here. As the hub of Indonesia's lucrative eastern oil and gas fields and a timber export centre, it has an airport serviced by international flights incoming from Biak. It is also the gateway to Raja Ampat, the mention of which sends divers into a swoon.

DIVING AT RAJA AMPAT

Although there are more than 1,500 small atolls in the **Raja Ampat** ⑩ group, there are four main islands: Waigeo, Batanta, Salawati and Misool. Raja Ampat ('Four Kings') gained notoriety when scientific data seeped out that the area may very well be the epicentre of oceanic biodiversity. Its position in the Coral Triangle – comprising Indonesia, Malaysia, the Philippines, the Solomon islands and New Guinea – is significant. According to research conducted by The Nature Conservancy, 1,320 fish species, 553 varieties of coral and 699 molluscs have already been recorded, and the discovery of new species – such as the walking shark – are common. Couple this with crystal-clear waters, rainforests and mangroves, and no amount of difficulty getting here seems to be too much trouble. Alfred Russel Wallace visited Raja Ampat in 1860 in search of birds of paradise, and this amazing area lies just east of the line named in his honour.

Infrastructure has developed rapidly in recent years, with an array of upscale dive resorts, generally only accessible by boat, and more affordable homestay accommodation (with the latter mostly on Kri and Gam islands). The area is particularly popular with live-aboard dive boats and cruises.

Diving, of course, is the main event; frequently encountered are manta rays, giant groupers and large schools of barracudas and jacks, as well as sharks, whales and dolphins. In the shallows are pygmy shrimp, octopus and nudibranchs. Most explorations are drift dives due to strong currents. But there are also other activities. Kayak4conservation is a community development project and offers homestay-to-homestay programmes for experienced kayakers and with a guide and support boats for the less adventurous. The homestays are owned by villagers, trained by Westerners. Snorkelling is included in the adventure. Birdwatching is as exciting as the undersea world. While the fabulous bird of paradise is at the top of most avian enthusiasts' must-see lists, there are lowland forest, mountain and riverine species to search for, as well as waders.

Raja Ampat is one of the best places in the world to dive.

Black-crested macaques in Tangkoko National Park.

INDONESIA

TRAVEL TIPS

TRANSPORT

GETTING THERE

By air

The vast majority of long-haul international flights arrive either at the huge and recently upgraded **Sukarno-Hatta International Airport** (also spelled Soekarno-Hatta), 20km (13 miles) west of **Jakarta** on Java, or **Ngurah Rai International Airport**, in Bali (technically listed as 'Denpasar' on flight databases, though it is in fact on the outskirts of Kuta). In addition, most other major Indonesian cities are served by short-haul international flights from neighbouring countries, especially Singapore and Malaysia, with more limited connections to Australia, Thailand and other parts of Southeast Asia.

⊙ Mobile ride-hailing apps

Local transport in urban Indonesia has been transformed by the emergence of the ride-hailing apps **Go-Jek** and **Grab**. Go-Jek was originally just a means of hailing *ojek* (motorbike taxis) in Jakarta, but it soon expanded to provide private minicabs and registered taxis. Both Go-Jek and Grab allow you instantly to request whichever transport mode you prefer from your current location, with the fare automatically fixed in advance. If you're travelling with a smartphone it's a great idea to install these apps. In smaller towns the service may not yet exist, and in some places (notably Bali) there has been resistance from traditional taxi operators. But coverage is continuously expanding.

The cost of internal flights in Indonesia has increased considerably in recent years, while short-haul regional links remain highly competitive. If you're heading to Sumatra, Kalimantan or Sulawesi, it may be cheaper to use **Kuala Lumpur** or **Singapore** as your long-haul destination, and then to book a flight with a regional budget airline such as AirAsia directly to your final destination, rather than heading to Jakarta or Bali and travelling onwards from there.

By sea

Other than the short hop from Singapore to **Batam** and **Bintan** islands (Sumatra), served by high-speed ferries, scheduled international passenger ferries to Indonesia are a thing of the past, thanks to cheap air travel. The old links between Malaysia and Sumatra have mostly been discontinued.

The archipelago is regularly visited by cruise ships, however. Cruise operators often offer fly/cruise arrangements that allow you to fly to Bali and other ports, then catch a ship on the way home, or vice versa.

By land

Indonesia has three land borders: with East Timor, Papua New Guinea, and Malaysia. There are official border crossings at each, with the major crossings (especially those with Malaysia) served by through public transport. Visas on arrival are available at the major crossings, but for entry at more obscure points it may be necessary to obtain a visa in advance. Regulations change frequently, so be sure to check the current status of a particular crossing before you travel.

GETTING AROUND

By road

In big cities Indonesia's urban transport network is rapidly modernising, with modern bus networks running between fixed stops becoming more common. But in smaller towns fleets of battered public minivans *(bemo)* are still the norm. They can be flagged down anywhere along loosely fixed routes. Enquire what the fare is before getting in. Mobile ride-hailing apps (see box) have transformed local transport and put traditional taxi companies under pressure. More traditional urban transport in the form of *becak* (pedicabs) and even horse-drawn *dokar* is sometimes encountered – be sure to agree the fare in advance.

Intercity transport is covered by **public buses**. Between major cities these are usually modern air-con coaches, but in more remote regions expect cramped, rattletrap vehicles packed with goods and passengers. These days, many Indonesians prefer to book intercity transport on '**travel**'; these are typically air-con minibuses or large cars, which run door-to-door. They are slightly more expensive than long-distance buses, but much more convenient (though in big cities they can spend a long time picking up passengers from scattered locations). Most hotels or travel agents should be able to make a booking for you.

The hire of a **car and driver** can be arranged through most hotels or guesthouses. Negotiate better rates if you are booking a vehicle for a week or longer, but note that you are responsible for the driver's food and lodging, and for the petrol.

By air

Indonesia has a vast domestic flight network, with online reservation usually possible, particularly between bigger cities. In particularly remote areas such as Maluku, Nusa Tenggara and Papua, many local routes are served by small propeller aircraft. Booking systems for these flights are often unreliable and impossible online, and the services themselves are prone to cancellation and delay. It may be necessary to go through a local travel agent to make reservations in these instances.

By sea

PELNI (Pelayaran Nasional Indonesia; www.pelni.co.id), the state-owned shipping company, serves about 30 ports, with each ferry accommodating 1,000–1,500 passengers in four classes. The vastly expanded flight network has reduced the demand for passenger ferries, with many private companies ceasing operation. But the subsidised Pelni network survives and is essential in remote eastern regions. As well as Pelni, the busy vehicle links between major islands are mainly operated by ASDP.

In bad weather, especially during the rainy season (Oct–Apr), the seas can be quite rough, particularly between Sumatra and Java, Bali and Lombok, and around Komodo, and all ferry runs may be cancelled. Enquire at the local ticketing office if the weather looks ominous.

By train

There is a reasonable railway network in Java, and a more limited

Horse-drawn carts in Denpasar

⊙ Domestic airlines

Indonesia's domestic flight network is always in flux, with new airlines appearing and vanishing from year to year. The following are the current major operators, nationally and regionally. Batik Air (www.batikair.com) has a growing domestic network. Citilink (www.citilink.co.id), a Garuda subsidiary, serves Jakarta and other major cities. Garuda (www.garuda-indonesia. com). The national flag-carrier has a generally reliable domestic network, though it's often more expensive than its competitors. Lion Air (www.lionair.co.id) Lion air has one of the biggest domestic

networks, though it has a poor reputation for punctuality and safety. Sriwijaya Air (www.sriwijayaair. co.id) has a good network of domestic routes and a reasonable reputation. Susi Air (www.susiair.com) runs a scheduled commuter service to remote destinations in Java, Sumatra, Kalimantan, Timor and Papua. TransNusa Air Services (www. transnusa.co.id) links Bali to Nusa Tenggara. Trigana Air (www.trigana-air.com) connects Denpasar and Lombok, and serves destinations in Kalimantan and Papua.

one in Sumatra, but train services are virtually non-existent elsewhere. (See Java and Sumatra below for more details.)

JAVA

By air

Jakarta is well served with long-haul flights and is a major domestic hub. There are more limited international connections to **Bandung**, **Yogyakarta** (Jogja), **Surakarta** (Solo) and **Surabaya**, all of which also have regular connections from Jakarta.

City transport in Jakarta

Jakarta is notorious for its traffic jams, but public transport in the city is slowly improving, and congestion in the centre seems to have eased slightly in recent years.

The modern TransJakarta Busway operates 10 corridors linking five Jakarta areas. More than 400 air-conditioned buses ply special car-free lanes for a fixed one-way fare. The Kota bus terminal is the point to alight for exploration of the old city. The Busway has now been joined by a new MRT metro system. At present there is a single route running south from the city centre, but it will be expanded in phases in the coming years. The old suburban train network has also been greatly modernised, with clean, fast trains running between city stations. The most useful route runs between Kota in the north, all the way to Bogor, with a useful central stop at Gondangdia. There is also a useful modern train service linking Kota station and the airport, the Soekarno–Hatta Airport Railink.

For short hops off the organised transport network, the vast majority of Jakarta residents now use the Go-Jek and Grab (see box) ride-hailing apps (the vast numbers of green-helmeted motorcyclists you'll see on the streets are Go-Jek and Grab drivers). If you have a smartphone, these apps are very useful – you can choose between a motorbike taxi, a private car or a licensed taxi (with the price ascending in that order). Reputable private taxi companies, which can be booked or hailed on the street, include Bluebird (tel: 021-7917 1234) or Pusaka (which is owned by the Bluebird Group) or its sister company, Silverbird (tel: 021-798 1234). Also recommended are Express (tel: 021-2650 9000) and

TransCab (tel: 021-5835 5500), which is equipped with cable TV.

By car

Chauffeur-driven cars are offered by many companies, the use of such cars can be arranged through your hotel. Hourly or daily rates are charged within the city; trips out of town are charged on a round-trip basis. The most reputable companies are: Avis, tel: 021-314 2900; Hertz, tel: 021-830 7460; White Horse, tel: 021-6385 5005; and Bluebird, tel: 021-797 1245.

By train

Java's train network, running from east to west, offers services to all its major cities (www.kereta-api.co.id). In the east, it connects with ferries to Bali, and in the west, with ferries to Sumatra.

There are two basic routes: (north) Jakarta–Cirebon–Semarang–Surabaya; and (south) Jakarta–Bandung–Yogyakarta–Surakarta–Surabaya. Slow economy trains can be fun for short hops, but for intercity travel book an express, which generally have two classes: comfortable eksekutif, featuring air-conditioning and reclining seats, and bisnis, which has padded upright seats and fans. There are both day and night express trains on the major routes. Jakarta to Surabaya takes around 10 hours; Jakarta to Yogyakarta is around seven hours. It is generally best to book tickets in advance, particularly at peak times. Gambir is the main long-haul station in Jakarta, with a helpful tourists' booking office.

By road

Java's main highways are well-maintained, and there are increasing numbers of fast intercity toll roads. Off the main routes expect a few potholes.

Intercity buses in Java are generally comfortable modern coaches with air-conditioning, and increasingly often with Wi-Fi. Smaller, less comfortable buses provide links to smaller towns and rural areas.

Jakarta has three main terminals: **Kalideres Terminal** (west Jakarta) operates services to Sumatra and West Java; **Kampung Rambutan Terminal** (in northeast Jakarta,

near the old Halim Airport) is the hub for services to Bandung, Bogor and southwards; while **Pulo Gadung Terminal** (Jl. Bekasi Timur Raya) has services heading to Central and East Java.

Increasingly, Indonesians use door-to-door 'travel' services for intercity transport. Pre-booked seats in large cars/air-conditioned mini-buses can be booked between most points in Java. Dozens of different companies serve these routes; ask at your hotel for help with booking. Amongst the companies operating from Jakarta are Day Trans (tel: 021-2967 6767; www.daytrans.co.id), X-trans (tel: 021-315 0555; www.xtrans.co.id) and Cipaganti (tel: 022-8600 8800; www.cipaganti.co.id).

It is also possible to charter a vehicle. With a group of four or five people, you can go from Jakarta all the way to Yogyakarta for about the same cost as flying, with the added bonus of being able to stop along the way. Work out the details in advance, including the amount you will give the driver every day for food and lodgings (tips are not mandatory, but will be appreciated). You may have to pay extra for a driver who speaks English. Count on an extra day's hire and a full tank of petrol for the driver to get home.

SUMATRA

Medan is Sumatra's largest city, with **international flights** arriving from Singapore and Kuala Lumpur, as well as from other points in Sumatra and elsewhere in Indonesia, at the modern Kualanamu International airport. There are also short-haul international links, and more extensive domestic connections, to Palembang, Pekanbaru, Batam, Banda Aceh and Padang. Other airports with domestic connections include Bandar Lampung, Bengkulu, Jambi, Pekanbaru, Bangka and Belitung.

International ferry services have mostly been discontinued, but there are still regular speedboats for the short hop between Singapore's Harbourfront Centra and Bintan and Batam. Ferry operators include Penguin (www.penguin.com.sg) and Dino/Batam Fast (www.batamfast.com). Note that you will have to go through Immigration upon arrival at Batam.

A Jakarta backstreet.

On mainland Sumatra, there are good highway systems in the north, west and south, but in the east, travel is more difficult. The long TransSumatra Highway is gradually being upgraded along its entire length, but conditions on remote sections can sometimes still be rough, and delays due to the upgrading work itself are frequent. For intercity journeys, pre-booked door-to-door 'travel' (passenger car/minibus) is the most popular option, though there is also an extensive bus network.

Sample journey times by express bus:
Medan to Banda Aceh – 11 hours
Medan to Prapat (Danau Toba) – 4 hours
Medan to Padang – 18 hours
Padang to Bukittinggi – 2 hours

There are three unlinked **rail systems** in Sumatra. The North line runs from Medan north to Banda Aceh and south to Rantauprapat; West, from Padang north to Bukittinggi and Payakumbuh and south to Solok and Sawah Lunto. In South Sumatra, the line begins at Tanjung Karang and runs north to Prabumulih, east to Palembang and west to Lubuklinggau. The trains that run on these routes are hot, slow and crowded, generally taking longer than buses serving the same destinations.

Sumatra's offshore islands

Nias

There are daily **flights** on Lion Air (operated by Wings Air) and Garuda to Nias island from Medan. Sibolga can be reached by **road** from either

Medan (in 9 hours) or Padang (10 hours). You can also take a boat from there; daily **ferries** make the 4–10-hour crossing to the Nias capital, Gunung Sitoli. Note: Storms are frequent and the waves can be quite dangerous. ASDP ferries depart nightly from Sibolga for the 10-hour journey to Gunung Sitoli.

Siberut

The 150km (90-mile) boat trip from Padang to Siberut island takes 12 hours. From Padang's Teluk Bayur Harbour, small passenger **ferries** depart twice a week for Muara Padang on Siberut. The boats can be very crowded, so book in advance (tel: 0759-21064; Siberut office, Jl. B.T. Arua No. 31, Teluk Bayur; tel: 0725-21941) or contact Regina Adventures (Jl. Pampangan No. 54, Padang; tel: 0751-781 0835; www. reginaadventures.com).

Batam island

AirAsia, Garuda, Sriwijaya and Lion Air have **flights** from Jakarta to Batam. **Ferries** frequently zip back and forth between Singapore and the Riau islands. Crossings from Singapore's Harbourfront Centre (the main terminal) take 30–60 minutes, depending on the type of boat and destination on Batam.

Bintan island

Tanjung Pinang, the capital of Riau on the southwest coast, is served by **high-speed ferries** from Singapore's Tanah Merah Ferry Terminal (45 minutes away), Johor Bahru (Malaysia), Batam and other Riau islands. In Bintan, you can obtain a visa on arrival (if appropriate) at Bandar Bentan Telani terminal on the western tip of the Bintan Resort area (Lagoi). Schedules and online booking for Bintan Resort Ferries are available at www.brf.com.sg.

Transport from the ferry terminal to the resort is generally included in hotel packages, which may also include ferry fares. Car hire companies are also located at the ferry terminal for trips to other parts of Bintan.

BALI

Getting there

Bali's **Ngurah Rai International Airport** (tel: 0361-935 1011) is

⊘ Carand motorbike hire

Indonesian traffic conditions are daunting and rural roads are often poorly maintained. Nonetheless, many travellers do self-drive, usually on a rented motorbike, less frequently with a car. Organised motorbike hire is generally available in major tourist centres, with daily rates and negotiable discounts for longer periods. Elsewhere it's usually possible to arrange informal hire through hotels or guesthouses.

Having your own wheels does allow for unrivalled freedom to explore and stop at will, but the hazards need to be taken very seriously. Indonesia – and especially Bali – is certainly no place for beginners. A helmet is essential and required by law, as is a valid international driving permit (police in Bali frequently stop foreigners to check their licenses). Self-drive car hire is also possible, particularly in Bali and Yogyakarta, but while much safer than motor-biking it is usually even more daunting, given the hectic conditions.

extremely well served by long-haul and regional international flights, with numerous direct links from cities in Europe, the US, Middle East, Australia and Asia, as well as many cities in Indonesia (links westwards to Sumatra and Kalimantan are more limited, and may require transit in Jakarta or Surabaya). The airport is very compact, with the domestic and international terminals within a few minutes' walking distance of each other. Domestic departure tax in Bali to other Indonesian cities is currently included in the ticket price.

Bali is well connected by bus to most cities in Java, usually running overnight services via the ferry link at Gilimanuk. There are also bus connections westwards into Nusa Tenggara, via the ferry from Padangbai. Reputable travel agents such as Perama (www.peramatour. com) runs some of its interisland services, and can also book tickets for long-haul buses, including transfers to the inconveniently located main bus terminal, northwest of Denpasar and the main resort areas.

The ferry link between Bali and Java is one of the busiest crossings in Indonesia. Be prepared for delays, particularly in bad weather and in peak season, and for long waits while cargo and passengers are offloaded. Ferries ply the 30-minute trip between Ketapang in East Java and Gilimanuk in West Bali. From Lembar Harbour in Lombok, ferries take 4 hours to reach Padangbai in East Bali. The ferry fare should be included in any through-transport booked along these routes.

Getting around

Balinese roads double as parade grounds for festival processions. They are becoming increasingly crowded, and traffic jams are frequent. Keep in mind that patience is a virtue.

Near-universal private vehicle ownership means that public transport within Bali is limited and unreliable. Public minivans (bemo) operate on fixed routes from terminals or marketplaces in major towns, and along some rural routes. There are no marked places to get off and on; just flag one down, and call out 'stop' when you want to get out. Fares are based on distance travelled (ask a local what the fare is while waiting). This mode of transport does take time, but allows you to meet the local people; beware of pickpockets, though. More useful are the private tourist shuttle buses, which offer prebooked door-to-door links between all the major accommodation centres. These can generally be booked directly through guesthouses or hotel receptions.

Bali's taxi companies are notorious for their protectionist approaches, which have to some extent limited the rise of the Go-Jek and Grab ride-hailing apps, ubiquitous elsewhere in Indonesia. They are still available in Bali, but are less reliable and their drivers are forbidden to operate in certain areas (Kuta, for example). Airport taxis have fixed rates, which are posted at the taxi counters outside the domestic and international terminals, where you pay. Few taxis, outside the Kuta-Legian-Seminyak area, cruise the streets for passengers, so call **Bali**

Taxi (tel: 0361-701 111) – owned by Jakarta's reputable Bluebird Group, it has the highest percentage of English-speaking drivers. If you can't get a Bali Taxi, **Praja Taxi** (tel: 0361-701 784) is also good.

In Ubud, the only taxis are the ones that have brought passengers from other areas and are hoping for a fare back. Your hotel can arrange private transport, or negotiate a fare with one of the men offering transport on the street. (See Vehicle with driver, below, for more details.)

Hiring a car or minivan with driver can be done by the half-day or full day. Tip: rates are cheaper if negotiated on the street rather than from your hotel; look out for young men who call out 'transport' and move their hands as if driving a car. Check the condition of the vehicle and get a feel for the driver before agreeing to anything. Rates vary according to the kind of vehicle, its condition, actual travel time and total number of hours. This amount should include fuel. Full-day rates generally range from Rp 400,000–500,000 during peak season. Half-day will cost Rp 250,000–300,000.

It is courteous to give your driver money for a meal if you pause for lunch or dinner. If you are pleased with his service, a tip of Rp 30,000–50,000 is appropriate and Rp 50,000–100,000 for English-speaking guides. You will usually get a better rate if you arrange to use the same driver for all the trips during your stay.

It is easy to charter a vehicle with a driver (and a guide, if needed) for an hour, day or month. Check with **Golden Bird Limousine & Car Rental** (24-hour reservations): tel: 701 111; www.bluebirdgroup.com. **Autobagus Rent a Car:** Jl. Tukud Balian Renon, Denpasar; tel: 7222 222; www.autobagus.com.

Self-drive cars are available throughout South Bali, for which you must have a valid international driving licence. It's also advisable to pay the extra costs to ensure you have full insurance coverage. Petrol is not included in the price. You can book a car through your hotel or from the companies listed above – they will deliver the car to you and pick it up at the end of the rental period. Always test-drive the car before paying. Note: drive on the left side of the road. Motorcycle hire is also widely available (see box), with discounted

rates negotiable for long rental periods. Daily rental rates typically begin from Rp75,000 per day.

You must have an international driving permit valid for motorcycles. Alternatively, go to the Denpasar Police Office to obtain a temporary permit, valid for three months on Bali only. Normally the person who rents you the motorbike will accompany you to the police office. Take your passport, driving licence from your home country and three passport-sized photos.

Bicycles are available for rent in many areas, especially Ubud and Sanur, and many hotels have them. The main roads of Bali are congested and full of potholes, and motor vehicles spew exhaust fumes into your face, so stick to the quieter country roads. Wear a helmet for extra safety, and try not to ride at night, because roads are very poorly lit, or not lit at all. Prices typically begin from Rp40,000 per day.

Lombok

Getting there

Lombok International Airport is in an isolated area, 40km (25 miles) south of Mataram. Visas on arrival are available here for qualifying nationalities. There are limited international connections from Australia and mainland Southeast Asia, and good domestic links, with very regular flights from Bali. Public (slow, overcrowded) **ferries** depart every 2 hours for the picturesque sea crossing between Padangbai Harbour (Bali) and Lembar Harbour (Lombok), about 20km (12 miles) south of Mataram; the crossing takes 4 to 5 hours. Note that on a windy day with high waves, the crossing will be choppy and uncomfortable. The public ferries are really only useful for those planning on exploring the main island of Lombok; for those heading to the Gilis by far the best option is a direct **speedboat** from Bali. On the other side of Lombok, a similar but much shorter ferry crossing connects Labuan Lombok with Poto Tano on Sumbawa. Most people make this crossing aboard a through bus from Mataram to Sumawa Besar or Bima, but local

buses serve the ports on either side for foot passengers.

Getting around

Motorbike rental is available in Senggigi and Kuta. Enquire at your hotel or any motorcycle shop on the main streets. A motorcycle licence is required – obtainable at the police station – as is a helmet. You can bring a motorcycle from Bali on the public ferry. Many hotels have bicycles for hire. Away from Mataram, Lombok's roads are much less crowded than those in Bali, though also generally in worse condition, with many potholes. Rental cars are available from www.lombokcarrentals.com or www.lombokrentcar.com. Most hotels can arrange a car with a driver.

Lombok Taxi (tel: 0370-627 000), owned by Jakarta's reliable Bluebird Group, operates light-blue taxis that are metered and have courteous drivers. Flag one down on the street, or phone ahead to book one. Hourly or day-rate hire also available. Minivans (bemos) and buses serve all the towns on the island, but they are slow and uncomfortable. The central terminal is at the crossroads at Sweta, just to the east of Cakranegara; there is a signboard displaying the fares to all destinations. **Perama** (www.peramatour.com)

⊘ Getting to the Gilis

Unless you want to explore the rest of Lombok en route, the best option for travel from Bali to the Gilis is a direct speedboat transfer. Padangbai is the main point of departure, but there are also speedboats from Sanur and Amed. Gili Cat (www.gilicat.com) is one of the more reliable operators. Tickets typically cost about the same as a flight from Bali to Lombok, but avoid the need for lengthy transfers from the airport.

From Lombok itself, Perama (www.peramatour.com) has daily shuttles to the Gilis from Mataram, Senggigi and Kuta (Lombok). Also check the dive shops for shuttle service. Public boats leave from Bangsal beach. Ignore the touts and go to the ticket office on the left by the jetty. Note that boats to the Gilis do not depart until they are full.

operates shuttle buses that connect to key places on the island.

Sumbawa

Lion Air and Garuda **airlines** serve both Sumbawa Besar (West Sumbawa) and Bima (East Sumbawa). **Ferries** from Lombok to West Sumbawa run regularly throughout the day. Long-haul **buses** to Bima or Sumbawa Besar can be booked from Denpasar or Mataram, with the ferry crossings included in the fare.

Komodo and Rinca

Komodo National Park can be reached only by sea. Labuanbajo in western Flores is the main entry point, with a modern airport, served by direct flights from Bali and Jakarta as well as from smaller airports in Nusa Tenggara. Labuanbajo is an increasingly sophisticated tourist town, with a wide array of accommodation options. An alternative approach to Komodo is from Bima on Sumbawa via Sape (1.5 hours by by public bus or hired vehicle along curving mountain roads), where there is basic accommodation and local boats available for charter.

The crossing from Sape to Komodo takes eight hours in calm seas, longer if the waves are strong. From Labuhanbajo, it's about three hours to Komodo and is a far more scenic crossing. Overnight stops with accommodation aboard the boat is possible. And there are various upscale liveaboard dive boats operating from Labuanbajo.

There is also a daily public ferry running between Sape and Labuanbajo (with departures usually in the early morning in each direction) which passes through the park but does not stop.

Foreigners visiting Komodo National Park must pay an entrance fee of Rp150,000 (Sunday and public holiday Rp305,000). There are additional tourist taxes for each of the main islands of Rp100,000, and a separate entrance fee of Rp150,000 for Padar Island.

Flores

As well as flights from Bali and Jakarta, TransNusa operates

Sanur beach.

extensive **flights** to Labuanbajo from other points in Nusa Tenggara, including Kupang (Timor) and Ruteng (Flores). TransNusa also flies to Bajawa, Ende, Larantuka and from Kupang and Ende. TransNusa's flights into Ruteng originate in Denpasar, Ende, Kupang and Labuhanbajo. PELNI **ships** have several routes to Labuanbajo.

Travelling overland across Flores should not be attempted with limited time. The Trans-Flores highway reaches from Labuanbajo in the west to Larantuka in the east – which can be done by public transport – but be aware that the 670km (400-mile) road is often shut down for hours or days due to landslides during the rainy season (Oct–Apr). There are gruelling through buses, but the journey is much better broken up over a week with overnight stops. With the exception of Riung, most of Flores' main destinations lie along the highway.

Elsewhere in Nusa Tenggara

There are regular **flights** to Kupang from Jakarta, Surabaya and Denpasar. Kupang is also the most important hub for onward flight connections within Nusa Tenggara. Be warned that small-aircraft flights in this area are frequently delayed or cancelled altogether. Flexibility and patience are essential to travelling here. TransNusa serves the Solor and

Alor archipelagos and Sumba from Kupang. Susi Air flies from Kupang to Rote and Savu. Tickets must be booked well in advance at the Susi Air office.

PELNI sails between the islands and there are also local **ferries** providing links to Rote, Sabu, Alor, Sumba and Flores. Note that the seas are rough in Jan and Feb. The large PELNI ships run whatever the weather, but private ferries are often cancelled when the sea is rough.

KALIMANTAN

Many travellers enter Kalimantan via **Balikpapan**, which has daily flights from Singapore, Jakarta, Manado and other Indonesian cities, as well as ferries from Java. The West Kalimantan gateway is **Pontianak**, connected by air with Kuching in East Malaysia, as well as major Indonesian cities. Visitors seeking orang-utans in Central Kalimantan can fly to Palangkaraya or Banjarmasin. Internal flights link these major cities with various smaller inland towns such as Putussibau. For more details on getting to Kalimantan, see below.

The road network within Kalimantan – long limited and in poor condition – is both expanding and improving, and has largely replaced the rivers as a long-distance transport network.

East Kalimantan

Balikpapan

Balikpapan has international flights from Singapore, and regular domestic connections from Jakarta and Surabaya, as well as air links to other towns within Kalimantan. There are also PELNI services to Surabaya in Java, to Makassar in Sulawesi and to Tarakan in northern East Kalimantan, near the Sabah border.

The Trans-Kalimantan highway extends from Batakan, south of Banjarmasin, to Balikpapan and then to Samarinda. It eventually connects to Bontang and Tarakan. Buses run from Banjarmasin to Balikpapan and Samarinda, as do 'travel' (prebooked door-to-door minibuses or cars). Boats – *taksi sungai* (river taxi) or *bis air* (water bus) – are popular forms of transport for short hops, but have largely vanished as a form of long-haul transport thanks to improved road and air networks.

Samarinda

Buses from Balikpapan make the journey to Samarinda in about two hours. Chartered **taxis** are much faster but more expensive. **Speedboats** depart Samarinda daily and arrive in Bontang about five hours later. **Water taxis** take about twice as long.

South Kalimantan

Banjarmasin

Garuda, Lion Air and Sriwijaya Air fly to Banjarmasin from Jakarta. PELNI **ferries** call at Banjarmasin on the run between Surabaya and Semarang in Java. From Balikpapan and Samarinda, overnight **buses** make the journey to Banjarmasin in 12 and 14 hours, respectively. Prebooked 'travel' (door-to-door shared cars or minibuses) also make the same trips, usually taking less time.

For river trips boats can be chartered upriver as far as Mauratewe. From there, switch to a canoe as you approach the headwater. A long trek northeast (you can shorten the journey by road) over swamps leads to Intu and finally to Long Iram on Sungai Mahakam. Samarinda is 36 hours away down the Mahakam River. But if you are game for more river

travel, on arrival in Long Iram go by boat up the Mahakam to the Dayak villages at Longbangun, through the rapids to Long Pahangai, Tiong Ohang and further.

Central Kalimantan

Palangkaraya

Garuda, Citlink and Sriwijaya fly to Palangkaraya from Jakarta. Garuda also flies in from Surabaya. By bus or car from Banjarmasin (on a good road) takes about eight hours, or travel the way the local people do, by *bis air* (water bus) or speedboat.

Pangkalanbun

There are daily flights between Pangkalanbun and Semarang, Jakarta and Pontianak.

Tanjung Puting National Park

Visitors must register with the PHPA (Forestry Department) office in Pangkalanbun to obtain a permit to go into the park. You will need a photocopy of your passport. Current registration fee is about US$18 (Rp250,000).

From Pangkalanbun, it is 20 minutes by taxi to Kumai, the riverside village that is the entry point into Tanjung Puting National Park. At Kumai Harbour, rent a *klotok* (motorised local boat) typically from around US$50 per day. If you plan to eat and sleep on the boat, you will pay extra for a cook. Be sure to buy food and water in Kumai before heading upriver.

West Kalimantan

Pontianak

Pontianak has daily flights from Kuching (Sarawak, Malaysia) and Kuala Lumpur, and regular flights from Jakarta and Surabaya, as well as the other main cities in Kalimantan. It also has links to smaller Kalimantan towns such as Putussibau and Sintang, useful for inland explorations to Dayak communities and national parks. There is also an increasingly limited number of ferry connections across the Java sea to Jakarta and Semarang, though these have largely been superseded by flights.

The **road trip** from Pontianak to Sambas takes five hours via Singkawang. There are buses

and 'travel' running along this route. Direct buses also connect Pontianak with Kuching in Malaysia via the Entikong border crossing (where visas on arrival are available).

The road inland to Sintang and Putussibau is now in excellent condition, traversed by both buses and 'travel', though the journey to Putussibau still takes at least 12 hours. From there another good road leads via the Danau Sentarum National Park to the Malaysian border at Badau. From the village of Lubok Antu on the Malaysian side, transport to Kuching can be arranged.

SULAWESI

Makassar is the provincial capital of Sulawesi and has the largest number of **flights**, including international connections to Kuala Lumpur and Singapore. However, there are good connections in Manado, serving the north and gateway to Bunaken, and in Palu, with more limited connections to Gorontalo. Kendari is the entry point for Southeast Sulawesi, including Wakatobi. By **sea**, PELNI is the main connection with other Indonesian islands.

Overland travel in Sulawesi is slow, because of the mountainous geography, and off the main cross-island highway road conditions are often poor. Travel by air is advised whenever possible. PELNI ferries schedule routes to the Wakatobi area, but are unreliable, making it best to use one of the fast boat services there.

South Sulawesi

Makassar

Confusingly, Makassar city was formerly called Ujung Pandang, and the airport still officially goes by this name. Several **airlines** originating in Jakarta and Surabaya serve Makassar, and there are international flights from Singapore and Kuala Lumpur. From the airport, it is about 40 minutes to town. To ride in an authorised taxi, purchase a coupon at the taxi counter outside the arrivals hall.

PELNI **ferries** operate routes to Makassar from Balikpapan, Bau-Bau and various points in Java and Flores.

For **short trips** in the city, *becak* (pedicabs) are an environmentally-friendly way to get around. To travel by air-con metered taxis, either hail one on the street or call one by phone (Bosowa Taxi; tel: 0411-454 545).

Boats to Samalona island or other places can be chartered from Pantai Benteng (across from Benteng Rotterdam) for about US$35 for a round-trip. The price to Kayangan island is US$3.50 by shuttle boat. Tickets can be purchased at kiosks across from Benteng Rotterdam.

Rantepao

Air-conditioned buses leave for Toraja morning and evening from Daya Bus Terminal in Makassar. The most comfortable buses are found at **Litha & Co.** (tel: 0411-324 847), **Alam Indah** (tel: 0411-586 717) and **Bintang Prima** (tel: 0411-477 2888). These days, however, most locals and many tourists avoid the hassle of traveling out to the bus terminal and book door-to-door travel services instead. In Sulawesi these are usually large SUV type vehicles seating up to seven passengers. Most hotels will be able to book these 'travel' for you. Though slightly more expensive than buses, they will drop you directly to your chosen accommodation at the other end.

Travel agents and hotels in Makassar can also arrange **chartered vehicles** for the 7–8-hour trip from Makassar to Rantepao via Pare Pare, a good place to stop for a seafood lunch overlooking the ocean. From there the road is winding and hilly and drivers are aggressive. Motion sickness medication is advised if you are susceptible.

Rantepao is small enough to explore on foot. You can also hop into a *becak* (pedicab) or ride around on a rented bicycle or motorbike. Minivans *(pete-pete)* make the 20-minute run between Rantepao and Makale several times throughout the day, starting their trip from Terminal Bolu, and can be flagged down anywhere along Jalan A. Yani for travel to nearby destinations.

Hiking is the best way to explore Tana Toraja. One-day walks can be made around the area, but several days are needed to see remote areas such as Mamasa Valley. May–Oct is the best time, otherwise your hike may well end up being just a long slog in the mud.

The livestock market at Rantepau, Sulawesi.

Central Sulawesi

Palu

Lion Air and Sriwijaya **fly** regularly from Makassar to Palu. PELNI passenger **ships** travel overnight from Balikpapan, Bitung, Makassar and Pare Pare. Daily public **buses** leave for Palu from Daya Bus Station in Makassar and from Rantepao.

To get the most out of Central Sulawesi, a combination of trekking, taxis, four-wheel-drive vehicles, buses and boats is required. For a hassle-free holiday, ask a tour operator to make all the arrangements for you.

Poso/Tentena

Buses make the journey from Palu to Poso in about 6 hours, but as the roads are rough, the journey is a tedious one. From Poso, there are regular minibuses to Tentena (a two-hour trip). A chartered taxi is a more comfortable option and can take you direct to Tentena.

Togian islands

The main entry point to the Togians is Ampana, from where daily public ferries run to the main town of Wakai, where small boats can be chartered to the resorts. There are also speedboats which run directly to various points around the archipelago from Ampana, and charter transfers direct to the resorts can be arranged. The other major entry point is Gorontalo, from where a public ferry makes the 10-hour crossing several times a week.

Private speedboat transfers can be arranged from several other points, including Marisa and Bunta, but this is generally arranged in advance when booking at one of the resorts, such as Black Marlin (www.blackmarlindiving.com).

Kendari

Kendari, the capital of Southeast Sulawesi, is a good place to break your journey because of its decent range of lodgings. Spend a day soaking and swimming at the spectacular seven-tiered waterfall at Morame.

Lion Air and Garuda fly to Kendari daily from Makassar, and there are also some **direct flights** from Jakarta. PELNI **ferries** sail from time to time between Makassar and Kendari.

As Kendari has only one main road, you can't get lost. *Pete-pete* (minivans) run frequently, stopping anywhere along the way for a low fixed fare; they can also be chartered to any destination in the city. There are also metered taxis and *becaks* (pedicabs) for shorter distances.

Bau-Bau

Wings Air and Garuda **flights** to Bau-Bau operate frequently from Makassar. PELNI **ferries** sail between Makassar and Bau-Bau (12 hours) a few times a week. Times vary radically.

Superjet and Sagori Express operate twice-daily **express boat services** to and from Kendari and Bau-Bau, taking five hours. Ticket prices are the same, but the Sagori boats are newer and more comfortable. Purchase your tickets at booths near the harbour.

Wakatobi

Getting there

Wangi-Wangi is the first island in the Wakatobi archipelago, and it is the main port of entry by air and sea. Wings Air **flies** to Wangi-Wangi daily from Makassar and Bau-Bau, and to and from Kendari each week.

There are **overnight ferries** between Bau-Bau and Wangi-Wangi, departing each destination daily at 9pm and arriving around 6am, but it is safest to check the current schedule for each destination before any trip. These are wooden boats, equipped with mattresses to sleep on in large communal areas. A few cabins are available for those wishing to pay extra, but the communal area is more spacious than the cramped cabins. Purchase tickets on the boat.

Passenger boats run between Kendari and Wangi-Wangi four times a week (10 hours), departing each destination at 9am and arriving around 7pm. The boats are similar to the Bau-Bau to Wangi-Wangi boats, only bigger. Tickets can be bought in the harbour or directly on the boat.

There are also some direct boats from Bau-Bau to Kaledupa and Bau-Bau to Tomia, but the times are variable and unpredictable. Get information on timetables at Bau-Bau Harbour.

Getting around

There are four main islands in Wakatobi, and daily public **speed-boat ferries** operate between three of them: Wangi-Wangi and Kaledupa, and Wangi-Wangi and Tomia.

The **Kaledupa boats** depart Kaledupa at 5am and arrive in Wanci (Wangi-Wangi's main town) at 7.30am, then head back from Wanci to Kaledupa at 9 or 10am and arrive there at about noon. Tickets can be bought on the boat, and the boats depart from Jembatan Mola.

Once on Kaledupa it is easy to charter a small boat across to Hoga island. The **Tomia boats** also depart from Jembatan Mola at 9 or 10am, and the journey to Tomia takes 2–3 hours. The boats from Tomia to Wanci depart Tomia at 10am and arrive in Wanci around noon. Tickets can be bought on the boat.

North Sulawesi

Manado

SilkAir **flies** from Singapore four times a week. Garuda and Lion Air arrive daily from Bali via Makassar, and Garuda and Lion Air service Manado several times daily from Jakarta.

Ships from Ambon, Sangihe, Talaud, Sorong, Ternate, Bau Bau and Banggai islands sail overnight to arrive in Bitung Harbour, one hour east of Manado city.

MALUKU AND PAPUA

The main entry points to **Maluku** are Ambon and Ternate. Daily return flights from Jakarta, Bali and Manado serve Ambon, the logistical hub of Maluku; intermittent flights serve other islands in the Maluku province.

Lion Air has direct **flights** from Jakarta, and also from Bali via Surabaya and Makassar to Ambon. Garuda and Sriwijaya depart daily out of Jakarta via Makassar or Surabaya. Be prepared to show your passport at the airport upon arrival. PELNI **sails** throughout the Maluku islands from many ports. Check with the local office for schedules, which are subject to changes, delays and cancellations.

Nearly all visitors arrive in **Papua** by air via Biak or directly into Jayapura. Before booking a flight into Jayapura, compare timetables, as most make many stops en route.

Garuda has direct flights to Jayapura from Jakarta. PELNI is the major carrier by sea. The only land crossing open to tourists is into Jayapura via Vanimo, Papua New Guinea.

Travelling into **Papua's interior** past the main coastal towns (ie Jayapura and Biak) requires a travel permit *(surat jalan)*. You must list on the permit every area you plan to visit. You can get the permit at police headquarters in Jayapura, Biak or Sorong, usually in one day, with two passport-sized photos, a copy of your passport and a small administration fee. While you are in the city, make plenty of passport and *surat jalan* photocopies to take with you, as hotels and tour operators may ask for them.

Jayapura/Sentani

Flights to Jayapura actually land at Sentani, a 45-minute drive from Jayapura. Garuda, Lion Air and Sriwijaya Air have frequent services. Flights from major cities in western Indonesia often transit through Makassar. Xpress Air serves Jayapura to Tanah Merah, Wamena, Nabire, Manokwari and Sorong. Garuda has a route from Jayapura to Timika before continuing on to Jakarta. Agats is served by twin-propeller aircraft from Timika and Merauke.

If you are in no hurry, the PELNI **ferry** sails from Jakarta to Jayapura and other points in Papua.

Manokwari

As the capital of West Papua province, Manokwari is linked by Sriwijaya Air. Susi Air connects Manokwari with other destinations on the Bird's Head peninsula and Biak.

Raja Ampat

Sorong, on the northwest tip of Bird's Head peninsula, is the entry point to Raja Ampat and is accessible on some international **flights** via Biak. Sriwijaya Air, Garuda and Wings are among the airlines that fly to Sorong from Jakarta.

Regularly scheduled **ferries** or chartered speedboats ply the waters between Sorong and Raja Ampat. Check with your Raja Ampat accommodation to determine if they provide transfers from the harbour.

⊙ Getting to Melak and Derawan islands

Melak, the starting point for Dayak expeditions, can be reached by ferry (20 hours) or bus (7–8 hours) from Samarinda. Xpress Air flies from Balikpapan to Melak daily. The roads around Melak are good, but there is no public transport. Hire a car or motorcycle to reach Kersik Luwai, Eheng and Tering.

To get to Derawan, Berau has regular flights from other parts of Kalimantan. A couple of hours east of Berau is Tanjung Batu, from where chartered speedboats cross to Derawan in about 30 minutes. The archipelago now has its own airport, on Maratua, currently served by daily flights from Balikpapan.

A

Accommodation

When it comes to accommodation, Bali and Java offer the full gamut, from basic backpackers' pads to the most luxurious resorts on earth. In terms of value for money in all price brackets, Bali is unrivalled, thanks to cut-throat competition, with even the cheapest options usually coming with an endearing dash of local style. In more remote areas, expect more basic conditions, and generally worse value. Jakarta and most other major cities are well supplied with high-end business hotels from international chains, but most urban centres

The rise of the domestic backpacking scene has seen old-fashioned budget guesthouses replaced in some places by hip modern hostels, often with pod-style beds, and Airbnb has made significant inroads, especially in Bali and Java. In more remote regions and small provincial towns, expect less innovation – with old-style budget and midrange guesthouses and hotels. The diving industry, however, has been responsible for spreading high-quality accommodation into unexpectedly remote places, with wonderful dive resorts scattered here and there on isolated shores across Indonesia.

Prices and bookings

Throughout Indonesia, advance reservations are recommended during the peak June–August and Christmas–New Year periods. Also be aware that prices are usually higher at these times or surcharges are added. In addition, during Indonesian public holidays and school breaks (June–July), all recreation areas plus Bali and Jogja are crowded with domestic travellers.

Look for better rates during 'low' (non-peak) season. In small establishments, it is perfectly acceptable to ask for a discount when they are not fully booked. Many larger hotels have special internet rates. When travelling from island to island within Indonesia, local travel agents can often get the best rates on two- and three-star hotels by booking with hotels they frequently do business with.

There is a government tax of 11 percent, which is charged by all but small establishments, and the larger ones also usually include a 10 percent service tax (in lieu of tipping).

Traditional Indonesian hotels typically offer a broad choice. Inexpensive and moderately priced hotels may have rooms without air-conditioning and hot water for budget travellers as well as rooms with all amenities, termed 'VIP'. Moderately priced and expensive hotels may also have 'presidential suites' or private villas. Check with individual hotels for current rates during the time of your visit.

Addresses

It can be difficult for visitors to find addresses in Indonesia, as villages often flow into one another with no apparent boundary demarcations in sight, particularly in Bali. To add to the confusion, street names often undergo official changes, but some establishments continue to use the old forms while others have switched to the new.

Admission charges

There are usually admission charges at museums and historical monuments, and there may be dual pricing systems, with a cheaper entry fee for Indonesian citizens and permanent residents (though with the exception of major attractions such as Borobudur, even the foreigners' prices usually remain modest).

B

Budgeting for your trip

Bottled beer: Rp35,000 (from a convenience store) to Rp100,000 (restaurant)
Glass of house wine: Rp130,000
Main course meal: Rp40,000 budget; Rp100,000 moderate; from Rp250,000 expensive
Hotel cost: from Rp150,000 budget; from Rp400,000 moderate; from Rp1.5 million expensive
Taxi ride: from Jakarta airport to city centre, Rp250,000
Bus journey: deluxe bus from Jakarta to Bandung Rp100,000; tourist shuttle bus from Kuta to Ubud Rp60,000

Business travellers

Big hotels in cities and towns have conference rooms and business centres that are internet- and email-friendly, can send and receive faxes, make appointments and handle typing, photocopy and other administrative chores. In larger cities, internet and email are available. Wi-Fi 'hotspots' are easily found in hotels, cafés and malls.

Business etiquette

The correct protocol is of the utmost importance when doing business in Indonesia. Apprise yourself of the rules by reading books on the subject. Here are a few pointers.

The terms *Bapak* or *Pak* ('Sir') and *Ibu* ('Madam'), are universally applicable in Indonesia and used to address business counterparts. Both men and women shake hands on introduction. If drinks are served, don't reach for yours until your host has gestured for you to do so. Observe the formalities until your Indonesian counterpart takes the lead to be more relaxed. At first meetings, business may not be discussed at all, paving the way for subsequent consultations.

Meetings usually begin with the conversation centring on social or predictable topics. Specific or personal enquiries are avoided. The best way to air a grievance is to talk politely around the subject until your business partner sees your point of view. Do not be too direct; rather than saying 'no' directly, most Indonesians would say 'belum', meaning 'not yet'. Consensus is fundamental to all relationships. Business with Indonesians requires endurance, and most negotiations on deals will take far longer than hoped or planned.

C

Children

Indonesians generally love children, and you'll get lots of friendly attention if travelling with kids. Reliable babysitters are available at major hotels, and even small inn owners are happy to look after youngsters. Many resort hotels in Bali have kids' clubs and children's programmes, and shopping malls in large cities

Drinks stalls outside the mosque at Banten, Java.

often provide pushchairs. Disposable nappies and baby food are scarce outside major cities.

Climate

The climate in Indonesia is warm and humid year-round, with temperatures typically around 30–35 degrees Celsius at sea level, though the year is broadly divided into two seasons: wet and dry.

November to April is the wet season in most of the country. It doesn't rain all day every day, but expect torrential cloud-breaks and thunderstorms most afternoons. Mornings are generally dry and often sunny, though humidity is high (75–100 percent).

May to October is the dry season in most of Indonesia, with much lower humidity, and generally sunny days. Occasional brief thunderstorms can occur all year round, however, particularly in the mountains.

In northern Maluku the seasons are reversed, with November to April being the main dry season.

Crime and safety

Indonesia is remarkably safe for a huge country with a great deal of inequality, though petty crime is an issue in major urban centres, and crime targeting tourists can be a problem in southern Bali. Pickpockets can be a threat in crowded areas, and bag-snatching by thieves on motorbikes is not unusual, particularly in busy areas

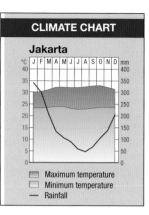

of Bali and in big cities. Report any theft immediately to police or security officers. (Without a police report, new passports and travel documents are difficult to obtain.) In some tourist areas, such as Jakarta, Jogja and Bali, there are English-speaking 'tourist police' in specially marked uniforms and cars who are trained to handle foreigners' questions and lend assistance.

Exercise caution by carrying photocopies of your passport, tickets and travel documents, and keep the originals in hotel safes. Tourists may also be exposed to scams and credit card/ATM fraud. There has been an increase in reports of violent crime in Bali, including muggings in the Kuta area, though these generally take place late at night around the nightlife scene.

All narcotics are illegal in Indonesia and prosecution means a long prison term – perhaps even death – and/or huge fines.

Indonesia has experienced a certain amount of domestic terrorism over the last two decades, mainly in Jakarta and Bali, though Surabaya also suffered an attack in 2018. Generally, the response of Indonesian security forces has been highly efficient, with a number of terrorist networks broken up by the authorities over the years. Exercise caution and check latest government warnings, but keep a sense of perspective: the threat of terrorism is probably no higher in Indonesia than in Europe.

Papua is the only region with ongoing separatist issues. This is generally at a low level, and as this is the one part of the country where travel restrictions are in place, tourists are usually kept well away from any affected areas. Indonesia is subject to a range of natural disasters including volcanoes, earthquakes, tsunamis and floods. You should pay close attention to emergency procedures and monitor local warnings.

The governments of the UK (www.fco.gov.uk) and US (www.travel.state.gov) provide current travel advisories.

Customs regulations

Each adult is permitted to bring a maximum of one litre of alcoholic beverages, 200 cigarettes, 50 cigars, or 100 grams of tobacco, and a reasonable quantity of perfume. Prohibited from entry are the following: narcotics, arms and ammunition, pornography and fresh fruit. There is no restriction on import and export of foreign currencies and travellers' cheques; however, import or export of Indonesian currency exceeding Rp 100,000,000 is prohibited. It is also prohibited to import or export products made from endangered species.

Visas and passports

All travellers to Indonesia must be in possession of a passport valid for at least six months after arrival and tickets proving onward passage. Some immigration officials will require six blank passport pages, so it's better to be safe than sorry.

Visitors from 169 countries, including most of Europe, North America, Australia and New Zealand, and other Southeast Asian members of ASEAN can enter Indonesia for up to 30 days without a visa. Citizens of many other countries not granted visa-free entry can obtain a visa on arrival, and those not able to make use of these facilities must obtain a visa (30 or 60 days) in advance from an Indonesian consulate.

Visa-free entry does not allow for a stay longer than 30 days, so if you wish to stay longer you should apply instead for a visa on arrival (which can, with considerable bureaucracy, be extended by a further 30 days in provincial capitals), or better still apply in advance for a 60-day visa from an Indonesian consulate overseas. A visa obtained in advance can, in theory, be extended by 30 days at a time up to a total of six months, though this requires much paperwork.

Travel permits

A *surat jalan* (travel permit) is required for visits to some parts of Papua, though restrictions have been much reduced in recent years. They are available from provincial police headquarters, with Jayapura the best place to apply.

Permits are also required to enter all national parks. In some parks there is an officer on the premises, but in others permits must be obtained prior to arrival. Check locally for regulations before visiting any national park.

E

Eating out in Indonesia

The staple for the majority of Indonesians is rice, although in the eastern islands corn, sago, cassava or sweet potatoes dominate, and in smaller towns and villages that's what you'll be served. Coconut milk and hot chilli peppers are popular cooking ingredients nationwide. Dishes range from very spicy meat, fish and vegetables, such as the Padang food found everywhere in restaurants called rumah makan Padang, to those that are quite sweet, for instance Jogja's speciality, *gudeg*. Almost all come with steamed white rice *(nasi puti)*. The most popular dishes among visitors are *nasi goreng* (fried rice), *mie goring* (fried noodles), *sate* or *satay* (grilled meat or chicken on skewers) and *gado-gado* (cold, steamed vegetables served with a peanut sauce). *Nasi campur* is a good choice for travellers because it is a complete meal, including rice, a vegetable and a piece of meat, usually chicken.

Chinese restaurants are found in almost every town and offer less spicy food and vegetarian dishes. In the main tourist centres and resorts, many restaurants cater for visitors and serve a wide variety of cuisines, including Western. All cities have American fast-food outlets such as KFC (Kentucky Fried Chicken), and larger ones have McDonald's and Pizza Hut.

Drinks

While the main local beer, Bintang, is reasonably priced, imported beers, cocktails and wine (only available in larger cities) are expensive and can

equal the price of a meal. Tap water is not safe to drink in Indonesia, and Indonesians do not drink it themselves. Bottled drinking water can be purchased everywhere. In tourist-centre restaurants, free room-temperature or cold water may be poured from a pitcher at the table *(air putih)*, which has been filled from a large mineral water container in the kitchen, saving you the cost (and environmental waste) of buying bottled water. In cheaper establishments, *air putih* may be served hot in a glass or in a thermos, indicating that it has been boiled and is safe to drink.

Hygiene and etiquette

Ice is generally safe, even at roadside food stalls, as is any water you are likely to be offered to drink (other than in the most remote rural areas, Indonesians invariably use boiled or filtered water). Be aware that the hygienic standards of *warungs* and street vendors are usually not what Westerners are accustomed to. Plates and cutlery are not washed with hot water and food may not be refrigerated until cooked. Proceed with caution. If visiting someone's home, for example in a village, you will almost always be offered a drink and a snack. It is impolite to refuse, so if unsure of cleanliness, stick with coffee or tea (which have been boiled), cooked food or fresh fruit.

Electricity

Electricity is usually 220V to 240V AC in Indonesia. Power failures are common and voltage fluctuates considerably, so using a stabiliser is advised. Wall plugs are the standard Western European variety: two round pins. International hotels may have adaptors for guests to use.

Embassies and consulates

Embassies are found only in Jakarta. In Bali, Medan (Sumatra), Jogja (Java) and Surabaya (Java), a few countries maintain small consular offices. Only addresses in Jakarta and Bali are given here.

Jakarta

(Telephone area code 021)
Australia: Jl. H.R. Rasuna Said, Kav. 15–16; tel: 2550 5555; www.indonesia.embassy.gov.au.
Canada: Jl. Jend. Sudirman, Kav. 29, World Trade Center 6th floor; tel:

2550 7800; www.canadainternational.
gc.ca.
New Zealand: Sentral Senayan
2, Floor 10, Jl. Asia Afrika, No. 8;
tel: 2995 5800; www.nzembassy.com/
indonesia.
Singapore: Jl. H.R. Rasuna Said,
Kav. X-4, No. 2, Kuningan; tel: 2995
0400; www.mfa.gov.sg/jkt.
United Kingdom: Jl. Patra Kuningan
Raya Blok L5-6; tel: 2356 5200; www.
ukinindonesia.fco.gov.uk.
United States: Jl. Medan Merdeka
Selatan, No. 5, Jakarta Pusat; tel:
3435 9000.

Bali

(Telephone area code 0361)
**Australia, Canada, New Zealand,
Ireland and Papua New Guinea**: Jl.
Tantular, No. 32, Renon; tel: 241 118;
www.dfat.gov.au.
France: Jl. Mertasari, Gang II, No. 8,
Sanur; tel: 285 485.
Germany: Jl. Pantai Karang, No. 17,
Sanur; tel: 288 535.
Italy: Lotus Enterprise Bldg, Jl.
By-Pass Ngurah Rai, Jimbaran; tel:
701 005.
Spain: Jl. Raya Sanggingan, Br.
Lungsiakan, Kedewatan, Ubud; tel:
975 736.
United Kingdom: Jl. Tirta Nadi, No.
20, Sanur; tel: 270-601.
United States (Consular): Jl. Hayam
Wuruk, No. 310, Denpasar; tel: 233
605; http://surabaya.usconsulate.gov/
bali2.html.

Etiquette

Indonesians are remarkably friendly
and courteous, but they may also be
conservative. Travellers who observe
a few basic rules of etiquette will be
assured of a warm welcome.

Using the left hand to give or to
receive anything is taboo (the left
hand is reserved for hygiene acts),
as is pointing or crooking a finger to
call someone.

Don't make any offers to purchase unless you intend to buy.
When bargaining, start at half the
asking price and then work out a
compromise. A small contribution
at a temple, a village or a cultural
conservation centre is appropriate
and will be appreciated. Begging is
not widespread (other than outside
major religious pilgrimage sites).
However, there is a very lively tradition of busking for money, particularly around clusters of food stalls
and on public transport. In roadside

The odalan festival, Bali.

eateries and around major bus terminals expected to encounter an
endless procession of buskers –
individuals or in groups. Some are
very talented (a number of famous
musicians have started out this way);
others much less so. After playing for a short they usually politely
approach diners/passengers with a
cup. Most Indonesians give a little
small change.

Hands on the hips indicates
defiance or arrogance, especially
when also standing with legs
apart. When sitting, feet should be
tucked away, not propped up with
the soles facing another person.
When visiting mosques and other
places of worship, dress modestly
and remove shoes.

F

Festivals

Indonesians love to gather with family and friends to celebrate practically any occasion, and these events
promise entertainment for everyone.
Many festivals and ceremonies are
based on religious or cultural calendars, meaning the dates change
every year. Enquire upon arrival if
there are any events being held in
your area, and you might get lucky.

Cultural festivals

Chinese New Year: Many cities
host elaborate festivals to celebrate
Chinese New Year (Feb/Mar). In
Manado (Sulawesi) the **Toa Peh
Kong Festival**, a large procession
including horses, decorated floats

and children in Chinese costumes,
begins at a Confucian temple if
the gods grant permission through
a ritual.
Dayak Erau Festival (Kalimantan):
Held throughout the region, the best
known is in Kutai Kartanegara, a
showcase for Dayak cultural arts,
dances and handicrafts. Scheduling
is based on auspicious dates chosen
by traditional leaders.
Pasola (Sumba): A mock-battle,
usually held Feb/Mar, at a date
determined by the annual migration of *nyale* sea worms. 'Warriors'
on horseback try to unseat their
opponents, and any blood spilled is
believed to fertilise the soil and benefit the next harvest. Held in three
areas: West Sumba's Wanakola
and Kodi districts, and Waingapu in
East Sumba. On Mandalika beach,
Lombok and in Sabu similar rituals
are held.
Lake Sentani Festival (Papua):
Usually in June, local dancers perform on floating dugout canoes;
there are drum competitions, lake
tours, fireworks, and bark-painting
and hair-weaving contests.
Lake Toba Festival (Sumatra): June
or July on Samosir Island, this festival features Batak art, cultural performances, boat and horse races,
and handicrafts exhibitions.
Labuhan (Java): In Jogja, every
25 Aug there is a procession to
Parangkusumo beach where
offerings are made to Nyi Roro
Kidul, Queen of the Southern Sea.
Similar ceremonies are held at
Gunung Merapi, Gunung Bromo
and Gunung Lawu, and throughout the country to give thanks for
successful harvests or catches
and to ask blessings for the
coming season.
Madura Bull Races (Java): Races
are held from Sep to Nov in East
Java and in Madura showcasing the
strength and speed of prized bulls.
In Oct in Pamekasan, the **Sapi Sono
Festival** is held to name the most
'beautiful' buffalo in the region.

Religious festivals

Waisak Day (Java): Thousands of
Buddhists from throughout Asia join
a procession from Mendut temple
to Borobudur to meditate in honour of the Day of Enlightenment
(June/July), the biggest day on the
Buddhist calendar.
Easter (Flores): Laruntuka's Easter
celebrations draw devotees by the

hundreds from nearby islands. On Good Friday, the ceremony begins with a procession through town led by shrouded bearers of Christ's coffin and the bathing of a Virgin Mary statue in a tradition dating back to Portuguese ancestors.

Sports festivals

Many sporting events are held during school holidays (June/July), at the height of the tourist season.

Raja Ampat Marine Festival (Papua): Promotes the beauty of culture, adventure and nature, held in Waisai in May. Activities include underwater orientation and photo competitions, parades, dragon-boat races and beach sports.

Indonesian Surfing Championship (Seminyak, Bali): June events include Pro, Junior, Women's, Master and Longboard competitions. Local and international surfers participate in a one-week championship competition and surfing film festival (www.isctour.com).

Bali International Triathlon: Held every June, Olympic and sprint-distance events, team relays and fun runs. Balinese bicycle blessing ceremony; post-race live music and beach party (www.balitriathlon.com).

Tour de Singkrak (Sumatra): An annual cycle race that draws participants from throughout Asia and Europe begins in Padang and traverses 743.5km (462 miles), ending at Lake Singakaral. Held in June or July.

International Kite Festival (Bali): Part of the **Sanur Village Festival** (June/July). Teams from Indonesia and abroad fly enormous kites up to 10 metres (33ft) long – taking as many as five men to launch – and compete in various divisions, including traditional Balinese and contemporary kite designs.

Darwin–Ambon Yacht Race: Held annually since 2007 (July–August) and attracting over 100 boats, the Darwin–Ambon Yacht Race (www.darwinambonrace.com.au) also inspires other marine festivals en route, such as **Sail Banda** and **Sail Wakatobi**, with game-fishing competitions, beach sports, diving tournaments and conferences.

August celebrations

Beginning the first week in August in every village, town and city, competitions and games are held in celebration of Indonesia's **Independence**

Day on 17 Aug, and visitors are always welcome. Two spectacular ones are:

Sanur Village Festival (Bali): An annual celebration held in July–August, drawing hundreds of locals and tourists to its many events. A four-day feast of contests includes water sports and an international kite-flying competition, music, dance and food, food, food. A great opportunity to mingle with the local people, hear some great music and eat some really good food (www.gotosanur.com).

Baliem Valley Festival (Papua): Fabulous mock battles held in August between tribes accompanied by traditional dance, music and art exhibitions and a pig feast.

Health and medical care

The health risks when travelling in a tropical country such as Indonesia depend greatly on how you choose to travel and where you are going to go. Nonetheless, you should not travel to Indonesia without comprehensive medical insurance.

Yellow fever vaccinations are required if arriving within six days of leaving or passing through an infected area. Check with your home physician regarding vaccinations for other ailments like typhoid, cholera and hepatitis A and B.

Always use mosquito repellent.

Diarrhoea and stomach upsets may be a problem, often a reaction to a change in food and environment. Tablets such as Lomotil and Imodium are invaluable, but offer only a temporary solution, best taken only when toilet facilities are lacking. A fever accompanying cramps and diarrhoea may require doctor-prescribed antibiotics.

Probably more stomach upsets are due to **dehydration** than anything else, as most people simply don't drink enough water. Drink more than you think you need, particularly if taking part in outdoor activities. Take precautions against the sun and the heat. Wear a hat as protection. Tanning oils and creams are expensive in Indonesia and difficult to find outside the big cities. Bring them from home.

Malaria is carried by night-biting mosquitoes. Prophylactics are increasingly questionable; strains are developing in Southeast Asia that are resistant to most medications; some, like Larium, can cause dizziness, stomach upset, even hallucinations. Before consulting a physician, first determine if you will be travelling in a malaria-infected area (antimalarial medication is not generally recommended for Bali, Java or major urban centres elsewhere). Upon arrival, minimise contact with mosquitoes by using repellent; and as mosquitoes are most active around dawn and dusk, wear long-sleeved shirts and long trousers

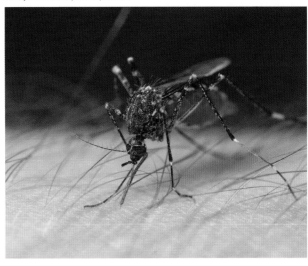

during those times. Sleep under a mosquito net in infected areas. All bites, cuts and abrasions can easily become infected in the tropics; treat them immediately.

Dengue fever, carried by daytime mosquitoes, is far more prevalent in Indonesia than malaria. There is no prophylactic; take the precautions described above if travelling in an infected area.

All **water** must be made safe before consumption. Bottled purified water is readily available in even the smallest villages, but if caught in a bind, bringing water to a rolling boil for 20 minutes is an effective method of sterilisation. All fruit should be peeled before eaten; avoid raw vegetables.

HIV and other sexually transmitted diseases are increasing in Indonesia. Act responsibly and use condoms, available over the counter at city *apotik* (pharmacies), supermarkets and mini-marts.

Most drugs are available at pharmacies *(apotik)* in major cities without prescription, but if you need special medication, bring adequate supplies with you. International-standard medical treatment and specialist care is available in Jakarta and Bali at hospitals and clinics.

Jakarta

The following clinics are of international standard and are popular with expatriates living in Indonesia. Both have staff who can handle problems in English.

SOS Medika (AEA International Clinic): Jl. Puri Sakti, No. 10, Cipete, Jakarta; tel: 021-750 6001 (24-hour emergency); www.sosindonesia.com.

MMC (Metropolitan Medical Center): Jl. H.R. Rasuna Said, Kav. C 20–21; tel: 021-520 3435; www.rsmmc.co.id.

Bali

Bali International Medical Centre (BIMC): Jl. By-Pass Ngurah Rai, No. 100X, Kuta; tel: 0361-761 263; www.bimcbali.com. Provides 24-hour general medical treatment and emergency medical evacuation.

International SOS Medika, Bali Clinic: Jl. By-Pass Ngurah Rai, No. 505X, Kuta, tel: 0361-720 100; www.internationalsos.com. Provides international-standard medical care, including specialist and ambulance services. Routine care, including

dental and psychological, and emergency care 24 hours a day.

Internet

Wi-Fi is ubiquitous in Indonesia, with virtually every hotel and eatery, and many retail outlets and even convenience stores offering a free connection for customers. Speeds may not be top-notch, but they are usually adequate for browsing. The mobile data network is generally reliable outside of remote areas, and if your phone lacks data roaming, prepaid data-ready SIM cards are available.

LGBTQ travellers

Although homosexuality is not illegal in Indonesia, and traditionally the country has been relatively accepting by the standards of other countries in the region, there has been some conservative agitation in recent years, with controversy whipped up over supposed LGBT activity on university campuses and in the media. Generally speaking this has no impact on travellers, and most Indonesian cities have lively – if partly underground – gay scenes. Bali, unsurprisingly, is most open, with a number of gay nightlife spots, mainly in and around Seminyak. This is, however, a largely conservative country, where public displays of affection even between mixed-sex couples are highly inappropriate, so behave appropriately. In Bali, same-sex couples sharing a room will usually encounter no problems. Elsewhere, it is not unusual for Indonesians of the same sex – especially women – to share rooms when travelling together, so if you are discreet you will be unlikely to encounter major difficulties.

In Java and Bali there are gay communities and establishments that cater for them. Utopia, the Asian Gay & Lesbian Resources Centre (www.utopia-asia.com), has excellent information on gay travel in Indonesia as well as other Asian countries.

Media

The Jakarta Post is the major traditional English-language newspaper, and there are various glossy magazines published in Jakarta and Bali in English. These have been joined by a plethora of digital media. Online-only regional news outlets including New Naratif (www.newnaratif.com) and Asia Times (www.asiatimes.com) provide some excellent Indonesia analysis.

Television is available everywhere, even in the most remote locations. Larger hotels have cable TV, so in addition to Indonesian channels, they receive CNN, MTV, at least one sports and one movie channel.

Money

Rupiah (Rp) come in banknote denominations of 100,000; 50,000; 20,000; 10,000; 5,000; 2,000 and 1,000. Coins come in 1,000, 500, 200, 100 and 50 rupiah.

Change is often not available in smaller shops – don't be surprised to be given a handful of sweets in lieu of very small change! Carry a variety of coins and small notes, especially when travelling outside cities.

Changing money

Bring only new notes (no coins), as practically no one will change dirty or marred bank notes. The best exchange rate is usually obtained at money-changers, found at the airports of all major cities. Hotels usually offer a lower rate, and banks often offer even worse rates.

Particularly in Bali, where illegal money-changers know every scam in the book, stick to those advertising themselves as 'Authorised'. Count your money before leaving the counter and get a receipt. It is advisable to convert most of your money in the cities before moving towards the interior. Leftover rupiah notes are easily changed back into foreign currency at departure.

Credit cards

MasterCard and Visa are accepted in most large hotels and shops, and increasingly in even remote areas. Diner's Club and American

A surf shop, Kuta, Bali.

Express are less prevalent. Don't be surprised if an additional 3–5 percent 'handling charge' is added to the bill; this is an acceptedpractice.

ATMs

ATMs are now ubiquitous in even fairly remote areas. If there are no banks at hand, you'll often find standalone ATMs linked to international networks in Indomaret and Alfamart convenience stores.

Tipping

Major hotels add a 10 percent service charge to bills. If it is not included in upmarket restaurants, a tip of 5–10 percent is appropriate if the service has been satisfactory.

In small-town eateries, tipping is not expected. Airport and hotel porterage is Rp 10,000 per piece. Tipping taxi and hired-car drivers is not mandatory, but rounding up the fare to the nearest 10,000 for longer distances is standard.

O

Opening hours

In most places, government offices are generally open from Monday to Thursday, 8am–3pm, and close at 11.30am on Friday. On Saturday, they close at around 2pm. Business offices are open from Monday to Friday, 8 or 9am until 4 or 5pm. A few companies work on Saturday mornings as well. Banks are open 8am–3pm on weekdays, but in Jakarta some have branches in shopping malls that are open at weekends. Private retail businesses typically open quite late – between 10am and 11am, but may stay open until 9pm or 10pm.

P

Photography

Most Indonesians love to be photographed, especially if they have children, but it's still nice to ask before shooting. Practically everyone understands 'Foto?' Just point at the camera and, if you get a nod or a smile, click away. Older people may be shy; if they indicate 'no', politely move on. It isn't polite to photograph people praying.

Digital-photo shops are abundant in cities; convenient for downloading photos from camera to USB devices.

Postal services

There are post offices in every major town and village. Hours are generally as follows: from Monday to Thursday 8am–2pm; Friday 8am–noon; and Saturday 8am–1pm.

Public holidays

Schools and government offices are generally closed during public holidays in Indonesia, but for the most part private businesses, including those aimed at tourists, and transport systems run as normal – with two major exceptions. The Idul Fitri celebrations at the end of Ramadan see a mass movement across Indonesia, as migrant workers and students head home. At this time transport is very heavily booked. During the weeklong Lebaran holiday that follows Idul Fitri, many business and virtually all offices are shut. The unique Balinese event of Nyepi, which takes place in March, sees the entire island completely shut down for 24 hours. No one is allowed outside – with tourists strictly confined to hotel grounds – and all transport stops, including international flights into Bali's international airport. It is a fascinating experience, but if you are travelling to Bali in March be sure to check the date of Nyepi (which varies each year) to avoid being caught by surprise.

1 January New Year's Day
January/February Imlek (Chinese New Year)
March Nyepi (Bali only)
March/April Good Friday
1 May International Labour May/June
May Ascension
May/June Waisak (Buddha's birthday)
1 June Pancasila Day
17 August Independence Day
25 December Christmas
Major Islamic festivals including Muharram, Maulid, Idul Fitri and Idul Adha are public holidays. Their dates are set according to the Islamic lunar calendar, so their dates change annually.

S

Smoking

Large cities are making an effort to ban smoking in public places. Look for smoking rooms in airports, and enquire if smoking is permitted in special sections of restaurants and hotels.

T

Telecommunications

The telephone service is fairly effective, and mobile network coverage is excellent.

Establishments such as hotels may have several telephone numbers, which may come in five to eight digits. Thus, listings never seem to match. Major hotels offer International Direct Dial (IDD). Dial 001, 007, 008 and 017 for an international line. Indonesia's cellular phone system is GSM. Prepaid SIM cards that can be inserted into your phone allow you to make local and international calls at lower prices than landline calls. These can be purchased in varying amounts at many kiosks and supermarkets in Indonesia's towns and cities. The international dialling code for Indonesia is +62.

Time zones

Indonesia is divided into three time zones following provincial boundaries:
Waktu Indonesia Barat (WIB, Western Indonesia Standard Time): Sumatra, Java, western half of Kalimantan. UTC +7 of Greenwich Mean Time (GMT).
Waktu Indonesia Tengah (WITA, Central Indonesia Standard Time): Eastern half of Kalimantan, Sulawesi, Bali, Nusa Tenggara. UTC +8.
Waktu Indonesia Timur (WIT, Eastern Indonesia Standard Time): Papua, Maluku. UTC +9.
Daylight saving time is never observed in Indonesia.
During non-daylight saving time in other countries:
At noon in Western Indonesia (WIB), it's 0.00 (midnight) the previous day in New York (ie New York is 12 hours behind Jakarta) and 5am on the same day in London (ie London is 7 hours behind Jakarta).
At noon in Central Indonesia (WITA), it's 11pm the previous day in New York (ie New York is 13 hours behind Denpasar) and 4am the same day in London (ie London is 8 hours behind Denpasar).
At noon in Eastern Indonesia (WIT), it's 10pm on the previous day in New York (ie New York is 14 hours behind

Jayapura) and 3am on the same day in London (ie London is 9 hours behind Jayapura).

Toilets

Most places catering to tourists have at least one Western toilet. In shopping malls, there is often an attendant who collects a small fee (from Rp500 up to 5,000) to pay for keeping toilets clean. Otherwise, and in remote areas, 'squat' toilets are the norm. Toilet tissue is often not available, as most Indonesians clean themselves with the water that's provided. Bring your own tissue and dispose of it in the bin next to the toilet, if there is one.

Tourist information

While there is plenty of information about Indonesia on the web, much of it is conflicting and a lot of it is just plain wrong. Unfortunately, most of the provincial government tourist information websites are either in Bahasa Indonesia only or have not been updated in several years. Note that the provincial tourist information offices are difficult to reach by telephone and they close at odd hours, ie for lunch, at weekends and during public holidays. The best bet is to drop by their offices before noon on a weekday. The official government tourism website, www.indonesia. travel, provides a good overview of attractions around the country, and allows for booking of accommodation and tours.

Java

Jakarta
Ministry of Culture and Tourism: Gedung Sapta Pesona, Jl. Medan Merdeka Barat, No. 17; tel: 021-383 8565; www.indonesia.travel.
Jakarta City Government Tourism and Culture Office: Jl. Kuningan Barat, No. 2; tel: 021-520 5455, 520 5454.
PHKA (Forest Protection & Nature Conservation): Manggala Wanabakti Building Blok I, 8th Floor, Jl. Jend. Gatot Subroto; tel: 021-573- 4818. Information about permits for Indonesia's national parks.
Visitor Information Centre: Jakarta Theatre Bldg (across from Sarinah), Jl. M.H. Thamrin; tel: 021-315 4094.

Bandung
For useful tourist information about Bandung, visit www.visitbandung.net.
Banten Tourism Office: Jl. Syech Nawawi, Palima Serang; tel: 0254-267 060.
West Java Provincial Tourist Office: Jl. R.E. Martadinata, No. 209, Bandung; tel: 022-727 1385, 727 3209.

Cirebon
Provincial Tourist Services: Jl. Brigien Darsono, No. 5; tel: 0231-208 856.

Solo
Provincial Tourist Services: Jl. Wisata Menanggal; tel: 031-853 1814/1816/1820/1821.

Surabaya
Tourist Information Centre: Balai Pemuda, Jl. Gubernur Suryo, No. 15; tel: 031-5340 4444.
Tourist Information Centre: House of Sampoerna, Taman Sampoerna, No. 6; tel: 031-353 9000; www.houseofsampoerna.museum; Tue–Sun 9am–1pm. For useful information about East Java, visit:
www.eastjava.com
www.sparklingsurabaya.info
www.eastjava.com

Yogyakarta
Yogyakarta Tourism Office: Jl Malioboro, No. 56; tel: 0274-587 486. For Jogja tourism information, visit www.yogyes.com.

Sumatra

Bandar Lampung
Lampung Tourism Office: Jl. Jend. Sudirman, No. 2, Bandar Lampung; tel: 0721-261 430.

Bengkulu
Bengkulu Tourism Office: Jl. P. Tendean, No. 17, Bengkulu; tel: 0736-21272.

Medan
North Sumatra Tourism Office: Jl. Jend. A. Yani, No. 107, Medan; tel: 061-453 8101.

Padang
West Sumatra Tourism Office: Jl. Khatib Sulaiman, No. 7, Padang; tel: 0751-705 5711.

Palembang
South Sumatra Tourism Office: Jl. Demang Lebar Daun, Kav. IX,

Palembang; tel: 0711-356 661, 311 345, 357 348.

Riau
Riau Tourism Office: Jl. Jend. Sudirman No. 200, Pekanbaru; tel: 0761-31452, 40356.
For useful Sumatra tourist information, also visit: www.medanku.com.

Bali

Denpasar
Denpasar Government Tourist Office: Jl. Surapati, No. 7, Denpasar; tel: 0361-231 422.

Kuta
Indonesia Tourist Information Center: Jl. Raya Kuta, No. 2, Kuta; tel: 0361-766 181, 0361-766 184; www.indonesiatic.com.

Legian
Bali Tourist Information: Century Plaza, Jl. Bensari, No. 7, Legian; tel: 0361-754 092.
Legian Tourist Information: Jl. Legian, No. 37; tel: 0361-755 424.
Provincial Tourist Services: Jl. S. Parman Niti Mandala, Renon; tel: 0361-222 387.

Singaraja
Singaraja Tourist Information Office: Jl. Gajah Mada, No. 117; tel: 0362 25141.

Ubud
Ubud Tourist Information Service: Jl. Raya Ubud, Ubud; tel: 0361-973 285.
Helpful tourist information can also be found at www.balicalendar.com, www.bali-tourism-board.com, www.karangasemtourism.com, www.godivingbali.com.

Nusa Tenggara

Flores
Flores DMO Marketing Office: Jl. Batursari 20SB, Sanur; tel: 0361 27 1145.
Useful tourist information websites: http://floresexotictours.blogspot.com, www.florestourism.com, www.komodonationalpark.org.

Sumbawa
Tourist Information Office: Jl. Sukarno-Hatta, Raba, Bima; tel: 0374-44331.
Tourist Information Office: Jl. Akasia, No. 2, Dompu; tel: 0373-21177.

Tourist Information Office: Jl. Bungur, No. 1, Sumbawa Besar; tel: 0371-261-658.

Timor
Tourist Office: Jl. Raya El Tari, No. 2, Kupang; tel: 0380-833104, 833650.
Kupang Klub House: Jl. Hati Mulia, No. 2/6, Kupang; tel: 0380-840 244; www.kupangklubhouse.com, online information directory for Kupang and East Nusa Tenggara.
Other useful websites for East Nusa Tenggara tourist information: www.alordiver.com, www.lavalontouristinfo.com.

Kalimantan
Useful tourist information websites include www.kalimantantours.com and www.extremeborneo.com.

Banjarmasin
Provincial Tourist Services: Jl. Pramuka, No. 4, Banjarmasin; tel: 0511-274 252.

Palangkaraya
Provincial Tourist Services: Jl. Tjilik Riwut, Km 5, Palangkaraya 73112; tel: 0536-323 1110.

Pontianak
Provincial Tourist Services: Jl. Letjen. Sutoyo, Km 17, Pontianak; tel: 0561-736 172.

Samarinda
Provincial Tourist Services: Jl. Sudirman, No. 22, Samarinda; tel: 0541-736 850, 747 241.

Sulawesi

Bau-Bau
Buton Tourist Office: tel: 0402-23588.

Kendari
Provincial Tourist Services: Jl. Lakidende, No. 9; tel: 0401-21764.

Makassar
Provincial Tourist Office: Jl. Jend. Sudirman, No. 23, Makassar; tel: 0411-872 366, 878 912; Mon–Fri 8am–4pm.
There is also a **Tourist Information Centre** inside Benteng Rotterdam organised by the Indonesia Tour Guide Association.

Manado
Tourism Office: Jl. Diponegoro 111, Manadoi; tel: 0431-851 723.

North Sulawesi Tourism Organisation; tel: 0431-824 445.
Useful tourist information websites for North Sulawesi: www.north-sulawesi.com, www.north-sulawesi.org, www.divenorthsulawesi.com.

Palu
Provincial Tourist Services: Jl. Dewi Sartika, No. 91; tel: 0451-455 260.

Rantepao
Government Tourist Office: Jl. A. Yani, No. 62; tel: 0423-21277.
Tourist Information: Toraja Decouverte, Jl. Pahlawan, No. 7 (behind Modern Foto); email: torajainfo@gmail.com. Organises tours, hiking, rafting, and car/motorbike rental.

Maluku
Tourism Information Centre: Jl. Bhayangkara, Tobelo, Ambon; www.halmaherautara.com.

Papua
Tourist Office: Jl. Raya Abepura, Dinas, Otonom Kotaraja, Jayapura; tel: 0967-583001, -586551.

Tour operators and travel agents

Java
Panorama Tours: Head Office, Panorama Building, 3rd Floor, Jl. Tomang Raya, No. 63; tel: 021-2556 5199; www.panorama-tours.com. Incoming tour operator in Jakarta with several branches in Java and Bali. Specialises in Java-overland-to-Bali tours with multilingual guides. Also does ticketing and hotel reservations.
Ndeso Adventure Consultant (www.exploredesa.com) is a volcano- and eco-adventure specialist committed to responsible travel principles and excellent customer service. Experienced guides lead volcano-climbing and walking expeditions and adventure trips throughout Java, which can include tailored trips to active **Gunung Bromo** and **Gunung Semeru** in the magnificent Bromo-Tengger-Semeru National Park.

Bali

Walking tours
There are three Ubud-based walking tour groups, and all are recommended.
Bali Bird Walks: www.balibirdwalk.com.

Keep Walking Tours: www.balispirit.com/tours.
Ubud Herb Walks: www.baliherbalwalk.com.

Cycling tours

A range of interesting outdoor activities are available, allowing visitors to enjoy the 'real Bali' via cycling through villages or walking through rice fields. For guided cycling geared to suit capabilities, contact I Wayan Kertayasa at **Bali Sport** (www.bali-cycling.com), member of both the Bali and the Indonesia Cycling federations.
Perama Tours: www.peramatour.com. With offices in all major Bali centres, as well as in Lombok, Perama has decades of experience, and offers everything from daily shuttle buses between resorts, to tailor-made tour packages.

Kalimantan

De'Gigant Tours: Jl. Martadinata Rauda 1, No. 21 RT 11, Samarinda; tel: +62 (0)81-258 46578; www.borneotourgigant.com. A full-service tour operator specialising in adventure tours throughout Kalimantan. Its website has the most complete information on the island available.

Sulawesi

Safari Tours & Travel: Jl. Sam Ratulangi, No. 176, Manado; tel: 0431-857-637; www.manadosafaris.com. A complete service tour operator and travel agency focusing on North Sulawesi, offers diving, trekking, horse riding, rafting and cultural tours.

Conservation and marine expeditions

Operation Wallacea (www.opwall.com) runs 2–10-week research conservation expeditions, July–Aug, for students and volunteers. Participants stay in villages and/or forest base camps, and do jungle training and data collecting – a great way to see a lot of wildlife and experience local community living.

The company also conducts marine biology research expeditions from Hoga island. Volunteers stay in rustic beach bungalows and dive/snorkel every day to help marine biologists collect data.

Papua

Raja Ampat
For further information about Raja Ampat's diverse species, visit the websites of **World Wildlife Fund** (www.worldwildlife.org), which also occasionally conducts tours, **Conservation International** (www.conservation.org) and **The Nature Conservancy** (TNC) (www.nature.org) or visit the TNC field office at Jl. Gunung Merapi, No. 38, Sorong; tel: 0951-323 437.

Travellers with disabilities

There is little awareness in Indonesia for the special needs of travellers with disabilities, and anyone looking other than 'normal' will certainly draw stares, maybe even laughter, which camouflages embarrassment. Wheelchair ramps and van lifts are not the norm, though large international chains may have facilities. Ask your tour operator in advance for extra assistance.

W

Weights and measures

Indonesia follows the metric system.

What to bring

Travel as lightly as possible, as there are many good buys to be found in Indonesia and never enough luggage space for them. Essentials are insect repellent, sunscreen, prescription medicines and perhaps an extra set of spectacles. Always hand-carry medicines, as checked-in luggage can get delayed or lost. Make sure all luggage is locked.

What to wear

Indonesians are concerned with how they present themselves, and are particularly mindful of modesty. As most Indonesians are Muslim, it is polite for women to keep their knees, midriffs and armpits covered. Strappy vests, halter tops, shorts and miniskirts are frowned upon, as are swimsuits anywhere other than on the beach or at the pool.

As the weather is hot and humid year-round, bring all-cotton clothing or the synthetic quick-dry variety for sale in camping stores throughout the world. Sandals or footwear that can be slipped off easily are a good idea, especially if planning to visit mosques or homes, as shoes are always removed before entering. Hiking boots may be required for trekking.

For formal occasions, men wear batik shirts and tailored trousers; women, modest dresses or ethnic outfits.

Women travellers

The increasing popularity of backpacker-style travel among young Indonesians means that the idea of women travelling for pleasure without male company is increasingly understood. However, very few Indonesians, male or female, travel solo for fun, and lone females may have to put up with being pestered by gregarious Indonesian men; young local women almost always move around in company. However, you will be quite safe as long as you dress and behave modestly; women with bare legs and minimal tops are considered disrespectful.

Take the usual precautions: don't walk down dark alleys or on beaches alone at night. In Bali and Jakarta, be wary of gigolos and 'cowboys' offering free rides.

LANGUAGE

Bahasa Indonesia – which simply means 'Indonesian language', and which is also known in English as Indonesian – developed from Malay, which has been the lingua franca throughout much of Southeast Asia for centuries. The construction of basic sentences is relatively easy. Indonesian is written in the Roman alphabet and, unlike some other Asian languages, is not tonal.

To show respect, an older man is addressed as bapak or pak (father or Sir) and an elder woman as ibu (mother or Madam). Bung (in West Java) and mas (in Central and East Java) roughly translate as 'brother' and are used to address younger men, or those of equal status; neng (West Java) and mbak (Central and East Java) are the equivalent terms for women. These forms of address are particularly useful for talking to hotel, restaurant or shop staff, or employees on public transport. Other regions have equivalent terms, but mas and mbak in particular may be used nationwide.

Much signage will also be in English.

PRONUNCIATION

a short as in 'father' (apa = what, ada = there is)
ai rather like the 'i' in 'mine' (kain = material, sampai = to arrive)
k hard at the beginning of a word as in 'king', but hardly audible at the end of a word (kamus = dictionary, cantik = beautiful)
kh (ch) slightly aspirated, as in 'khan' or the Scottish 'ch' in 'loch' (khusus = special, khabar = news)
ng as in 'singer', never as in 'danger' or 'Ringo' (bunga = flower, penginapan = cheap hotel)
ngg like the 'ng' in 'Ringo' (minggu = week or Sunday, tinggi = high, tall)
r always rolled (rokok = cigarette, pertama = first)
u as in 'flute', never as in 'bucket' (umum = public, belum = not yet)
y as in 'you' (saya = I or me, kaya = rich)
c like the 'ch' in 'church' (candi = temple, kacang = nut)
e 1. often unstressed as in 'open' (berapa sounds like b'rapa = how much?) 2. sometimes stressed, somewhere between the 'e' in 'bed' and 'a' in 'bad' (boleh = may)
g hard as in 'golf', never as in 'ginger' (guntur = thunder, bagus = good)
h generally lightly aspirated (hitam = black, lihat = to see)
i mid-length, halfway between i in 'pin', and 'ee' in 'meet'; usually slightly longer as the first letter in a word (minta = to ask for, ibu = mother)
j as in 'John' (jalan = road or street, jahit = to sew)

SPELLING

Indonesian spelling is delightfully logical and consistent, with one minor complication: in some personal names, old-fashioned Dutch-style spelling is occasionally retained (oe for u; tj for c; j for y; and dj for j). These older spellings are also sometimes used by businesses to convey a 'heritage' effect (much as in 'Ye Olde Englande').

Less important are the subtle distinctions in Central Java between the liquid sounds of 'l' or 'r', 'v' interchanged with 'w' and 'p' substituted for 'f'. The niceties are of interest only to experts in phonetics, but in practical terms, it means that the Siva (also spelled Siwa) temple at Prambanan may be written (in its popular form) as Lara Janggrang, Loro Jonggrong or Roro Jonggrang and they are all correct.

GREETINGS AND CIVILITIES

Thank you Terima kasih
Good morning Selamat pagi
Good day Selamat siang
Good afternoon/good evening Selamat sore (pronounced soray)
Goodnight Selamat malam
Goodbye Selamat jalan (to person going)
Goodbye Selamat tinggal (to person staying)
I'm sorry Ma'af
Welcome Selamat datang
Please come in Silakan masuk
Please sit down Silakan duduk
What is your name? Siapa nama Anda
My name is... Nama saya...
Where do you come from? Berasal dari mana?
I come from... Saya berasal dari...

PRONOUNS/FORMS OF ADDRESS

I Saya
You (singular) Anda
He, she Dia
We (excluding the listener) Kami
We (including the listener) Kita
You (plural) Kalian
Mr Pak/bapak
Mrs Ibu/bu
Miss Nona

DIRECTIONS/TRANSPORT

left kiri
right kanan
straight terus
near dekat
far jauh
from dari
to ke
inside di dalam
outside di luar
here di sini
there di sana
in front of di depan/muka
at the back di belakang
next to di sebelah
pedicab becak
car mobil
bus bis
train kereta api
bicycle sepeda
motorcycle sepeda motor
Where do you want to go? Mau kemana?
I want to go to... Saya mau ke...
Stop here Berhenti di sini
Bank bank
post office kantor pos
Immigration department Departemen immigrasi
tourist office kantor pariwisata
embassy kedutaan

EATING OUT

restaurant restoran/rumah makan/resto
food makanan
drink minuman
breakfast sarapan pagi
lunch makan siang
dinner makan malam
boiled water air putih/air matang
iced water air es
tea teh
coffee kopi
milk susu
rice nasi
noodles mie/bihun
fish ikan
prawns udang
vegetables sayur
fruit buah
egg telur
sugar gula
salt garam
pepper merica, lada
cup cangkir
plate piring
glass gelas
spoon sendok
knife pisau
fork garpu

SHOPPING

shop toko
money uang
change (from a bill) uang kembali
to buy beli
price harga
expensive mahal
cheap murah
fixed price harga pas
How much is it? Berapa?/Berapa harganya?

SIGNS

open buka
cashier kasir
closed tutup
entrance masuk
exit keluar
don't touch jangan pegang/sentuh
no smoking dilarang merokok
push dorong
pull tarik
gate pintu
ticket window loket
ticket karcis
information informasi
city kota
market pasar

NUMBERS

1 satu
2 dua
3 tiga
4 empat
5 lima
6 enam
7 tujuh
8 delapan
9 sembilan
10 sepuluh
11 sebelas
12 dua-belas
20 dua-puluh
100 seratus
200 dua ratus
2,000 dua ribu
1 million satu juta
First pertama
Second kedua
Third ketiga

GLOSSARY OF TERMS

A

adat customary law
alang-alang (or lalang) tall grass used for roof thatching
aling-aling a short wall designed to deflect troublesome spirits
Anak Agung title given to someone of the Balinese princely caste
arak strong spirit from sugar palm

B

bale (also balai) open-air pavilion with roof
Bali Aga 'mountain Balinese'; indigenous Balinese communities with pre-Hindu culture
banjar neighbourhood association; the basic social and political unit
banten religious offerings (Bali)
barat west
Barong mythical beast representing good; danced by two men inside an ornate costume (Bali)
bemo public minibus
Brahmana the priestly caste; highest of the four Balinese castes
brem a sweet rice wine (Bali)
bukit a hill or hilly area

C

candi bentar split entrance gateway to a Balinese temple
Cokorda title of a Balinese prince or king

D

dalang puppet master
danau lake
desa village
dewa generic name for god
dewi generic name for goddess
Dewi Sri Goddess of Rice
dokar two-wheeled pony cart

E

endek Balinese ikat cloth

G

gado-gado steamed vegetables served with peanut sauce
Galungan Balinese New Year according to the Wuku calendar; celebrated every 210 days
gamelan percussion orchestra
gang small lane or alley
garuda mythological bird, the vehicle of the Hindu god Wisnu
geringsing rare double ikat cloth woven in Tenganan, Bali
gunung mountain
Gusti title given to members of the Balinese Wesia caste

I

ikat traditional handwoven textile

J

jalan street, road; to walk
jukung Balinese outrigger sailing boat

K

kain cloth; also sarong
kantor office
kepulauan archipelago
keris ceremonial dagger with a wavy blade
klotok motorised local boat
kulkul hollow wooden drum to summon villagers (Bali)

L

leyak a witch or sorcerer (Bali)
legong Balinese dance; also the name given to the dancer
lingga a Hindu phallic symbol
lombok chilli
lontar a species of palm; also refers to a palm-leaf manuscript
losmen small guesthouse
lumbung a traditional rice barn

M

Mahabharata Hindu epic
Melasti purification ceremony
meru holy Hindu mountain; also a Hindu temple's pagoda-style roof

N

naga dragon, water serpent
nusa island (also called *pulau*)

Nyepi Hindu Day of Silence; Balinese New Year according to the Saka calendar

O

odalan Balinese temple anniversary festival
ogoh-ogoh huge papier-mâché monsters (Bali)
ojek motorcycle taxi

P

padi rice in the husk, when growing in the field
pantai beach
paras sandstone used in building temples and for stone-carving
pasar market
pedanda Brahmana high priest
pemangku temple lay priest
PHKA Department of Forest Protection & Nature Conservation
puputan Balinese fight to death or ritual suicide
pura temple
pura dalem temple of the dead
puri palace

R

Ramayana Hindu epic
Rangda the widow-witch representing evil (Bali)
rumah sakit hospital

S

satria Balinese princely class, second in ranking to Brahmana
sawah rice field
selatan south
subak Balinese irrigation society
sudra lowest of the four Balinese castes; also called *jaba*
sungai river

T

taman garden
teluk bay
tenggara southeast
timur east
topeng mask
tuak palm wine

U

utara north

W

wantilan open pavilion used as a hall in a village or temple (Bali)
wartel telecoms office
warung simple café where food and drinks are served
wayang Javanese puppet
wesia the third and lowest of the Balinese aristocratic class

Y

yoni Hindu symbol of female sexual organs

FURTHER READING

FICTION

Beauty is a Wound by Eka Kurniawan. Eka Kurniawan is one of the first novelists from Indonesia to make waves on the international literary scene. His debut is a surreal, ribald historical epic, with shades of Gabriel Garcia Marquez. His other books include Man Tiger, Vengeance is Mine and All Others Pay Cash.

The Buru Quartet by Pramoedya Ananta Toer. Pramoedya was Indonesia's best-known 20th-century writer, and this four-part series (*This Earth of Mankind, Child of All Nations, Footsteps, House of Glass*) was his major work. The series tells the multifaceted story of Indonesia's birth as a nation through the eyes of a Javanese journalist called Minke.

Twilight in Djakarta by Mochtar Lubis. Along with Pramoedya, Lubis was one of the towering figures of mid-20th-century Indonesian literature. This novel, with its varied cast of characters, is a snapshot of uncertain life in a new postcolonial state.

Saman by Ayu Utami. Daring in both style and subject matter, this beautifully written novel is the best-known translated work from the leading light of an informal grouping of woman writers who emerged during the post-Suharto reform period.

Home by Leila S. Chudori. An epic novel of contemporary Indonesian experience, and the dark shadows still cast by the political violence of the 1960s.

The Rainbow Troops by Andrea Hirata. This popular Indonesian novel, later made into a successful film, is a poignant but ultimately uplifting tale of childhood on a sleepy island. It did wonders for the tourist industry in Belitung, where it is set.

Love, Lies and Indomie by Nuril Basri. A light-hearted take on life as a millennial in contemporary Jakarta from one of Indonesia's emerging young novelists.

The Year of Living Dangerously by Christopher Koch. Set in the turbulent mid-1960s, this iconic novel (later made into a film starring Mel Gibson) provided a ready stock of clichés for subsequent foreign writers and journalists tackling Indonesia, but it remains gripping and richly atmospheric.

MEMOIR AND TRAVEL WRITING

Indonesia, Etc. by Elizabeth Pisani. A wry and fast-paced account of a journey around the archipelago which doubles as an insightful portrait of 21st-century Indonesia,

⊘ Send us your thoughts

We do our best to ensure the information in our books is as accurate and up-to-date as possible. The books are updated on a regular basis using local contacts, who painstakingly add, amend and correct as required. However, some details (such as telephone numbers and opening times) are liable to change, and we are ultimately reliant on our readers to put us in the picture.

We welcome your feedback, especially your experience of using the book "on the road". Maybe you came across a great bar or new attraction we missed. We will acknowledge all contributions, and we'll offer an Insight Guide to the best letters received.

Please write to us at:
Insight Guides
PO Box 7910
London SE1 1WE

Or email us at:
hello@insightguides.com

written by an experienced observer of the country.

Fragrant Rice – A Tale of Love, Marriage and Cooking in Bali by Janet De Neefe. What started with De Neefe's desire to put together a collection of Balinese recipes developed into the fascinating story of her life in Ubud, with food as the main ingredient.

Crazy Little Heaven by Mark Heyward. This finely written book is both a travelogue recounting a hardy journey through the forests of Kalimantan, and an affectionate memoir of several decades of life in Indonesia.

In the Time of Madness by Richard Lloyd Parry. This gripping journalist's memoir recalls travels in the turbulent years that surrounded the fall of Suharto in the late 1990s, cataloguing ethnic violence in Kalimantan, unrest in Java and the chaos that ensued as East Timor split from Indonesia.

Java: The Garden of the East by E.R. Scidmore. This travel book written by an American visitor to Java in 1899 helped opened the eyes of the English-speaking world to a little-known island in the East. Her journey during the heyday of colonial rule is both astonishing and amusing and brings to life a world of yesteryear.

GEOGRAPHY AND NATURAL HISTORY

A Dark Place in the Jungle: Science, Orangutans and Human Nature by Linda Spalding. Spalding went to Kalimantan to follow the trail of orang-utan researcher Biruté Galdikas and discovered an unholy mix of foreign scientists, government workers, tourists, loggers, Dayaks and half-tame orangutans vying for control of the jungle.

Tropical Herbs and Spices of Indonesia by Wendy Hutton. This handy pocket-sized book with photos is ideal for identifying the exotic spices used in Indonesian cooking and their scientific classifications.

Zoo Quest for a Dragon by David Attenborough. A classic travel tale of Attenborough's journey to Indonesia in the 1950s to capture Komodo dragons for London Zoo, the people he met and the animals he saw.

HISTORY AND CULTURE

A History of Modern Indonesia since c.1200 by M.C. Ricklefs. The standard text for students of Indonesian history, this heavyweight academic overview gives impressive detail on happenings across the archipelago since the arrival of Islam. Ricklefs is also the author of numerous other works, particularly focusing on the history of religion and royalty in Java.

A Brief History of Indonesia: Sultans, Spices and Tsunamis by Tim Hannigan. A light narrative history, giving an accessible overview of the history of the archipelago from the arrival of the first modern humans to the 21st century.

Indonesia: Land Under the Rainbow by Mochtar Lubis. This is a most interesting book and the first popular history of Indonesia through the eyes of a distinguished Indonesian author to appear in English. It covers the maritime trade that put the archipelago on the world map from the beginning of time to the 20th century.

Krakatoa: The Day the World Exploded August 27, 1883 by Simon Winchester. In this highly readable popular history, Winchester puts an entirely new perspective on the iconic 1883 eruption of Krakatoa that was followed by an immense tsunami that killed nearly 40,000 people, with a wealth of cultural, historical and geological context.

Nathaniel's Nutmeg by Giles Milton. An endlessly entertaining popular history covering the early years of the spice trade, and the appallingly bloody saga of early European interventions in Maluku, with the Dutch and English facing off for control of the world's nutmeg supply.

Bandit Saints of Java by George Quinn. Highly readable and unexpectedly funny, this fascinating book – part anthropology, part history, part travel writing – explores the Javanese tradition of pilgrimage to the tombs of Muslim 'saints', and draws some unexpected conclusions in the process.

A Short History of Bali by Robert Pringle. This engaging history of Bali covers the story of Bali from before the Bronze Age to the presidency of Megawati Sukarnoputri and the tragedy of the Kuta bombings in 2002.

A Little Bit One o'Clock: Living with a Balinese Family by William Ingram. A beautifully written mini-memoir explores the web of relationships between a foreigner and a Balinese family.

Bali: A Paradise Created by Adrian Vickers. This fascinating scholarly book examines how the world's image of Bali as a paradise island came into

being, and considers how that image is often at odds with local perspectives.

Bali: Sekala & Niskala Volumes I and II by Fred B. Eiseman, Jr. Essays by a long-time Bali resident: Volume I is an exploration of Balinese religion, rituals and performing arts; Volume II covers the geography, social organisation, language, folklore, as well as Bali's material culture.

The Island of Bali by Miguel Covarrubias. First published in 1937, this book arguably did more than any other to popularise the idea of Bali as a uniquely artistic and paradisiacal place. Beautifully illustrated and engagingly written, it remains highly informative.

Jamu: The Ancient Indonesian Art of Herbal Healing by Susan-Jane Beers. The culmination of 10 years' research, Beers provides a comprehensive look at the background, materials and applications of the holistic *jamu*, herbal tonics, massage oils and creams used by Indonesians for hundreds of years.

Jogja: Sites out of Site by M. Rizky Sasono, et al. A treasure trove of information about the obscure temple remains near Prambanan, Borobudur and the Gunung Merapi plains compiled by archaeologists and anthropologists. In English, French and Indonesian, with maps.

Demokrasi: Indonesia in the 21st Century by Hamish McDonald. This book examines the country's ongoing transformation of one of the world's youngest democracies.

TEXTILES

Batik Belanda 1840–1940 by Harmen C. Veldhuisen. A detailed, illustrated account of Dutch influence on Javanese batik, complete with history and stories.

Contemporary Tie and Dye Textiles of Indonesia by Kim Jane Saunders. A comprehensive look at hand-woven and hand-spun textiles as a dynamic art form, this is an introduction to the diversity of the textiles of each of Indonesia's main weaving islands as they exist in modern times.

Indonesian Textiles by Michael Hitchcock. Hitchcock examines the survival of traditional designs, significant colours, techniques and types of decorative applications in Indonesian textiles, with illustrations.

Lurik: The Magic Stripes by Nian S. Djoemena. One of the few compilations in existence of *lurik* motifs and

colours and their symbolism, this book is Djoemena's attempt to keep alive this traditional Yogyakarta handwoven cloth, perhaps older than batik.

Story Cloths of Bali by Joseph Fischer. Story cloths are used as ritual decorations and offerings in Balinese temples. Indonesian art expert Fischer describes how to appreciate Balinese culture via its array of textiles.

THE ARTS

Balinese Paintings by A.A.M. Djetantik. A concise but well-documented guide to traditional Balinese painting, including the work of Ubud's Pitamaha painters and Batuan and Penestanan's Young Artists.

Dance and Drama in Bali by Beryl de Zoete and Walter Spies. Spies lived in Bali for 12 years from 1927 and was an accomplished expert; De Zoete was trained in European dance. This important ethnographical book documents the history of Balinese dance and drama.

A House in Bali by Colin McPhee. First published in 1947 and one of the most enchanting books ever written about Bali, this is the story of how, in 1929, a young Canadian-born musician chanced upon rare gramophone recordings of Balinese gamelan music that were to change his life for ever.

Offerings, the Ritual Art of Bali by Francine Brinkgreve and David Stuart-Fox. This beautifully illustrated book provides a rare glimpse into the pageantry, ritual and devotion that accompany the creation of offerings in Bali.

OTHER INSIGHT GUIDES

Insight Guides comprehensively cover the Southeast Asia region, with titles including Bali and Lombok; Malaysia; Singapore; Southeast Asia; Myanmar; Vietnam; Laos and Cambodia; Thailand; Thailand's Beaches & Islands; and the Philippines.

Insight Explore Guides advise on the best and most rewarding things to see, including up to 20 tailor-made itineraries exploring the main attractions. Southeast Asian titles include Bali, Bangkok and Singapore.

The laminated *Insight FlexiMaps* have an informative easy-to-read approach. *FlexiMaps* to Bali, Bangkok, Phuket and Kuala Lumpur are available.

CREDITS

PHOTO CREDITS

COVER CREDITS

INSIGHT GUIDE CREDITS

Distribution
UK, Ireland and Europe
Apa Publications (UK) Ltd;
sales@insightguides.com
United States and Canada
Ingram Publisher Services;
ips@ingramcontent.com
Australia and New Zealand
Woodslane; info@woodslane.com.au
Southeast Asia
Apa Publications (SN) Pte;
singaporeoffice@insightguides.com
Worldwide
Apa Publications (UK) Ltd;
sales@insightguides.com
**Special Sales, Content Licensing and
CoPublishing**
Insight Guides can be purchased in
bulk quantities at discounted prices.
We can create special editions,
personalised jackets and corporate
imprints tailored to your needs.
sales@insightguides.com
www.insightguides.biz

Printed in China by RR Donnelley

All Rights Reserved
© 2020 Apa Digital (CH) AG and
Apa Publications (UK) Ltd

First Edition 1983
Eighth Edition 2020

Every effort has been made to provide
accurate information in this
publication, but changes are
inevitable. The publisher cannot be
responsible for any resulting loss,
inconvenience or injury. We would
appreciate it if readers would call our
attention to any errors or outdated
information. We also welcome your
suggestions; please contact us at:
hello@insightguides.com

www.insightguides.com

Editor: Sian Marsh
Author: Linda Hoffman
Head of DTP and Pre-Press:
Rebeka Davies
Updated By: Tim Hannigan
Managing Editor: Carine Tracanelli
Picture Editor: Tom Smyth
Cartography: original cartography
Cosmographics, updated by Carte
Layout: Dan May

CONTRIBUTORS

This new edition of Insight Guides
Indonesia was copyedited by **Sian
Marsh** and updated by **Tim Hannigan**.
Tim lived in Indonesia for five years
working as a teacher and journalist.
He is author of the best-selling *A brief
history of Indonesia* and several other
books about the country. This edition
builds on the comprehensive work of
Linda Hoffman and a team of experts

she assembled from across Indonesia,
including **Jacky Djokosetio**, **Joan
Suyenaga**, **Nia Fliam**, **Andy Shorten**,
Lucas Zwall and **Robert Arung**.
The bulk of the photographs were
the work of **Corrie Wingate**, who
spent months travelling around Java,
Bali, Lombok, Sumatra, Kalimantan
and Sulawesi to capture the images
that bring the pages to life.

ABOUT INSIGHT GUIDES

Insight Guides have more than 45
years' experience of publishing high-
quality, visual travel guides. We
produce 400 full-colour titles, in both
print and digital form, covering more
than 200 destinations across the
globe, in a variety of formats to meet
your different needs.
 Insight Guides are written by local
authors, whose expertise is evident in
the extensive historical and cultural

background features. Each destination
is carefully researched by regional
experts to ensure our guides provide
the very latest information. All the
reviews in **Insight Guides** are
independent; we strive to maintain an
impartial view. Our reviews are
carefully selected to guide you to the
best places to eat, go out and shop, so
you can be confident that when we say
a place is special, we really mean it.

Legend

City maps

- Freeway/Highway/Motorway
- Divided Highway
- Main Roads
- Minor Roads
- Pedestrian Roads
- Steps
- Footpath
- Railway
- Funicular Railway
- Cable Car
- Tunnel
- City Wall
- Important Building
- Built Up Area
- Other Land
- Transport Hub
- Park
- Pedestrian Area
- Bus Station
- Tourist Information
- Main Post Office
- Cathedral/Church
- Mosque
- Synagogue
- Statue/Monument
- Beach
- Airport

Regional maps

- Freeway/Highway/Motorway (with junction)
- Freeway/Highway/Motorway (under construction)
- Divided Highway
- Main Road
- Secondary Road
- Minor Road
- Track
- Footpath
- International Boundary
- State/Province Boundary
- National Park/Reserve
- Marine Park
- Ferry Route
- Marshland/Swamp
- Glacier   Salt Lake
- Airport/Airfield
- Ancient Site
- Border Control
- Cable Car
- Castle/Castle Ruins
- Cave
- Chateau/Stately Home
- Church/Church Ruins
- Crater
- Lighthouse
- Mountain Peak
- Place of Interest
- Viewpoint

INDEX

MAIN REFERENCES ARE IN BOLD TYPE